# INVESTMENT ANALYSIS
## Techniques of appraising the British Stock Market

## MICHAEL FIRTH

Department of Accountancy and Business Law
University of Stirling

Harper & Row, Publishers
London    New York    Evanston    San Francisco

Copyright © 1975 Michael Firth

Standard Book Number 06-318028-6

Designed by 'Millions'
Typeset by European Printing Corporation, Dublin
Printed and bound by R J Acford Ltd, Chichester

To My Parents

# Contents

# Preface

Over the past ten years there has been a significant growth in investment analysis and the numbers now employed in it are such that it has become a profession in its own right. This growth has been occasioned by (1) the realisation by investors, financial institutions and take-over-minded companies of the benefits of rigorous investment analysis (2) the improvements in analytical methods and the recent derivation and application of quantitative techniques to share selection and portfolio management (3) the gradual increase in personnel skilled in the various disciplines of investment analysis.

The book sets out to describe the methodologies of investment analysis and to discuss some of the recent analytical techniques that can be applied to investments. By bringing together the various disciplines relevant to investment analysis in one book it is hoped that the process of learning will be speeded-up. The various quantitative methods available to investment analysis have up to now been mainly published in academic journals and so, again, the description of such techniques and of their application to stocks and shares in a single volume will help speed the flow of knowledge to the financial community.

The aim of the book therefore is to disseminate knowledge of the methods of investment analysis in an essentially practical manner. Obviously, no single text can hope to thoroughly review all the particular disciplines or to discuss all the various advanced academic concepts and theories: the book does, however, give a consistent basic coverage of the framework necessary for the evaluation of investments.

The level of the book has been pitched such that no prior knowledge of accountancy, economics or mathematics is required. The book is intended to be comprehensive and no additional material is vitally necessary. References have been made to major texts and articles on specific topics which can be followed-up by the interested reader. The references have been restricted to the major studies so as not to clutter the book. By the end of the book the reader will readily appreciate the changing nature of the factors influencing investment decision making and the need to keep abreast of these. In order to help in the reading of the text a glossary has been included which defines some of the technical terms.

The book will be found helpful for everyone working in or studying investment analysis and corporate forecasting. Specific uses include the following.

1 As a text for new recruits to investment analysis. The use of the book along with the practical work pursued in the research department

should enable the individual to quickly master the methodology of investment analysis.

2   As a formal description of the methods of investment analysis and as a review of the recent strides made in quantitative analysis. This will be useful for practising investment analysts employed by stockbrokers, financial institutions and in the corporate planning departments of industrial companies.

3   For undergraduate studies in accountancy, business administration and economics, where investment analysis is becoming an increasingly popular elective: additionally, investment analysis is an integral part of studies in corporate planning and business forecasting. The book also caters for financial courses in postgraduate business studies programmes. Many of the major professional bodies are now including investment analysis in their examinations and the degree of competence required is likely to grow. The book should therefore be useful to those studying for accountancy, actuarial, banking and chartered secretarial qualifications. The Stock Exchange now requires any new members to have passed an examination. One of the papers is titled 'The Technique of Investment' and the book should help prepare students for this examination.

The book opens with a general introductory chapter on the role of the stock market in the economy. Following this the forecasting of corporate profits and share prices is discussed. Chapter 7 describes the building of portfolios whilst Chapter 8 discusses the appraisal of investment performance. There then follow chapters on taxation and investment mathematics which expand upon matters mentioned in the earlier chapters. Finally, the theories of share-price behaviour are described and the implications of these for investment analysis is discussed.

I would like to take this opportunity to express my gratitude to the typing office of the University of Stirling who typed the manuscript.

# Chapter 1
## Introduction

The main socio-economic role of the Stock Market is the allocation of the ownership of an economy's capital stock. This is a mechanism which exerts considerable influence on the assignment of scarce capital resources to various projects and the deployment of these resources in the form of fixed capital formation is a major determinant of growth rates and of standard-of-living performances. Many of the 'Western world's' economies have substantial proportions of their total assets valued in the Stock Market and thus the proper functioning of Stock Exchanges is vital if their economic welfare functions are to be maximised. The fact that the number of people directly or indirectly investing in Stock Exchange securities has been growing rapidly, and that the proportion of various economies' assets being valued in the Stock Market has been rising, is evidence that the Stock Exchange has provided at least a reasonable medium for resource allocation.

## Perfect market conditions

Whilst there are numerous theories regarding the measurement of the socio-economic welfare function, most would acknowledge that to maximise the benefits from a Stock Exchange requires a perfect market. The traditional view of a perfect market requires:

1 Homogeneity of the goods.

2 Many buyers and sellers.

3 Freedom of entry and exit.

4 Unlimited supplies of stocks and shares.

5 Perfect knowledge.

1

No existing markets meet the above criteria precisely but the Stock Exchanges of the United States and of Great Britain do in broad terms comply with some of the requirements. Specifically, there is homogeneity of the goods; an ordinary share in ICI confers the same rights and liabilities as any other ordinary share in ICI.

## Buyers and sellers and the jobbing system

There are many buyers and sellers in shares of the larger quoted companies and all but a few of the smaller firms attract investor attention. The matching of purchases and sales is conducted through the jobbing system where the jobbers act as principals owning various shares in which they will deal. The system has come in for some criticism over the past ten years or so, the arguments being largely based on the lack of competition as the number of jobbers decline. The decline in numbers from seventy-two in 1963 to twenty-six in 1973 represents a fairly drastic fall such that only one jobber may be dealing in some of the smaller quoted securities with the obvious impact on competitive pricing. The fall in the numbers of jobbers has been occasioned by the amalgamation of various firms who sought to reduce costs by obtaining the economies of scale. The profitability of jobbing firms has been under pressure due to both inflationary administrative costs and to the ever-increasing finance required to take up stocks and shares. To counter this trend the Stock Exchange has recently allowed jobbing and broking firms to obtain limited-company status and several firms have taken advantage of this by attracting additional investors*. This initiative will hopefully end the decline in jobbing firms as the smaller the number of firms in existence, the weaker the competition.

## ARIEL

A recent development which will affect the jobbing system is Automated Real-Time Investments Exchange Ltd (ARIEL). This is a computer-based system which will enable institutional investors to deal directly with each other and completely by-pass the Stock Exchange. The aim behind the operation is that of reducing the costs of dealing, and ARIEL appears to be attracting a lot of interest – indeed, it is backed by seventeen accepting houses which represent the largest of the City merchant banks. The Stock Exchange has criticised the scheme on a number of points including:

1 ARIEL facilitates the transfer of large blocks of stock in one transaction and this may be against the shareholders' and the general public's interest. In particular, it can exaggerate the profits available from having inside knowledge.

2 The market will be fragmented and the prices made by the jobbers will not reflect the whole of the activity in a stock.

3 The Stock Exchange has no regulatory powers over ARIEL and so standards may lapse.

*One firm of jobbers, Smith Brothers, has recently obtained a Stock Market quotation.

Certainly, the reduced costs of dealing through ARIEL will create a greater competitive strain on the jobbing system and further amalgamations may be necessary. It will probably be the mid-1970s before the initial impact of ARIEL can be assessed, and it will be interesting to examine the advantages of reduced dealing costs against a reduced (?) jobbing system.

The requirement of many buyers and sellers does not apply to many of the smaller quoted companies. In these cases the controlling shareholders, who are invariably the directors of the company, often have no desire to see an active quotation but nonetheless like to have the quote for acquisition or status reasons. There has been recent Press comment that such poorly marketable shares should be suspended. This has been based on the premise that the controlling shareholders can manipulate the company without accounting to the remaining shareholders and that the market quote should represent recent dealings in the shares.

**Costs of Stock Exchange transactions**

The third requirement of a perfect market is that of freedom of entry and exit and whilst this does not exist for Stock Exchange transactions the expenses are at fixed rates and do represent some service. The introduction of ARIEL described earlier was initiated by the large institutions whose main aim was to cut down the large commissions they were paying.

**Number of shares in issue**

The fourth requirement, unlimited supplies of stock, does not exist as companies have fixed capitals. The amount of stock that is actively being traded varies from stock to stock but rarely would it amount to 10 per cent of the total unless there were exceptional reasons such as major fundamental news, oil strikes or takeover negotiations. Although this is an imperfection it does not act as a limiting factor for many of the larger companies.

**Perfect knowledge**

The final requirement is that of perfect knowledge. This is the greatest weakness of the Stock Exchange and, indeed, of the commodity markets in general. Perfect knowledge is the main requirement for the correct valuation of securities and this, of course, is the job of the investment analyst. The values placed upon capital assets and earnings potential are very important as they determine, in some part, whether resources are channelled into these particular activities. The correct pricing of shares will also help investor confidence so that they will put up funds for new issues. Whilst much needs and can be done to improve the workings of the Stock Market it is out of the province of a book describing the methods and techniques of investment analysis.

**Value of quoted securities**

Table 1.1 shows the nominal and market values of all securities quoted on the London Stock Exchange as at 31 December 1973. As can be seen, the ordinary share capital accounts for by far the largest proportion of quoted securities. The column showing the market value of the shares

**Table 1.1**

Nominal and market values of securities quoted on the London Stock Exchange as at 31 December 1973

| | No. of securities | Nominal amount £m | % of total | Market valuation £m | % of total |
|---|---|---|---|---|---|
| Gilt-edged and foreign stocks | 1,488 | 33,788 | 53 | 23,222 | 12 |
| Loan capital UK-registered | 2,517 | 6,972 | | 4,752 | |
| Loan capital Non UK or Irish-registered | 47 | 274 | 12 | 231 | 3 |
| Loan capital Republic of Ireland | 28 | 36 | | 25 | |
| Preference and preferred capital UK-registered | 1,620 | 1,094 | | 525 | |
| Preference and preferred capital Non UK or Irish-registered | 72 | 220 | 2 | 174 | 1 |
| Preference and preferred capital Republic of Ireland | 78 | 12 | | 6 | |
| Ordinary share capital UK-registered | 3,202 | 12,385 | 19 | 40,519 | 22 |
| Ordinary share capital Non UK or Irish-registered | 375 | 8,769 | | 108,775 | 58 |
| Ordinary share capital Republic of Ireland | 99 | 125 | 14 | 423 | |
| Shares of no par value Non UK-registered | 33 | | | 6,995 | 4 |
| | | 63,675 | | 185,647 | |

Note 1 Loan capital includes convertible securities
    2 Ordinary share capital includes deferred share capital

*Source:* Stock Exchange Fact Book, 31 December 1973

reveals quite clearly the growth in share prices from their nominal values (it should be noted, of course, that new issues are usually priced above their nominal value). The gilt-edged and fixed-interest securities have, however, fallen below their nominal values and show up the inadequacy of the interest rates to account for inflation. One yardstick against which to measure the importance of the equity market is that of the total market value of UK-registered company ordinary shares at 31

December 1966, which amounted to £27,148 million, and this compares against an estimate for national wealth at that date of £140,000 million[1]. Although the statistic for national wealth is capable of different interpretations the above figures do indicate that a significant proportion of the country's assets are valued in the Stock Market. Along with the growth in the market value of quoted ordinary shares the percentage of turnover to the total turnover of all securities has also been rising. This is quite significant given the enormous transactions conducted in gilts, as investors switch between various fixed-interest securities.

The above statistics give some idea of the value of economic resources valued in the Stock Market. These assets are owned in varying amounts by millions of investors whose ownership is direct or indirect.

**Share ownership**

Table 1.2 gives estimates of equity ownership in the UK. This shows a clear trend of increasing institutional investment at the expense of private shareholders. The number of private investors has been growing at a steady pace but in terms of market value it is the financial institutions who have become the dominant influence. The growth in institutional business has occurred as more individuals have begun to save, and they have channelled these funds through insurance companies, pension funds and unit trusts. The Stock Market therefore provides an important avenue of savings for individuals and one which should continue to grow as long as investors have confidence in the workings of the Exchange. With the rates of inflation experienced since the war, equity investment has provided amongst the best returns possible to investors and only the risk of certain individual years giving bad performances has deterred even greater investment. The two objectives of providing an attractive savings channel and of valuing projects for resource allocation must be the over-riding social goals of the Stock Exchange.

**Stock Market influence on resource allocation**

The Stock Market affects the process of asset formation by direct and indirect means both of which wield considerable influence. Direct influence is exerted through the new-issue and the rights-issue markets and to a lesser degree the fixed-interest market. Indirect influence is exerted by the share-price performance and by investor comment. Table 1.3 which was derived from the 'Annual Abstract of Statistics' discloses the sources of finance of publicly-quoted companies in the years 1966 to 1971.

The increase in short-term credit represents temporary finance to the company although, as there was an increase in every year during the 1960s, firms have been able to rely on it as a semi-permanent addition. The ratio of proceeds of new issues to total financing showed a dramatic reduction in 1969 and 1970 largely due to the low level of the market indices which have deterred companies from entering the capital market. The normal rate of new capital raising to total financing would appear to be in the range 10 to 20 per cent. The recent introduction of the imputation system of company taxation should

5

**Table 1.2**

Institutional equity holdings in UK-registered and managed companies

| £m 31 December | 1966 | 1967 | 1968 | 1969 | 1970 | 1971 |
|---|---|---|---|---|---|---|
| Insurance companies | 2,600 (11.7) | 3,366 (11.8) | 5,313 (12.9) | 4,724 (13.6) | 4,595 (14.1) | 6,885 (15.1) |
| Private pension funds | 1,452 (6.6) | 1,920 (6.7) | 2,850 (6.9) | 2,417 (7.0) | 2,341 (7.2) | 3,416 (7.5) |
| Public pension funds | 421 (1.9) | 602 (2.1) | 893 (2.2) | 828 (2.4) | 917 (2.8) | 1,484 (3.3) |
| Local-authority pension funds | 208 (0.9) | 291 (1.0) | 485 (1.2) | 438 (1.3) | 431 (1.3) | 754 (1.7) |
| Investment trusts | 1,625 (7.3) | 2,156 (7.6) | 3,158 (7.6) | 2,671 (7.7) | 2,462 (7.6) | 3,547 (7.8) |
| Unit trusts | 453 (2.1) | 664 (2.3) | 1,142 (2.8) | 1,095 (3.2) | 1,034 (3.2) | 1,635 (3.6) |
| Others | 15,390 (69.5) | 19,555 (68.5) | 27,360 (66.4) | 22,441 (64.8) | 20,718 (63.8) | 27,796 (61.0) |
|  | 22,149 (100.0) | 28,554 (100.0) | 41,201 (100.0) | 34,614 (100.0) | 32,498 (100.0) | 45,517 (100.0) |
| Combined pension funds | 2,081 (9.4) | 2,813 (9.8) | 4,228 (10.3) | 3,683 (10.7) | 3,689 (11.2) | 5,654 (12.4) |
| Combined institutions | 6,759 (30.5) | 3,999 (31.5) | 13,841 (33.6) | 12,173 (35.2) | 11,780 (36.2) | 17,721 (39.0) |

*Source:* Dobbins, R., 'Institutional Shareholders in the Equity Market', Unpublished MSc. thesis, University of Bradford

**Table 1.3**

Sources of finance of quoted companies

| No. of companies | 2,109 | | 1,993 | | 1,829 | | 1,701 | | 1,308 | | 1,239 | |
|---|---|---|---|---|---|---|---|---|---|---|---|---|
| | 1966 | | 1967 | | 1968 | | 1969 | | 1970 | | 1971 | |
| | £m | % total | £m | % total | £m | % total | £m | % total | £m | % total | £m | % total |
| Proceeds from the issue of loan and share capital | 482 | 20.2 | 519 | 19.3 | 421 | 13.5 | 343 | 9.2 | 274 | 6.9 | 505 | 18 |
| Retained profit plus depreciation | 1,395 | 59.3 | 1,615 | 60.1 | 1,839 | 58.8 | 1,841 | 49.2 | 1,988 | 50.3 | 2,241 | 79.6 |
| Increase in short-term credit | 481 | 20.5 | 552 | 20.6 | 870 | 27.7 | 1,556 | 41.6 | 1,693 | 42.8 | 67 | 2.4 |
| TOTAL | 2,358 | | 2,686 | | 3,130 | | 3,740 | | 3,955 | | 2,813 | |

induce greater dividend payouts and so an increase in capital raising activities may well accrue.

Whilst internally-generated funds form by far the largest source of finance, the new issue and loan capital markets still account for a significant part of the total cash flow to the company. Rights and new issues are often chosen by firms as the last alternative in obtaining finance and these usually enable larger increases in short-term credit to be obtained. In some cases, of course, it is the already high level of short-term credit that forces the company to come to the market for permanent capital. The considerable funds generated by rights and new issues could never have been raised if the Stock Market had not believed in the particular company's efficiency. Whilst prospectuses issued when raising money do not give detailed information on capital projects, investors do appraise the offers by looking at the company's past performance and by looking at the record of the industry within which it operates. The issuing houses sponsoring the issue usually have access to the company's internal records during the investigation prior to the issue and they and the reporting accountants' audit act as some safeguard against excessive claims by company management.

## Criticisms of the new-issue market

A recurring criticism of the new-issue market has been that concerned with the stagging profits available from the first day of dealings. This can represent a significant under-valuation of the company and often exceeds the total of all the direct-issue expenses. When the difference between the new-issue price and the price on the first day of quotation is large the under-valuation is serious as the company could have raised significantly more money without having to have further diluted its equity. During 1973, stagging profits disappeared and a number of loss situations arose. Whilst this was partly due to the particular market conditions it perhaps also represents greater skill and judgment being exercised by the financial institutions. The heavy academic and Press comment of the pricing ability of the issuing houses may therefore have had some effect.

## Rights issues

When a company makes a rights issue the Stock Market will make an assessment of the impact on profitability and stability. As with new issues the information issued by companies is not very detailed and this may be an area for tightening regulations. Normally, a rights issue is accompanied by a fall in price, partly as shareholders may not have cash available to take up their entitlement, and partly because of the information content. Companies tend to raise cash in order to increase earnings by undertaking new projects or to reduce falls in profits by an injection of working capital or by replacement of obsolete plant. Investors assess what is the real cause of the capital raising and adjust their forecasts of company profitability accordingly. In practice, the impact of rights issues often follows the average market sentiment so one will find that during some years all rights issues are poorly received whilst in others the sentiment will be positive. However, within these trends individual companies will find that investors are examining their prospects, and it will pay the company to have properly researched its projects or its cash position, if there is a liquidity problem.

**Loan capital**

The raising of fixed-interest capital is directly influenced by the Stock Market as investors may not underwrite or subscribe to the issue or may require very high interest rates to offset the risk. Thus, the fixed-interest market acts in a small way to prevent a mis-allocation of resources.

**The ramifications of a poor share price performance**

Indirect influence by the Stock Market on the use of funds is exerted by the performance of share prices. The reasoning here is that poor share prices represent poor profit performance and bad management. Eventually the poor market price will attract the attention of a more efficient company who will take it over and attempt to make it more profitable. Alternatively, the poorly-managed company will itself bring in new management which will more efficiently deploy its assets. Although there has been little empirical testing of this argument of indirect influence it has a logical conceptual backing and is commonly acknowledged as being a significant determinant of resource allocation.

### The role of investment analysis

The role of investment analysis is to evaluate the worth of a share, to forecast future share-price performances and to build portfolios suitable to the requirements of the investor. Some aspects of investment analysis such as charts and mechanical strategy rules look solely at past share-price performance and forgo any attempt to value a company's worth or its portfolio characteristics.

**Influence in resource allocation**

From a socio-economic viewpoint investment analysis can justify itself as an influence in resource allocation and in providing a more stable investment environment for the investing public. Although investment analysts working in financial institutions do not have the same detailed information regarding capital projects as the companies have themselves they do bring a detached, profit-orientated judgment. The analyst will base his judgments on past performance which measures managerial ability and on prospects for the industry and on the particular company's projects. The company's own management is obviously biased to some extent and this may outweigh the knowledge advantages they have over investment analysts employed by financial institutions. Analysts' opinions are in even greater demand when rights and new issues are made as the company is increasing its resources, and from an investor's viewpoint such issues represent occasions to significantly increase or decrease their relative holdings. As mentioned earlier, however, analysts often have specific reactions to rights issues, regardless of individual circumstances.

**Investor confidence**

For individual investors investment analysis helps create a more stable pattern of prices. This gives more confidence for individuals to invest in stocks and shares for, whilst some individuals have a high risk preference, the vast majority are risk averters. Risk aversion is facilitated when the market has few violent fluctuations and when there seems to be some long-term association between a company's growth in terms of earnings per share (EPS) and its stock price. Investors' aversion to risk is emphasised in the many cases where individuals are using equity investments as a vehicle of saving for their retirements. Without the competitive framework of investment analysis speculative elements in the Stock Market will grow and investor confidence will decline. The withdrawal of investors from the Stock Exchange in large numbers would produce not only a market crash but would drain away business and monetary confidence to a crisis degree. The repercussions of a wildly speculative stock exchange would seriously affect business activity both through the capital-raising markets and through a general ebbing of confidence. Keith Funston, a former President of the New York Stock Exchange, has remarked:

*The spread of corporate ownership among additional millions of people willing to undertake the risks of stock investments – in return for the rewards – is not only a measure of the country's economic vitality, but an indication that the goals of the future, which will require enormous quantities of risk capital, can be achieved[2].*

Funston argued that the Stock Exchange provided a safe medium for the allocation of ownership of a country's assets and at the same time urged greater vigilance on the part of the stock market to inspire the public's confidence in investment.

## Success of investment analysis

Whether the increased resources devoted to analysing shares has resulted in more efficient resource allocation and more stable share prices is difficult to determine. This is due to the gradual build-up of investment research activities and the gradual growth in assets quoted on the Stock Exchange; this makes comparisons of what the situation might have been with significantly less investment analysis almost impossible to ascertain. There is virtually no published research on the economic value of investment analysis although the proponents of the Efficient Markets Theory, which is described later, would appear to implicitly argue that investment analysis has made the Stock Exchange more 'perfect'. Additionally, the build-up of research departments indicates that investors desire investment analysis and this is maybe due to it being inherently valuable: alternatively it is sometimes suggested that the increased commitment to research is purely for promotional reasons[3] and that no intrinsic value is obtained in the form of better investment advice. Although the success of investment analysis to date has not been established it is argued that any lack of success is due to both the weakness of the techniques being used and in the personal judgment and experience of the analyst. Thus, if the art and science of investment analysis is improved sufficiently, sounder resource allocation and more stable share prices will ensue: it is contended that such improvements can be made.

**Jobbing system**

The jobbing system on the London Stock Exchange developed in order to match buyers and sellers of various shares. They do this by taking positions in shares themselves and act as principals in dealings with stockbrokers. As described earlier there has been a large cutback in the number of jobbers during the past ten years and there has been a growing concern over the competitive element of the system. To some extent investment analysis has offset this lack of competition by influencing a more stable market which (1) reduces the risk to the jobber and therefore giving him more confidence in taking positions in stock, and (2) increases the confidence of investors in buying and selling.

**Growth of investment analysis and its implications**

Investors have always analysed shares to some extent, i.e. they must have had a reason(s) for selecting a particular stock, but until recently it had not warranted full-time attention. However, with the rapid growth of institutional investment in equities, investment analysis has become a paying proposition and has led to a new profession. Professional investment analysts are employed mainly by the financial institutions and by firms of stockbrokers although a growing number are being employed by industrial companies especially for their corporate planning activities. The growth of the profession of investment analysts, the increase in statutory controls on companies and on their reporting of financial results and the rise of regulatory bodies should tend towards more stable share-price behaviour. This has led many authors to conclude that the Stock Market is as near perfect a market as could be practically hoped for, given the large number of shares dealt in and the uncertain nature of future economic events. The theory of share prices being formed by the dynamic equilibrium model of the varying views of competing analysts and investors has received considerable attention from empirical researchers. The prevailing academic (and professional?) description of share-price behaviour is the 'efficient market model'.

**Efficient Markets Theory**

The theory argues that in a fully competitive market one would expect share prices to fully and accurately adjust to all publicly-available information. Such a market has been termed 'efficient' by its protagonists. Fama described that such share price processes provide accurate values for resource allocation, that is a market in which firms can make production-investment decisions, and investors can choose among the securities that represent ownership of firms' activities under the assumption that security prices at any one time fully reflect all available information[4]. This hypothesis is based on the accuracy and time taken for share prices to adjust to new information. Considerable empirical proof has been obtained which supports a weaker definition of the efficient markets model – one that says that share prices of the major quoted companies are determined in a fully competitive environment and that without inside information further investment analysis is generally not worth while. The Efficient Markets Theory and other concomitant models are described in Chapter 11 and the various statistical studies investigating such processes are reviewed.

## Review of the book

The usual chronological order of evaluating shares starts with an examination of the company's accounts. This provides an initial resumé of the company's business, its earnings progress and its book net asset worth. Chapter 2 explains the contents and the make-up of the general form of Annual Accounts. The analysis and interpretation of the data appearing in the Annual Accounts is described in Chapter 3. This chapter also discusses areas for improvement in Annual Reports.

Chapter 4 describes methods of forecasting company profits. These range from short-term estimates to long-range projections employing various forecasting techniques.

Once the forecast of a company's earnings have been made, the analyst will then need to determine what this means in terms of share-price performance. Chapter 5 describes various valuation models and the less 'scientific' but more market-orientated methods. This type of evaluation is known as fundamental analysis as it attempts to attach a value to a share. However, there is another branch of analysis which has many advocates, and this looks solely at past data and does not involve deriving a 'true worth' for a share. This is known as technical analysis and Chapter 6 describes many of the more commonly-used techniques.

Chapter 7 discusses the building of portfolios and the various practical difficulties likely to be encountered. The chapter also reviews some of the recent advances in the mathematical programming techniques of portfolio theory.

The measurement of investment and portfolio performance is, perhaps, more complicated than many would imagine. The various problems in measurement and the methods of overcoming these are discussed in Chapter 8.

A brief description of corporate taxation is given in Chapter 9. This will include pre-imputation and the imputation system of corporation tax.

Chapter 10 gives a basic introduction to some of the mathematical and statistical techniques which have been referred to throughout the book. This prevents the main body of the book being cluttered with appendices and enables the reader to turn-up the relevant statistical methodology without having to refer to other texts.

Chapter 11 gives a more detailed account of the Efficient Markets Theory and summarises the research that has been carried out on this topic. The impact of the Efficient Markets Theory for investment analysis will be discussed. For readers who are more interested in the various hypotheses of share-price movements this chapter could be read next.

Although Stock Market mechanisms vary from country to country the techniques of investment analysis are much the same. Obviously major differences lie in accounting methods and disclosure requirements and in the techniques of technical analysis. Hopefully, however, the reader will be able to apply the methodologies described in the book to share-price evaluation in the various Stock Markets around the world.

## References

1   'National balance sheets and national accounting', Revell, J. and Roe, A. R., *Economic Trends*, May 1971.

2   'Who owns American Business? Census of Shareholders', New York Stock Exchange, 1956.

3   For some illuminating quotes from leading stockbrokers on this point see: Braham, M., 'The growing impact of stockbrokers' research', *Money Management and Unitholder*, June 1972.

4   Fama, E. F., 'Efficient capital markets: A review of theory and empirical work', *Journal of Finance*, May 1970.

The texts given below relate to the functions and the workings of the British Stock Markets. For an American text on the role of the stock market and the economy see Baumol, W. J., 'The Stock Market and Economic Efficiency', Fordham University Press, 1965.

Briston, R. J., 'The Stock Exchange and Investment Analysis', George Allen & Unwin Ltd, 1970.

Morgan, E. V. and Thomas, W. A., 'The Stock Exchange, Its History and Functions', Elek Books, 1962.

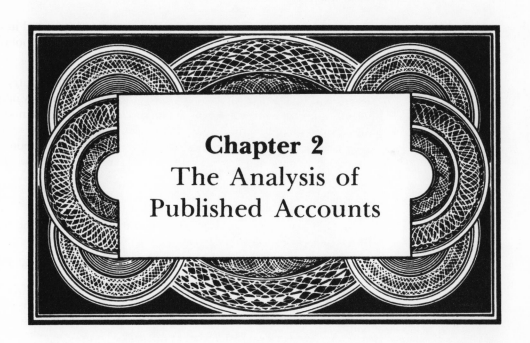

**Chapter 2**
The Analysis of
Published Accounts

The most obvious source of company data for analysts is the firm's Annual Report and Accounts. These must be prepared in compliance with the Companies Acts of 1948 and 1967 which lay down minimum disclosure requirements. The Acts however, give few rules on the accounting conventions to be adopted in preparing Accounts and the accountancy profession has been left to draw-up its own guidelines. The Annual Accounts are subjected to an audit by professional accountants who have to express an opinion as to whether they show a 'true and fair view' of the state of affairs of the company at the year-end and whether they comply with the Companies Acts of 1948 and 1967.

## Uses of Accounts in investment decision making

The main uses of the Accounts can be classified thus:

1 They provide a brief resumé of the business and its operations.

2 They provide a financial record of the stewardship of the management. The trend of past performance can be used as one indicator of managerial capability.

3 They give a net book asset value of the company. Although in many cases this figure may be far from the true worth, the Balance Sheet does give an idea of the asset structure.

4 They indicate certain key areas affecting profitability. For instance, the impact of financial gearing on earnings can be measured.

5 They sometimes specify intangible and deferred revenue assets. Although the valuation of these assets are in many cases very tenuous

13

they do acknowledge their existence and the fact that they may contribute towards or indicate future earnings.

6   Accounts provide bases from which projections of past figures and trends can be made. The automatic projection of past data into the future should be taken with caution as it is at best only a short-term forecasting technique. Some studies have shown that even short-term extrapolation of accounting data has no relevance at all and this has been attributed to both accounting methodologies and to the variability in business fortunes.

## Improvements in Accounts

The value of Accounts can, however, be improved considerably and this would further reduce the elements of risk in investment. The main areas for improvement include an increase in disclosure requirements and a re-examination of the principles and concepts used in preparing Accounts. One of the main arguments against increased disclosure requirements is that important data would be given to competitors. This view will be strengthened where there are foreign competitors as in many cases they do not have to reach the same disclosure levels. However, similar arguments were put forward against the 1967 Act but since its coming into operation the only criticism has been that it did not go far enough! Suggestions for the improvement of accounting information will be given at the end of Chapter 3 after the present methods of financial reporting have been explained and discussed.

The chapter will develop by giving a brief introduction to the Profit and Loss Account, the Balance Sheet and Group Accounts. This is followed by a hypothetical set of accounts for ABC LTD and will incorporate the various Companies Acts' requirements. The various items will be explained and their importance for investment analysis discussed. Following on from this Chapter 3 will describe the interpretation of Accounts which will involve the re-arrangement of data and the use of ratios.

### Profit and Loss Accounts and Balance Sheets

The Profit and Loss Account measures the stewardship of the company's funds over the particular period (usually one year). As accounts are prepared on a consistent basis shareholders can use them to measure management's performance over various periods. There is a body of opinion which says that the Profit and Loss Account should reflect all the changes in values between one Balance Sheet date and the next. These same people also argue for the Balance Sheet items to be recorded at current market, inflation adjusted or replacement values and that all items recording changes in these values should be entered in the Profit and Loss Account. At present, permanent changes in the value of assets are recorded either as an 'extraordinary item' in the Profit and Loss Account or as a movement in the company's reserves. However, the re-valuation of assets is not a common occurrence with historical cost forming the main valuation base.

14

The Balance Sheet gives a statement of the financial affairs of the company at one particular date. The net asset value attributable to the ordinary shareholders is given by the total of ordinary shares and reserves and represents the 'value' of the firm after repaying all debts. As the Balance Sheet values are usually recorded at cost price less amounts written off (which rarely reflects the market value) the net asset figure is not a current market value. Even using current market values will not give a true cash equivalent value for the firm as the realisation of assets will involve heavy expenses as well as accepting higher than, or more probably lower than, market prices. It is important to note that Balance Sheets give the financial position at one particular date and this can give a misleading picture of the general position. This is especially likely to occur in seasonal businesses. For instance, a greetings-card company with a year-end on say 28 February shows large cash balances and very low stock and debtor levels. This may not, however, be indicative of the usual financial position. The Christmas trade of the card manufacturer may account for around 50 per cent of business and thus by the end of February the stocks and debtors would be abnormally low and the cash balances exceptionally high. A competitor with a year-end on, say, 30 November would show a quite opposite position and so, clearly, the analyst has to be aware of trade customs when comparing Balance Sheets which have been drawn-up to different dates*.

## Subsidiaries

Most quoted companies have a subsidiary(ies) and so consolidated accounts have to be prepared. A subsidiary is defined as a company which has one shareholding company which owns over 50 per cent of the ordinary share capital. The investing company is usually referred to as the parent (where it trades itself) or the holding company (where it does not trade itself). Consolidated accounts combine the assets and profits of the subsidiary along with those of the parent. The Companies Act 1948 requires that a company publish a consolidated Profit and Loss Account, a consolidated Balance Sheet and a Balance Sheet of the parent (or holding) company.

## Consolidated accounts

The following example briefly shows the consolidation process. Company *A* and company *B* have the following Balance Sheets.

|  | *A* | | |
| --- | --- | --- | --- |
|  | £ | | £ |
| Capital – 30,000 @ £1 each | 30,000 | Cash | 100,000 |
| Reserves | 70,000 | | |
|  | £100,000 | | £100,000 |

*This is used as an example. In practice the Balance Sheets of greetings-card companies will not be as clear cut as above as sales of Christmas cards will be made, and stocks delivered, from around July onwards.

**B**

| | £ | | £ |
|---|---|---|---|
| Capital – 20,000 @ £1 each | 20,000 | Fixed assets | 50,000 |
| Reserves | 10,000 | | |
| Liabilities | 20,000 | | |
| | £50,000 | | £50,000 |

Book net asset value per share = £1.50p

If *A* uses its cash to buy more than 50 per cent of *B*'s ordinary shares, say 75 per cent at £1.50p, then it has to prepare consolidated accounts. *A*'s unconsolidated Balance Sheet after acquiring the shares in *B* would appear as:

**A**

| | £ | | £ |
|---|---|---|---|
| Capital | 30,000 | Cash | 77,500 |
| Reserves | 70,000 | Shares in *B* | |
| | | 15,000 @ 1.50 | 22,500 |
| | £100,000 | | £100,000 |

The consolidated Balance Sheet will exclude the item 'Shares in *B*' and in its place will be inserted the assets and liabilities taken over. *A*'s consolidated Balance Sheet would thus appear:

**A**

CONSOLIDATED

| | £ | | £ |
|---|---|---|---|
| Capital | 30,000 | Cash | 77,500 |
| Reserves | 70,000 | Fixed assets | 50,000 |
| Minorities | 7,500 | | |
| Liabilities | 20,000 | | |
| | £127,500 | | £127,500 |

The minorities item represents the value of those *B* shares not held by *A*, i.e. 5,000 × £1.50p. If *A* had paid more than £1.50p for each share in *B* then a goodwill item would have appeared in the consolidated Balance Sheet as the purchase price is above the book net asset value. Thus, if *A* had paid £2 for every *B* share it would have paid out £30,000 in acquiring its stake but the assets it acquired would still be the same as before, i.e. £22,500 (75 per cent of £50,000 − £20,000). The consolidated Balance Sheet would now look like:

**A**

CONSOLIDATED

| | £ | | £ |
|---|---|---|---|
| Capital | 30,000 | Cash | 70,000 |
| Reserves | 70,000 | Fixed assets | 50,000 |
| Minorities | 7,500 | Goodwill | |
| | | 30,000–75% | |
| Liabilities | 20,000 | (50,000 − 20,000) | 7,500 |
| | £127,500 | | £127,500 |

**Accounting conventions**

There are a number of ways of accounting for business data although certain conventions and concepts have become virtually unanimously accepted in different countries. The UK is no exception and most quoted companies adhere to the standards set. The following paragraphs set out the standard concepts.

1   The going-concern basis which assumes there is no intention to liquidate the company and that it will continue in its existing form. This concept has been used as an argument against the regular re-valuing of assets on the grounds that as the company is not going to liquidate current values are of little relevance in financial accounts.

2   The accruals or matching of costs and revenues concept. This defers writing-off expenditure in the Profit and Loss Account until the appropriate revenue has been received. Judgment has to be exercised in determining whether the revenue will ever arise and its value if it does.

3   Consistency. This requires the accounting treatment of like items to be consistent. This is often used as a defence against adopting improved methods of recording or valuing assets.

4   Prudence. This concept requires that profits are only taken when they appear in the form of cash or of other assets whose ultimate realisation in cash can be forecast with reasonable certainty. Provisions are made for all known liabilities whether the amounts are known with certainty or not. This concept may act to understate the true worth of a business and therefore acts to the benefit of creditors and potential shareholders and to the detriment of the existing investors.

5   The use of cost as the major measurement of Profit and Loss Account and Balance Sheet items. This accounting base has been the subject of considerable criticism in its use of valuing assets as in the majority of cases historical cost bears little resemblance to current market values, or replacement values.

**Criticisms**

These concepts have come in for considerable criticism during the past few years and the accounting bodies are waking up to the challenge on existing ideals. Although many of the criticisms are valid the various alternative concepts proposed have not been greeted with any general approval. One major area of criticism has been the use of historical cost as the method of valuing assets and the Accounting Standards Steering Committee (ASSC) has drawn up proposals for accounting for inflation[1]. The methods advocated by the ASSC have themselves come in for considerable criticism by parties who have proposed a number of alternatives.

**Disclosure of accounting policies**

Following an Institute of Chartered Accountants (ICA) statement, companies have been recommended to include in their notes to Accounts or in their Directors' Report a note on the accounting policies adopted for material items affecting the Profit and Loss Account and the Balance Sheet[2]. Additionally, if the standard accounting concepts of going concern, accruals, consistency and prudence, have been departed from, this should be stated.

**Need for understanding accounting conventions**

It has to be recognised that accounting for business transactions is an estimation process and that no system can consistently and accurately portray the real value of the enterprise. In economic terms the value of a business is the discounted value of all future benefits and, as we shall see, this is what fundamental analysis sets out to achieve. The economic profit of a company is defined as the change in the discounted value of future benefits between the Balance Sheet dates. This value of the enterprise cannot, of course, be known with certainty. Accounting conventions use historical or inflation-adjusted costs as the basis of measurement and do not attempt to measure the future cash flows that will result from a company's transactions: this, it is argued, is the role of the investor. Within the traditional concepts and conventions there exist many ways of recording and valuing transactions and these can lead to significantly different earnings figures[3]. Thus it is important for the analyst to have an understanding of the various possible ways of recording accounting data so that he can interpret financial results knowing what the bases and what the limitations are.

**Explanation of accounts**

This section was written for readers with only a perfunctory knowledge of accountancy and thus describes in detail the items usually found in published Accounts. For those who have no knowledge of book-keeping at all and who wish to get a grasp of the subject they are recommended to some of the elementary texts[4]. Graduates in accountancy can skip this section of the book and can skim through the following chapter. Chapter 3 explains how the analyst makes use of the information given in Annual Accounts.

The Accounts of ABC LTD are set out opposite. They contain the usual items found in published Accounts and have been set out in vertical form which is now the accepted form of presentation. The accounts have followed the Companies Acts provisions[5] and have incorporated the commonly accepted standards in financial reporting. Readers can easily obtain copies of published Annual Reports simply by writing to the company or to their registrars*.

---

*The annual 'Survey of Published Accounts' published by the ICA provides a useful reference of the financial reporting methods of major quoted companies.

## ABC LTD
### Consolidated Profit and Loss Account for the period ended 31 December 1972

| 1971 £'000 | | | Notes | | 1972 £'000 |
|---|---|---|---|---|---|
| 9.800 | | Group turnover | 1 | | 10,600 |
| 1,000 | | Group profit before taxation | 2 | | 1,536 |
| | | Share of profit *less* losses of | | | |
| 120 | | associated company | | | 162 |
| 1,120 | | Profit before taxation | | | 1,698 |
| | 350 | Taxation: Investing company and subsidiaries' | 5 | 620 | |
| 368 | 18 | associated company | | 62 | 682 |
| 752 | | Group profit after taxation | | | 1,016 |
| 10 | | Minority interests | | | 20 |
| 742 | | Profit after taxation before extraordinary items | | | 996 |
| | | Extraordinary items (group proportion after taxation and minority interests and including share of associated company's items) | 3 | | |
| — | — | | | | 116 |
| 742 | | Profit attributable to members | | | 880 |
| 200 | | Dividends | 7 | | 200 |
| 542 | | Net profit retained | | | 680 |
| | 432 | ABC LTD | | 520 | |
| | 30 | Subsidiaries | | 60 | |
| | 80 | In associated company | | 100 | |
| | 542 | | | 680 | |
| | 36.2p | Earnings per share | 6 | 44.9p | |

### Notes on Profit and Loss Account

1 Group turnover
  This excludes all inter-group transactions

| 2 Trading profit is arrived at after charging | 1972 £ | 1971 £ |
|---|---|---|
| Depreciation | 431,000 | 398,000 |
| Interest: Bank interest | 27,192 | 41,252 |
| Interest on loans repayable within five years | 5,100 | 4,983 |
| Interest on loans repayable in excess of five years | 25,400 | 15,400 |
| | 57,692 | 61,635 |
| Hire of plant & machinery | 4,256 | 4,352 |
| Auditors' remuneration | 5,250 | 4,750 |
| Directors' emoluments (See note 4) | 25,000 | 17,500 |
| Exceptional and non-recurrent expenditure: | | |
| Exceptional stock losses | 55,000 | – |
| Exceptional Foreign Exchange fluctuations | 25,000 | – |

*Investment analysis*

|  | 1972 £ | 1971 £ |
|---|---|---|
| And after receiving | | |
| Income from quoted investments | 6,100 | 5,950 |
| Income from unquoted investments | 10,000 | 10,000 |
| Income from rents of land | 500 | 500 |
| Income transferred from development grant account | 10,000 | |

3 Extraordinary item

| | | |
|---|---|---|
| Loss on sale of assets of machine tool division | 116,530 | |

4 Directors' emoluments

| | | |
|---|---|---|
| Fees | 1,000 | 500 |
| Management remuneration | 24,000 | 17,000 |
| | 25,000 | 17,500 |

of which the

| | | |
|---|---|---|
| Chairman's emoluments amounted to | 1,000 | 1,000 |
| and that of the highest paid director to | 8,250 | 5,500 |

Directors' emoluments classified in multiples
of £2,500 are as under:

| | | |
|---|---|---|
| 0–2,500 | 1 | 1 |
| 2,501–5,000 | 1 | 3 |
| 5,001–7,500 | 2 | 1 |
| 7,501–10,000 | 1 | |

5 Taxation

| | | |
|---|---|---|
| UK corporation tax at 40% | 450,000 | 300,000 |
| *Less*: Foreign tax relief | 50,000 | 40,000 |
| | 400,000 | 260,000 |
| Add foreign taxes | 100,000 | 80,000 |
| | 500,000 | 340,000 |
| Transfer to deferred taxation account | 120,000 | 10,000 |
| | 620,000 | 350,000 |

6 Earnings per share
The calculation of EPS is based on earnings of
£996,000 (£742,000 1971) and on the weighted average
of 2,220,000 ordinary shares after adjustment of
the number of shares in issue prior to the rights
issue on 1 July 1972 by the factor

$$\frac{100\text{p cum rights}}{98\text{p ex rights}}$$

The EPS figure for 1971 has been adjusted accordingly

7 Dividends (gross)

| | | |
|---|---|---|
| Interim paid 4p per share (4p–1971) | 80,000 | 80,000 |
| Final proposed 5p per share (6p–1971) | 120,000 | 120,000 |
| | £200,000 | £200,000 |

## ABC LTD
## Consolidated Balance Sheet as at 31 December 1972

| 1971<br>£'000 | | Assets | | | Notes | 1972<br>£'000 |
|---|---|---|---|---|---|---|
| 1,836 | | Fixed assets | | | 1 | 2,479 |
| 220 | | Goodwill | | | 2 | 220 |
| 161 | | Investments | | | 3 | 261 |
| | | Current assets: | | | | |
| | | Stocks and | | | | |
| | 805 | work-in-progress | 1,081 | | 4 | |
| | 683 | Debtors | 970 | | | |
| | 58 | Cash | 47 | 2,098 | | |
| | 1,546 | | | | | |
| | | Current liabilities: | | | | |
| | 380 | Creditors | 460 | | | |
| | 200 | Taxation | 340 | | | |
| | 600 | Bank overdraft | 60 | | | |
| | 120 | Proposed dividend | 120 | 980 | | |
| 246 | 1,300 | | | 1,118 | | |
| | | Net current assets | | | | 1,118 |
| 2,463 | | | | | | 4,078 |
| | | *Financed by*: | | | | |
| 500 | | Share capital | | | 5 | 600 |
| 231 | | Share premium account | | | 6 | 481 |
| 1,052 | | Reserves | | | 7 | 1,732 |
| 1,783 | | | | | | 2,813 |
| 120 | | Minority interests | | | | 140 |
| 240 | | Loan capital | | | 8 | 340 |
| 60 | | Deferred taxation | | | | 180 |
| 260 | | Amount set aside for future taxation | | | | 405 |
| | | Development grant account | | | | 200 |
| 2,463 | | | | | | 4,078 |

## Balance Sheet as at 31 December 1972

| 1971<br>£'000 | | Assets | | | Notes | 1972<br>£'000 |
|---|---|---|---|---|---|---|
| 1,449 | | Fixed assets | | | 1 | 2,099 |
| 161 | | Investments | | | 3 | 261 |
| 593 | | Subsidiary companies | | | 9 | 520 |
| | | Current assets: | | | | |
| | | Stocks and | | | | |
| | 600 | work-in-progress | 830 | | 4 | |
| | 450 | Debtors | 660 | | | |
| | 60 | Cash | 3 | 1,493 | | |
| | 1,110 | | | | | |

| 1971 £'000 | Assets | | Notes | 1972 £'000 |
|---|---|---|---|---|
| | Current liabilities: | | | |
| 200 | Creditors | 300 | | |
| 170 | Taxation | 200 | | |
| 500 | Bank overdraft | 20 | | |
| 120 | Proposed dividend | 120 | 640 | |
| 990 | | | 853 | |
| 120 | Net current assets | | | 853 |
| 2,323 | | | | 3,733 |
| | *Financed by*: | | | |
| 500 | Share capital | | 5 | 600 |
| 231 | Share premium account | | 6 | 481 |
| 1,062 | Reserves | | 7 | 1,582 |
| 1,793 | | | | 2,663 |
| 240 | Loan capital | | 8 | 340 |
| 60 | Deferred taxation | | | 180 |
| 230 | Amount set aside for future taxation | | | 350 |
| | Development grant account | | | 200 |
| 2,323 | | | | 3,733 |

## Notes to the Balance Sheet

### 1 Fixed assets

GROUP £'000

| | Freehold property | Long leasehold property | Plant & machinery | Total |
|---|---|---|---|---|
| Cost at 1.1.72 | 300 | 200 | 2,386 | 2,886 |
| Additions | | 150 | 1,410 | 1,560 |
| Disposals at cost | | (58) | (528) | (586) |
| | 300 | 292 | 3,268 | 3,860 |
| Accumulated depreciation | | | | |
| Balance at 1.1.72 | | 60 | 990 | 1,050 |
| Written off during year | | 5 | 426 | 431 |
| Disposals | | | (100) | (100) |
| | | 65 | 1,316 | 1,381 |
| Net | 300 | 227 | 1,952 | 2,479 |

COMPANY £'000

| | Freehold property | Long leasehold property | Plant & machinery | Total |
|---|---|---|---|---|
| Cost at 1.1.72 | 300 | 85 | 1,687 | 2,072 |
| Additions | | 100 | 1,366 | 1,466 |
| Disposals at cost | | | (520) | (520) |
| | 300 | 185 | 2,533 | 3,018 |
| Depreciation | | | | |
| Balance at 1.1.72 | | 25 | 639 | 664 |
| Written off during year | | 5 | 350 | 355 |
| Disposals | | | (100) | (100) |
| | | 30 | 889 | 919 |
| Net | 300 | 155 | 1,644 | 2,099 |

Valuations: freehold property was re-valued at 30.4.65     172
           Additions at cost         <u>128</u>
                                                             <u>300</u>

No depreciation has been charged on freehold property

2   Goodwill

This amount represents the excess cost over book value of businesses acquired and not written off.

3   Investments

|  | GROUP | | COMPANY | |
|---|---|---|---|---|
|  | 1972 | 1971 | 1972 | 1971 |
|  | £'000 | £'000 | £'000 | £'000 |
| Quoted at cost | 36 | 36 | 36 | 36 |
| Market value in UK† | *(60)* | *(48)* | *(60)* | *(48)* |
| Associated company* | 200 | 100 | 200 | 100 |
| Unquoted at cost: shares | 15 | 15 | 15 | 15 |
| loans | 10 | 10 | 10 | 10 |
| Directors' valuation† | *(15)* | *(15)* | *(15)* | *(15)* |
|  | <u>261</u> | <u>161</u> | <u>261</u> | <u>161</u> |

ABC LTD holds 25.6% of the ordinary share capital of ALPHA LTD, a company quoted on the London Stock Exchange

| | | | | |
|---|---|---|---|---|
| *Quoted at cost – Associated Company | 20 | 20 | 20 | 20 |
| Group's proportion of post acquisition Retained Profits | 180 | 80 | 180 | 80 |
|  | <u>200</u> | <u>100</u> | <u>200</u> | <u>100</u> |

†Figures in italics are the market value and directors' valuation of shares.

4   Stocks

Stock is valued at cost or net realisable value whichever is the lower. A proportion of overhead allowance is included in the work-in-progress figure.

5   Share capital

| | 1972 | 1971 |
|---|---|---|
| Authorised | | |
| 4,000,000 ordinary shares of 25p each | £1,000,000 | £1,000,000 |
| Issued and fully paid | | |
| 2,400,000 ordinary shares of 25p each (2,000,000–1971) | 600,000 | 500,000 |

During the year 400,000 ordinary shares were issued via a rights issue

6   Share premium account

| | £ |
|---|---|
| Balance at 1.1.72 | 231,000 |
| Premium on shares issued via rights issue during the year | 250,000 |
| | 481,000 |

7   Reserves

| | 1972 £'000 | 1971 £'000 | 1972 £'000 | 1971 £'000 |
|---|---|---|---|---|
| Balance at 1.1.72 | 1,052 | 510 | 1,062 | 630 |
| Retained profit for the year | 680 | 542 | 520 | 432 |
| | 1,732 | 1,052 | 1,582 | 1,062 |

8   Loan capital

| | 1972 £ | 1971 £ |
|---|---|---|
| 7% debenture stock 1981/5. Secured by a first charge over the freehold properties | 220,000 | 220,000 |
| 10% loan notes 1975. Secured by a floating charge over the company's assets | 20,000 | 20,000 |
| 10% debenture stock 1990 issued during year. Secured by a second mortgage on the freehold property and a floating charge over the remaining company assets | 100,000 | |
| | 340,000 | 240,000 |

9   Shares in subsidiary company
DEF LTD.

| | 1972 £'000 | 1971 £'000 |
|---|---|---|
| At cost | 520 | 520 |
| Amounts due by subsidiaries | 1 | 76 |
| | 521 | 596 |
| Amounts due to subsidiaries | 1 | 3 |
| | 520 | 593 |

ABC LTD own 300,000 ordinary shares in DEF LTD which represents 75% of the total ordinary 25p shares in issue of that company

*The analysis of published accounts*

**Directors' Report**

1   Accounts and dividends. The directors submit accounts for the year ended 31 December 1972 and recommend the payment of a final dividend of 5.0p per share. If approved the final dividend will be paid on 28 February 1973. An interim dividend of 4p per share was paid on 31 August 1972 in respect of the shares outstanding at 30 June 1972.

2   The principal activities of the group consisted of general engineering products to the automobile and aircraft industries. Exports amounted to £230,000 (£195,000 in 1971).

3   Employees. The average number of employees of the group in each week during the period was 1,842 and their aggregate remuneration in respect of the year was £2,180,000.

4   Charitable and political contributions. Gifts amounting to £600 were made to charitable organisations. No political contributions were made.

5   Directors. The present directors of the company are set out on p. 123. The interests at 31 December 1972 and 31 December 1971 of persons who at those dates were directors, in the shares of the company as shown by the register kept by the company are:

| Name | 1972 | 1971 |
|------|------|------|
| L | 120,000 | 110,500 |
| M | 87,500 | 90,000 |
| N | 50,000 | 45,000 |
| O | 10,000 | 10,000 |
| P | 10,000 | 10,000 |

6   The directors are of the opinion that the current market value of properties is not significantly different from the book value and consider that a revaluation at the current time would not be worth while.

7   So far as the directors are aware the company is not a close company within the meaning of the Income and Corporation Taxes Act 1970.

8   Auditors. The auditors Messrs z have signified their willingness to continue in office.

The Accounts of ABC LTD were made up to 31 December 1972, pre the imputation system of corporation tax. The changes in financial accounts to take account of the imputation system of company taxation will be described in this chapter and in Chapter 9.

**Turnover**

Until the 1967 Companies Act, firms did not have to publish their turnover statistics although many in fact did so. The Act requires companies to state their turnover in the Profit and Loss Account and the method used in computing it as a note thereto. Certain exemptions from disclosure were granted, i.e. shipping, banking and discounting firms and for companies with a turnover which does not exceed £50,000. This last item is virtually non-applicable to quoted companies. No definition of turnover is given by the Companies Act of 1967 and the analyst will have to look at the Notes to the Accounts to see how the figure has been arrived at. Companies usually exclude inter-group sales but other factors are often not easy to ascertain, e.g. the treatment of agency sales, royalties, customs and excise duty. Turnover should be shown net of any value added tax (see SSAP5 'Accounting for Value Added Tax', Accounting Standards Steering Committee, May 1974).

## Categorisation of turnover

The division of turnover into product groups, if material, must be given in the Directors' Report. This split-up can often be extended by an investigation of the subsidiaries' accounts (if any). Exports are dealt with in the Directors' Report.

### Profit before taxation

Most companies' first reference to profits occurs under the above heading although a few do give some information on the cost of sales. However, under the Companies Acts of 1948 and 1967 disclosure of certain expenses has to be made and these provide some useful information for analysts. The items requiring separate disclosure are:

1   Income from rents of land.

2   Income from investments distinguishing between income from quoted and income from unquoted investments.

3   Directors' emoluments, Chairman's emoluments and emoluments of employees receiving more than £10,000 per year. The emoluments must be classified into multiples of £2,500.

4   Auditors' remuneration.

5   Interest payable differentiating between those relating to bank loans, overdrafts and loans repayable within five years and those relating to all other loans.

6   Amounts incurred for the hire of plant and machinery.

7   Provision for depreciation.

The company normally discloses the above information by way of a Note to the Accounts.

## Interest payments

The interest payments are used in calculating various ratios which are useful to analysts. As mentioned previously the Balance Sheet items represent the financial position at one specific date and as this may not be indicative of the general structure, analysts may tend to place more attention on the interest payments. The division of loans into amounts repayable within five years and those repayable after five years gives a further breakdown of the gearing structure. Further divisions, especially of loans repayable under five years, would be desirable, however.

## Plant hire

Plant hire charges can be useful as an explanation as to why two similar companies may have substantially different plant and machinery assets.

## Depreciation

The depreciation figure appearing in the vast majority of accounts represents the measure of use that the trading period has had of the life of the particular fixed asset. This view usually entails adopting a consistent policy of writing down the value of assets. However, there are other interpretations of how depreciation should be measured, these often being based on the diminution of current market value of the asset. Another method involves measuring the fall in current market value and the additional amounts necessary to replace the asset.

## Depreciation methods

The first method involves using constant depreciation rates which enables the write-offs to be forecastable and creates a more stable profits trend. However, it does not represent the diminution of value where the asset to be sold and thus the Balance Sheet will not reflect the current market value. The argument for replacement depreciation is that, due to inflation, the cost of replacing a similar-capacity machine will be far in excess of the old. If the company has only provided depreciation based on the original cost then insufficient capital may be available for the replacement. The valuation of replacement costs is very difficult and often a matter of personal judgment and here lies one of its main weaknesses. The replacement method will invariably involve a higher charge than either of the two other methods. The introduction of a depreciation figure based on replacement values will, however, not be possible as under Company Law only the part based on original cost or a revaluation can be included: any additional amounts set aside to cover the cost of replacement will be regarded as a reserve and must be shown separately. The replacement method can therefore be used by splitting the charge into two parts, one being recorded in accumulated depreciation to date, the other as a reserve. Unfortunately, few companies have adopted these procedures and so the analyst must make the best estimate he can of whether the retained profits will be sufficient for any asset replacement.

The depreciation charge shown in profit and loss accounts will be based upon the original cost or on any revaluation figure to record current market values. Apart from property companies, however, few companies adopt the current market value approach. This method requires a valuation each year and can fluctuate widely thereby making the profit figure more erratic. The usual methods of depreciation are the reducing-balance and straight-line techniques. The reducing-balance method involves writing-off a constant percentage of the outstanding balance each year. The annual charge under this method will be the highest in the first years of the asset's life. Straight-line depreciation charges a constant amount to the Profit and Loss Account. Any sale of assets will be compared against its written-down value (i.e. the cost less cumulative depreciation to date) and the resultant profit or loss will be transferred to the Profit and Loss Account or, occasionally, reserves if it is a very large sum. Separate disclosure of profits or losses accruing from the sale of fixed assets need only be given if the amounts are material and the concept of materiality in accountancy is really one of judgment on the part of management and the auditors.

*Example*   A company pays £1,000 for a machine. The depreciation rate set by management is 10 per cent (straight-line) or 20 per cent (reducing balance). At the end of three years the machine is sold for £200. The following depreciation write offs will have occurred in the three years.

|        |                      | Straight line<br>£ |                   | Reducing balance<br>£ |                            |
|--------|----------------------|--------------------|-------------------|-----------------------|----------------------------|
|        | Cost                 | 1,000              |                   | 1,000                 |                            |
| Year 1 | Depreciation         | 100                | constant amount   | 200                   | constant percentage (20%)  |
|        | Written-down value   | 900                |                   | 800                   |                            |
| Year 2 | Depreciation         | 100                |                   | 160                   |                            |
|        | Written-down value   | 800                |                   | 640                   |                            |
| Year 3 | Depreciation         | 100                |                   | 128                   |                            |
|        | Written-down value   | 700                |                   | 512                   |                            |
| Year 3 | Sales proceeds       | 200                |                   | 200                   |                            |
|        | Loss on sale of assets | £500             |                   | £312                  |                            |

## Disclosure of depreciation policies

Very few companies disclose the methods they use in depreciating assets. Some companies, however, do give both the methods and the rates of write off and good examples can be found in the field of television renters (in this case the depreciation figures are an important determinant of company profitability). Most companies do not provide for depreciation of freehold land as there almost never is any fall in value*. However, companies must state whether or not depreciation has been charged on freeholds.

Depreciation reduces the profits available for distribution but as no cash leaves the company the funds represented thereby are invested in fixed or current assets. The amounts provided for by depreciation are very large and represent over 25 per cent of the total gross trading profits, and finance an even greater proportion of industry's expenditure on fixed assets.

### Investment grants

Regional development grants created by the Industry Act of 1972 are available for certain types of capital expenditure. The company

*The evidence of 1974 shows, however, that property values can fall quite markedly in some periods.

receives a cash grant and there are a number of ways of recording the transaction. The ASSC in their exposure draft ED9 'The Accounting Treatment of Grants under the Industry Act 1972'[6] looked at the principal treatments which are:

1 To credit to Profit and Loss Account the total amount of the grant immediately.

2 To credit the amount of the grant to a non-distributable reserve.

3 To credit the amount of the grant to revenue over the useful life of the asset by:
(*a*) Reducing the cost of the acquisition of the fixed asset by the amount of the grant; or
(*b*) Treating the amount of the grant as a deferred credit, a portion of which is transferred to revenue annually.

The first two alternatives do not match the receipt of the grant into the Profit and Loss Account and the depreciation of the asset to which it relates and are therefore rejected in practice. This is an example of the matching of revenues and expenditures concept. Both the applications of the third method are met frequently in published Accounts. The ASSC in their statement of standard accounting practice on the subject have come down in favour of the deferred credits method where the annual transfer to the Profit and Loss Account is made, 'on a basis which reflects the benefit over the expected useful life of the asset'. The advantages of this method are that assets acquired at different times and locations are recorded on a uniform basis, that control of expenditure is based on cost value and because capital allowances are calculated on the cost price of an asset before the deduction of any grant. This is likely to become the prevailing method and thus each year a proportion of the grant will be credited to the Profit and Loss Account. Where the credit transferred to the Profit and Loss Account is material, it should be separately disclosed.

### Exceptional items

If regular business transactions have for some reason exceptionally and materially affected profits the companies are expected to disclose such in the accounts or in a note thereto (ASSC proposed statement of standard accounting practice, ED7, 'Accounting for Extraordinary Items'[7]). This classification would for instance include exceptional bad debts or stock losses and abnormal profits or losses through fluctuations in Foreign Exchange rates. Companies should disclose the specific exceptional item and the amount involved. These items often explain unexpected profits news and are of considerable use to analysts. In interpreting Accounts, analysts will very probably exclude exceptional items from cost structure analyses and from performance ratios. This is because the items tend to fluctuate erratically and thus distort any underlying fundamental business trends.

### Treatment of the results of associated companies

By law companies must, with certain exceptions, consolidate profits and losses of subsidiaries. Until recently, where an investment of 50 per cent or less has been held, only the investing company's share of the dividend has been included in the Profit and Loss Account. In 'Accounting for the Results of Associated Companies', January 1971, the ICA have recommended that the attributable earnings of associated companies be consolidated. This recommendation was made on the basis that it provided better information for investors to evaluate management performance and future prospects. Although the statement has had its opponents there is now a good deal of acceptance, and it is likely to become the prevailing practice within the next few years.

**Definition**

An associated company is defined thus:
A company (not being a subsidiary of the investing group or company) is an associated company of the investing group or company if:
(*a*) the investing group or company's interest in the associated company is effectively that of a partner in a joint venture or consortium; or,
(*b*) the investing group or company's interest in the associated company is for the long term and is substantial (i.e. not less that 20 per cent of the equity voting rights), and, having regard to the disposition of the other shareholdings, the investing group or company is in a position to exercise a significant influence over the associated company.

In both cases it is essential that the investing group or company participates (usually through representation on the board) in commercial and financial policy decisions of the associated company, including the distribution of profits.

**Inclusions in investing Company Accounts**

The recommendation proposes that the investing company's Accounts should include only the dividend receipt which is the existing practice. In the consolidated accounts, however, the share of profits less losses of the associated company should be included. If no consolidated accounts are prepared then the investing company's Accounts should include this item and exclude the dividend receipt.

**Accounting periods**

The Accounts of the associated company which are to be used should be the audited accounts either coterminous with those of the investing company or made up to a date which is not more than six months before, or shortly after, the date of the investing group or company's Accounts. In the absence of such audited Accounts (for which there should be justifiable cause), unaudited Accounts may be used provided the investing group is satisfied as to their reliability. If Accounts not coterminous with those of the investing company, or unaudited Accounts, are used, the facts and the dates of year-ends should be disclosed.

Adjustments should be made to group Accounts to exclude unrealised profit on stocks transferred to or from associated companies and to achieve a 'reasonable consistency with the accounting practices adopted by the investing group'.

**Disclosure requirements**

The disclosure requirements of reporting of associated company results are as set out in the ICA recommendation as follows.

### Profit and Loss Account items

*Profits before tax*  The investing group should include in its consolidated accounts the aggregate of its share of before-tax profits less losses of associated companies. The item should be shown separately and suitably described, e.g. as 'share of profits less losses of associated companies'.

*Taxation*  The tax attributed to the share of profits of associated companies should be disclosed separately within the group tax charge in the consolidated accounts.

*Extraordinary items*  The investing group's share of aggregate extraordinary items dealt with in associated companies' accounts should be included with the group share of extraordinary items, unless the amount is material in the context of the group's results when it should be separately disclosed.

*Net profit retained by associated companies*  There should be shown separately the investing group's share of aggregate net profits less losses retained by associated companies.

*Other items*  The investing group should not include its attributable share of associated companies' items such as turnover and depreciation in the aggregate amounts of these items disclosed in its consolidated accounts. If the results of one or more associated companies are of such significance in the context of the investing group's Accounts that more detailed information about them would assist in giving a 'true and fair view', this information should be given by separate disclosure of the total turnover of the associated companies concerned, their total depreciation charge, their total profits less losses before taxation, and the amounts of such profits attributable to the investing group.

### Balance Sheet items

Unless shown at a valuation, the amount at which the investing group's interests in associated companies should be shown in the consolidated Balance Sheet is: (1) the cost of the investments less any amounts written off, and (2) the investing company or group's share of the post-acquisition retained profits and reserves of the associated companies.

The investing company which has no subsidiaries, or which does not otherwise prepare consolidated accounts, should show its share of its associated companies' post-acquisition retained profits and reserves by way of note to its Balance Sheet.

Information regarding associated companies' tangible and intangible assets and liabilities should be given, if materially relevant for the appreciation by the members of the investing company of the nature of their investment.

The amount at which the investing group's interests in accumulated reserves is shown in the consolidated accounts should distinguish between profits retained by the group and profits retained by associated companies. If retained profits of associated companies overseas would be subject to further tax on distribution, this should be made clear. It will also be necessary to take account of and disclose movements on associated companies' other reserves, e.g. surplus on revaluation of fixed assets.

The Accounts of ABC LTD have followed the above disclosure recommendations.

### Disclosure of particulars of associated companies

The investing group or company should give particulars of the names of, and its interests in, companies treated as associated companies, and of any other companies in which it holds not less than 20 per cent of the equity voting rights but which are not treated as associated companies.

Many companies have adopted the associated company recommendation and now include the relevant items in their Accounts. The information is useful to the analyst although he could have arrived at the figures by examining the Accounts of the 'associated' companies. Where the 'associated company profits' are large, one would expect the analyst to look at their Accounts and evaluate their prospects so as to build up data on the investing company.

### Taxation

The Companies Act requires disclosure of the charges for:

1   UK corporation tax before deduction of any double taxation relief and the basis of computation.
2   UK income tax and the basis of computation.
3   Charge for overseas taxation.

The charges are based on group taxable income before extraordinary items and therefore include subsidiary profits and attributable associated company earnings. The taxation charge will rarely appear as the standard rate multiplied by published pre-tax profits as different bases are used in computing profits for the Inland Revenue. A description of taxation charges and reasons why they usually differ from the standard rate on pre-tax profits is given in Chapter 9. A further item which will appear in the Profit and Loss Account, or in the Notes thereto, is any charge for deferred taxation. The mechanics of deferred taxation are described later in the chapter. The taxation charge for the year will also include any amount for irrecoverable advance corporation tax and tax attributable to franked investment income (under the imputation system).

## Minority interests

Many companies have subsidiaries who are not wholly owned and the parent or holding company is therefore only entitled to a certain percentage of their profits. The figure for profits before tax includes all the profits (losses) of the subsidiary and so the item 'minority interests' represents the after-tax profits attributable to outside shareholders. Companies do not usually differentiate the minority interests into dividends and retentions although the Balance Sheet may give an indication of the division.

## Extraordinary items

ED7 referred to previously also set out proposed standards for the reporting of extraordinary items[8]. The definition of extraordinary items given is:

*Extraordinary items, for the purposes of this Statement, are those material items which derive from events or transactions outside the ordinary activities of the business and which are not expected to recur frequently or regularly. They do not include items which, though exceptional on account of size and incidence (and which may therefore require separate disclosure), derive from the ordinary activities of the business. Neither do they include prior-year items merely because they relate to a prior year.*

The emphasis is on the word 'outside' the ordinary business transactions of the company. Examples can include the closing down of a substantial part of the company's manufacturing capacity, a major 'permanent' re-alignment of currency values and the writing off of intangibles due to unusual events.

Extraordinary items appear after the 'profit after tax' figure and are therefore net of any tax relief/charge. The company should disclose the specific nature of the extraordinary item.

Prior to the ASSC statement, extraordinary items appeared either in the Profit and Loss Account (disclosed separately or not) or as an adjustment to reserves. The ED7 recommendation has thus advocated a consistent basis and has called for a description of the items involved. Some judgment has to be used in deciding whether an item is extraordinary, exceptional or neither and whether it is material. Nevertheless, the consistency and disclosure requirements give basic information which an analyst will need in evaluating business cycles and trends and in determining future fortunes of the company.

## Dividends

Prior to the introduction of the imputation system of corporation tax dividends paid and proposed were reported gross. Under the imputation system, which is described in Chapter 9, the dividends paid and proposed will be shown net and there will probably be a note inset giving details of the amount of the tax credit attributable to the dividend. The paid dividend usually represents the interim dividend while the proposed final dividend will not be declared officially until the Annual General Meeting (AGM) when the shareholders vote. The proposed dividend appears in the Balance Sheet as a provision.

In the Accounts of ABC LTD the dividend is shown gross as the year end was 31 December 1972, before the introduction of the imputation system. Under the new system the dividends are shown net and the tax thereon imputed to the corporation tax charge for the year.

### Retained profits

These are the profits for the year after all expenses and after the dividend appropriation. The figure is classified into profits retained by the parent company, those retained by subsidiaries and those representing the company's share of the associated company's retained profits.

Some companies bring the balance on the Profit and Loss Account at the beginning of the year into the current year's Account just after the dividend appropriation. The total of this figure and the retained profit for the year is then carried into the Balance Sheet. Most companies, however, follow the approach adopted by ABC LTD and add retained profits for the year to the balance on the Profit and Loss Account in the Notes to Accounts section on movements in reserves.

### Earnings per share (EPS)

Most companies now disclose the EPS based on the accounts for the year. The usual basis of computation adopted is that advocated by the ICA in their Statement of Standard Accounting Practice No. 3, February 1972. The actual basis used is normally shown in the accounts and this is especially helpful if there have been any capital issues during the year. The Accounts of ABC LTD show the details that are required to be disclosed. The details of the calculations and the derivation of the EPS for ABC LTD is explained in the next chapter.

### Fixed assets

The usual items found under this heading include properties and buildings, plant and machinery, furniture and fittings. These assets tend to be those which provide the productive capacity of the company and are usually long-term items. Trade investments and goodwill are two other items which are often included in the fixed asset total. The fixed asset figure appearing in the Balance Sheet is usually an aggregate total and the analyst will have to turn to the Notes to the Accounts to obtain the split-up.

## Movements of fixed assets

Since the 1967 Companies Act, firms must show the movement of fixed assets during the year. This means that purchases and sales of assets must be disclosed. The Act requires the following disclosures for each class of fixed asset heading:

1   Cost or last revaluation of the asset. Details of the date of revaluation must be given and for any revaluations during the year being reported upon there must be given additional information on who did the revaluation and what the bases of valuation were. The most usual revaluation is that conducted on properties and this almost invariably shows a surplus. Methods of valuation might, for instance, be current market value or perhaps market value incorporating anticipated development of those properties with detailed planning permission. The profits on revaluations are usually credited to Reserves and shown in the Movements on Reserves Note.

2   The total depreciation written off the assets since their acquisition. If there has been no depreciation provided for during the year this must be stated.

3   Particulars of additions and disposals of fixed assets in the period. Some companies give additional information on the additions to fixed assets. A fairly common example is the cost being split up into assets paid for in cash and those acquired via a takeover of an existing company. The methods used in presenting information on the value of assets disposed of varies; some show the net book value after depreciation, others show the cost value, accumulated depreciation and net book value. ABC LTD has shown the cost value and the accumulated depreciation to date on its sale of assets.

4   Corresponding figures for the prior year have to be shown in common with other Balance Sheet and Profit and Loss Account items. Some companies interpret this by showing the aggregate figure as done in the Accounts of ABC LTD whilst others give the preceding financial year's figures split up according to the various assets and classified by cost, depreciation, disposals and additions and net values.

## Land

The Companies Act 1967 requires specific information on land held as fixed assets. The interests in land should be classified into the following:

1   Freehold.

2   Long leaseholds, i.e. those having more than fifty years to run at the Balance Sheet date.

3   Short leaseholds.

This requirement has given additional information to the analyst although it is still very difficult to obtain an accurate view of the asset backing. Companies with substantial property assets could perhaps reveal a lot more about their values, locations, details of lease agreements, state of repairs and tenancy occupants.

**Development grants**

Development or investment grants are now shown as deferred credits but until recently the most popular accounting treatment was to deduct the grant from the cost of the asset. A few companies may still adopt this method and so the Notes to the Accounts should indicate the grants received and deducted from the cost of fixed assets. The impact on the Profit and Loss Account may well be the same under either method as the rate of transferring the deferred credit may be the same as the depreciation rate.

*Example*   A company buys an asset for £1,000 and receives a development grant of £200. The straight-line depreciation rate is 10 per cent. The two accounting methods (for two years) are shown below.

---

**Deferred Credit Method:**
*Extract from Balance Sheet, year 1*

| | | | |
|---|---|---|---|
| Development grant | 180 | Asset cost | 1,000 |
| | | *Less*: Depreciation | 100 |
| | | | 900 |

*Extract from Profit and Loss Account, year 1*

| | | | |
|---|---|---|---|
| Depreciation | | Transfer development | |
| (10% × 1,000) | 100 | grant account | 20 |
| | | (10% × 200) | |

*Extract from Balance Sheet, year 2*

| | | | |
|---|---|---|---|
| Development grant | 160 | Asset cost | 1,000 |
| | | *Less*: Accumulated | 200 |
| | | depreciation | |
| | | | 800 |

*Extract from Profit and Loss Account, year 2*

| | | | |
|---|---|---|---|
| Depreciation | | Transfer development | |
| (10% × £1,000) | 100 | grant account | 20 |
| | | (10% × 200) | |

---

**Deduction from Asset Account Method:**
*Extract from Balance Sheet, year 1*

| | | |
|---|---|---|
| | Asset cost | 1,000 |
| | *Less*: Development | 200 |
| | grant | |
| | | 800 |
| | *Less*: Depreciation | 80 |

*Extract from Profit and Loss Account, year 1*

| | |
|---|---|
| Depreciation | |
| (10% × 800) | 80 |

*Extract from Balance Sheet, year 2*

| | |
|---|---|
| Asset cost less development grant | 800 |
| *Less:* Accumulated depreciation | 160 |
| | 640 |

*Extract from Profit and Loss Account, year 2*

| | |
|---|---|
| Depreciation (10% × 800) | 80 |

## Depreciation

Provision for depreciation will appear as a deduction from the relevant asset classification. Aggregate amounts provided must be shown in the Accounts. Amounts set aside for replacement values in excess of cost or revaluation are shown in the section headed 'reserves'. Few companies in fact set up such reserves but where they do they may provide analysts with useful factual information on the amounts which will be needed to replace assets and to maintain existing capacity. Provisions for bad debts and the decline in value of stocks will be written off the appropriate asset values–no separate disclosure is generally given.

### Goodwill and intangible assets

The Companies Acts require that expenditure for goodwill, patents and trade marks should be shown separately in the Accounts (as an aggregate item or separately) so far as they have not been written off. The Companies Acts' provisions relating to the classification of fixed assets do not apply to goodwill, patents and trade marks although the basis used in arriving at goodwill is required to be shown.

## Goodwill on acquisitions

Goodwill tends to arise in many companies when they acquire subsidiaries. The acquisition often entails paying a price above net asset value and a goodwill item is needed to balance the Accounts*. Many companies write-off the goodwill item to the Profit and Loss Account or to reserves either immediately or over some period of years. It is the usual practice to find amounts written off goodwill being disclosed. Goodwill does not represent a physical asset but in some cases may represent to some degree the under-valuation of assets acquired (i.e. the assets acquired may be at book value and not at a revaluation for the takeover). In this case 'goodwill' may be a surrogate for the under-valuation of the company. Premiums over asset values are also paid as the acquired company may have good managerial talent or that the combined prospects of the group are far better than those of the separate entities. Goodwill arising from the latter items are sometimes referred to as capitalised future earnings power.

*The section on consolidated accounts covered earlier in the chapter showed how goodwill arises in acquisitions.

## Other goodwill items

Goodwill also arises from other transactions such as the acquisition of a trade name or a patent right. Here the amount appearing in the Balance Sheet is the actual payment made, less any write offs. Such assets may have a market value but this will be difficult to determine as is really a capitalisation of future earning power. Because of the difficulty in placing values on such items, companies usually write them off.

## Analysis of goodwill

The analyst should normally write off goodwill relating to future earning power when computing asset values although if he is reasonably sure that the amount relates to the under-valuation of acquired assets he could incorporate it. Thus, when forecasting future profitability the analyst may find that the existence of, and the value placed on goodwill has some usefulness. This, however, will almost certainly require a breakdown of the goodwill figure. As with Research and Development expenditure, however, detailed breakdowns will be difficult to obtain and so the importance of the goodwill figure will be severely reduced.

### Initial and issue expenses

When a company obtains a quotation it incurs heavy expenses for professional services and underwriting commissions. Occasionally, companies decide to capitalise such items: the more normal practice is to write off the expenditure immediately against reserves or as an extraordinary item. This item does not represent present physical assets nor can it be described as a right to, or capitalisation of, future profits. Analysts should write this amount off for any analytical purposes.

### Advertising expenses

When a company undertakes a very heavy promotional campaign near its year-end it may decide to capitalise this expenditure. This is defended on the grounds that the impact of the campaign may take some months to accrue and that to write off the expenditure in the year it accrued would produce a widely fluctuating profits record. The counter-argument is that sales income arising from the campaign may never accrue. There are, however, relatively few cases of this deferring of revenue expenditure. When it does appear it is the result of the judgment of management and the auditors that future sales will be more than sufficient to cover the expenses. The analyst should be wary if the item becomes very large in relation to the other assets.

### Research and Development expenditure

When companies expend a large proportion of their resources on the Research and Development of products it is often found that they capitalise part of the expenditure. It therefore appears in the Balance

Sheet as an asset (often referred to as a deferred debit) as opposed to writing it off in the Profit and Loss Account. The idea behind this basis of accounting is that such items can be extremely large and if they are written off to the Profit and Loss Account in the year they occur erratic profits figures can be obtained, which the management may feel gives a wrong impression of the company's affairs. When the company starts to earn profits from exploiting the invention or product it then writes off the expenditure. This produces a 'smoothed profits' trend, a technique which has both its advocates and adversaries. Whilst the values represent actual expenditures, whether they will be recouped from future sales is a contentious point. Some authors call this deferral of revenue expenditure 'capitalised future earnings'. This is a misnomer, however, as the value relates to the expenditure and does not attempt to measure the future earnings it will generate.

**Analysis of Research and Development**

The analyst should deduct such expenditures from the Balance Sheet when measuring the asset backing but the figure could prove valuable in forecasting future profitability. As the Research and Development figure is gross and does not describe the various projects it is financing the analyst will have to dig deeper in order to assess its impact. Some simple correlations between past expenditures and profitability may give an insight into the success rate of Research and Development expenditures but in all probability the relationship will be more complicated than this. The main advantage of a company capitalising Research and Development costs is that it discloses the expenditure. If it was written-off in the Profit and Loss Account it might probably not be separately disclosed.

### Trade investments

Many companies have investments in quoted and unquoted securities. These investments are sometimes made in companies who operate in similar industries or who may be trade suppliers or trade customers. If such investments are made for the long term they are usually described as 'trade investments' and appear separately in the Balance Sheet just under the 'fixed assets' figures.

### Other investments

If a company has surplus funds it may invest them in quoted stocks and shares pending their use in the business. The investments are not held with a view to their being long term and so they are usually included separately in the current assets section of the Balance Sheet.

**Disclosure requirements**

The Companies Act 1967 requires investments, whether described as trade investments or whether included in current assets, to be classified into quoted or unquoted investments and the income from each class is to be shown separately in the Profit and Loss Account. The aggregate market value of the quoted investments is required to be shown with a subdivision between those quoted on the United Stock Exchange in the

UK and those outside. Unquoted investments should show the aggregate value of the amounts written off cost prices. The directors must give a valuation to the unquoted investments or, if not, details of the investment's financial performance must be disclosed. In the vast majority of cases a directors' valuation appears.

**Valuation**

Investments appearing in current assets are normally valued at cost or market value, whichever is the lower. Trade investments are valued at cost but if the market price appears to have fallen permanently and significantly below cost, companies usually write off the discrepancy.

**Disclosure of investments**

Where an investing company holds more than 10 per cent of the equity class of another company or holds shares in another company which accounts for more than one-tenth of the investing company's total assets, the accounts must show the name of the company, the class or classes of shares and the proportion owned. For a fuller description see the ICA's 'The Accounting Requirements of the Companies Acts 1948–1967'.

### Shares in subsidiary companies

A holding company must prepare a Balance Sheet in the Annual Accounts and amongst the assets will appear an item showing the shares in, and the aggregate amounts owing from, subsidiaries. The aggregate amounts owed to subsidiaries by the holding company must be separately disclosed by that company. The amounts appearing in the accounts are usually at cost price with any adjustments being explained. Loans to subsidiaries and loans from subsidiaries are sometimes grouped separately in current assets and current liabilities, although they more usually appear in a separate group in the Balance Sheet. The Balance Sheet of ABC LTD shows the cost of the shares owned in the subsidiary and the amounts due to and due from the subsidiary as one aggregate amount. The split-up is given in Note 9 to the Balance Sheet.

**Details of subsidiaries**

Companies have to give various particulars of their subsidiaries including their names and the identity and proportion of the nominal value of the issued shares held. 'The Accounting Requirements of the Companies Acts 1948–1967' deals concisely with the details and exemptions. The Guide also gives details of the requirements of subsidiary companies which are not consolidated. In such cases additional financial information is required.

### Current assets

These items represent assets which are expected to be sold within the year. They are usually ranked in descending order of liquidity starting with stocks and work-in-progress. None of the items apart from stocks, require much explanation. The debtors figure is stated net of any provision for doubtful debts. Sometimes companies invest cash balances in stocks and shares pending the use of the funds in the business. In such cases the market value of the investments will be shown in the Accounts. The disclosure requirements relating to investments have already been discussed.

## Stocks

There is no Company Law requirement to differentiate the stock figure into raw materials, work-in-progress or finished stocks and generally an aggregate figure is given. The stock figure of some companies could therefore include substantial raw materials and commodities, fast-moving finished stocks and long-term contracts stretching over many years. There appears to be a need to subclassify the stocks figure into the component parts especially differentiating between raw materials, finished stocks and work-in-progress of short- and long-term contracts. The ASSC recommends separate disclosure of the various items making up the stock figure but few companies have yet adopted the standard (Proposed Statement of Standard Accounting Practice 'Stocks and Work in Progress' ED6).

## Stock valuation

The Companies Act 1967 requires a Note to the Accounts stating the method by which stocks and work-in-progress have been computed. The usual methods employed in valuing stocks are:

1 At the lower of cost or net realisable value. Realisable value is the market value less expenses to be incurred in selling it.

2 Replacement cost. This is rarely found as it will never usually be below the cost or net realisable value.

Cost includes the raw materials, direct manufacturing expenses, direct labour and can include a provision for overhead allowances. The provision for overhead allowances allows a fair leeway for management to value stocks although the accounting principle of consistency will prevent the constant changing of methods.

## Work-in-progress

Work-in-progress on long-term contracts are valued as above but they often include a proportion of the expected profit. This anticipation of profits is an example of the adoption of the accruals concept. The disclosure requirements recommended by the ASSC on long-term contracts are fairly comprehensive and many companies are adopting them. The proposals advocate that the following information be given.

### Balance Sheet

1 The separate amounts included in respect of cost and attributable profit.

2 The amount deducted in respect of anticipated losses.

3 The further amount provided for anticipated losses on those contracts where the total anticipated losses exceed the costs to date.

4 Cash received and receivable at the accounting date as progress payments on account of contracts.

41

### Profit and Loss Account

The amount of profit or loss arising from long-term contracts distinguishing between:

1   The net amount provided in the year for anticipated losses.

2   The profits less losses relating to contracts which had been treated as completed at the close of the preceding financial year.

3   Other profits and losses on long-term contracts.

### Current liabilities

The items are largely self-explanatory and call for little comment. The general yardstick for assessing whether a liability is current or not is to determine if the liability is payable within one year. If so, then it is included in current liabilities. This yardstick has no legal standing but is a generally accepted rule. When loan or debenture capital falls due for repayment in the year the amount is occasionally transferred into the current liabilities section although it more commonly retains its existing position. Bank overdrafts appear under the current liabilities heading although for some ratio measurements they are regarded as being permanent capital. In the accounts of ABC LTD the amount appearing in current liabilities for taxation represents the amount due on 1 January 1973.

### Share capital

The Balance Sheet or the Notes thereto must distinguish between the various classes of capital and give details of the authorised number of shares, their nominal value, the number of shares issued and whether they are fully paid-up or otherwise. The authorised capital relates to the maximum number of shares that can be issued as set out in the company's memorandum. However, any restrictions can easily be changed as required. The authorised capital is therefore a somewhat redundant item in financial analysis as is the designation of a monetary value (known as the nominal value) to the ordinary shares. Shares of no par value (i.e. no monetary denomination) are prevalent in the US and this practice may eventually extend to the UK. The inclusion of these items in the Balance Sheet does make the information easily available, however.

**Preference shares**

Preference shares are a form of fixed-dividend security and the individual rights attached to the shares should be checked (from the company's Articles, the Annual Accounts or the Stock Exchange Official Year Book). Generally they rank immediately before the ordinary capital in a winding-up. In the event of a winding-up the preference shares may be entitled to be repaid at a premium. The dividend on the shares may be cumulative so that if there are insufficient profits to pay a preference dividend in one year, the following year's earnings have to bear two year's preference dividends before anything can be paid to the ordinary shareholders. Some preference shares have participating rights attached to them so that after their fixed dividend payment they participate in the remaining profits in some relation to the ordinary shareholders. After the 1965 Finance Act preference shares went out of favour because of the bias against dividends and in fact many were converted into debentures. It is unlikely that many preference issues will be made again as other forms of security, the debenture and the convertible loan stock, offer either greater security or greater participation in the equity.

Under the Finance Act 1972 the gross rate of preference dividends were reduced to 70 per cent of the former rate. This has required some alteration in the description of the shares in the Balance Sheet. The ASSC in their statement of taxation under the imputation system discussed the matter thus[9],

*Any dividend right established before April 6th, 1973 at a gross rate or a gross amount was reduced by the Finance Act 1972, Schedule 23, paragraph 18\*, to seven-tenths of its former rate or amount. Steps should therefore be taken to distinguish, for example, a 10 per cent preference share issued before April 6th, 1973 on which the dividend is now 7 per cent, from such a preference share issued after that date. A change in the basic rate of income tax and a corresponding change in the rate of ACT would not affect this once-for-all 'netting down'. Thus a former 10 per cent preference share may in the future yield, with related tax credit, either more or less than 10 per cent on nominal value. The new rate of dividend on preference shares (including participating preference and preferred ordinary shares where the former rate of dividend forms part of the title), should therefore be incorporated in the description of the shares in the balance sheet, e.g.:*

|  | Authorized | Issued |
|---|---|---|
| 100,000 10 per cent (now 7 per cent + Tax credit) Preference shares of £1 | £100,000 | £100,000 |

## Other types of shares

There are a number of other types of shares that can be issued which have different rights and entitlements. One example is deferred shares which may only entitle shareholders to dividends after a certain number of years or after the ordinary shareholders have received a certain level of dividend. The analyst should carefully check the various terms of these issues. The usual sources of information are the Annual Report and Accounts, the company's Articles of Association or the Stock Exchange Official Year Book.

### Share premium account

This arises when shares are issued at a price greater than their nominal value. Nearly all quoted companies have a share premium account

*\*Subsequent changes in the rate of ACT have varied the rate of tax credit but not the amount of the cash dividend payable to shareholders.*

although if shares of no par value were introduced this account would disappear. The share premium account must be shown separately in the Balance Sheet. There are restrictions on the uses to which the share premium account can be applied and these are set out in Section 56 of the 1948 Companies Act. The main provisions of the Act are:

1 *Where a company issues shares at a premium, whether for cash or otherwise, a sum equal to the aggregate amount or value of the premiums on those shares shall be transferred to an account, to be called "the share premium account" and the provisions of this Act relating to the reduction of the share capital of a company shall, except as provided in this section, apply as if the share premium account were paid-up share capital of the company.*

2 *The share premium account may, notwithstanding anything in the foregoing subsection, be applied by the company in paying up unissued shares of the company to be issued to members of the company as fully paid bonus shares, in writing off –*
*(a) the preliminary expenses of the company; or*
*(b) the expenses of, or the commission paid or discount allowed on, any issue of shares or debentures of the company;*
*or in providing for the premium payable on redemption of any redeemable preference shares or of any debentures of the company.*

3 *Where a company has before the commencement of this Act issued any shares at a premium, this section shall apply as if the shares had been issued after the commencement of this Act:*

*Provided that any part of the premiums which has been so applied that it does not at the commencement of this Act form an identifiable part of the company's reserves within the meaning of the Eighth Schedule to this Act shall be disregarded in determining the sum to be included in the share premium account.*

In practice the main use made of share premium accounts is in the issue of bonus shares (capitalisation or scrip issue).

**Reserves**

These represent accumulated profits of the company which have not been distributed and the share premium account. They accrue from accumulated balances on the Profit and Loss Account, from profits less losses of transactions not included in the Profit and Loss Account and share premiums. One example of a transaction being recorded directly to reserves is the revaluation of property. This item rarely goes into the Profit and Loss Account except where it is a relatively small item. Such a revaluation can represent realised profits or can be unrealised. The definition of a reserve as given by the Companies Act 1967 shall not include:

1 Any amount written off or retained by way of providing for depreciation, renewals or diminution in value of assets.

2   Any amount retained by way of providing for any known liability.

3   Any sum set aside for the purpose of its being used to prevent undue fluctuations in charges for taxation.

Any amount dealt with under **1** or **2** above which, not being an amount written off fixed assets before 1 July 1948, is in excess of that which in the opinion of the directors is reasonably necessary, shall be treated as a reserve.

## Classification of reserves

Prior to the 1967 Companies Act, reserves had to be classified into capital reserves, revenue reserves and share premium account. The distinction between capital and revenue reserves has been ended but share premium accounts and capital redemption reserves still have to be separately disclosed. A capital redemption reserve is a fund that is required to be made where redeemable preference shares are repaid, unless the repayment is by way of a new issue of shares when no such fund need be made. Some companies still differentiate between capital and revenue reserves and this is sometimes the result of a requirement of the firm's Articles of Association.

The reserves together with the ordinary share capital represent the book value of the ordinary shareholders' funds and when divided by the number of shares in existence gives the book asset value per share. The computation and use of asset values in investment analysis is described in Chapter 3.

## Movements on reserves

The 1967 Act requires that the movements on reserves are to be shown. Specifically the source of any increase and the application of any decrease must be stated unless immaterial. In the Accounts of ABC LTD the retained profit for the year is added to the balance of reserves brought forward. This is disclosed in Note 6.

### Minorities

The group accounts will include all the assets and liabilities of subsidiary companies. Where the subsidiaries have shareholders other than the parent company a share of the net assets will belong to them. The item 'minority interests' appearing in the accounts represents the proportion of ordinary capital and reserves (i.e. the net assets) which belongs to the minority shareholders of the subsidiary companies.

### Convertible loan stock

These have become a popular method of raising finance during the past few years. They provide greater security than ordinary shares and yet allow the owners to convert into ordinary shares, and participate in the equity, at their option on specified dates. The typical convertible loan stock is unsecured and is convertible at one period, possibly stretching to one month, in each of a number of years. The owner receives a fixed-interest payment until he converts and this rate is usually somewhat below the prevailing rates for debentures. The conversion rate is normally pitched some way above the current market price[10]. The individual rights attached to the securities, including conversion terms and dates, need to be examined. The Stock Exchange Official Year Book gives the details of such issues for quoted companies. Convertible loan stocks appear under the heading of loan capital which of course has to be classified into the various stocks and loans issued. This is normally done by way of a Note. When the loan stock is converted the share capital account will increase by the number of shares issued and the share premium account will increase by the amount of the premium on the shares issued. ABC's financial structure does not include convertible loan stocks.

**Loan capital**

This represents long-term fixed interest finance for the company. When the loans are secured by a fixed or floating charge on the assets of the company they are usually referred to as 'debentures'. The analyst must look at the trust deed to obtain the details of repayment dates, premiums, provisions for default on interest payments, and the security. If the loan is secured on assets of the company this must be stated. Both debentures and loans can be offered at a discount and can be repayable at a premium. This has advantages for those investors who prefer paying capital gains tax as opposed to income tax. The details relating to repayment dates and other matters are often not given in the Accounts and the analyst can most easily check by reference to the Stock Exchange Official Year Book. When a loan or debenture becomes repayable within one year it is usually still classified as a loan even though any other short-term finance, defined as being repayable within one year, is classified as a current liability. The analyst's particular interest in loan capital will centre around the impact of gearing on both the earnings and the liquidity of the company. The asset structure will indicate whether any additional gearing can be obtained.

**Provisions**

Certain items appear in accounts under the description 'provisions for . . .'. These constitute amounts set aside for the depreciation or diminution in value of certain assets or to meet a specific liability. The Companies Act 1967 defines a provision as:

*(a) any amount written off or retained by way of providing for depreciation, renewals or diminution in value of assets*
*(b) any amount retained by way of providing for any known liability of which the amount cannot be determined with substantial accuracy.*

*The expression 'liability' in this context includes all liabilities in respect of expenditure contracted for and all disputed or contingent liabilities.*

*Excess provisions are to be treated as reserves.*

The provision must be made against a real liability. This differentiates a provision from a reserve. As with reserves the Companies Act 1967 requires movements on provisions to be separately disclosed. The sources of any increase and the applications of any decrease must be shown, unless immaterial.

Short-term provisions appear in the current liabilities section of the Balance Sheet. For example, proposed dividends are not legally binding until voted upon at the Annual General Meeting (AGM) but they still appear in the Balance Sheet and are strictly a provision. Longer-term provisions are often those representing depreciation and they are usually deducted from the appropriate asset value. The creation of provisions prevents management from distributing these funds as dividends and they represent substantial finance for the company.

### Deferred taxation*

This account normally arises when the capital allowances given by the Inland Revenue are greater than the depreciation charged in the Accounts. This usually means that the tax charge as a percentage of pre-tax profits is below the prevailing rate of corporation tax. The deferred taxation account is created by transferring a portion of the profit for the year. This represents the difference between the tax rate on the reported profits and the actual tax charge.

**Deferred taxation methods**

There are two main methods of computing the deferred taxation, one the 'deferral' method, the other the 'liability' method. The first method regards the item as a deferred expenditure for that year and is not revised on changes in taxation rates. The liability method regards timing differences in taxation as liabilities for taxes payable in the future.

The ASSC, in their proposed statement of standard accounting practice, ED11, 'Accounting for Deferred Taxation' have recommended the use of the deferral method. This statement should be consulted for a description of the methods. The debit in the Profit and Loss Account appears separately disclosed in the taxation charge. This reduces the distributable profits and may lead to a higher level of sources of funds in that management cannot pay the amounts out as dividends.

The argument for the creation of the deferred tax reserve is that at some future time the tax charge as a percentage of profits will be greater than the corporation tax rate. This will be because capital allowances will have fallen below the depreciation charge in the accounts. At this point a transfer out of the deferred taxation account will be made so increasing the distributable profit. Such techniques produce a smoothing effect on EPS. There are, however, many opponents to the deferred taxation account, some believing that their companies will always be paying a below-average tax rate.

*Sometimes called the tax equalisation account.

## Potential capital gains taxation

Another amount which may appear in the deferred taxation account is potential capital gains tax pertaining to revalued assets. When a company revalues its properties the surplus which usually accrues is added to reserves. As the property has not been realised in cash no capital gains tax is payable. On a future sale, however, the tax would be payable and companies therefore often provide for it in the deferred taxation account. This treatment is not universal, however.

The reserve represents a long-term source of funds and the account is usually presented under the heading 'deferred taxation' on the sources section of the Balance Sheet.

### Provision for future taxation

As will be described in Chapter 9 taxation on the profits of the year being reported will not normally be paid until the 1 January in the year following (i.e. if a year ran from 1 January 1968 to 31 December 1968 the corporation tax would be payable on 1 January 1970) or, in the case of young companies, nine months after the year-end. The amount of taxation is only provisional at the Balance Sheet date as no final assessment will usually have been made and it is therefore referred to as a provision. The amount usually appears separately disclosed in either the current liabilities or in a section on its own just above the current liabilities in the horizontal form of Balance Sheet. In the vertical form presentation of the Balance Sheet the item appears in the sources of funds section or as a current liability.

In the accounts of ABC LTD the UK corporation tax due for the year to 31 December 1972 will not be payable until 1 January 1974 and has therefore been grouped with the sources of funds.

### Development grant account

The accounting for investment grants has been described previously. The grant is credited to the Profit and Loss Account over a number of years and the item appearing in the Balance Sheet represents the amount yet to be transferred.

### Directors' Report

This must accompany the Accounts in the Annual Report. Its content generally consists of statutory items with the comment of the company's performance and future prospects being dealt with by the Chairman in his report. The 'Guide to the Accounting Requirements of The Companies Acts 1948–1967' gives a good summary of the items required to be shown. The directors' Report of ABC LTD covers some of the more commonly-found items none of which require much explanation. Note 3 relates to information on employees working in the UK. The 'close company' provisions of the Income and Corporation Taxes Act 1970 rarely apply to quoted companies.

If a company has substantial overseas divisions they often give a geographical split of the figures or percentages of its trading operation. Companies who have obtained a Stock Market quote since June 1966 have been required by the Stock Exchange to give this information and many companies quoted before this date have also followed this rule.

## Analysis and interpretation of accounts

This chapter has briefly described the contents and the make-up of Annual Accounts. The descriptions have been necessarily general and the special items and accounting conventions relating to specific industries have not been considered. The interested reader should refer to the specialised accounting texts for a description of accounting for particular business enterprises; however, the chapter should enable the reader to understand most Annual Reports. The next step in investment analysis is to interpret the data given in the Accounts. Accounts give historical data on the stewardship of a company's funds but the analyst's job is to use the data for forecasting the future. Chapter 3 describes the interpretation of financial data appearing in the Annual Report and Accounts.

## References

1   SSAP No. 7 'Accounting for changes in the purchasing power of money', May 1974. The proposal involves adjusting values by the Retail Price Index and is known as the Current Purchasing Power (CPP) method. The Accounting Standards Steering Committee (ASSC) is made up of members of the senior accounting bodies in the UK (The Institute of Chartered Accountants in England and Wales [ICA], Scotland and Ireland, the Association of Certified Accountants [ACA] and the Cost and Management Accountants [ICMA]). The ASSC was set up to examine accounting practices and their statements of standard accounting practice are expected to be supported.

2   'Disclosure of Accounting Policies', Statement of Standard Accounting Practice, No. 2, SSAP2, November 1971.

3   See: Spacek, L., 'Business Success Requires an Understanding of the Unsolved Problems of Accounting and Financial Reporting', Address to the Financial Accounting Class, Harvard Business School, 25 September 1969. This gives examples of how different earnings per share can be reported by using different accounting methods on business transactions.

4   For instance:
Gambling, T., 'A One Year Accounting Course', Parts I and II, Pergamon, 1969.
Bierman, H. and Drebin, A. R., 'Financial Accounting: an introduction', MacMillan, 2nd edition, 1972.

For an intermediate text see Lee, G. A., 'Modern Financial Accounting', Nelson, 1973.

5 A very useful concise guide to the accounting provisions regarding accounts is given in: 'Accounting Requirements of the Companies Acts 1948–1967', published for the ICA by Gee & Co. This should be referred to.

6 Subsequently released as SSAP4, 'Accounting Treatment of Government Grants', May 1974.

7 Subsequently released as SSAP6, 'Extraordinary Items and Prior Year Adjustments', May 1974.

8 Now the subject of a statement of standard accounting practice, SSAP6, Extraordinary Items and Prior Year Adjustments', May 1974.

9 'The Treatment of Taxation under the Imputation System in the Accounts of Companies', SSAP8, ASSC, September, 1974.

10 For a description of convertible loan stocks issued by companies and of their pricing see Skerratt, L. C. L., 'Convertible Loan Stocks 1958–1968: an empirical investigation', *Journal of Business Finance*, Vol. 3, No. 3, Autumn 1971.

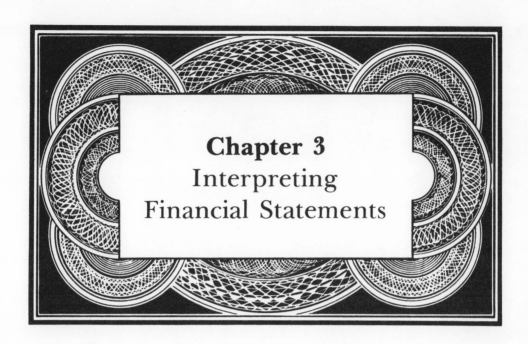

# Chapter 3
## Interpreting
## Financial Statements

The last chapter described the various items usually found in published Accounts and noted those specifically required to be disclosed by Company Law. Various terms were explained in detail as their make-up is not obvious to students who have little experience of financial reporting.

This chapter sets out to explain how the Annual Accounts can be helpful to analysts in their forecasting of corporate profits and share prices. The normal form of Accounts give a financial record of past performance: an examination of these figures may provide an analyst with a base for arriving at the net worth of the company, provide indicators of managerial performance, operating efficiency and key areas of weaknesses and strengths, and provide bases for projecting trends and ratios. In using published figures, analysts are likely to re-arrange and re-group certain items. This is done to build up data on the important factors affecting profits, to provide consistent data for comparative analyses and to account for exceptional or non-recurring items (thus to 'normalise' profits).

**Sources and uses of funds**

A statement of sources and uses of funds is a common analysis derived from the Accounts by investment analysts. This analysis shows the source of finance raised during the year and the use to which it has been put. A small but growing number of companies are now including such a funds statement in their published Accounts and this could become common practice in the near future. A description of the derivation of a sources and uses of funds statement is given later.

**EFFAS standards**

The re-arrangement of published figures into a standardised form has been recommended by the European Federation of Financial Analysts Societies (EFFAS)*. This involves adjusting published Balance Sheets and Profit and Loss Accounts to arrange items in particular formats and to facilitate the computation of a sources and uses of funds statement (which they term a financing table). Although such a standardised form has gained little acceptance yet in either Europe or the UK there are a number of prominent practitioners advocating its use.

## Ratio analysis

Analysts use published figures to derive certain ratios the more common of which will be described later. Ratios are used as yardsticks of asset structure, managerial performance and operating efficiency. The measurement of liquidity is a major indicator of insolvency and as such is used extensively by credit analysts. Ratio analysis is also used in inter-firm comparison but here the analyst needs to be very wary. Intracompany ratio analysis is a reasonably useful tool as one can expect, except where the Accounts state otherwise, the accounting principles and policies to be consistent from one period to the next. However, when different companies are evaluated, the accounting policies adopted and the specific business transactions involved may vary considerably and so render comparisons invalid. Inter-firm comparison can, however, throw up useful data, especially if the trends of ratios over a number of years are compared. The analyst must be aware of the limitations of this analysis and weigh his decisions accordingly. Ratio analysis gives concise, quantitative yardsticks which can be used, given the limitations due to accounting measurement, for comparison against other shares†.

## Projections

Certain items in the published Accounts and the ratios derived therefrom are used by analysts in projecting current trends into the future. In doing so they take account of various factors which may alter the growth of past trends and the projections are often framed in a range of outcomes depending on different assumptions. Obvious examples of projections include sales, net profits before interest, and net profit ratios. The extent to which analysts will rely on projections will depend upon the prior success of using the projection. Some companies and industries have certain items which have fairly consistent growth patterns and thus projecting trends into the future can give an immediate 'region of probability' before a detailed analysis commences. The various techniques used in projections are given in Chapter 4. This chapter will concentrate on the main information content given in Accounts and on the important figures for projection. The prevailing accounting conventions of the accruals basis and

*See 'Proceedings of the Second Congress, 1963', European Federation of Financial Analysts' Societies. This conference set up a Permanent Commission on Standardisation. The subsequent congresses at Noordivigk (1966) and Wiesbaden (1968) approved the Commission's work.

†This is an argument for greater standardisation of accounting conventions.

consistency make for a 'smoothing of profits' which are, of course, more amenable to linear projections. However, analysts will find they have to re-arrange many items in the accounts so as to obtain better bases for projection. These will be described later. As future profit figures will be based on consistent accounting concepts, projection of past figures has some validity. Projections that are made are obviously more accurate in the short-term although its use as a technique in long-term forecasting is comparatively greater.

### Sources and uses of funds statement*

This is a table showing for the period under investigation the sources of additional funds and the uses to which they have been applied. The statement provides information as to how the activities of the enterprise have been financed and how its financial resources have been used during the period covered. It does not, however, purport to show the capital requirements of a business nor the extent of seasonal peaks of debtors, creditors, stocks, etc. It has become an increasingly important analysis as modern methods of financing have become more diverse and complex, and the normal form of Profit and Loss Account and Balance Sheet have not given the necessary information. Few British companies give a sources and uses of funds statement although pressure is being brought to bear from certain bodies for its compilation and disclosure†. The sources and uses tables which have been presented in published Accounts are of a very diverse nature making immediate comparisons difficult. This can be demonstrated by the difficulty of reconciling many statements with the figures appearing in the Accounts. Analysts will, therefore, have to formulate a table themselves until the disclosure by companies becomes standard. This section will outline the main items that need to be recorded.

**Construction of a statement**

The table shows the sources and uses of finance and the balance between these two represents the net movement in liquid assets (defined by the ASSC to include investments held as current assets). The sources will start with the profit before extraordinary items. Extraordinary items are then shown as a deduction from profits, thus highlighting the impact of these special events. To the sources are added non-cash expenses, i.e. items which affect profits but do not entail cash outlays. Funds raised from other than the normal company operations are then added to give a total figure for the sources of finance.

The ASSC's ED13 recommends showing dividends as a use of funds

---

*Sometimes called a financing table, a funds statement or a sources and applications of funds statement.

†The ASSC have recently issued an exposure draft (ED 13, May 1974) which recommends the preparation and disclosure of a sources and applications of funds statement. The draft also recommends a layout for the statement. Another influential report which relates to the topic is, 'The Funds Statement', Accountants International Study Group, 1973.

although some textbooks advocate deducting them from profits under the 'sources' subheading. Other uses of funds include purchases of fixed assets, redemptions of debentures, acquisition of investments and movements in working capital balances. Thus, whilst increases in stocks and debtors do not affect the profits they do tie up additional cash and are therefore an application of funds. Increases in creditors and tax liabilities can be shown as a source of funds or as a deduction from the uses of funds (advocated by the ASSC). The net difference

### ABC LTD
### Sources and Uses of Funds Statement For the Year Ended 31 December 1972

#### Sources of Funds

|  | 1972 £'000 | 1971 £'000 |
|---|---|---|
| Profit before extraordinary items | 996 | |
| Extraordinary items | 116 | |
|  | 880 | |
| Adjustments for items not involving the movements of funds: | | |
| Minority interests in the profits for the year | 20 | |
| Depreciation | 431 | |
| Loss on sale of assets | 116 | |
| Profits retained in associated company | (100) | |
| Increase in deferred taxation | 120 | |
| Total generated from operations | 1,467 | |

| Funds from other sources | | |
|---|---|---|
| New issue of shares for cash | 350 | |
| Debenture issue | 100 | |
| Sale of fixed assets | 370 | |
| Development grant received | 200 | 1,020 |
| Sources of funds | | 2,487 |

#### Uses of Funds

| Dividends paid and proposed | 200 | |
|---|---|---|
| Purchase of fixed assets | 1,560 | |
| Increase in stocks | 276 | |
| Increase in debtors | 287 | |
| Increase in creditors | (80) | |
| Increase in current taxation | (140) | |
| Increase in future taxation | (145) | 1,958 |
|  | | 529 |

| Movement in net liquid funds | | |
|---|---|---|
| Decrease in bank overdraft | 540 | |
| Decrease in cash balances | (11) | 529 |

*Note:* Comparative figures for prior-year sources and uses of funds should be given between the sources and uses of funds will add up to the net movement in the cash and overdraft balances and the liquid asset balances.

The sources and uses statement for ABC LTD shows the method of financing the various expenditures throughout the year (ED13 has been followed as regards layout)*. The sources include the non cash 'expenses' of depreciation, the loss on the sale of assets and the increase in deferred taxation. These amounts have reduced the 'profit before extraordinary items' figure, but they did not involve any cash outlay. The profits earned by associated companies have been included in the opening profits figure of £996,000; however £100,000 of the associated company's profits were kept by the associated company and do not therefore add to ABC's sources of funds. The profits attributable to minority interests have been left inside the business and so these are a source of funds. Funds obtained from other than the normal operating sources have been separately shown. These include the cash proceeds of the sale of assets, the cash proceeds from the issue of shares and the issue of debentures and cash received for development grants (this totalled £210,000 but £10,000 of this has been included in the profit before extraordinary item figure). In future years the transfer to the Profit and Loss Account of the development grant will have to be excluded or deducted from the opening profits figure as the funds were all received during 1972. The increases in creditors and tax liabilities have been shown as deductions from the uses of funds as they in fact represent a short-term increase in finance.

**The analysis of the table**

The advantages of the sources and uses of funds statement are that it shows the financing of the company's expenditures, and areas of financial strain may be revealed. For example, a large increase in fixed assets in one year may have incurred little financial burden from a quick examination of the Profit and Loss Account and the Balance Sheet and therefore heavy future capital expenditures might be thought feasible. The increase in fixed assets might, however, have been met largely from new capital monies and from decreases in working capital requirements. This may not have been readily apparent from the Profit and Loss Account and the Balance Sheet but would have been highlighted by the sources and uses of funds statement.

**Uses of the table**

The analyst in using the statement for forecasting purposes will need to assess the possibilities of further capital raising, possible changes in the stock, debtors, creditors and taxation accounts, the need to replace assets or to increase physical capacity. Thus, he will be interested in projecting the various items making up a sources and uses statement. The analyst should be aware that the statement is drawn-up at a specific date and this may not be representative of the company's normal financial structure. Similarly, the statement does not budget for any critical times that a company is likely to go through during a year.

*Comparative figures for 1971 have not been included. This requires knowledge of the Balance Sheet at 31 December 1970.

ABC LTD's statement showed large capital expenditures during the year which required new issue monies and proceeds from the sale of substantial assets. The analyst will therefore have to estimate whether this level of capital expenditure is likely to recur. If, possibly due to heavy replacement of obsolete machinery, it does recur then a serious financing problem might arise.

### Breakdown of accounts by subsidiaries

Where a company is involved in a number of quite different activities it becomes very important to obtain as much data as possible on those various businesses. This is because some activities may be enjoying 'boom' conditions whilst others are depressed: the conditions may be long-term or the result of irregular influences such as, say, commodity shortages. In projecting future earnings the analyst requires an analysis of the present position and past record of each activity. He can then use industrial and economic statistics to project the separate areas of business and estimate an aggregate future trading profits position for the firm. This, subject to the financial gearing and the cost structure gearing, will provide a basis in arriving at estimated earnings per share (EPS). There are two main difficulties for the analyst in analysing businesses by activities. Firstly, there is the problem of defining what are the important differences in activities. Chapter 4 deals briefly with the identification of the important differences in business activities. It must be realised that the analysis given in the Directors' Report on the firm's activities is often not precise enough and can be misleading. Business activities can be classified by products, input requirements, labour intensity, sales markets and by many other factors. The important identification factor for the analyst will be to use the classification which acts as the major constraint on profitability especially where it is relatively uncorrelated profitwise with the other activities of the company. As will be seen the important classification of activity is often the marketing outlets and not the product grouping which is the usual criterion in the activity differentiations used in Directors' Reports.

**Obtaining data**

The second problem encountered by the analyst will be to obtain relevant data on the different areas of activities as defined by the analyst. The Annual Accounts give information on the principal activities usually on the basis of products and the turnover and pre-tax profits or losses relating to each. This information may not, however, represent the really critical areas of the business activities. For example, it is often the markets, and not the products themselves, which are the real determinants of profitability and thus it is information on the marketing outlets which is required.

**Subsidiaries' accounts**

When companies engage in substantially different activities they often form separate limited liability subsidiaries for each business. The divisionalising of a group is usually along the lines of product, market or geographical differentiation. Thus, the breakdown of consolidated accounts into the separate subsidiaries usually provides the best basis available for arriving at the state of affairs of the importantly different activities. The Annual Report presents a consolidated Profit and Loss Account, a consolidated Balance Sheet and the holding company's Balance Sheet. The analyst will extract the names of the subsidiaries from the Annual Report and investigate their Accounts at Companies House (in Cardiff for English-registered companies and in Edinburgh for Scottish-registered companies). The Accounts of limited liability subsidiaries will comply with Company Law in the same way as those of the parent company. Accounts have to be filed at Companies House within forty-two days of the Annual General Meeting (AGM) and so the analyst may have to wait some while after receiving the published consolidated accounts before obtaining data on the subsidiaries. This delay is therefore around two months (the published accounts being sent out at least twenty-one days before the AGM) and can be much longer. This is because of non-strict compliance with the Companies Acts provisions and because subsidiary companies' AGMS may be at different dates to the parent company. This delay may prevent the analyst from completely re-evaluating a security immediately upon receiving the Annual Accounts.

In extracting subsidiary accounts the analyst should aggregate the figures to see if they compare with the published consolidated accounts. There will be many occasions when there are substantial differences and these can be due to numerous reasons the more common of which will be described later.

## Consolidated accounts

Group accounts can come in two types: (1) where the parent company trades itself as well as owning subsidiary companies; and, (2) where the parent company's sole activity is to hold shares in subsidiaries. The parent in the latter case is usually termed a holding company. Further classification includes whether the subsidiaries are wholly owned or not. Whether a parent company trades or not can usually be determined by looking at its Balance Sheet. If it contains plant and machinery or stocks then the parent company can be assumed to trade.

## Consolidated Profit and Loss Accounts

The consolidated Profit and Loss Account will be filed at Companies House but there is no provision for the parent company's own Profit and Loss Account to be separately disclosed. The actual items belonging to the parent company's operations must be found by deducting the aggregate amounts of the various subsidiaries. In the case of a holding company there are, of course, no trading operations but it may provide various group services, i.e. financial, property, management.

For example, (1) a parent company XYZ LTD may show earnings of £10,000 with a breakdown of subsidiaries thus:

|   | £ |
|---|---|
| A | 5,000 |
| B | 2,000 |
| C | 1,000 |

Thus the parent company's activities have produced £2,000 of profit which could have been derived from management charges to *A*, *B* and *C* or from a trading operation. If the Balance Sheet of XYZ LTD showed stock and plant and machinery then it is reasonable to assume it trades (although it may still have made management charges).

**Overseas subsidiaries**

A complete analysis cannot be made if there are overseas subsidiaries as these do not file accounts in the UK. If the parent company is a holding company with no income of its own then the deduction of UK subsidiary figures from the total will give the foreign earnings. When the parent company trades and also has foreign subsidiaries then it is the aggregate of this figure which can be determined and not the individual components.

For example, (2) a parent company XYZ LTD has earnings of £10,000 and the following subsidiaries:

|   | £ |
|---|---|
| *A* | 5,000 |
| *B* | 1,000 |
| *C* | 1,000 |
| *D* | Not known – *D* incorporated abroad |

The parent company plus *D* have produced £3,000 profit (10,000 − *A* + *B* + *C*). Whether the parent company has traded can be reasonably established from the Balance Sheet but how much of the £3,000 accrues to it and how much to the foreign subsidiary is impossible to say.

If any of the subsidiaries consolidate foreign subsidiaries of themselves then the assessment of foreign earnings will be very difficult.

For example, (3) a parent company XYZ LTD has earnings of £10,000 and the following group structure:

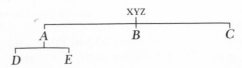

Profits may be shown as:

1

|   | £ |
|---|---|
| *A* | 5,000 |
| *B* | 1,000 |
| *C* | 1,000 |
| *D* | 1,000 |
| *E* | 1,000 |
|   | 9,000 |
| Parent company profit | 1,000 |
|   | £10,000 |

Subsidiary companies are not required to publish consolidated accounts although many do.

**2** Or *A* may consolidate *D* and *E*'s earnings thus:

|  | £ |  |
|---|---|---|
| *A* | 7,000 | (consolidated) |
| *B* | 1,000 | |
| *C* | 1,000 | |
|  | 9,000 | |
| Parent company profit | 1,000 | |
|  | £10,000 | |

*A*'s profit can be deduced by the extracting of profits of *D* and *E*.

**3** If *D* and *E* paid dividends of £500 and £200 to *A* then the analysis may look thus:

|  | £ | (trading profits 5,000) |
|---|---|---|
| *A* | 5,700 | (dividends 700) |
| *B* | 1,000 | |
| *C* | 1,000 | |
| *D* | 1,000 | less dividends (500) |
| *E* | 1,000 | less dividends (200) |

Thus care must be taken to extract dividend income from other subsidiaries.

If *E* was a foreign subsidiary then the complete breakdown of profits of *A* would not be possible. Here the deduction of *D*'s profit (£1,000) would give a total earnings figure for *A* and the foreign subsidiary *E* of £6,000. No further breakdown could be made.

## Problems associated with intragroup transactions

When analysing subsidiary company Accounts many ratio comparisons become meaningless due to the methods of accounting for intragroup transactions. Even the trends of ratios can be of little value in many cases. Intragroup accounting is especially prevalent when: (1) the subsidiaries rely on other subsidiaries for goods and services. This is very common in 'vertically integrated' companies; (2) there is a service company which may provide management or director expertise (or at least make a charge for such), own the property on which other subsidiaries are sited, or provide finance.

## Aggregation of subsidiary accounts differing from consolidated accounts

The aggregation of the various subsidiaries' profits may not equal the consolidated earnings due to the elimination of stock profits. Such 'profits' will normally arise when intragroup sales are made. For example, subsidiary *A* sells a product to subsidiary *B* for £10 and makes a profit of £2. *B*'s accounts will show stock of £10 at the year end in respect of this item (assuming it has not been re-sold). As stocks are usually recorded at cost price the consolidated accounts will include the product at a value of £8 thus eliminating the profit of £2 'made' by *A*. This is a major reason for discrepancies in profits figures between the aggregation of subsidiaries and consolidated accounts. Sales figures, financing charges, hire of plant and machinery and other items in subsidiary accounts also may not add up to the consolidated figures. This would be because there are intragroup items which have been cancelled-out in the consolidated accounts. Thus, if subsidiary company *A* hires plant out to fellow subsidiary company *B* for £100, *A* will show it as turnover and *B* as an expense. In the published Accounts these amounts will probably be cancelled against each other.

## Comparative analysis

Any comparative analysis of subsidiary accounts should be treated very warily. If there have been no intragroup transactions then an analyst may place some reliance on the figures. If the activities of the subsidiary company obviously have no relationship with the fellow subsidiaries and if there is no service company or, if there is, the scope of the services is known, and if there are no intragroup loans, then there is a good possibility that the accounts show a fair, 'at arm's length' picture of the subsidiary's performance and book net worth. Partly-owned subsidiaries are more likely to deal at 'arm's length' with the parent company as they have to account to the minority shareholders. The turnover attributable to specific activities can be taken from the subsidiary accounts. Even where there are intragroup sales the problem of transfer pricing may not be too disruptive if the products all go to one market, i.e. all outputs going to the same market, therefore having the same growth prospects. Profitability and asset ratios are probably very tenuous if substantial intragroup transactions take place: the analyst can, however, derive various trends in ratio analysis, and if they bear some resemblance to industry averages then he may feel they represent a fair picture. If they do not bear any resemblance then it may be due wholly or partly to intragroup transactions and the analyst will be unable to distinguish whether and to what extent this is so. Examples of intragroup transactions are:

## Intragroup transactions

1 Finance being given by one subsidiary. The rates and terms may differ from market rates and may vary between various subsidiaries.

2 Management charges may vary significantly between subsidiaries and could bear no resemblance to the actual service.

3 Rents charged to subsidiaries for property owned by the service company may vary enormously.

4 Directors' fees may be apportioned on a basis other than the value of the work done.

The reasons for the various services not being priced at competitive rates include:

1 Management's desire to make interfirm comparisons untenable for competitive reasons.

2 The rates may have been fixed on a fair basis many years ago. The effort of revising the rates to account for changing circumstances may not have been thought worth while.

3 The rates may be based on various standards such as proportions of turnover or labour intensity.

4 The services may be provided free because of the difficulty of allocating them to divisions.

Unless the analyst can be fairly sure of the extent and effects of intragroup transactions then extreme care should be used in handling ratios and other performance yardsticks of subsidiaries of a parent company. However, turnover figures and 'accurate ratios' provide valuable disaggregated data which is essential information to the analyst if a company has substantially different activities.

**Ratio analysis**[1]

The main uses of ratios are:

1 To compare intracompany trends. These may then be projected into the immediate future to give estimates of future performance. In doing so, they may indicate current and future areas of financial weakness.

2 To compare against other firms and industry averages. This may indicate the potential improvement that could be obtained given different management or asset deployment. It may also highlight areas where the company is ultra-efficient and may therefore expect increased competition.

**Comparison statistics**

Comparisons can be made against specific competitors and against industry averages. There are numerous tables of industrial statistics which can be used as yardsticks (e.g. Business Ratios, National Economic Development Council reports, trade organisation surveys and general financial surveys). However, the analyst may want to employ different statistics than those available and this will involve analysing individual company Accounts.

**Caveats in comparison statistics**

As has been mentioned previously the use of ratios has to be handled with care especially for interfirm comparisons where accounting policies differ significantly and where finding comparable companies can be difficult. Chapter 2 explained the importance of excluding or at least acknowledging exceptional and non-recurring items and this is especially relevant in ratio analysis and trends of ratios. An additional factor which needs to be recognised is the industry cycle within which the firm operates. For some companies the industrial cycle produces large fluctuations in profits and the performance ratios of successive years become erratic and difficult to interpret*. One way of overcom-

*The analysis of industry and trade cycles is described in Chapter 4.

ing this problem is to measure the ratios over the length of the cycles (often four or five years). This, however, makes ratio analysis less sensitive and is possibly of less predictive use in short-term extrapolation.

**Profitability ratios**
**Profit margins**

Since the Companies Act 1967 disclosure of turnover has had to be made and this statistic has enabled a number of useful ratios to be calculated. One of the most important is the gross profit margin. This is defined as the ratio of trading profit to turnover. The trading profit can be taken before or after the various items separately disclosed in the Profit and Loss Account, the analyst deciding which figure to use after experimentation on which provides the most useful forecasting tool. For example, many analysts would use profits before depreciation as this charge is somewhat arbitrary and is usually at a rate unconnected with profit margins. Similarly, long-term interest charges may be added back to profits as it is a fixed expense and is a function of the firm's financing policy, not its trading performance.

**Computation**

The profit margin for ABC LTD is computed after adding back to the group profit before taxation, depreciation £431,000, interest charges £57,700, directors' emoluments £25,000, exceptional items £80,000 and deducting income from investments £16,100 and development grant receipts £10,000. For example, ABC LTD

$$\frac{\text{Trading profit}}{\text{Sales}} \times 100 = \text{Profit margin}$$

$$\frac{2,103,600}{10,600,000} \times 100 = 19.8\%$$

**Uses of profit margin ratios**

The movement in this ratio over a number of years gives an indication of the changing profitability of the company's trading activity. The analyst can use this trend to:

1 Project short-term and tentative long-term estimates of gross trading profits.

2 Compare against like companies to see if there appears to be scope for improvement or whether there is a danger of increased competition. The obvious caveats should be taken account of, i.e. projection of trends will be very tenuous if the past figures show considerable variability; the change in profit margins may be due to an alteration in the proportion of sales of different products or activities and not an actual change in individual profit margins; the difficulty of identifying suitable companies for interfirm comparisons. The breakdown of a group into the various subsidiaries will considerably assist the usefulness of this ratio.

Another important aspect of the examination of profit margins is that it shows the degree of trade 'gearing'. This 'gearing' is a measure of the responsiveness of profits to changes in variable costs or changes in sales. Highly 'trade' or 'operationally geared' companies are often characterised by having relatively large fixed overheads and these magnify the impact on profits of changes in sales volume or contribution margins*. A company that has a high profit† margin is less susceptible, profitwise, to an increase in costs and likewise any alterations in price will have less impact (assuming there is no change in volume). For a company with low margins any movements in prices or costs will have a strong impact on profits. Such companies will have strongly fluctuating profits and are often more difficult to forecast. This 'gearing' is of considerable use to the analyst as he may have knowledge of movement in sales prices (i.e. standard retail price changes are given in trade journals) and a good idea of cost charges and volume production (i.e. industrial inflation indices and trade statistics). This especially applies to one-product companies.

*Example*

|  | Company A | Company B |
|---|---|---|
| Profit margin (%) | 25 | 10 |
| Increase in sales price (trade journal) (%) | 10 | 10 |
| Volume increase (trade journal) (%) | 5 estimate | 5 estimate |
| Cost increase (trade statistics) (%) | 8 | 8 |
| Percentage increase in profit | 38 | 83 |

The above example shows two companies experiencing similar percentage increases in volume, prices and costs. However, company B starts off with a profit margin considerably lower than company A and is thus more highly cost geared (A and B are equally efficient in their respective trades.) The impact of the gearing is quite clear with company B showing an increase of 83 per cent in gross profit to A's 38 per cent. It is apparent from the example that the determination of profit margins, especially where they are low, is of considerable importance to the analyst.

## Return on Capital Employed (ROCE)

This is the prime measure of profitability but one which is hard to define. Basically the ratio expresses the earnings generated by the permanent capital. Permanent here means the net assets which are not required to meet immediate liabilities (i.e. those due for repayment within one year). The differences in definitions arise as both the

---

*Contribution margin being the sales price minus the variable costs per unit of goods.

†'High' and 'low' are used in a relative sense. This is relative to industrial sectors.

numerator (earnings) and the denominator (capital employed) are capable of numerous meanings.

**Definitions**

Capital employed is capable of several interpretations and the usage of these depends from which angle the ratio is being looked at. The important factor to remember is to use the earnings figure appropriate to the capital employed definition adopted. The most common method of defining capital employed is the total of the issued ordinary capital, reserves, preference shares, minorities, loan capital, future tax provisions and bank overdrafts minus intangible assets. Other interpretations leave out items roughly in order starting from overdrafts. The reason for including overdrafts in the capital employed figure is that for many companies this item is permanent (some analysts in fact include only a part of the overdraft, usually a proportion based on the average of a number of years' overdrafts). Many analysts, however, leave bank overdrafts out of the calculation altogether. Future tax is another contentious source of funds although there is less argument over deferred taxation accounts as these are usually outstanding over many years. Other common definitions would include the value of intangible assets, or perhaps, some part of them. The criterion here may be whether a reliable value can be attached to the asset. In many cases the asset values appearing in the Balance Sheet do not reflect market values and, if current figures can be obtained, these should be substituted in the capital employed. The most obvious examples here are to use the market value of quoted investments and the market value of property (where this is given but not incorporated in the Accounts). As return on capital employed measures earnings against the resources owned, the current market values should be used so as to compare the returns against other forms of investment. If current values cannot be obtained then comparison of the returns between two similar companies may be completely different and this could be due to their having bought assets at different periods. Some economic texts advocate the use of replacement costs in place of the historical cost Balance Sheet values. This therefore uses today's cost price of the plant and equipment and, it is argued, allows valid interfirm comparison (the replacement cost values of identical plant and machinery are the same). Against this, however, is the fact that one would expect older machinery, even though physically identical, to be eventually less efficient and one would expect lower returns. Using current market values, assuming there is a rational, well organised secondhand market, acknowledges that machinery deteriorates with age but the replacement method does not. Few companies give replacement values and so this adjustment will be no easier than the more correct current market values. The analyst could possibly use general indices* of replacement values to adjust the Balance Sheet items but these will be very tenuous and the analyst will have little idea of whether the adjustments are correct.

*In the twenty-year period 1950 to 1970 the general index of capital goods prices rose by over 70 per cent.

## Earnings in the numerator

The earnings used in the numerator should be in accord with the method of computing capital employed, i.e. where bank overdrafts are included in capital employed the earnings should be those before bank interest charges. Similarly, if preference capital were to be left out of capital employed along with other fixed interest stocks then the earnings figure should be that of pre-tax profits less the grossed-up equivalent of the preference dividend. Earnings are usually taken pre-tax although there may be occasions when after-tax figures are required. This will enable the efficiency of the firm to be assessed before any external factors such as taxation.

## Dates for measuring capital employed

Another point which has to be established is to choose a date at which capital employed is to be measured. The possible alternatives include the opening Balance Sheet values, the closing Balance Sheet values, and half the total of the opening and closing Balance Sheets' values. If the profits accrue evenly throughout the year and major payments (i.e. tax, dividends and capital expenditure) also accrue evenly, then the latter method of measuring capital employed may be the most appropriate. However, any of the methods if used consistently will give similar trends. The caveat to this, of course, is when there is an exceptional occurrence such as a rights issue or the raising of a loan. The impact of these on earnings ratios will be explained later but the analyst may well have to ignore the ROCE figures for these years.

*Example*

The return on capital employed for ABC LTD is computed below:

| ABC LTD | 31.12.72 | 1.1.72. |
|---|---|---|
| *Capital employed* | £'000 | £'000 |
| Share capital | 600 | 500 |
| Share premium | 481 | 231 |
| Reserves | 1,732 | 1,052 |
| Minorities | 140 | 120 |
| Loan capital | 340 | 240 |
| Development grant A/C | 200 | |
| Amount set aside for future taxation | 405 | 260 |
| Deferred tax | 180 | 60 |
| | £4,078 | £2,463 |
| | | |
| Market value of investments minus Balance Sheet figure | 24 | 12 |
| Overdraft | 60 | 600 |
| | 4,162 | 3,075 |
| *Less* goodwill | 220 | 220 |
| *Capital employed* | 3,942 | 2,855 |

*Investment analysis*

| Earnings | £'000 |
|---|---|
| Profit before taxation | 1,698 |
| Add back interest | 57.7 |
| Add back exceptional and non-recurrent expenditure | 80.0 |
| | 1,835.7 |
| *Less* transfer from development grant account | 10.0 |
| | 1,825.7 |

$$\text{ROCE} = \frac{\text{Earnings}}{\frac{1}{2}\begin{array}{c}\text{(Capital employed at beginning}\\\text{of year plus capital employed}\\\text{at the end of the year)}\end{array}} = \frac{1,825.7}{\frac{1}{2}(3,942 + 2,855)}$$

$$= \frac{1,825.7}{3,398.5} = 54\%$$

## Computation capital employed

The capital employed definition used in the example on ABC LTD included the overdraft figure and the various deferred credits and liabilities (deferred taxation, amounts set aside for future tax and development grants). Goodwill has been deducted as this item related to the acquisition of subsidiaries. Its value is very tentative; it may give some indication of the under-valuation of assets acquired but in general it is intangible. It is not fair to compare two companies, one of which does not have a goodwill item and therefore the item has been ignored. The directors stated in their report that the current market values of freehold properties are not significantly above book value. An adjustment is made to incorporate the current market value of investments and in this case the adjustment is small (some would argue that it is not worth while making the adjustment especially as market values can easily swing say 10 per cent in a matter of weeks). No other adjustments to values were made. As there was a rights issue and an issue of debentures during the year the capital employed figure has been derived by aggregating the Balance Sheet values of 1971 and 1972. This value is then divided by two to obtain the average capital employed. The analyst can derive other fractions by determining how long the company has the money. This still will not show a truly accurate figure as it may take time to deploy the money and more time still for the assets purchased to become revenue earning. The average of the two Balance Sheet values was felt to be the best way of deriving the capital employed; however, the use of ROCE when there has been a large increase in capital employed should be treated with caution.

## Computation earnings

The earnings figure started with the figure 'profit before tax' which appeared in the consolidated Profit and Loss Account. To this figure are added the interest on the loan capital and bank overdraft as these figures are used in computing capital employed. Also added to the profit is the item exceptional and non-recurring expenditure as these tend to fluctuate erratically and upset any patterns that may be evident. The transfer of the deferred development grant to the Profit and Loss Account is left out.

## Alternative computations

The other definitions of capital employed could have been used. For instance, investments could have been left out as these are funds which are not employed in the mainstream business of the company. For ABC the ROCE calculation would become:

| | | 31.12.72 £'000 | | 1.1.72 £'000 |
|---|---|---|---|---|
| Capital employed as before | | 3,942 | | 2,855 |
| Less investments | 261 | | 161 | |
| Less current market adjustment | 24 | 285 | 12 | 173 |
| | | 3,657 | | 2,682 |
| Earnings as before | | 1,825.7 | | |
| Less income from investments | 16.1 | | | |
| Less income from associated company | 162.0 | 178.1 | | |
| | | 1,647.6 | | |

$$\text{ROCE} = \frac{1,647.6}{\frac{1}{2}(3,657 + 2,682)} = 52\%$$

The reader is left to consider ROCE figures produced by other methods.

## Additional factors

Whilst ROCE is one of the most useful ratios it is one which can be the most difficult to measure. Apart from problems mentioned above there are a number of other items which can significantly affect the comparisons of the ratio:

1 The raising of new capital will make a ROCE calculation very difficult to establish. The capital employed can be time weighted but the earnings figures will not reflect the benefit of the new monies as it takes time to deploy resources. Similarly, any exceptional capital expenditure will considerably affect the ratio. The effects of these may last beyond the year of occurrence, e.g. the deployment of new capital into revenue producing fixed assets may take a number of years if it involves (say) the building of a new plant or is a payment for exploration rights.

2 Book asset values may not be equivalent to current market values. This is a significant problem with respect to freehold and leasehold properties.

3 Profits may not be 'normalised'. An example of this may be a sale and leaseback agreement which may contain a provision that the company does not pay rent for a given number of years. In this case the reported profits would exceed the real economic return on the assets.

67

4   Valuation of intangible assets. These are normally left out. However, in some cases goodwill reflects the under-valuation of acquired assets and should therefore be included in the capital-employed figure. The difficulty is in establishing what proportion of goodwill is attributable to under-valued assets and so the normal practice has arisen of excluding intangibles altogether.

## Implications of ROCE

ROCE is important as a measurement of managerial performance. A poor return can be expected to continue if management is unchanged although such a company may be the target for a takeover bid which will probably be at a substantial premium on current share price (unless discounted). If a new management team arrives in a company with a poor ROCE this may suggest an improvement in earnings performance as there will be substantial scope for this to occur. A very high ROCE ratio may suggest that the company has had a substantial lead over competitors. In the majority of cases this high return will eventually be eroded by increasing competition and the analyst should be wary of companies maintaining high returns. Both the trend of capital employed and interfirm comparisons will provide indicators of relative performance. There are numerous trade journals available which give return on capital employed statistics. These are computed in a consistent manner although the underlying Accounts are based on various principles and policies. An ultimate ramification of a poor ROCE is that the company should be wound up. Such a process would involve considerable expenses especially since the advent of redundancy payments but nevertheless it is an eventual outcome of continuous low returns. Despite the drawbacks of measurability the trend of ROCE can give guidelines for future performance. Interfirm comparisons should, however, be treated with extreme caution with the analyst making a detailed investigation of the Accounts and the computational methods used (this obviates the use of published statistics).

### Sales to capital employed

This and the similar ratios of sales to fixed assets, sales to current assets and sales to current assets less current liabilities, examines the asset structure which a company uses to generate sales. The 'capital employed' used in the ratio should exclude trade and other investments as they are not intended to create turnover. High ratios of sales to capital employed may indicate that the firm's asset base is too narrow and that further capital may be required to finance sales. Over-trading can be especially disastrous if a slump ensues as can be the case in say the one-product fashion industry where the stock becomes difficult to sell and debtors are slow to pay. A low ratio suggests that there is an under-employment of assets and usually reflects poor management. By breaking the capital employed figure up into fixed assets and net current assets, the analyst may determine which is the constraint. If it is fixed assets this may be more important as it usually takes some time to either redeploy or acquire assets.

*Example* ABC LTD

$$\frac{\text{Sales}}{\text{Capital employed}} = \frac{10,600,000}{3,597,000} = 2.95$$

|  |  |  | £ |
|---|---|---|---|
| Capital employed | As before |  | 4,078,000 |
|  | *Less*: Goodwill | 220,000 |  |
|  | Investments | 261,000 | 481,000 |
|  |  |  | £3,597,000 |

The multiple combination of profit margin ratio and sales over net assets employed will give the return on capital employed (assuming similar 'profits' and capital-employed figures are used). This gives the relative contribution of profit margins and turnover to the total return on capital employed.

*Example* ABC LTD

$$\frac{\text{Sales}}{\text{Capital employed}} \times \frac{\text{Gross profit}}{\text{Sales}} \times 100 = \frac{\text{Gross profit}}{\text{Capital employed}} \times 100$$

$$\frac{10,600,000}{3,597,000} \times \frac{2,103,600}{10,600,000} \times 100 = \frac{2,103,600}{3,597,000} \times 100$$

$$2.95 \quad \times \quad 0.198 \quad \times 100 = \quad 58.41\%$$

## Asset value per share

This figure gives the book value of the assets of the company, after repaying all debts, available to each ordinary share. It is represented by the ordinary share capital plus reserves divided by the number of ordinary shares. Many authorities state that the above asset value is the worth of the share to an investor if the company is wound up and it is therefore used as a yardstick below which the share price should not be consistently placed. However, book asset values in the majority of cases do not give a fair representation of what the company would be worth in a break-up. Firstly, it does not take into account the enormous sums of money that would have to be paid in redundancy settlements and the expenses of liquidating the company. Secondly, book asset values are frequently far from the current market prices that could be obtained. In certain situations, however, book asset values are a reliable pointer to the value an acquirer would pay. Generally, this applies to companies with a high proportion of assets in the form of properties which are valued in the accounts at current market values and a lowish number of employees. For instance, major store groups have substantial properties and virtually no plant and machinery. The current assets of stocks and debtors should be easily realisable at near to Balance Sheet values. Additionally, the properties are likely to be used as stores by the acquirer and so staff would be retained thereby obviating redundancy payments.

*Investment analysis*

If there are substantial property assets but they have had no recent revaluation the asset values will probably afford little information although analysts can and do make estimates of current worth of freeholds and leaseholds.

**Include current market values**

In computing net asset values the current market values of securities and properties (where given) should be substituted. Similarly, debt repayments should be deducted at the repayment amounts, i.e. although a debenture is quoted at its nominal value in the Balance Sheet it may be repayable at a premium and it is this figure which should be included. This information is not always shown in the Accounts and the analyst will have to look at the appropriate statistical records. The treatment of intangibles is again difficult – most analysts leave them out especially with regard to goodwill.

*Example*   ABC LTD

$$\text{Asset value per share at } 31.12.72 = \frac{\text{Net assets (revalued)}}{\text{Number of shares in existence}}$$

| *Net assets* | £ |
|---|---|
| Net assets per Balance Sheet | 2,813,000 |
| Addition due to market value of investments | 24,000 |
| | 2,837,000 |
| *Less*: Goodwill | 220,000 |
| | 2,617,000 |
| Number of shares in existence | 2,400,000 |

$$\text{Asset value per share} = \frac{2,617,000}{2,400,000} = 109p$$

**Implications of ratio**

If the asset value is substantially below the share price this may indicate that the company has excellent management in earning high returns on capital. A high asset value (in relation to share price) is evidence of inefficient use of resources and thus poor management. As with poor returns on capital employed it indicates the possible returns that could be made with a new management team and the susceptibility to a takeover bid.

Companies in the property sectors and the investment trust sector are in fact valued in relation to the underlying asset values and such firms often give much more up-to-date information on their current values. These companies are therefore valued in a different way to the ordinary industrial share.

**Stock turnover**

This is the ratio of turnover to stocks.

*Interpreting financial statements*

*Example* ABC LTD

$$\text{Stock turnover} = \frac{\text{Sales}}{\text{Stock at end of year}}$$

$$= \frac{10,600,000}{1,081,000} = 9.81$$

Another method which may be used is to take the average of the opening and closing levels of stock. Thus:

$$\frac{\text{Sales}}{\frac{1}{2}(\text{Opening stock } (1.1.72) + \text{Closing stock } (31.12.72))}$$

$$= \frac{10,600,000}{\frac{1}{2}(805,000 + 1,081,000)} = 11.24$$

This will probably give a better estimate of average stock turnover.

Stock turnover can also be described in terms of the number of months for which stock are held on average. The expressions are:

$$\frac{\text{Stock at } 31.12.72}{\text{Sales}} \times 12$$

or

$$\frac{\frac{1}{2}(\text{Stock at } 31.12.72 + \text{Stock at } 1.1.72)}{\text{Sales}} \times 12$$

*Example* ABC LTD

(1) $\dfrac{\text{Stock}}{\text{Sales}} \times 12 = \dfrac{1,081,000}{10,600,000} \times 12 = 1.2$ months

or (2) using the average of opening and closing levels of stock:

$$\frac{\frac{1}{2}(\text{Stock at beginning of year} + \text{Stock at end of year})}{\text{Sales}} \times 12$$

$$= \frac{\frac{1}{2}(805,000 + 1,081,000)}{10,600,000} \times 12$$

$$= 1.06 \text{ months}$$

## Interpretation of stock ratios

Stock turnover ratios can give an idea of the operating efficiency of the business and is sometimes used as an indicator of managerial efficiency. For example, if the ratio becomes extremely high it may indicate the presence of obsolete lines of stock. Interfirm comparisons will be very tenuous due to differences in stock valuations and differences in the make-up of aggregate stocks (i.e. raw materials, work-in-progress, finished goods). Few companies give break-ups of their stocks into raw materials, work-in-progress and finished goods and so the ratios computed have to be aggregates. If companies are eventually required to differentiate between stocks then more apposite ratios can be constructed, i.e. raw material stocks compared against cost of goods sold (if this figure is also given) and finished goods expressed as a ratio of sales. This type of increased disclosure will be extremely helpful

71

especially in highlighting an area which often leads to insolvencies. If the business has a seasonal bias then the analyst should be careful to compare only those companies with similar year-ends.

The figures computed for ABC LTD should be compared with other companies in the same business and the trend of the ratio over a number of years examined. Subject to this the stock ratios of ABC LTD appear to be fairly good.

### Credit granted to debtors

This measures the average length of time debtors take to pay-off amounts due. Like the previous ratio, this statistic is an indicator of managerial efficiency. A very high figure may lead an analyst to suspect that there is a likelihood of substantial bad debts.

*Example* ABC LTD (Figures in £'000)

$$\frac{\text{Debtors at } 31.12.72}{\text{Sales}} \times 12 = \frac{970}{10,600} = 1.1 \text{ months}$$

or

$$\frac{\frac{1}{2}(\text{Debtors } 31.12.71 + \text{Debtors } 31.12.72) \times 12}{\text{Sales}}$$

$$= \frac{\frac{1}{2}(683 + 970) \times 12}{10,600} = 0.94 \text{ months}$$

This ratio can also be described in terms of the turnover of debtors to sales, i.e.

$$\frac{\text{Sales}}{\text{Debtors at } 31.12.72} = \frac{10,600}{970} = 10.93$$

or

$$\frac{\text{Sales}}{\frac{1}{2}(\text{Debtors } 31.12.71 + \text{Debtors } 31.12.72)} = \frac{10,600}{\frac{1}{2}(683 + 970)} = 12.83$$

The turnover figures used should be the credit sales. As few companies differentiate between cash and credit sales the total turnover will have to be taken.

**Seasonal business** If sales are seasonal it is quite likely that the average length of credit granted as calculated above will be unrepresentative. This is similar to the stock ratio problems of seasonal business. The analyst should therefore take care in making interfirm comparisons between seasonal businesses. ABC's debtor ratios are quite reasonable for an engineering firm although further information such as the trend of the ratio is required.

### Liquidity ratios

These ratios measure the ability of the company to meet its short-term commitments as they become due.

The working capital ratio is calculated by dividing current liabilities into current assets.

*Example* ABC LTD (Figures in £'000)

|  | 1971 | 1972 |
|---|---|---|
| $\dfrac{\text{Current assets}}{\text{Current liabilities}}$ | $\dfrac{1{,}546}{1{,}300} = 1.19$ | $\dfrac{2{,}098}{980} = 2.14$ |

If the ratio is greater than 1 this implies that the company can meet its obligations as they fall due. The analyst will have to investigate beyond this crude statistic and some of the more common items to be looked for are mentioned below. ABC's working capital ratio has improved significantly during the year, this being largely due to the fall in the bank overdraft.

**Quick assets ratio**

A more strict yardstick of liquidity is given by quick assets ratio (acid test). This excludes stocks from current assets. Stock values tend to be the least reliable of the current assets and, more importantly, they take much longer to realise.

*Example* (Figures in £'000)

|  | 1971 | 1972 |
|---|---|---|
| $\dfrac{\text{Current assets} - \text{Stocks}}{\text{Current liabilities}}$ | $\dfrac{741}{1{,}300} = 0.57$ | $\dfrac{1{,}017}{980} = 1.04$ |

One can see that if substantial amounts of stocks were unsaleable then the company's apparent good liquidity position would deteriorate considerably. ABC LTD appears to have sufficient working capital to meet its output although any further heavy capital expenditure would alter the position.

One method of assessing whether there are substantial obsolete stocks is to measure the ratio of

$$\frac{\text{Stocks}}{\text{Current assets}}$$

If this ratio grows significantly over a period of years it may indicate the presence of old, unsaleable stocks. In general, however, the analyst will be relying on the Annual Accounts and the auditor's certificate as showing the correct stock values. Few of the more recently publicised company crashes due to stock deficiencies could have been foreseen from the Annual Accounts.

**The use of liquidity ratios**

Both the working capital and acid tests may be unrepresentative of the liquidity position if the company is involved in a highly seasonal business. The analyst should be aware of normal trade terms for seasonal products when comparing like-industry companies which have different year-ends to assess the differences in liquidity ratios. The main use of these ratios to the analyst is that they may indicate a shortage of working capital. In conjunction with the company's trading record and with conditions for raising capital, the analyst can assess the impact on earnings and share prices of having to raise fresh capital.

The analyst may adjust the figures appearing in both the numerator and the denominator of the ratio so as to incorporate further near-term liabilities and easily realisable assets. For example, the analyst may want to include taxation on profits of the year even though not payable for at least twelve months. Similarly, debenture repayments which are due within one year, but not entered in current liabilities, may be entered as a liability in the ratio. The analyst could add quoted trade investments or a part of them to current assets as these are often easily realisable should a liquidity squeeze ensue.

In measuring the liquidity position the analyst should note the trend of the ratio and not be too concerned with the magnitude of the ratio. If, for instance, ABC LTD realised £900,000 of debtors and used the proceeds to pay off liabilities, the working capital ratio would soar.

That is:

$$\text{1972}$$
$$\text{£'000}$$
$$\frac{\text{Current assets (2,098)} - \text{Debtors realised (900)}}{\text{Current liabilities (980)} - \text{Those paid (900)}} = \frac{1,198}{80} = 14.97$$

The figure 14.97 compares with the earlier computed figure of 2.14. This shows up the need to look at the trend of the ratio.

### Ratio of fixed assets to net assets

This expresses the degree to which fixed assets are financed by shareholders. Fixed assets should exclude investments as these are reasonably easy to realise. Net assets (also known as net worth) is the issued ordinary capital and reserves.

*Example* ABC LTD

| | 1972 | 1971 |
|---|---|---|
| Fixed assets = | £2,479,000 | 1,836,000 |
| Net assets   = | £2,813,000 | 1,783,000 |

$$\frac{2,479,000}{2,813,000} = 0.88 \qquad \frac{1,836,000}{1,783,000} = 1.03$$

If the trade investments were felt to be difficult to liquidate easily at current market prices then they could be included in the ratio. This, for example, may occur with large stakes in unquoted companies. The ratio for ABC LTD would then look like:

$$\frac{2,479,000 + 261,000}{2,813,000} = 0.97 \qquad \frac{1,836,000 + 161,000}{1,783,000} = 1.12$$

The ratio can be extended to show the relationship of fixed assets to long-term capital (net worth plus minorities plus loan capital plus deferred taxation).

## Analysis of the ratio

Too high a ratio indicates that long-term commitments are being financed by short-term finance, a position which could create a funding crisis if the company's fortunes turn bad or in a credit crisis. A low ratio suggests that not enough of the company's assets are being invested in productive capacity, thus not realising the full potential of the company. Apart from the usual problem of valuing assets, problems can arise in interfirm comparisons as some companies lease property and hire machinery whilst others own their assets. The treatment of investment grants and depreciation can also seriously distort comparisons.

A concomitant ratio which highlights the division of assets between productive and working capital is the ratio of fixed assets to total assets.

*Example*  ABC LTD

|  | 1972 | 1971 |
|---|---|---|
|  | £ | £ |
| Fixed assets | 2,479,000 | 1,836,000 |
| Trade investments | 261,000 | 161,000 |
|  | 2,740,000 | 1,997,000 |
| Current assets | 2,098,000 | 1,546,000 |
| Total assets | 4,838,000 | 3,543,000 |

$$\text{Ratio of fixed to total assets} \quad = \quad \frac{2,740,000}{4,838,000} \quad = \quad \frac{1,997,000}{3,543,000}$$

$$= \quad 0.57 \quad = \quad 0.56$$

A high ratio indicates that a company may be expanding too rapidly with consequent pressure upon liquidity. A low figure suggests the under-utilisation of funds in productive resources. The analyst must be aware of the structure of the firm he is analysing and only compare similar-industry firms. For instance, a wholesale business would expect to have a very low ratio as they have no manufacturing assets and they carry high levels of stocks and debtors.

A major drawback to this ratio is that current liabilities are ignored altogether. The relationship can, however, highlight differences between similar industry companies.

### Other ratios

There are numerous other ratios an analyst can devise which may help him in forecasting future profitability. He will investigate the use of such and, if they aid forecasting, then they should be incorporated within the framework of the analysis. For example, the ratio of sales to total wages can give relevant information when analysing labour-intensive industry. A rising trend may be indicative of increased efficiency of the labour force or an increase in capital equipment intensity. This latter explanation could be assessed by examining the ratio of plant and machinery to the number of employees.

*Investment analysis*

*Example*   ABC LTD

|  | 1972 | 1971 |
|---|---|---|
| Sales | 10,600,000 | 9,800,000* |
| Wages | 2,180,000 | 1,900,000 |
|  | = 4.86 | = 5.16 |

The ratio indicates that the amount of sales earned for every pound spent on wages has fallen in 1972. The figure should be compared with those in the same industry although because of the difficulties in interfirm comparisons the trend of the intracompany ratio will be of more importance.

**Wages**

The ratio of total wages to total numbers of employees indicates the level of wage inflation.

*Example*

|  | 1972 | 1971 |
|---|---|---|
| Wages | 2,180,000 | 1,900,000* |
| Number employees | 1,842 | 1,700 |
|  | = £1,180 | = £1,120 |

The average wage earned has increased from £1,120 to £1,180. This statistic is fairly crude as a measure of wage inflation as wages could have risen due to overtime working or different-quality jobs. These statistics will only be available for employees working in the UK.

**Financial gearing**

An important item in a company's financial structure is the amount of fixed-interest borrowings, this having a magnifying effect on the fluctuations in trading profits. Generally speaking, companies with more volatile trading profits patterns can afford only a small level of fixed-interest bearing stocks as investors on average are risk averters. The effect of fixed-interest borrowings on the earnings capacity can be seen in the example.

*Example*

|  | Method of finance | | |
|---|---|---|---|
|  | *A* | *B* | *C* |
|  | £ | £ | £ |
| Ordinary shares & reserves | 100,000 | 500,000 | 1,000,000 |
| 10% Debentures | 900,000 | 500,000 |  |
|  | £1,000,000 | £1,000,000 | £1,000,000 |

*From the previous year's accounts.

|  | £ | £ | £ |
|---|---|---|---|
| Profit (1) Return on capital of 8% | 80,000 | 80,000 | 80,000 |
| Debenture interest | 90,000 | 50,000 | |
| Profit (loss) available to ordinary shareholders | (10,000) | 30,000 | 80,000 |
| Earned on ordinary share capital | (−10%) | 6% | 8% |
| Profit (2) Return on capital of 12% | 120,000 | 120,000 | 120,000 |
| Debenture interest | 90,000 | 50,000 | |
| Profit | 30,000 | 70,000 | 120,000 |
| Earned on ordinary share capital | 30% | 14% | 12% |
| % change on 1 | − | $\frac{14}{6} = 233\%$ | $\frac{12}{8} = 150\%$ |
| Profit (3) Return on capital of 20% | 200,000 | 200,000 | 200,000 |
| Debenture interest | 90,000 | 50,000 | |
| Profit | 110,000 | 150,000 | 200,000 |
| Earned on ordinary share capital | 110% | 30% | 20% |
| % change on 1 | − | $\frac{30}{6} = 500\%$ | $\frac{20}{8} = 250\%$ |

Notes
(1) Taxation has been ignored
(2) In practice it would be difficult to obtain a financial structure similar to *A*'s

## The impact of financial gearing

The impact of gearing can be clearly seen from the example. This shows three methods of financing capital of £1 million, the first being the highest geared, the second having equal fixed interest and equity investment and the last having no gearing whatsoever. Three levels of profitability are then assumed and the earnings attributable to the ordinary shareholders are shown. These vary enormously with the degree of gearing. Thus, the highly geared financial strategy of *A* gives a negative return to shareholders when the return on capital employed is 8 per cent but shows a return of 110 per cent on a ROCE of 20 per cent. This represents a more than doubling of investors' wealth in one year. The volatility of *A*'s financial strategy is enormous, both the ROCE's of 8 and 20 per cent are fairly attainable by industrial companies. Financing strategy *B* does not show a loss on the three assumed rates of return but the growth in EPS is far less than method *A*. Strategy *C* as can be seen is the most conservative of all. The impact of fixed interest gearing is fairly obvious, i.e. it bears a fixed charge regardless of the level of profit and the ordinary shareholders take all the additional increase or decrease in profit.

## Interpretation of gearing ratio

Figure 3.1 shows the three financing strategies *A*, *B* and *C* and measures the earnings for differing ROCE. The graph shows that the three financing methods give similar earnings when the return on capital employed reaches 10 per cent. This is because 10 per cent is the debenture interest rate and, with a return on capital employed of 10 per cent, the different financing strategies have the same impact on EPS. It can be realised that the determination of the amount and stability of the return on capital employed is extremely important for highly

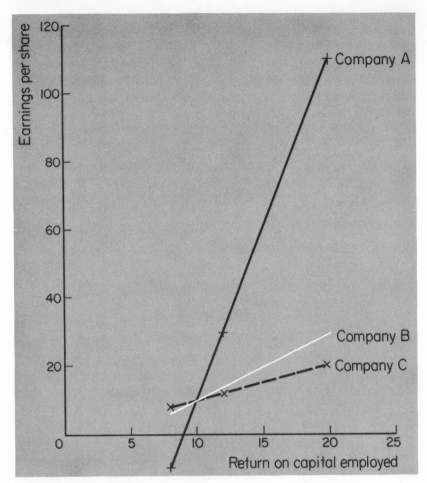

**Figure 3.1**

The impact of financial gearing on earnings per share

geared companies. Highly geared companies will have a more volatile profits performance than a similarly placed firm with little fixed interest borrowings and will be a more risky investment. This is because dividends may be reduced in the downswings of the business cycle and thus investors who rely on dividend income will be less inclined to own such shares. A further point is that the Stock Market usually places a heavy emphasis on near future profits and so a volatile profits profile may also have a more volatile share price pattern and thus deter some investors. Additionally, if profits are more difficult to forecast (because they are more volatile) investors may be prejudiced against them for although there may be as many good shocks as bad, investors are risk averters. In common with investor behaviour theory one would expect highly geared companies (comparative to similar firms) to be on lower Stock Market ratings, thus giving greater scope for better returns. There are exceptions, however, these usually being property and investment trust companies.

## Traditionally highly geared companies

The companies who can obtain the greatest gearing are firms with more stable earnings patterns and whose asset values are both stable or rising and marketable (as seen later both earnings and assets are important items in measuring gearing)[2]. For cyclical industries the level of gearing has to be lower as losses are likely at the bottom of the cycle if a company has heavy interest commitments. Although investors gain more when the cycle is at the top these gains will have to substantially outweigh the losses for investors to give the company a reasonable share-price status.

Property companies are typically highly geared as they satisfy the criteria of steady profits growth with a continually rising trend of asset values. The rental income increases steadily as reversions take place, the management charges are small and reasonably predictable and the interest charges can be ascertained. Besides the steady trend in profits growth the asset values are relatively easy to forecast. Property values have risen in virtually every period for the past twenty years and the market for transferring property is fairly sophisticated so that assets can be sold quickly at or near current market values. Property is one of the few continually appreciating assets and thus provides excellent security for the loans*.

Investment trusts are also highly geared and again they show the characteristics of stability and marketability. Their income usually rises year by year and although the asset backing is more volatile than property shares the investments are easily liquidated and do form some hedge against inflation over longer periods of time.

Cyclical industries are typically lowly geared as the trading profits figures are volatile and liquidity crises can occur if large interest payments have to be met. Further, their assets in the form of plant and equipment, depreciates rapidly.

## Gearing by industrial sectors

The Stock Market normally allocates an approximate gearing level for particular industries and thus companies will find it difficult to obtain fixed interest borrowings greatly in excess of its industry average. Recognition of the impact of financial gearing is extremely important in the forecasting of earnings and in helping to understand why shares stand on particular yields. For example, two companies with similar earnings per share and asset values may be priced very differently. This may be due to heavy financial gearing on the part of one company with the Stock Market giving it a premium if a property company or giving it a discount if it is a cyclical-earnings firm.

There are two main financial 'gearing ratios', one dealing with the asset structure, the other with the appropriation of pre-interest profits (known as priority percentages).

*There is no guarantee of rising values, however. This was experienced during 1974 when several property companies revalued their properties downwards. In some cases the high level of gearing forced companies to sell off properties, the values of which were already falling.

## Asset structure

The gearing factors given by the asset structure can be arranged in a number of ways but as long as the analyst is consistent the ratios give viable information. The method used to establish the gearing of ABC LTD is to divide the ordinary share capital plus reserves into long-term loan capital plus preference share capital.

*Example*  ABC LTD. Figures in £'000.

$$\frac{\text{Long-term loan capital}}{\text{Ordinary share capital plus reserves}} = \frac{340}{2,813} = 12.1\% \qquad \frac{240}{1,783} = 13.5\%$$

(with the years 1972 and 1971 labelled above the respective fractions)

ABC LTD is relatively lightly geared although any substantial increase in long-term borrowings may be difficult to obtain as the properties are fully mortgaged.

## Inclusion of bank borrowings

A possible refinement that could be made is to include bank overdrafts (or a portion thereof) with long-term loan capital plus preference capital. Thus the gearing for ABC LTD would look like:

|  | 1972 £'000 | 1971 £'000 |
|---|---|---|
| Long-term loan capital | 340 | 240 |
| Bank borrowings | 60 | 600 |
|  | 400 | 840 |

$$\text{Gearing ratio} \qquad \frac{400}{2,813} = 14.2\% \qquad \frac{840}{1,783} = 47.1\%$$

The fixed interest borrowings for 1971 rise considerably when bank overdrafts are included and the company becomes relatively highly geared. By the end of 1972, however, the ratio was little above that shown by the previous definition.

## Other factors in asset gearing

Other methods have been advocated which include minority interests and future tax provisions as part of the equity capital available to meet fixed interest borrowings. Sometimes the denominator of the ratio uses ordinary share capital plus reserves plus the long-term loans (and minority interests and tax provisions). However, the ranking order of gearing and the trends evident therein would be unchanged.

## Hire and rental gearing

If the analyst had information available on rental and hire agreements taken out by the company these could be incorporated into the gearing ratios and priority tables. Amounts paid under these commitments are fixed for a number of years hence and would take priority pro rata with the unsecured loan stock shown in the example. Such data is rarely available, however.

## Limitations in using annual accounts for gearing ratios

An obvious drawback in the above measurements is that Balance Sheet asset values may be far away from market values. Some analysts have advocated the use of the market values of securities as the surrogates of current values of assets. Thus, M.S. Rix[3] suggests the ratio:

Nominal value of fixed interest securities
  Market value of ordinary share capital

By using the nominal value of fixed interest stocks the ratio ignores the rate of interest payable. Solomon[4] recommends the substitution of the market value of the fixed interest securities in the numerator of the above ratio. This is on the ground that the market value reflects the interest rates paid on the securities. The ratio thus becomes:

$$\frac{\text{Market value of fixed interest securities}}{\text{Market value of ordinary share capital}}$$

or

$$\frac{\text{Market value of fixed interest securities}}{\text{Market value of ordinary share capital and market value of fixed interest securities}}$$

By using market values the ratio will of course change from day to day but this may make it a more sophisticated tool. The above market value orientated approaches can take into account bank overdrafts of course.

## Priority percentages

Gearing factors can also be derived based on the interest charges and the company's profits. These are known as priority percentages. Priority percentages are normally made out in the form of a table which starts with pre-interest profits and successively deducts the fixed interest borrowings in their order of priority. The following table shows the compilation of priority percentages for a company with debentures, convertible loan stocks, minority interests and preference capital.

| | Available profits | Income requirement of charge | Cumulative total | Percentage of profit taken | Priority percentage |
|---|---|---|---|---|---|
| Debenture interest | 80,000 | 10,000 | 10,000 | $12\frac{1}{2}$ | $0–12\frac{1}{2}$ |
| Convertible loan stock (unsecured) | 70,000 | 6,000 | 16,000 | 20 | $12\frac{1}{2}–20$ |
| Minorities (grossed up) | 64,000 | 14,000 | 30,000 | $37\frac{1}{2}$ | $20–37\frac{1}{2}$ |
| Preference dividend (grossed up) | 50,000 | 7,000 | 37,000 | 46 | $37\frac{1}{2}–46$ |
| Ordinary dividend (grossed up) | 43,000 | 14,000 | 51,000 | 64 | 46–64 |
| Retentions (grossed up) | 29,000 | 29,000 | 80,000 | 100 | 64–100 |

The company made £80,000 profit pre all charges. Debenture interest has the first charge on profits and takes the first $12\frac{1}{2}$ per cent. The next charge is the unsecured loan stock interest. It has no charge on the company's assets and therefore ranks with other trade creditors. The debenture and loan stock interest take the first 20 per cent of the profits with the loan stock having a priority percentage of $12\frac{1}{2}$ to 20 per cent of the profits. The minority interests take the next charge on profits*. This item as well as the preference and ordinary dividends and retentions are grossed up in order to show the pre-tax level of profits that are required to service the various charges or appropriations.

The example shows that a fall in profits of 37 per cent would leave the ordinary dividend uncovered and a fall of 55 per cent would produce a negative earnings per share figure.

The percentage priority table for ABC LTD is given below:

|  | £'000 |  | % of profit available |
|---|---|---|---|
| Profit pre-priority interest[1,2] |  | 1,756 |  |
| Loan interest | 31 |  |  |
| Bank interest[3] | 27 | 58 | 0 – 3 |
|  |  | 1,698 |  |
| Minorities grossed-up[4] |  | 33 | 3 – 5 |
|  |  | 1,665 |  |
| Dividends grossed-up |  | 333 | 5 – 24 |
|  |  | 1,332 |  |
| Retentions grossed-up |  | 1,332 | 24 – 100 |

Taxation assumed at 40%

[1]Profit before taxation per accounts £1,698,000
Add interest payments 58,000
1,756,000

[2]The extraordinary item has been left out of the computation.

[3]Some analysts would leave out the bank interest on the grounds that overdrafts are not long-term capital and that the bank interest charge is variable.

[4]There is a case for leaving out minorities as no cash leaves the company and such a 'charge' does not impose any drain on liquid resources.

The analyst can modify the items he includes in his gearing tables to suit his particular requirements.

An alternative approach is to multiply the pre-tax charges by the net of tax factor which with corporation tax at 40 per cent would be 0.60. The debenture and loan stock interest is therefore multiplied by 0.6. No adjustment to the after-tax items is now necessary. The same priority percentages will be arrived at as previously.

The priority percentages table of ABC LTD shows a very lightly geared capital structure. When allied to the ratio of loan capital to total equity funds and the liquidity ratios, ABC LTD would appear to be capable of obtaining further fixed interest borrowings. The analyst would want to assess the trends in gearing and in profitability during different

---

*Minority interests rank after the debenture holders and loanstock holders of the particular subsidiary. This requires a priority percentage table to be derived for each subsidiary. The above analysis on the consolidated accounts may give an accurate picture of the situation, however.

periods of the trade cycle in order to obtain a better picture. An additional factor which might weigh against ABC LTD is that it has little security to offer to any lenders.

**Additional considerations**

The priority percentage tables offer the best measure of the shorter-term assessment of 'gearing' whilst the study of the asset structure is needed for longer-term forecasts. One drawback in the use of priority percentage tables is that they do not incorporate the company's reserves. If a company cannot meet its interest commitments from the current year's profits it can make recourse to its retained profits. Although the position would be serious the direct comparison between companies based on priority percentages is biased if one firm has large reserves whilst the other has none. Another factor that an analyst should examine is the state of the liquid assets; even though the Profit and Loss Account can bear the interest charges the payments of such may be difficult if there is a liquidity shortage. Finally, the analyst should be aware of the financial structure of subsidiaries some of whom can be in a very different state of affairs to the parent company.

Another ratio sometimes found in gearing considerations is that of liabilities to net worth. This can be broken down into the component parts of current and long-term liabilities. The latter division is of course the normal gearing ratio. A high ratio of current liabilities may indicate a liquidity shortage although it is the liquidity ratios mentioned earlier which give the most efficient indicators.

### Earnings per Share (EPS)

This is the major ratio used by analysts in measuring a company's performance and in making interfirm comparisons. Over a number of years a fairly accurate picture of the firm's earnings may be obtained, for whilst accounting policies vary, the differences are often related to the allocating of profits to a particular year. The ratio is computed by dividing the number of ordinary shares in issue into earnings available for the equity shareholders, i.e. earnings after tax, minority interests and preference dividends. As equity capital in the UK has to have a nominal value the earnings can be expressed as a percentage of the nominal capital.

**Definition**

The definition given to earnings available for the ordinary shareholders can vary but it is recommended that extraordinary items should be excluded. This is the method recommended by the ICA in their Statement of Standard Accounting Practice No. 3[5]. An analyst may also decide that exceptional and abnormal expenses should be excluded from the calculation for, whilst they are a normal business transaction, they are exceptional due to their size. The 'normalised' earnings figures would appear to be the most suitable with which to compare against prior years, for interfirm comparisons and as a basis of projection. Thus, exceptional items may be excluded if they are very volatile. Until the change to the imputation system of corporation tax the computation of EPS, earnings and dividend yields, cover and P/E ratios were fairly straightforward. However, the imputation system has given rise to a number of possible EPS computations and thus different ways of expressing yields. There are three methods of calculating earnings:

1   On a full distribution basis which notionally assumes that all the year's profits are distributed. This has very few protagonists.

2   On a nil distribution basis which takes the earnings figure after all foreign and UK corporation tax but assumes no dividend pay-out, thus excluding excess ACT* or irrecoverable foreign tax arising from a dividend distribution. This method has been advocated by the Society of Investment Analysts.

3   On a net basis which is the balance left after all foreign and UK corporation tax, including excess ACT or irrecoverable foreign tax, arising from a dividend distribution. The net basis has been recommended by the ICA.

The distinction between net and nil distributions lies in the treatment of excess ACT and irrecoverable foreign tax arising when companies have insufficient UK corporation tax.

*Example*

|  | 1<br>Full<br>distribution<br>£ | 2<br>Nil<br>distribution<br>£ | 3<br>Net<br>basis<br>£ |
|---|---|---|---|
| Profits | 1,000 | 1,000 | 1,000 |
| Tax[3] | 500[1] | 500 | 550[2] |
|  | 500 | 500 | 450 |
| Dividend net | 500 |  |  |
| Dividend gross | 714 |  |  |
| Number of shares | 10,000 | 10,000 | 10,000 |
| Earnings per share | 7.14p | 5p | 4.5p |

[1]The tax includes ACT of 214
[2]Includes unrelieved ACT and irrecoverable foreign tax
[3]Corporation tax at 50%

The three methods of computation are shown in the example. It is the net basis that has been adopted by the *Financial Times* for its statistics and thus will probably be the method in general use. In the majority of cases, however, the net and nil figures will be exactly the same; it is mainly companies with large amounts of overseas earnings where there will be a difference. It is recommended that the net basis be used for general analysis work although the nil basis could be used on occasions and specifically for companies with high foreign taxes.

*This is advance corporation tax. When a company pays a dividend it must pay tax to the Inland Revenue which is regarded as an advance payment of corporation tax. This is discussed in Chapter 9.

However, for some yields different EPS figures may be chosen and these will be disclosed in due course.

## Complications in calculating EPS

A major problem in calculating earnings arises when there has been a change in the equity structure of the company. The ICA recommendations on EPS[5] cover a fairly comprehensive list of adjustments that are necessary for various types of equity capital finance raised during the year. This should be read. The two most common adjustments are for capitalisation issues and for rights issues.

### Capitalisation issues and EPS

Capitalisation issues involve the capitalising of reserves into share capital. The shares are issued pro rata and free of charge to the existing shareholders. No cash accrues to the company and the share price should, *ceteris paribus*, reduce in proportion to the number of new shares created. A similar capital restructuring is involved with share splits which arise when a company reduces the nominal value of its shares and increases the number of shares in existence so as to maintain the issued share capital. As with capitalisation issues they are a mere book-keeping entry and should have no effect on the company's market capitalisation.

## Computation

Where there has been a capitalisation issue or a share split during the year the earnings should be apportioned over the number of shares outstanding after the issue. Corresponding figures for earlier periods should be adjusted accordingly.

*Example*

Capitalisation issue

Issued share capital 31 December 1971
1,000,000 ordinary £1 shares                                    £1,000,000

On 31 March 1972 the company made a capitalisation issue of 1 for 2.

| | 1972 | 1971 |
|---|---|---|
| Trading results – profit after tax | £125,000 | £100,000 |
| No. of ordinary shares at 31.12.71 | 1,000,000 | 1,000,000 |
| Capitalisation issue 31.3.72 | 500,000 | 500,000 |
| | 1,500,000 | 1,500,000 |
| Earnings per share = | $\dfrac{125,000}{1,500,000}$ | $\dfrac{100,000}{1,500,000}$ |
| = | 8.3p | 6.7p |

In the Accounts to 31.12.71 before the capitalisation the EPS would be given as 10p, i.e.

$$\frac{\text{Earnings } (100,000)}{\text{Number of shares in existence } (1,000,000)}$$

### Share split

Issued share capital 31 December 1971
1,000,000 shares of £1 each        £1,000,000

On 31 March 1972 a share split took place where the existing £1 shares were converted into shares of 50p

|  | 1972 | 1971 |
|---|---|---|
| Trading results – profit after tax | £125,000 | £100,000 |
| Number of ordinary shares at 31.12.71 | 1,000,000 | 1,000,000 |
| Share split 31.3.72 | 1,000,000 | 1,000,000 |
|  | 2,000,000 | 2,000,000 |

$$\text{Earnings per share} = \frac{125,000}{2,000,000} \qquad \frac{100,000}{2,000,000}$$

$$= 6.25\text{p} \qquad 5\text{p}$$

In the Accounts to 31.12.71 before the share split the EPS would be given as 10p, i.e.

$$\frac{\text{Earnings } (100,000)}{\text{No. of shares in existence } (1,000,000)}$$

### Rights issues and EPS

The adjustments needed for a rights issue require a knowledge of the share price of the company at the last cum rights day or at the first ex rights day. The example shows the usual technique employed.

*Example*

### Capital

100,000 shares of 50p each 31.12.71        £50,000

On 1 March 1972 the company made a rights issue of 1 for 2 at 75p = 50,000 shares bringing in £37,500

|  | 31.12.72 | 31.12.71 |
|---|---|---|
| Earnings | £150,000 | £120,000 |

Market price of ordinary shares on last day of quotation cum rights = 100p

**A**    The factor for adjusting past earnings per share:

The holder of 1,000 ordinary shares would subscribe £375 in taking up his entitlement of 500 shares at 75p. Assuming no other change in circumstances the investor will now hold 1,500 shares worth £1,375 or 91.7p per share.

|  | £ |
|---|---|
| 1,000 at market value of £1 each | 1,000 |
| 500 at 75p | 375 |
|  | £1,375 |

The conversion factor of past earnings is therefore:

$$\frac{\text{Theoretical ex rights price}}{\text{Actual cum rights price}} = \frac{91.7}{100}$$

$$\text{Reported EPS for 1971} = \frac{120,000}{100,000} = 120\text{p}$$

$$\text{Adjustment for rights issue} = 120 \times \frac{91.7}{100} = 110\text{p}$$

**B**  Earnings per share for 1972

$$\text{No. of shares } 100,000 \times \frac{3}{12} \times \frac{100}{91.7} = 27,263$$

$$150,000 \times \frac{9}{12} \qquad\quad = 112,500$$

Weighted average no. of shares  $\underline{139,763}$

$$\text{Earnings per share} = \frac{\text{Earnings}}{\text{Weighted average number of shares}} = \frac{150,000}{139,763}$$

$$= 107\text{p}$$

Rights issues are normally made at a price below the current market value and so the distribution includes a 'bonus' element which is equivalent to a capitalisation issue. The adjustment to past earnings for the bonus element is made by calculating the theoretical ex rights price. This adjustment is computed by the ratio:

$$\frac{\text{Theoretical ex rights price}}{\text{Actual cum rights price on last day of quotation cum rights}}$$

**Adjustment factor**

This adjustment factor is shown in the example at point **A**. There are other methods that could be used in the adjustment process. For instance, the actual ex rights price on the first day of quotation ex rights and the theoretical cum rights price could be used. Another method that has been advocated is the ratio of assets per share before and after the issue.

**Time weighting**

As the proceeds from the issue were only available to the company for the nine-month period between 1 April and 31 December it is necessary to weight the number of shares in issue by the time factor. This is shown at point **B** in the example. Here the reciprocal of the conversion factor is multiplied by the number of shares in issue before the rights and by the fraction of the year prior to the issue.

The weighted average number of shares is divided into the earnings to obtain the EPS for the year. The analyst should take care when interpreting EPS during or just after a rights issue year as the deployment of the proceeds of the issue into revenue earning assets may take some time.

The EPS calculations for ABC LTD are as follows:

Market price pre rights issue       100p

Rights issue of 1 for 5 at 87.5p on 1 July

Theoretical ex rights price $= \dfrac{587.5p}{6} = 98p$

Earnings per share 1971:

    Pre adjustment $= 37.1p$

    Adjustment for rights issue $37.1 \times \dfrac{98}{100} = 36.2p$

Earnings per share 1972:

    No. of shares   $2,000,000 \times \dfrac{6}{12} \times \dfrac{100}{98} = 1,020,000$

$$2,400,000 \times \dfrac{6}{12} \qquad \dfrac{1,200,000}{2,220,000}$$

$$\frac{\text{Earnings}}{\text{No. of shares}} = \frac{996,000}{2,220,000} = 44.9p$$

## Issues at full market prices and EPS

Companies sometimes make an issue of shares at the full current market price. This usually happens when the shares are used as consideration for the purchase of a business. The computation of EPS involves using the time weighted average number of shares. The example shows the methodology.

*Example*

Issued share capital = 100,000 25p shares = £25,000.

On 31 August 1972, 50,000 25p shares were issued in consideration for the acquisition of a competitor. The shares were valued at market price.

| *Weighted average number of shares* | 1973 £ | 1972 £ | 1971 £ |
|---|---|---|---|
| Shares outstanding at 1 January | 150,000 | 100,000 | 100,000 |
| Issued 31 August 1972 | | | |
|   50,000 × 1/3 | | 16,666 | |
| | 150,000 | 116,666 | 100,000 |
| Earnings of parent | 60,000 | 60,000 | 60,000 |
| Earnings of acquired competitor | 20,000 | 5,000 | |
| | £80,000 | £65,000 | £60,000 |
| Earnings per share | 53.3p | 55.7p | 60p |

The shares should be assumed to have been issued as from the date when profits of the acquired company have been included in the group's earnings. As with capital issues for cash the analyst has to use considerable judgment in interpreting earnings per share figures after the acquisition of a business for shares.

## Convertible loan stocks and EPS

Many companies have issued convertible loan stocks during the last ten years and the analyst needs to acknowledge the eventual effect of these on EPS and earnings yields. In expressing the EPS for the year an analyst will want to calculate the EPS assuming full conversion. The adjustments will include adding back to profit the interest paid on the loan stock and dividing the 'new earnings' figure by the total number of shares after dilution.

The example follows the recommended accounting practice of showing EPS on existing share capital and on the capital assuming a complete conversion at the next available opportunity. The information relating to conversions in 1975 and 1976 is not used.

*Example*
Capital structure

| | |
|---|---:|
| 10,000,000 ordinary 25p shares | £2,500,000 |
| 1,000,000 £1 10% convertible loan stock, convertible on the following terms at the dates shown | £1,000,000 |

| | | |
|---|---|---|
| 1974 | 200 shares per £100 loan stock | |
| 1975 | 180 shares per £100 loan stock | |
| 1976 | 150 shares per £100 loan stock | |

| | 1971<br>£ |
|---|---:|
| Profits before interest and tax | 450,000 |
| Loan stock interest | 100,000 |
| | 350,000 |
| Tax at 40% | 140,000 |
| | £210,000 |

$$\text{Basic EPS} = \frac{210,000}{10,000,000} = 2.1\text{p}$$

| | £ |
|---|---:|
| Fully diluted EPS: | |
| Profits before tax | 450,000 |
| Tax at 40% | 180,000 |
| | £270,000 |

| | |
|---|---:|
| No. of shares in issue | 10,000,000 |
| Issued on assumed conversion | 2,000,000 |
| | 12,000,000 |

$$\text{Fully diluted EPS} \qquad \frac{270,000}{12,000,000} = 2.25\text{p}$$

## Interpreting EPS after new issues of shares for consideration

The interpretation of EPS figures after a new issue for cash or as consideration for the acquisition of a business requires considerable judgment on the part of the analyst. The deployment of the proceeds of the issue into revenue earning assets or the rationalisation of an acquired business can take a number of years to complete and thus to establish a 'normal' earnings pattern. If the new issue is extremely large the analyst may well feel that the EPS calculations are of little value at that time in measuring performance. In such cases analysts can only rely on the past trends if they wish to use earnings per share in their analysis.

## Cover for ordinary dividends

This is the ratio of the maximum dividend which can be paid from the year's earnings to the actual dividend paid and proposed. Thus the 'earnings' figure to be used is that based on a full distribution. If a company made profits of £1,000 all of which were derived in the UK the maximum gross dividend payable would be £714*. This follows from the example showing the various computations of EPS. If the actual gross dividend paid was £600 the cover would be the ratio:

$$\frac{714}{600} = 1.19$$

In the US the reciprocal of cover, the payout ratio, is the more common statistic quoted for the relationship between dividends and earnings. The payout ratio in the above example would be:

$$\frac{1}{\text{Cover}} = \frac{1}{1.19} = 84\%$$

## Market yields

These are usually the first ratios quoted in initial stock selection comparisons, the common denominator being the current market price of the share. They express the particular returns to the shareholder at that point in time. The main market yields are: (1) the earnings yield; (2) the P/E ratio; and, (3) the dividend yield.

## Earnings yield

This expresses the EPS figure as a percentage of the share price. The EPS figure adopted by the *Financial Times* in its statistics on earnings yields is that based on a full distribution, and this method is also recommended by the Society of Investment Analysts.

*Example*
A company makes £1,000 profits pre-tax which accrue solely from the UK and has 10,000 ordinary shares in issue which are valued in the market at 85p. The relevant EPS figure is that based on a full distribution, i.e.

$$\frac{714}{10,000} = 7.14\text{p}$$

$$\text{Earnings yield} = \frac{\text{EPS}}{\text{Share price}} = \frac{7.14}{85} = 8.40\%$$

*Assuming corporation tax at 50% and income tax at 30%.

90

### Price/Earnings (P/E) ratio

This ratio involves dividing the EPS figure into the share price. Thus, it represents the number of years' purchase of current year profits. The EPS used is either the net or nil basis. The *Financial Times* uses net in most circumstances, although for companies with high overseas earnings the nil basis may provide better comparison yardsticks. Until the imputation system the P/E ratio was the reciprocal of the earnings yield. Now, however, different EPS figures are used.

*Example*
A company has a 'net' EPS figure of 5p. If the current share price is 85p then P/E ratio will be:

$$\frac{\text{Share price}}{\text{EPS}} = \frac{85}{5} = 17$$

### Dividend yield

This is the dividend per share divided by the market price and represents the annual cash return to the shareholder for the current value of his investment. Dividends under the imputation tax system will be shown net of ACT. The dividend yield will, however, be based on the gross* basis by the various Stock Exchange statistical services.

*Example*
If a company pays a gross dividend per share of 6p and the market price is 85p the dividend yield will be:

$$\frac{6}{85} = 7\%$$

The dividend yield multiplied by the cover will give the earnings yield.

### Improvements in accounts

Improvements in Annual Accounts can take the form of improved accounting principles embodying both new concepts and measurement techniques; increased disclosure of significant transactions, i.e. items having a significant impact on business efficiency and activity; and forecasts of future profitability and disclosure of longer-term strategies adopted by the company.

### Accounting principles

The underlying concepts embodied in the preparation of periodic financial accounts are the going concern basis, prudence, consistency and the accruals basis or matching of cost and revenue. The major accounting base used in valuing assets is historical cost. All of these have been criticised either in their entirety or because of their dogmatic application[6].

*That is the net payment plus income tax at the basic rate.

**Going concern**

The going concern concept has led to the practice of not revaluing assets whose current market values have significantly departed from the book value. Although the Companies Act 1967 calls for the directors to state the market value of land where it differs substantially from the book value it is largely a matter for the directors to decide when the difference is significant. The value of most plant and machinery tends to fall very quickly and the rates of depreciation used by most companies often fails to match this. This becomes serious when plant becomes obsolete or nearly obsolete and yet management persists in writing down the asset over its original expected life.

**Prudence**

The prudence concept can tend to under-state the real worth of a company and can make it more difficult for present and potential investors to evaluate future prospects. Some companies adopt a policy of only taking profits when they have been realised in cash and this can seriously under-state earnings which are certain.

**Consistency**

The consistency concept is in general acceptable but there are cases where companies stick dogmatically to outmoded or even incorrect practices. Thus the rigid application of the consistency concept can eventually do considerable harm in financial reporting and in some extreme cases can far outweigh any comparison advantages.

**Accruals**

The accruals concept matches costs with revenues and the resultant profits or losses are entered into the Profit and Loss Account. This concept justifies both deferment and anticipation to achieve proper 'timing'. The American Accounting Association has for instance said: 'Accounting is thus not essentially a process of valuation, but the allocation of historical costs and revenues to the current and succeeding fiscal periods'[7]. This concept leads to a 'smoothed profits' trend by deferring large costs until the appropriate revenue is received. The main arguments against the accruals concept are that future revenues may not be received or may be smaller than thought and that it takes no account of the time taken for 'appropriate' revenues to be received.

The general view is that the concepts are the most reliable there are but that they should not be rigidly applied in every case. Management and auditors should use their judgment when it appears that the application of a particular concept to a transaction would lead to poorer information than some other method.

**Objectives of financial statements**

Perhaps of more fundamental importance is the question of the objectives of periodic financial accounts. In the past, Accounts were prepared largely for the owner-directors of the business and to satisfy creditor requirements. More recently, accounts have been concerned with the stewardship of the management during the year. However, many authorities are now questioning these objectives of financial reporting. There is now a greater awareness that Accounts are being used by existing and potential investors and analysts in evaluating future prospects[8]. This usage of Annual Accounts requires the Balance Sheet values to signify more accurately the true value of the assets and places a far greater demand for disclosure of financial information. Although investment decisions are to be made by investors in their role as risk takers, the Accounts should provide as much information as possible on which investment decisions can be made. Thus, there is a growing body of opinion which regards the purpose of Accounts as being to communicate information on the value and nature of the resources of the business, the ownership of these resources, and the changes in the nature and value of these resources from one period to another. This objective will involve a constant re-thinking of accounting concepts and bases so as to best convey data regarding the value of the resources of a business. Such an objective in financial reporting should more enable rational economic decision taking to take place in society.

The use of historical cost as a valuation method has the one advantage of being certain, but otherwise it has been strongly criticised. For instance, two similar companies with the same earnings potential and physical assets can have significantly different Balance Sheet structures because the assets were bought at different times.

## Inflation adjusted accounts

There are a number of other ways of valuing assets and as stated in Chapter 2 the ASSC have recommended that Annual Accounts now contain a statement showing the financial position adjusted for the effects of inflation by their Current Purchasing Power Method[9]. The process basically consists of converting historical figures, $£h$, into terms of current purchasing power $£c$, which is to be represented by the Index of Retail Prices (IRP). The historical figures are thus multiplied by the IRP at the terminal date of the accounts and divided by the IRP at the date of the original transaction. Various approximations will have to be made to obtain a date for transactions within the year, e.g. revenue items may be assumed to have occurred evenly throughout the year. The ASSC recognised that other methods of accounting for inflation, notably the use of replacement cost accounting or specific index methods, existed. However, because of the greater complexity and the subjective nature of these methods, the ASSC have come down on the side of the current purchasing power method for the immediate future. The ASSC's recommendation has not been received with general acceptance; the Society of Investment Analysts, for example, advocate the use of replacement accounting. It may be some time, therefore, before there is any broad agreement on the method of accounting for the impact of inflation.

### Disclosure

## Companies Acts

The Annual Reports and Accounts rarely give much more information than is required under the Companies Acts of 1948 and 1967. The Stock Exchange requests additional information for new quotations and the ASSC have made recommendations as to extra disclosure. This level of disclosure, however, does not give adequate enough knowledge to the analyst. Obviously, no amount of historical data is going to make forecasting completely accurate but there are many important variables which, if disclosed, would enable investors to make better investment decisions and create a more 'perfect' market.

## Proposed company law reform

During 1973, the then Government issued a White Paper on Company Law reform and the subsequent Bill was published just before Christmas, 1973. The Bill was expected to become law by the end of summer, 1974. The intervening election brought a change in Government and the Labour Party has stated that a new Companies Bill will be introduced. This is expected to extend the Conservatives' Bill on Company Law reform especially in the area of employee participation. Up to date no explicit proposals have been released on Labour's ideas: the Conservatives' proposals are outlined below as the eventual Companies Act may well incorporate many of the provisions, albeit in some revised form.

## Classification and powers of companies

Part I of the Bill was concerned with the classification and powers of companies. It was proposed that companies would have had to disclose their status of: (1) public company by the letters 'PLC'; (2) private company by the letters 'LTD'; (3) companies which were neither public nor private, the words 'company limited by guarantee' or the letters 'CLG'. Disclosure requirements were to be less onerous for private companies.

## Insider dealing

Part II related to share capital and debentures. The Secretary of State was to have laid down minimum levels of paid-up capital required by various classes of company. This was to be effected via a statutory order.

Part II imposed restrictions on insider dealing. Persons who are connected with the company and in possession of price sensitive information were not to deal in, or arrange for others to deal in, the company's shares for profit. Offenders were to be liable for up to seven year's imprisonment, or an unlimited fine, and would have been required to compensate other parties to the transactions. The Bill laid down definitions of who 'insiders' were and what amounts to 'insider dealing'. The proposed legislation would have helped deter 'insider trading' although it is difficult to see how any laws can substantially prevent the practice. Directors were to notify the Stock Exchange of any dealings of theirs in the shares of their company within three days (as opposed to fourteen days). The level at which an individual shareholding must be disclosed to the company was to be lowered from 10 to 5 per cent. The disclosure was to be made within three days as opposed to fourteen days. Further, quoted companies were to have the right to require any shareholder to disclose the beneficial owner of the shares. This was to enable companies to discover the real identity of nominee shareholders. The 'warehousing' of strategic stakes in companies by the use of nominee shareholders has come in for much criticism and the proposed legislation should have resulted in much greater information to investors. However, there is not a great deal that can be done to prevent companies acting in concert in warehousing stakes. Additionally the provision would have no effective bearing on foreign nominee shareholdings and thus a growth in these may have arisen.

Further provisions of this section included the virtual banning of quoted companies issuing shares with voting restrictions. Companies were also to have given reasons when they refused to register a transfer of shares.

## Directors and officers

Part III of the Bill dealt with the law relating to directors and officers. In the event of a winding-up, reckless conduct or breach of duty to the company were to be grounds for disqualification of a director. Weighted voting rights on resolutions to remove directors were to be abolished.

A most controversial part of the Bill intended to prevent a person being a director of a company which controls another business in which he or a member of his family had an interest. This provision was included to deal with abuses which can come about between a director's public and private interests. Transitional arrangements were provided by the Bill in order to effect the ruling. This was necessary as it would have taken some time for directors to rearrange their various interests.

## Accounts

Part IV made important changes and alterations in respect of accounts and auditors. Public companies were to publish their accounts within seven months of the year end* and private companies within ten months. In each case a three-month extension was to be granted where there were overseas subsidiaries. The Bill provided penalties for non-compliance and these fell mainly on the directors. The legislation together with the hoped-for improvement in administration (incorporating the move of Companies House to Cardiff) was intended to reduce the abuse of companies not filing returns or filing them late.

## Year end

Companies were to have registered their year-ends with the Registrar of Companies, otherwise a 31 December year-end would be implied. Provisions were also made in the Bill relating to accounting records which must be sufficient to give a 'true and fair view' of the state of affairs of the company and to explain its transactions.

## Auditors

Under the Bill, auditors had to be re-appointed every year by the shareholders and the company had to give a special notice to its members of any appointment of an auditor, other than one already appointed in general meeting. An auditor may have resigned with immediate effect by giving written notice to the client's registered office. The resignation notice was to contain either a statement that there were no circumstances connected with his resignation which he considered should be brought to the notice of the members or creditors of the company: or a statement of any such circumstances. The company was to send a copy of the auditor's resignation notice to the

*The Stock Exchange requires companies to publish accounts within six months of their year end.

Registrar of Companies and to every shareholder. Resigning auditors could have requisitioned an extraordinary meeting to consider the circumstances of resignation.

The Bill proposed that auditors of a holding company should have access to information about the audits of subsidiaries. This especially applies where there were overseas subsidiaries. The Secretary of State was to have power to specify the contents of Accounts, Directors' Reports, audit reports and annual returns. Such increased disclosure may have included reports on industrial safety and employees' welfare.

## Management and administration

Part V of the Bill related to the management and administration of companies. This included important clauses relating to winding-up procedures and to the conduct of inspectors. Provisions relating to dividends and reserves were also enacted. Specifically these were:

1 Unrealised capital profits are not distributable as dividends.

2 Dividends may be paid out of revenue profits and realised capital profits less any revenue losses and realised capital losses not already written off. This was subject to the ruling that no capital profit may be distributed unless the net assets after distribution are worth at least their book value.

3 Unrealised capital profits may not be used to write off revenue losses or realised capital losses.

The above provisions would have affected the accounting policies of many property companies and was an area of some contention.

The remaining five parts to the Bill related to the registration of charges; winding up procedures and receiverships; overseas companies; unregistered companies and companies with registered offices in Wales; and miscellaneous and supplementary details.

## Reasons against greater disclosure

The reason given by companies for not disclosing greater amounts of information than is necessary is that such data would be of vital importance to competitors. They cite pricing policies, marketing efforts and various operating efficiencies as major areas where competitors could gain vital data. Most companies are against greater disclosure even if enforced by Company Law. Although all UK companies would be disclosing similar types of information the inertia and secret-mindedness of businessmen have made them oppose any such move. Foreign companies may gain some competitive advantage from any wider disclosure requirements for UK companies. From a macro-economic viewpoint, however, the greater the disclosure, the better the information for portfolio investment decision making. The increased disclosure would also tend to make the efficient firms stand out more and possibly increase competition from the less efficient companies.

## Improvements in disclosure

Specific areas of disclosure which might be improved upon include:

1 Revaluation of assets to incorporate current market values and rates of

inflation, statements of the replacement costs and the likelihood of significant asset replacement. Although there are various views on the subject of accounting for inflation, statements of current market values and replacement values should at least be given, if materially different from the figures appearing in the Profit and Loss Account and the Balance Sheet. A statement of the state of repair of fixed assets and possible dates of replacement would be useful. A breakdown of 'plant and machinery' assets into various types of plant might be useful. This would be especially useful if the specific items of plant and machinery were used for different product outputs or where the replacement values of equipment varied considerably between the different types.

2   The disclosure of average stock, debtor and cash levels. This would be especially useful for businesses with seasonal biases.

3   A more consistent breakdown of activities possibly using the categories used for Government statistics.

4   An inclusion in the Profit and Loss Account of the cost of sales, classified by the area of activity.

5   In some instances more detailed information on the valuation of stocks, bad debt provisions and of current liabilities would be useful. The accounts should disclose the details of doubtful debts and any outstanding litigation.

6   The disclosure and classification of expenses, possibly by totals, into fixed, semi-fixed and variable expenses. This information will enable the analyst to assess the gearing impact of expenses.

7   Statements on managerial objectives could be useful. This could contain the long-term strategies of the firm. Such a statement could, of course, be misused by management who would have the opportunity to make wildly optimistic claims and so safeguards would have to be introduced.

8   A statement should be made of the research and development and other 'intangible' expenditures. This could contain information on how near the projects are to commercial application.

9   A sources and uses of funds statement. This is given by some companies but has not reached a general level of acceptance.

10   More detailed analyses of future capital expenditure and of contingent liabilities may prove valuable.

11   Profits forecasts and cash flow projections.

12   Various statistics and reports relating to the contribution of the company to social and national economic goals.

The above includes some of the more relevant items which could lead to a better understanding of a company's financial position and of its future prospects. There are disadvantages especially as regards the giving of information which may reveal areas of comparative efficiency. Some of the items also increase the scope for management to make excessive claims for their companies. Difficulties would also be encountered in the implementing of the above areas for improvement. However, these and other suggestions for more relevant disclosure do indicate areas which can help improve financial reporting and further research on these topics can help to overcome the practical problems of implementation.

## References

1   For a text on ratio analysis see Westwick, C. A., 'How to Use Management Ratios', Gower Press, 1973.

2   See: Prusman, D. and Murphy, G., 'Gearing in British quoted companies', *Business Ratios*, Winter, 1968.

3   Rix, M. S., 'Investment Arithmetic', Pitman, 1964.

4   Solomon, E., 'The Theory of Financial Management', New York: Columbia University Press, 1963.

5   'Earnings per Share', Statement of Standard Accounting Practice, No. 3, SSAP 3, Feb. 1972.

6   For a fairly advanced text on accounting theory see: Hendriksen, E. S., 'Accounting Theory', Irwin, 1970.

7   In: 'The Search for Accounting Principles', American Institute of Certified Public Accountants, 1964.

8   This was acknowledged, for example, by the Trueblood Report on 'Objectives of Financial Statements' prepared for the American Institute of Certified Public Accountants, 1973.

9   'Accounting for Changes in the Purchasing Power of Money', Provisional SSAP, No. 7, Accounting Standards Steering Committee, May 1974.

# Chapter 4
## Forecasting of
## Corporate Profits

The purchase of a share entitles the holder to receive future cash dividends from the company and it is investors' expectations of these dividends and earnings that form the main determinant of share prices. Dividends and earnings are the most important factors in the stock selection techniques of regression models, price/earnings (P/E) relationships and the intrinsic value approach. Given accurate forecasts of future earnings and dividends the results from the various model approaches will significantly improve and investment decision making will become more of a science. For instance, Figure 4.1 shows the relationship between the percentage change in pre-tax company profits and the percentage change in the FTA All Share Index and the absolute level of FTA 500 Index P/E ratio. The patterns evident in the graph indicate that the Stock Market indices and yields follow closely the percentage movements in corporate profits. As company profits are normally announced around four to six months after the year-end date to which they relate, the Stock Market appears to be discounting corporate financial performance up to six months in advance. It is apparent that any accurate profits forecasting prior to this date will yield significant Stock Market profits. Forecasting of company profitability is therefore of vital importance for fundamental analysis and forms the major work conducted by analysts.

**Forecasting periods**

Forecasts can be made for various periods and the techniques employed may vary as the time horizon lengthens. Obviously, forecasting beyond three or four years becomes significantly less accurate and many assumptions have to be made. However, such longer-term

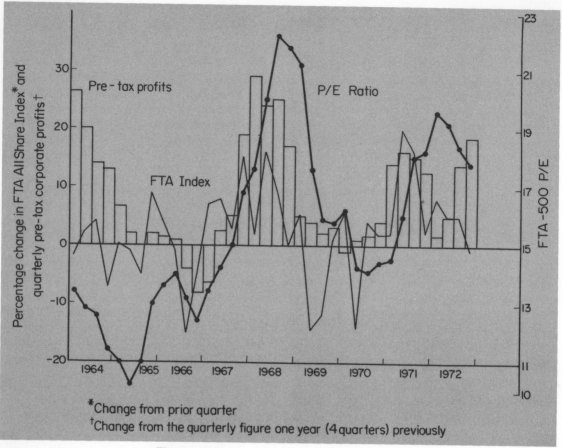

**Figure 4.1**

The relationship between the F.T.A. all share index and quarterly pretax corporate profits

forecasts can significantly improve the various stock selection techniques described in Chapter 5, this especially applying to the intrinsic value approach. The more commonly used forecasting periods can be classified as:

1   Following-year profits plus subsequent growth rate(s) which are usually based on past performance or on some industrial forecast. This is the type of forecast used in the P/E models although care must be taken that profits are 'normal', i.e. not at the peak or trough of a volatile cycle.

2   Forecasting for two or three years ahead with subsequent growth rate(s). This will involve taking into account the trade and industrial cycles and an assessment of economic factors. The intrinsic value approach of share selection would use such forecasts.

3   Five or more years' forecasts with subsequent growth rate(s). As the period gets farther into the future less detailed analysis will be

conducted and more assumptions will have to be made. For some industries, longer-term forecasts are easier to make, e.g. property companies where individual years' profits and growth rates may show a more stable pattern.

The length of the forecasting period will depend upon the stock evaluation techniques used and more importantly, on the degree of accuracy the analyst feels he can achieve. As seen from above, the analyst will also be concerned with the forecasting of aggregate industrial and economic factors. These predictions are especially important in arriving at growth rates attached to companies.

## Techniques used in forecasting

Techniques of forecasting include basic projections of earnings per share (EPS), the breakdown of business activities and cost structures, the use of industrial and economic statistics as indicators of company performance, econometric models of various factors affecting profitability, simulation models and probabilistic forecasting which produces ranges of forecasts. The chapter will commence with the forecasting of individual items which affect company profitability, this involving the use of the analyses described in Chapter 3 and use of industrial statistics. Following these will be a brief introduction to economic forecasting as it affects the firm. A discussion on the life-cycle of the firm and on methods of longer-term forecasting will then be given. Finally, specific computer-based techniques will be introduced and their impact on investment analysis discussed.

### Analysis and projection of corporate profits

## Simple projection of earnings per share (EPS)

The basic projection of EPS merely involves taking the EPS figure for the year and applying a growth rate. This rate is usually arrived at by taking some relationship of past performance or by using a forecast prepared by the appropriate trade society. It does not involve the breakdown or analysis of the various factors affecting profitability and represents the crudest of forecasting methods. Its main use is for when an immediate assessment is required or for the analyst who has to monitor large numbers of shares. There have been a number of statistical studies on the correlation of changes in EPS reported by companies. These have found that the correlation is very poor and that earnings changes are random[1]. The implication of these results, of course, is that simple extrapolation of past-earnings data is unlikely to lead to any better prediction than random forecasts. Any simple extrapolation therefore has to be regarded with caution.

## Analysis of activities, cost structures and constraints

The first step an analyst will take in a detailed breakdown of the company will be to examine the past financial performance of the company extracted from the Annual Reports and Accounts. At the same time he will study any press-cutting file kept on that company. From these sources the analyst will get an idea of industries within which the company operates, the markets in which it sells, possible constraints on expansion, the financial structure of the company and critical factors which affect profitability. The financial history can be quickly compared against economic and industrial indices to obtain an initial impression of relative performance. The susceptibility of the firm's profits to economic and industrial cycles can be ascertained and the relevance of trade indices can be established. The analyst may well decide to summarise five or maybe ten years of financial data and draw-up various ratios, trends of ratios and statistical analyses of the time series. These computations will be helpful in highlighting relative intra- and intercompany performance and perhaps shed some light on the important factors affecting profitability. The latter could include the impact of financial gearing and the effect of volume production on costs. The analyst should of course be aware of the various accounting concepts and conventions used in drawing up Accounts especially as regards the valuation of assets.

## Turnover

The turnover figure should be broken down into its various products or the markets these products serve. In many cases it is the markets which prove to be the real constraint on sales and in these cases it should form the basis for breakdown analyses. For example, an engineering firm may supply identical components to the UK motor car industry, to the shipbuilding industry and to the jute industry in India and Pakistan. The analyst will only have a small interest in the prospects for engineering companies in general but will be vitally concerned with forecasts for the motor industry (i.e. home and overseas demand, foreign competition, labour relations), for the shipbuilding industry (i.e. orders on hand, Government assistance, shortages of shipping) and for the jute industry in the East (i.e. foreign governments' attitudes to imports, political stability, Foreign Exchange conditions). The classification is necessary as, say, the motor industry might be experiencing boom conditions whilst the jute industry is in rapid decline. No one industrial statistic will be relevant in showing the conditions in both these markets. In this case the analyst gains far more information from studying the markets to which the products go as opposed to the products produced. Such 'market' breakdowns are especially relevant for multi-product companies whose various customers' demand functions are poorly correlated. The breakdown will allow the analyst to use the apposite industrial statistics both for obtaining measures of relative performance and for forecasting purposes.

## Breakdown of turnover

The analyst can establish the breakdown of sales in the following ways:

1 Studying the breakdown of activities given by the directors in the Accounts. These, however, are normally very broad product-based categories.

2 A breakdown of consolidated accounts. Separate companies are often formed for significantly different parts of the group's activities.

3 Sales catalogues, advertising brochures or public relations handouts.

4 Company visits by the analyst where the management will be ready to give some information on its activities. Occasionally managements

speak to a conference of analysts and talk about their company. The Society of Investment Analysts often arranges such seminars.

5   Trade journals may quote various products and relevant statistics and indices.

6   For a company which has recently obtained a Stock Market quote the prospectus relating to any new issue of shares will give details of activities which will still be relevant.

7   Correlating the various sales components with seemingly appropriate trade statistics. This may give some indication of the validity of the breakdown and of the specific trade and economic indices which are relevant.

The above sources will be useful for the other stages in forecasting although initially they provide data on the specific products made and the markets operated in. As with many forecasting methods the above process will be an ongoing exercise with feedback coming from the success of the predictions. In an established research department there will be considerable data and possibly analyses on companies from which a new analyst will be able to work.

## Use of trade statistics

The analyst will now be in a position to project the various sales figures by using industrial statistics. In the example mentioned earlier the analyst will obtain statistics and published trade prospects for the UK motor industry, the shipbuilding industry and the jute industry in India and Pakistan. In some cases an appropriate index might be difficult to find; in these cases the analyst should experiment with nearly appropriate statistics, possibly making combinations of, or weighting the indices, to see if they aid the forecasting. If not, then the analyst will have to rely on other methods of estimation. Trade statistics are useful in that they can be projected themselves by statistical means to show the expected growth in the particular markets the company is operating in. The analyst will then have to decide whether the company will increase, maintain or decrease its market share and by how much. Many trade indices are published quarterly and some monthly. This information is then projected to the company's sales. For example, if new-car registrations showed a 5 per cent increase in January, February and March over the corresponding months a year earlier, the analyst will be able to extrapolate with some degree of certainty some increase in sales for a particular manufacturer. The 'leading indicator' approach, which is the term applied to the above use of trade statistics, gives initial forecasts for the company. These, however, have to be adjusted for items peculiar to the firm; for instance, although the motor vehicle registrations have risen this could be due to a relative increase in imports or a sudden rush of new models introduced by competitors. Other factors such as labour troubles or trade supplier constraints may act to make the company buck the industrial trend. The analyst should therefore use trade indices and any forecasts made by trade associations as an initial guide for the company but must be aware of the individual company's circumstances and characteristics.

**Type of industrial statistics**

Trade statistics can vary enormously and so some will be of far more use to the analyst than others. The indices can be produced in quantity, price, and in total revenue terms at weekly, monthly, quarterly or yearly intervals. Trade statistics are published at varying dates after the event; obviously the sooner the better for analytical purposes. Some trade associations publish long-term forecasts for their industries which have been based on statistical models or from detailed question-naire replies from the organisation's member firms*. These will be extremely useful to the analyst in establishing longer-term growth rates although it should be recognised that the trade associations are likely to be somewhat biased.

**The applicability of industrial statistics**

The analyst may have a plethora of statistics from which to work and the criterion here is to use the one or the combination of indices which give the best forecasts. Initially the analyst can use correlation measures to establish the most relevant statistics although the feedback from his forecasts may make him adapt these figures. Different indices are likely to be of use at separate parts of the forecasting process. In investigating a brick manufacturer, the analyst may use statistics of brick production for the current year sales, use the figures for housing starts for estimating the following year sales and use published forecasts of the housing and property markets for the longer-term period. Statistics of forward order positions and capital expenditure plans are especially relevant for the two to three year forecasts. The same analyses are carried out on these series as those above.

**Economic statistics**

In analysing some companies there may be no trade statistics available and so recourse will have to be made to general economic indices. Although these statistics are aggregates over various industries and in some cases relate to events many months previous, they do give some general indication of business activity. Amongst the most useful economic statistics are those relating to employment, sales, banking and industrial output. Unemployment statistics are produced monthly after a delay of two or three weeks. They give indications of the turning points in the business cycle (i.e. output being partially a factor of labour) and of wage inflation (i.e. the rate of wage inflation falls as unemployment grows). Monthly statistics and indices of retail sales are produced by the Department of Trade and Industry and the data is broken down into the particular segments of the retail trade. Statistics relating to the Retail Price Index are also useful as a measure of price inflation. These statistics relate to specific goods and are not therefore weighted by the actual purchases (i.e. consumers will substitute products in order to save paying higher prices). Generally speaking,

*A few stockbroking firms have evolved econometric models but these mainly relate to the economy as a whole. This is because of the cost of constructing individual company models and because stockbrokers, unlike trade associations, do not have enough detailed information with which to build models.

increases in the index of consumer prices (weighted by purchases) are about 90 per cent of those shown by the Retail Price Index. Monthly statistics of bank clearings will be of obvious use in analysing financial companies but they are also a rough guide to business activity as a whole: some degree of correlation has been found between spending in the economy and bank clearings. Statistics relating to industrial production are usually published three months or so in arrears and even so they are only estimates. However, they do give some indication of industrial activity and, in the absence of more appropriate trade indices, they will have to be imputed to individual companies.

## Cyclical trends in statistics

The analyst will need to interpret the projected figures in the light of the known existence of trade and industrial cycles. These cycles are often of four or five year's duration and there may be significant magnitude between the peaks and troughs. The analyst should attempt to ascertain whereabouts in the cycle the industry is presently situated and estimate the direction and rate of change. This is an extremely important analysis for companies within very cyclical industries. The usual methodology used in examining the position in the cycle is to compute the percentage change in the indices. Monthly or quarterly data is normally compared against the data one year earlier and the percentage difference noted. This procedure removes the seasonal bias although for companies who have stable sales throughout the year the monthly or quarterly data could be compared against the prior month or quarter. When monthly statistics are available they are often formed into a three-month moving average, an example of which is shown in Table 4.1 and Figure 4.2. The three-month moving average is computed by adding the figures for three months and dividing by three. This value is then attributed to the middle month. The technique averages-out unusual highs and lows and smoothes the results as shown in Figure 4.2. The average tends to lag behind the

### Table 4.1

Moving averages

|  | Sales | 3-Month Total | Average |
|---|---|---|---|
| January | 1,500 | – | – |
| February | 1,050 | 3,850 | 1,283 |
| March | 1,300 | 3,850 | 1,283 |
| April | 1,500 | 4,150 | 1,383 |
| May | 1,350 | 4,550 | 1,517 |
| June | 1,700 | 4,900 | 1,633 |
| July | 1,850 | 5,950 | 1,983 |
| August | 2,400 | 6,350 | 2,117 |
| September | 2,100 | 6,500 | 2,167 |
| October | 2,000 | 5,250 | 1,750 |
| November | 1,150 | 4,650 | 1,550 |
| December | 1,500 | – | – |

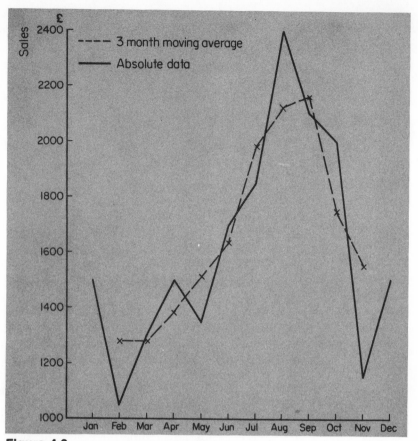

**Figure 4.2**

Smoothing of time series statistics

trend, however, and is possibly not as good a forecasting method as some more complex systems. Moving averages can, in certain cases, obliterate periodic fluctuations in the data and so care should be exercised. A further drawback in the method is that it gives equal weight to the data independent of time. A commonly-used forecasting technique which gives greater weight to more recent data is exponential smoothing. This takes the form:

New average $= \alpha$ (new value) $+ (1 - \alpha)$ old average

or

$$M_t(x) = \alpha x_t + (1 - \alpha)m_{t-1}(x)$$

where $x_t$ is the value of the series in time period $t$

$M_t(x)$ is the moving average (smoothed value) of the series in time period $t$

$m_{t-1}(x)$ is the moving average (smoothed value) of the series in the time period immediately prior to period $t$

$\alpha$ is the smoothing constant which is in the range, $0 < \alpha < 1$

$M_t(x)$ is a linear combination of past data and the weight given to the figures decreases geometrically the further away they get from the present[2].

These and other more advanced statistical models[3] help smooth out the monthly figures which otherwise may be so erratic that percentage differences become spurious as a method measuring trend.

**The use of turning points in statistical time series**

An example of measuring turning points in a time series is given below (Table 4.2 and Figure 4.3). The absolute figures for the sales of item $X$

**Table 4.2**

Analysis of turning points in a time series

| Date | Sales £'000 | Percentage change on previous year |
|---|---|---|
| **1970** | | |
| January | 200 | |
| February | 225 | |
| March | 250 | |
| April | 237 | |
| May | 250 | |
| June | 275 | |
| July | 262 | |
| August | 288 | |
| September | 300 | |
| October | 350 | |
| November | 375 | |
| December | 400 | |
| **1971** | | |
| January | 375 | $+87.5$ $\left(\text{i.e. } \dfrac{375-200}{200}\right)$ |
| February | 362 | $+60.9$ $\left(\text{i.e. } \dfrac{362-225}{225}\right)$ |
| March | 350 | $+40.0$ $\left(\text{i.e. } \dfrac{350-250}{250}\right)$ |
| April | 375 | $+58.2$ |
| May | 400 | $+60.0$ |
| June | 400 | $+45.5$ |
| July | 375 | $+43.1$ |
| August | 350 | $+21.5$ |
| September | 362 | $+20.7$ |
| October | 375 | $+7.1$ |
| November | 375 | $-$ |
| December | 412 | $+3.0$ |
| **1972** | | |
| January | 350 | $-6.7$ |
| February | 275 | $-24.0$ |

*Notes:*
1  No prior figures available for 1970
2  The figures are raw data – no smoothing has been done

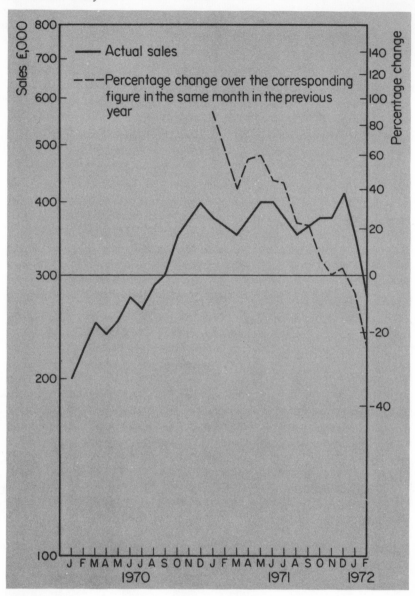

**Figure 4.3**

Time series: absolute and percentage change statistics

are given on the left-hand scale of the graph and the percentage change over the figure appearing in the corresponding month in the previous year is shown on the right-hand scale. The absolute figures show a steady increase in absolute sales and there is no sign of a decline until the last two months. The percentage changes, represented by the broken line, had started to fall from January 1971. By plotting the changes as in the graph the analyst could have predicted the reduction in sales. Care is needed in handling the statistics, however, as incorrect conclusions can be easily drawn. Semilog paper is generally used for showing such statistics as it gives equal space to equal proportions. Thus, an increase from 300 to 600 and from 400 to 800 are given equal spaces on the graph as both represent percentage increases of 100 per cent.

The use of percentage changes helps predict the turning points or the rate of continuing increase or decrease in absolute figures. The use of additional statistics such as orders received or of industrial surveys such as those produced monthly by the *Financial Times* will give further information to the analyst in his evaluation of trade cycles. The absolute figures will give perhaps the best indication of long-term trends and the percentage changes in the data will reveal the direction and stage of the cycle. Chapter 5 discusses the more common stock selection techniques and as will be seen some rely upon a single EPS figure which is projected at a constant growth rate. In such cases it is extremely important to know whereabouts in the trade cycle the company is as its EPS may be at one of the extremes.

The length and duration of a cycle is often more difficult to forecast than the turning points. An initial guide can be gained from measuring past data. The analyst must then use various economic, trade and company news and statistics to assess whether the conditions were similar to those of the past. It must be acknowledged from the outset that the forecasting of sales (and profits) in cyclical industries will be very difficult.

## Quantity statistics

If possible the analyst should obtain quantity statistics relating to the company's output or an industry's output. This will enable the analyst to determine how much of a sales increase was due to price inflation and how much to increased consumer demand. Price inflation is a statistic which is hard to project (above a certain long-run average) as consumer resistance and the substitution of alternative goods may arise. In this case, knowledge of the elasticity of demand would be required and this is a very difficult figure to assess with any degree of accuracy. Increases in sales which arise by way of increased consumer demand have a much more secure base and the analyst may feel more confident in any projections he makes. If quantity statistics are not available the analyst may, in a few cases, be able to estimate them. This will apply in a one-product company where the prices charged are known, i.e. launderette companies have just one product and the price charged is fixed at a national level. In most cases, however, the analyst will only be able to obtain quantity statistics from industry totals but these can still throw light upon the reasons for increases in sales. There are numerous other factors that an analyst will need to look at when forecasting sales. Many of these will be peculiar to the company and the analyst will soon pick these up. Some of the more common factors are dealt with below.

## Long-term contracts

Certain companies, notably those in the civil engineering and process plant industries, have substantial contracts which take several years to complete. As profits and net book assets are formally drawn-up once a year, difficulties arise in accounting for these long-term contracts. Chapter 2 described the ASSC recommended accounting treatment but a good deal of judgment and estimation is required. Some companies do not take any profit until the completion of the contract, whilst others take a proportion of the estimated total profit. For smaller companies who may only have one major contract in existence at one time, the timing of the completions and the accounting treatments adopted have critical importance. The Accounts will state in very broad terms the accounting treatment used and the analyst will have to be aware that judgments and assumptions will have played a large part in the measuring of profits. If no profits are taken until completion the analyst will have an even harder task in evaluating a company. Company visits, analyses of previous years' performance and the Chairman's statement may all give some clue to the profitability of contracts. Companies which rely heavily on long-term contracts are inherently difficult to forecast because of inflation in respect of fixed-cost clauses, Foreign Exchange rates, Government investment decisions and technological developments. Such uncertainty is reflected in the share prices of these companies as they are often below companies with similar earnings and assets.

**Geographical location**

The geographical split of a company's sales and profits will be needed if the foreign elements are substantial. This will be required as the prevailing economic conditions in the UK and the assumptions which are used in reaching forecasts may not be relevant for foreign countries. By knowing the degree of operation and the assets employed abroad in the separate countries the investor can evaluate his risk far better. Typical recent instances of investors' cautiousness over foreign assets and earnings has included the expropriating of assets by nationalist Governments, the remittance of earnings to the UK and the erratic nature of Foreign Exchange rates. Although the Stock Exchange now requires new companies to give a geographical split-up of their operations in the prospectus this soon becomes out of date and in any event is rarely detailed enough. If the foreign business is large in relation to the company then the analyst should pursue as many avenues as possible to obtain the geographical breakdown. The analyses of subsidiaries' accounts, company visits and the news media should all be screened for information.

**Foreign exchange rates**

Besides an intrinsic assessment of export markets, analysts will also need to evaluate and forecast Foreign Exchange rates. The price elasticity of the export market will have to be estimated if changes in exchange rates are expected. The job of forecasting the movement in currency rates will probably fall to the economist team and the predictions should be consistently used by the various specialist sector analysts. The reader will readily appreciate the importance of exchange rates on imports into the UK. Many of our imports are of basic raw materials which we cannot produce, or cannot produce enough of, ourselves. We therefore have to import these goods and in a period of widely fluctuating exchange rates, as has been encountered during the earlier 1970s, the profitability and liquidity positions of substantial importers became very volatile and consequently difficult to predict. The impact of substantial foreign currency realignments are likely to affect most of British industry as although many companies are neither exporters nor importers themselves, their customers and trade suppliers often are.

## Indirect taxation and credit controls

In managing the economy one of the main weapons at the Government's disposal is taxation. This especially applies to indirect taxation in the form of Customs and Excise duty and value added tax. Some sectors of consumer spending are very sensitive to changes in these indirect taxes and to changes in credit regulations such as hire-purchase terms. By increasing these rates the Government can bring about swingeing cuts in domestic demand (deflation) or, by decreasing them, can bring about a dramatic rise in demand. The analyst will first of all have to ascertain how sensitive the sales of the company's products are to changes in customs duties, VAT, hire-purchase regulations, etc. and this will involve examining past data. Forecasts of Government policies will then have to be made to obtain estimates of likely tax rates and credit restrictions. The general course of the economy and Press comment will themselves suggest when deflationary or reflationary policies are likely to be adopted; the existence of the business cycle implies that the Government will always be having to adopt some deflationary or reflationary measures. By examining past history and from an assessment of political comment, the analyst will forecast the type of measures he thinks will be imposed for the prevailing economic conditions. These forecasts together with knowledge of the company's sensitivity to tax changes and credit controls will provide further information for predicting sales and profit margins.

## The importance of profit margin analysis

Although total sales figures may be static and price levels and costs kept constant gross profit margins sometimes vary significantly. This will often be because of a change in the product mix of goods sold by the company. For example, although the total revenue of a company is the same as in the previous year, larger quantities of items which have a greater profit margin may have been sold and quantities of low-profit margin products reduced. The analyst in these cases must keep a watch on quantity and price level indices given in trade journals. The breakdown of a company's activities as previously described should be useful in evaluating the impact of a change in sales mix as significant differences in profit margins are mainly likely in items which go to separate markets. The introduction of a new product which is more than a variant of an existing line will create additional sales and earnings forecasting difficulties. Fortunately, such goods often only account for a small portion of a company's output initially and so their impact is reduced. When the product reaches a greater level of acceptance the analyst should have built up data to enable him to make a forecast. This methodology implies that the analyst should not worry too much about new products in their initial stages. This of course

111

means that major growth companies may be by-passed at their 'cheapest' stage (e.g. Rank Organisation with its Xerox franchise). However, for the number of successes that could have been picked up at their inception stage, there are likely to have been many more spurious 'growth' stocks. The recognition of major growth companies at their very early stages is extremely difficult and fraught with disaster although it has been the base of some investors' fortunes. A description of a company's life-cycle is given later.

**Cost of sales**

The next stage in the process is to forecast the costs of the expected sales and this involves computing the fixed-cost gearing. The breakdown of costs into variable, semi-fixed and fixed expenses will be extremely difficult but as shown in the example it can be of great importance.

*Example*

|  | Company A £ |  | Company B £ |  |
|---|---|---|---|---|
| Sales | 100,000 |  | 100,000 |  |
| *Less*: Variable costs | 30,000 |  | 70,000 |  |
|  | 70,000 | 70% | 30,000 | 30% |
| *Less*: Fixed costs | 50,000 |  | 10,000 |  |
| Profit | £20,000 |  | £20,000 |  |

Here, both sales and profits are the same but the cost structure is different. In cost accounting terms company *A* has a contribution margin of 70 per cent whilst that for *B* is 30 per cent. The contribution margin per unit is defined as the sales price minus variable costs and this is the amount that goes towards meeting the fixed overheads and the profit. If sales rose by 50 per cent the figures will look like:

|  | A £ |  | B £ |  |
|---|---|---|---|---|
| Sales | 150,000 |  | 150,000 |  |
| *Less:* Variable costs | 45,000 |  | 105,000 |  |
|  | 105,000 | 70% | 45,000 | 30% |
| *Less:* Fixed costs | 50,000 |  | 10,000 |  |
| Profit | £55,000 |  | £35,000 |  |

Both sales and variable costs for *A* and *B* have risen by 50 per cent but the fixed costs are static as they do not vary with turnover. As *A* has a much higher contribution margin his profits have risen substantially above those of *B*. If sales fell by 50 per cent *B* would become the more profitable; indeed *A* would make a loss.

|  | A £ |  | B £ |  |
|---|---|---|---|---|
| Sales | 50,000 |  | 50,000 |  |
| *Less:* Variable costs | 15,000 |  | 35,000 |  |
|  | 35,000 | 70% | 15,000 | 30% |
| *Less:* Fixed costs | 50,000 |  | 10,000 |  |
|  | Loss £15,000 |  | Profit £5,000 |  |

## Cost structure

*A* has higher 'fixed cost gearing' and this operates in the same way as financial gearing. Examples of fixed costs might include depreciation due to time, certain administrative costs, computer facilities, rents and rates. These will not be fixed for all levels of sales, however. For example, if sales increased substantially, additional premises would be required and this would increase rent and rates. Variable expenses include purchases of raw materials and components, factory labour, power for the machines and wear-and-tear depreciation. All of these expenses contribute directly towards the cost of goods sold. Semi-variable costs are items which vary in relation to turnover but usually at lesser rates. The analyst will find it almost impossible to obtain complete detailed information of the cost structure but there are a number of ways in which he can reduce the uncertainty:

1 Details of financial gearing are given in the Accounts. The analysis of interest charges and asset structure was described in Chapter 3.

2 Details of a few charges are given in the Accounts. Directors' emoluments, for example, are probably a semi-variable expense of profits. Income from investments and property is separately disclosed and does not usually vary with output. Depreciation is a variable or semi-variable cost although if there is any depreciation on properties this can be taken as being fixed. Exceptional and non-recurrent items, if material, are separately disclosed.

3 Company visits and knowledge of the 'traditional' cost structure of specific industries can help in determining the volatility in earnings to small changes in turnover.

4 Examining past data to see whether profits fluctuated greatly for certain levels of change in turnover.

The above process should give some idea to the analyst of cost structure and highlight companies that have very high levels of fixed costs.

The analyst will use his knowledge of the cost structure to assess the profit margin on sales. In the last example, the profit margin for *A* was 70 per cent and that of *B*, 30 per cent. However, published Annual Accounts will not give sufficient data for a detailed breakdown and the procedure for estimating the types of costs involved given above will have to be used. The profit margins computed will usually be based on profits before tax minus investment and property income and plus financial charges, directors' remuneration and possibly depreciation. Depreciation, although a semi-variable expense, can be dealt with separately. Exceptional and non-recurrent expenditure should be left out of the calculations.

## Additional factors in profit margin analysis

The profit margin so computed will have to take account of a number of factors before it can be applied to the predicted sales. The principal items are:

1 Changes in sales price. These can often be gleaned from trade journals and company pricelists.

2    Changes in the product mix which can be very important for companies with large sales ranges. The analyst should also be on watch for announcements of sales of, or the closing of, unprofitable divisions or products lines.

3    Changes in the factors of production. The analyst will have to estimate the make-up of costs, i.e. labour, raw materials, fuel and power and components. Companies have to disclose the number and aggregate pay of UK employees but other costs will have to be estimated. The analyst can then look at the appropriate statistics to measure rates of inflation, ascertain possible stock shortages, assess Foreign Exchange rates and so on. There are usually trade statistics and prospects available for future costs and the general news media should be screened for political decisions which may affect factors of production.

Labour costs account for around 75 per cent of the total costs in the economy and therefore forms a major factor in determining company profitability. Even companies that do not have large labour forces will be deeply affected by wages movements as their purchases of products and services are likely to have borne heavy labour charges. Since the Second World War strong rises in wage rates have been associated with falling profitability and so a detailed examination of wage settlements will help indicate possible changes in earnings at an early date. Economic data exists which provides general trends of wage settlements. Although individual trade unions bargain for wage increases there is a surprisingly high correlation between the various wage agreements, and thus the economic indices give valuable information. Additionally, the British workforce has displayed significant mobility and this has further made for uniformity in wage settlements. The analyst should study the monthly unemployment statistics and keep abreast of recent wage settlements which affect the industry being investigated and those that affect their suppliers. A long-term factor which the analyst will have to bear in mind is the increase expected in Department of Health and Social Security contributions from companies. The number of retired people as a percentage of the population is rising dramatically and the funding of pensions is likely to be largely met by employers. Another factor that an analyst will have to take account of is the productivity of labour. This has been rising at an annual rate of around $3\frac{1}{4}$ per cent over the past decade and some projection of this figure will be needed for long-term forecasts. The major reason for the increase in output per labour hour is the increased mechanisation of business and so statistics and expectations of capital expenditure may be used to confirm or modify the growth rate in labour productivity assumptions.

4    Stability of profit ratios in the past five or ten years. If they have been reasonably stable the analyst may feel confident in his projections. If the profit margins have been erratic this may have been due to high fixed costs; if not, the analyst may have to accept that any estimates of the company's profit margins will be tenuous.

5   Special factors may exist such as with long-term contracts where the prices are set at the outset and which will have been based on various cost assumptions. These cost estimates made by companies over long periods can easily be far out and the analyst without the access to the details may find profit margins extremely difficult to establish. Another factor is that of companies who, besides manufacturing, also deal heavily in the commodity markets where the often wide price fluctuations can result in large profits and large losses. It will be virtually impossible for the analyst to foretell the outcomes of these operations. In times of erratic raw material prices, similar product firms may show significantly different profits due to different stockholding policies. Again, the analyst will find it difficult to estimate the impact. By talking to management and examining historical performance the analyst may obtain an idea of the presence of these special factors and if he knows the firm's policies he may be able to make a fair estimate of the outcome. When management is not so forthcoming about the prevalence of special items the analyst should recognise the greater uncertainties.

## Depreciation charge

Depreciation charges are usually semi-variable with sales as the diminution in value is a function of both time and usage. The charges are disclosed in the Annual Accounts and these form the basis for forecasting purposes. Unless there has been a significant increase or decrease in physical assets during the year the depreciation charge should not be far removed from those of the prior year. The analyst should therefore keep himself up to date with Press releases of important capital expenditure plans or substantial sales of assets by the company. The latter item, the sale of assets, may result in heavy losses attributable to the year which might be included in depreciation or disclosed separately as an exceptional item. Abnormal depreciation can occur due to technical obsolescence and trade journals should be perused to indicate possible major write offs. Recent heavy depreciation and obsolescence examples include television rental companies increasing the depreciation rates on monochrome sets as coloured television has captured such a large part of the market, and computer equipment which has become outmoded by the introduction of later-generation models.

## Interest charges

Whilst the interest charges on debentures and loan stocks are known, bank interest will vary according to the level of overdrafts during the year. From the analysis of the changes expected in the asset structure of the company during the year the analyst will have a figure in mind for bank and other borrowings. The interest rates prevailing during the year should be applied to the expected average borrowings. Any additional long-term finance obtained will, of course, increase the interest charge and loans raised abroad will occasion a review of Foreign Exchange rates. The analyst may make adjustments to the interest charges and to the asset structure if the terms of a convertible loan stock allow for conversion during the year. It will be difficult to estimate the conversion that will take place (except when the equivalent share price is below the nominal loan stock value when no conversion is likely). In such cases the analyst may decide to show the interest charges and the EPS figures under varying levels of conversion.

**Investment and associated company income**

The analyst will need to forecast investment income for companies who derive substantial earnings from this source. The names of 'associated companies' as defined by the ASSC have to be shown in the Accounts, along with details of the shares held and the attributable profits. The analyst is therefore in a position to analyse and forecast the results of the associate. The attributable proportion of the estimated pre-tax profits is then added to the company's expected profits. The same procedure applies to subsidiary companies. When a subsidiary is not wholly owned, the amounts attributable to minorities need to be calculated. This involves no difficulty unless the parent company has altered its holdings during the year. This will generally only arise if the subsidiary has a Stock Market quote. Details of stakes in companies which amount to more than 10 per cent of that company's equity capital or more than 10 per cent of the investing company's assets have to be disclosed. Subsidiary and associated companies come within this definition but they have already been dealt with on an earnings basis. If the investment income is significant the analyst should separately analyse the investment's prospects. This will give valuable data in building up the Profit and Loss Account and in estimating the value of the investments. Where the investment income is derived from companies who have not come within the above categories no information is likely to be given in the Accounts on the investments held. The analyst in these circumstances should apply the Stock Market average dividend increase or decrease to the previous year's income. In forecasting investment income consideration should be given to that earned on short-term surplus funds. The amounts earned in money markets and deposit accounts can be quite significant and an analysis of the liquidity position allied to the analyst's knowledge of future expenditure plans will enable some forecast of surplus funds to be arrived at. The average interest rates are then applied to the average surplus funds to obtain short-term investment income. If any funds are kept abroad then knowledge of foreign currency rates and the prospects for these rates is required. The analyst will need to keep himself up to date with news of additions or disposals of subsidiaries, associated companies and large investment stakes. For significant changes in these items the parent company may have to consult its shareowners and will almost certainly give Press releases.

**Corporation tax**

The tax charge usually takes a fairly standard proportion of profits for most companies and the projection of such will form the basis for the estimated charge. The percentage of pre-tax profits paid in tax should not be all that different from the standard corporation tax rate. If it is, then the analyst should try to see why this is so and assess whether the conditions are likely to continue. If well above average capital expenditure takes place during the year the actual tax charge as a proportion of pre-tax profit will probably fall significantly. This is because the capital allowances granted by the Inland Revenue are usually far higher than the depreciation rates charged by the company. The company will in most cases, however, operate a deferred taxation account and this should bring the ratio of tax charge to pre-tax profits to somewhere in the region of the prevailing corporation tax rate. In any longer-term earnings forecasts the analyst will probably assume a continuation of the present day tax rate.

## Dividends

Dividend forecasts are needed as they are an important factor in share price determination; indeed, they form the basis used in the intrinsic value approach and in many computer-based stock evaluation models. Many investors rely upon the regular receipt of dividends for their day-to-day living expenses and therefore base investment decisions on dividend performances. The formal stock evaluation methods usually require forecasts of dividend performance for at least one year ahead (more if possible) and then an estimated growth rate(s).

Companies tend to raise dividends only when they believe they can be maintained[4]. Thus, a large increase in earnings in one year will not necessarily be accompanied by an increase in the dividend rate and similarly a fall in profits does not necessarily entail a reduction in the dividend. The usual pattern of dividend payouts will be of the rate moving up in steps.

## Dividend growth

Analysts will probably project dividends by assuming some constant ratio to the forecast earnings. To attempt to forecast 'stepwise' increases in dividends would probably not prove fruitful in the medium to long term. In using a constant payout ratio, the analyst must be aware of other factors influencing dividend decisions. These include the liquidity position of the firm and the need to retain earnings to replace capital assets. The strong rates of inflation since the war have meant that to replace machinery with similar-capacity new machines has cost considerably more money. In order to protect the net worth per share of the business, managements may be forced to lower the pay-out ratios. The analyst can assess the liquidity position of the firm by using the various analyses described in Chapter 3. An additional factor is dividend restraint exercised by the Government. Any long-term restrictions are likely to have a significant impact on the Stock Market.

The analyst will now be in a position to forecast earnings and dividends per share for the following and perhaps more, years. They will be based upon as many projections of individual Profit and Loss Account and Balance Sheet items as the analyst can identify and thinks relevant. The forecasts will therefore incorporate numerous economic factors and business variables. The analyst will then compare his forecasts against estimates derived by others and seek to find out reasons for any differences. The final forecasts will be eventually evaluated against the published figures and again the discrepancies should be examined. Company visits will provide an ideal time for the analyst to assess the reasons for shortfalls in his forecasts as well as providing the opportun-

117

ity to discuss future prospects. This feedback mechanism is one of the most valuable aids in investment analysis and should be approached in a professional fashion.

**Interim results**

Projected EPS can be revised during the year with the publication of the half-yearly results. Unfortunately these results are unaudited and usually only disclose the earnings and the dividend figures and occasionally turnover. Nevertheless, they do provide some feedback on margins and can indicate serious discrepancies in the analyst's forecasts. Interim results are of especial use in projecting the earnings of companies with volatile profits profiles as they can indicate the direction and possibly the magnitude of profits which otherwise are very unpredictable. Again the analyst should use other factors in association with the interim earnings figures: as with yearly changes in earnings the simple extrapolation of interim figures may be tenuous[5].

**Capital expenditure**

Besides analysing the profit and loss items for the year the analyst will also want to forecast the levels of capital expenditure and the asset structure of the Balance Sheet. This will suggest possible future sources of revenues and indicate likely strains on working capital and liquidity. The Annual Accounts have to disclose amounts of capital expenditure contracted for and the amounts of capital expenditure authorised by the directors but not contracted for, at the year end. These figures may give some indication of likely capital expenditure during the year. The analyst can measure previous figures for capital expenditure appearing in Accounts against the eventual total amount for the year. If there is a roughly stable ratio this will indicate the reliance and extent of prediction capable from looking at the capital expenditure plans at the year end. Company visits, trade journals, Chairman's reports and Press comment will all be helpful in keeping track of substantial projects. The trend and variability of capital expenditures in past years will be found useful as many firms make consistent commitments in increasing and replacing capital assets.

If possible, capital projects should be differentiated between those that represent increases to capacity and those that represent replacements*. The former can lead to substantial additional profits whilst the latter may add very little. The longer-term growth prospects of the company will be largely determined by net new investment and capital expenditure programmes give advance notice of possible sources of future profits. The analyst may find it illuminating to correlate net increases in assets with profitability. The association in many cases is likely to be somewhat vague because of the different time lags for investments to become revenue earning but, nevertheless, some interesting relationships may be found.

**Age and life analysis of assets**

Another rough method for forecasting capital expenditure requirements is to estimate the average age and the average expected life of

---

*This is a differentiation which perhaps ought to be included in published Accounts.

the company's assets*. For example, if the average age of assets is seventeen years and the expected life is, say, twenty years, then some quite heavy replacement is likely in the near future if the firm is to continue its rate of output. The figures computed above could be arranged as a ratio, i.e. 17:20 and if this is found to be increasing then greater asset replacement may be thought likely.

The methods of computing the average age and the average life of assets are very crude and the reader will easily recognise the wide, sweeping assumptions involved. The age of the asset can be calculated thus:

$$\frac{\text{Accumulated depreciation charge at the year end}}{\text{Depreciation charge for the year}}$$

Thus, if the accumulated depreciation figure appearing in the Balance Sheet is £12,000,000 and the depreciation charge in the Profit and Loss Account is £800,000 then the average age of assets is:

$$\frac{12,000,000}{800,000} = 15 \text{ years}$$

The average expected life of an asset can be derived from the following expression:

$$\frac{\text{Gross book value of assets at the year end}}{\text{Depreciation charge for the year}}$$

e.g. 
$$\text{Gross book value} = £20,000,000$$

$$\text{Depreciation for year} = £800,000$$

$$\text{Average expected life of assets} = \frac{20,000,000}{800,000} = 25 \text{ years}$$

For analytical purposes the above figures assume that (1) all the company's assets are depreciated at the same constant straight-line† rate (in the above case 4 per cent); (2) that the accumulated depreciation figure includes only the normal annual depreciation charges (i.e. no exceptional write offs for obsolescence); (3) that assets are scrapped or sold at the end of their expected life (i.e. the gross book value does not include items for which no depreciation is now being written off); (4) that the company's assets have the same length of life.

Besides indicating whether greater or lesser amounts of physical asset replacement over previous years is likely, some approximate idea of the cost of replacement may be obtained. This can be derived by measuring the price inflation which has occurred over the age of the assets and applying this to the gross book value of the assets to obtain their current replacement costs. If the analyst estimates that £800,000

---

*This should be conducted on depreciating assets. Thus, property assets should be omitted.

†This method of depreciation was discussed in Chapter 2.

of gross book value assets need to be replaced during the year he can calculate the cost by applying an appropriate inflation rate to the £800,000 (this may be the inflation that has occurred in twenty-five years, i.e. assuming it is the first assets bought which are to be replaced. The analyst can decide upon an appropriate inflation index). This sort of analysis is useful in determining cash flow and liquidity requirements; the impact on the profits of the company may be small as no new capacity is obtained*.

Apart from the immediate year's financing of asset replacement, the above analysis will indicate longer-term requirements. The re-statement of assets at their replacement values indicates the amounts of money that would be required to replace assets at the current time. By examining the resources of the company and its profitability (i.e. possible retentions to meet replacement and whether the returns are likely to attract investors if the company goes to the capital market) the analyst will have some idea as to the company's ability to at least continue in its present form.

The ASSC have recently advocated that companies should include in their Annual Report a supplementary statement showing the accounts as adjusted for inflation. These statements will give the replacement values of assets (based on the index of retail prices†) and so the above estimation procedures will not be needed as regards calculating replacement values. The CPP Accounts do not give information on the age of the assets (although the average can be roughly estimated by dividing the historical figure into the CPP figure and seeing how many years on the inflation index this represents) or on when the assets are to be replaced. The above analyses should augment the simple extrapolation of past capital expenditure plans especially as regards the replacement items.

## Liquidity and financing position

The other side of capital expenditure projects is financing and any liquidity problems that arise will have an immediate impact on profitability and may create a credibility crisis which may not allow the capital projects to come to fruition. In order to assess the financing strategies possible a sources and uses of funds statement will be found useful. This, along with the various liquidity ratio tests (as described in Chapter 3) and a knowledge of the existing state of the capital markets, will indicate whether the working capital requirements can be met. Analyses of creditors will indicate whether further trade credit can be obtained. The funds generated within the business, i.e. profits before depreciation, will have already been estimated by the analyst. Bank borrowings form a major source of finance for working capital

*There will be some impact on profits, however, i.e.: (1) the assets should be more efficient to run; (2) depreciation charges will be greater; (3) the tax charge should be reduced because of high initial capital allowances.

†This is known as the current purchasing power (CPP) method. CPP figures will only be approximations of the replacement values.

requirements although the banks are usually more reluctant when it comes to the permanent financing of capital assets. An assessment of the Balance Sheet structure, the existence of high-grade security and the general attitudes of banks towards lending will help the analyst decide whether increases from these sources can be expected. Additional long-term fixed interest capital will depend upon the financial state of the business, and upon the availability of security, which generally means unencumbered properties. The expected interest rates payable on long-term borrowings can easily be assessed by looking at existing market yields. The final source of funds is via an equity issue. The likelihood of an issue of new shares will be governed largely by market sentiment and by the existing share price. Companies will be reluctant to make issues when their share price is low and the Stock Market as a whole is usually less keen on rights issues made during bear markets. Nevertheless, the rights issue is the source of funds that has to be used when all else fails. If the analyst forecasts that a rights issue will be required and this has not been discounted by the market he can use this information, often alone, in making investment decisions. This is because market sentiment prevails very heavily in raising rights capital and so all issues made in the same period will be greeted initially with the same response which is often unenthusiastic.

## Analysis of return on capital employed

A 'quick' method of forecasting is to extrapolate the earnings on capital employed and then by adjusting for the various methods of financing, determine the EPS. The capital employed should, if possible, use current market values or even replacement costs instead of Balance Sheet values as otherwise this approximate forecasting method may become very poor indeed. Additionally, for very cyclical companies an average annual return on capital employed over the length of the cycle may have to be used. The protagonists of this method claim that returns on capital employed tend to be steady over periods of time, more so than with EPS. A refinement to the method which shows whether the ratio is steady is to measure the marginal return on investment. This examines the increase in profits and the increase in capital employed over a particular time period, probably the industrial cycle. The marginal rate of return so computed is then measured against the actual performance.

*Example*  Four-year cycle company

|  | £m |
|---|---|
| Increase in gross profits 1968 – 1972 | 14.0 |
| Increase in capital employed 1967 – 1971 | 70.0 |
| Marginal return on capital employed $\frac{14}{70}$ = | 20% |

The measurement of capital employment has been lagged one year behind the measurement of profits. This is an allowance to take account of the time required for assets to become revenue-earning. This is an arbitrary assumption, however, and the analyst can perhaps think of more appropriate adjustments for specific companies. The analyst will compare the marginal return with the actual average return on capital employed earned during the period 1968/72. If these are similar then the average can possibly be extrapolated into the future although the usual caveats relating to simple projections need to be acknowledged. If the marginal rate is below the average then this will act as a signal that returns are likely to fall: if above the average, then a rise in future returns is implied. It must be emphasised that this is a quick appraisal method and that it should only be used as one part of a detailed analysis. It could possibly be used to identify companies which are worth analysing in greater detail. The rate of return on capital employed also gives some useful data on future earnings as: (1) high rates are unlikely to be maintained over long periods due to competition; (2) poor returns may indicate takeover possibilities or suggest that existing or subsequent management may eventually increase earnings as there is substantial scope to do so.

## Economic forecasting

An assessment of economic activity is necessary in investment matters and, whilst for individual investors this may be a very rough subjective judgment that is not consciously made, large firms of stockbrokers and financial institutions will have extensive economic research departments. Companies operate within the economic environment and are subject to various Government legislation. Trade cycles which form a real part of a company's life are affected significantly by economic events and fiscal policies. The analyst or his firm should formulate views on economic events and the forecasts made should be used by the analysts in their specialist areas. It is important that analysts working in the same firm of brokers should be using similar economic assumptions, otherwise clients may be confused and the broking firm would have to admit at the outset that some company forecasts will be based on wrong assumptions.

Forecasting of the private sector of the economy, i.e. companies, can in fact be built up from the forecasts pertaining to individual companies. The aggregate earnings, variability of earnings and the forecasts of such data into the future all provide major information for the economic forecasts of the private sector. Aggregate and industry sector company profit forecasts prepared by Civil Service economists provides background data against which the analyst can compare his forecasts for company earnings. The analyst will need to both forecast and assess actual Government economic and fiscal measures. These include credit restrictions, Bank of England interest rates and deposit ratios, prices and incomes policies and tax rates. In order to assess whether such legislation is likely the analyst should look at the various items which the Government may hope to control to some extent. For example, Balance of Payments crises, rates of unemployment and concern over growth rates have been major events which the UK

Government has acted upon to influence in recent years. The analyst, by looking at the relevant statistics, by examining current opinion and by measuring past Government reaction to economic events, can estimate likely legislation and the consequent effect on company profitability and share prices.

## Money supply

Some studies have been made into determining the relationship between the change in money supply and Stock Market levels[6]. It has been hypothesised, for example, that excess money supply in the economy may act to drive up ordinary share prices without the presence of any other factors. Some studies have found there to be a relationship although it is rather tenuous; the Seventh Congress of the European Federation of Financial Analysts' Societies (1972) which discussed the relationship between money supply and share prices at length, concluded that the difficulties to this approach were so great, at the present time, that any predictive ability was very doubtful. Excess liquidity or money supply figures can be derived from domestic banking statistics (growth in net UK bank deposits, for example). Adjustments for rates of economic inflation can be made to obtain rates of 'real' growth in money supply. The analyst can, however, experiment with the various statistics in many ways, in order to obtain a better 'predictive measure' of money supply.

## Interest rates

The interest received on deposits or paid on overdrafts figures quite large in many companies' Accounts and so accurate forecasts of interest rate movements will greatly aid the prediction of corporate earnings. For financial companies such as banks, hire-purchase firms and insurance brokers the changes in Bank Rate and in other interest rates are major determinants of profitability and are one of the major variables the analyst will attempt to forecast. Interest rates vary mainly with the velocity of circulation of money which can be thought of as the turnover of the total volume of money. Past experience has shown there to be a strong correlation between the velocity of circulation and interest rates. The velocity can be measured by relating the money supply or volume of money to the gross national income. To predict interest rates therefore requires accurate forecasts of national income and money supply. Whilst national income can be forecast with some degree of accuracy, even by simple extrapolation, the forecasting of money supply is more difficult. This is represented by currency in circulation with the public and by the net deposits held with banks by UK residents. Statistics relating to bank deposits are issued monthly and act as feedback on forecasts made. In forecasting money supply the analyst will have to appraise the policies of Government borrowing and estimate growth in bank advances and growth in corporate and individual lending to the banking sector. Factors which will have to be taken into account will include the rates of inflation, Balance of Payments positions and returns available from other investments. Such forecasting is very tenuous and many analysts will therefore rely upon the estimates published by Government departments and by economic advisory firms.

### Longer-term economic forecasting

For longer-term forecasts the projection of Gross National Product (GNP) provides as feasible an approach as any to the assessment of company profitability. It acts as a guideline to the longer-term growth rates of companies after the analyst no longer finds it practical to forecast sales and profit margins. It should be recognised, however, that the growth in GNP over a number of years acts as a line around which corporate profits will wander. GNP is likely to grow steadily, but company profits will be more erratic as sales prices take time to catch up with costs and vice versa. Although forecasting GNP into the future is fraught with difficulties it is perhaps easier to predict than other variables*. GNP represents the total domestic expenditure for the year at market prices adjusted to overall national product by adding exports and income received from abroad and deducting imports and income paid abroad, valued at factor cost (that is deducting indirect taxation). The figure equals the total incomes received by the factors of production including corporate profits and this is a frequently-used method of computing GNP. It therefore gives the total growth in the economy in money terms and statistics of growth in real terms are derived therefrom. The projection of GNP forms a parameter to sales growth of companies and in the very long term a firm's growth rate could not substantially exceed that of GNP. The forecasting of GNP will therefore be useful in describing the economic environment in which a company will have to operate. The comparison of the expected growth rate of the company in earnings and dividends with the forecast growth rate of GNP will give useful data on the firm's efficiency.

There are a number of texts which describe methods for forecasting GNP and these should be consulted by the interested analyst[7]. However, most analysts will prefer to make use of existing models drawn up by industrial and Civil Service economists. The expense of building one's own model and the running of it will normally be considered to be prohibitive. In using published forecasts, however, the analyst needs to be aware of how they were derived and the various assumptions used. The analyst will then have to draw the implications for companies from the GNP forecast. This will involve estimates of corporate taxation, dividend policy, replacement of assets and the split of GNP into the various income groups.

**Economic growth**

Growth in economic output per head of the population will be largely determined by the proportion of the GNP devoted to investment and the productivity and efficiency of the workforce. The annual growth in output per man hour over the past decade has been in the order of $3\frac{1}{4}$ per cent and this has been attributable to both the increased investment

---

*There are three ways of measuring national product, namely by output, by spending, and by incomes. The difficulties of measurement involved are highlighted by the slightly different figures for GNP given by these methods; 'incomes' tending to give higher estimates of GNP, 'expenditure' fluctuates around the average and 'output' gives low estimates.

in plant and machinery and the greater skills of labour and management; Figure 4.4 shows the recent trend of capital per worker. Comparisons of growth rates between economies have shown that the major determinant in expansion has been the proportion of the national product allocated to capital investment: Britain has lagged behind other developed nations largely because of its small level of capital expenditure. In forecasting GNP the analyst will therefore need to make assumptions about the percentage of the nation's output each year which is devoted to long-term capital expenditure. Figure 4.5 shows the recent trend. Whilst analysts should be wary of extrapolating the rate of increase shown over the past forty years, some increase in the proportion of the national product used in capital formation can be assumed.

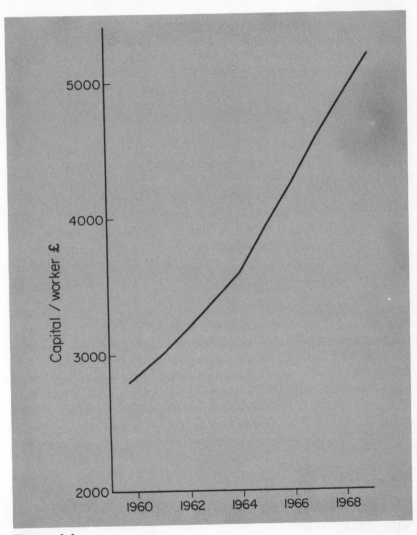

**Figure 4.4**

Fixed capital per worker

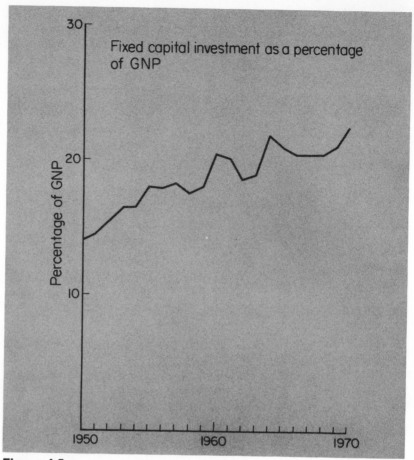

**Figure 4.5**

Fixed capital investment as a percentage of G.N.P.

### New companies and new products

The analyst may find more difficulty in forecasting the performance of a young company engaged in marketing a new product. This is because there is little prior data relating to consumer acceptance of the products or of managerial ability. The interest in analysing such companies is that to invest in major growth companies at their embryonic stage can lead to enormous profits. On the other hand, young companies have a higher 'death' rate and the risk of an investor losing most of his money is quite significant. This is a prime case of high returns being associated with high risks and the selection of the good stocks is a challenge which is often all time consuming for some analysts.

**Life-cycle of the firm**

The life-cycle of the firm is traditionally shown in the form of Figure 4.6. In the early part of its life the company expands very quickly, then the pace slackens as competition arises, and finally a stabilisation period

126

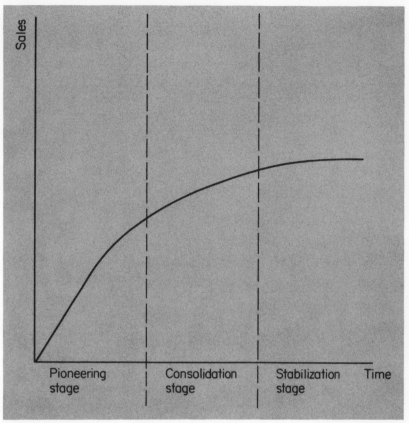

**Figure 4.6**

Life cycle of an industrial company

is encountered which is evidenced by market saturation and substitution of alternative products. The company will then grow at around the rate of GNP growth as the products cater for the replacement market. Further expansion will depend upon new-product development and managerial ability to diversify or create additional demand. The early part of a company's life as shown in Figure 4.6 is relevant to firms who had completely new products (i.e. not adaptions of existing goods) so that competition takes time to arrive. If the new products are slow to gain consumer acceptance or if they have to compete with similar existing products, then the early stage of growth will not be nearly as dramatic as in the figure[8].

**New products**

In making an evaluation of new products the analyst should consult various trade journals and possibly technical or marketing consultants in the specific fields. An appraisal of management is also needed and if they have had prior commercial ventures these will provide some indication of their ability. Many new ventures are characterized by the individual entrepreneur with a marketing idea which can blossom in a few years. However, it is these companies which often provide the eventual business collapses. This is typically due to overstocking and over reliance on the original idea in spite of consumer habits having changed. For young companies manufacturing advanced-technology goods the analyst must decide whether these products are sufficiently needed by consumers to make them fully commercial. Many such technical companies are poor on market research and on the financial control of research expenditure. The above considerations should help the analyst in evaluating new companies but it still does not reduce the risk to that enjoyed by long-established businesses.

## Research and Development

The analyst can attempt to measure the Research and Development expenditure of the company, the probabilities of commercial application and the returns therefrom. Many companies write off their research expenditure during the year it was incurred and do not disclose the expense. The analyst in these cases has no data from which to work and will have to derive assumptions on the research effort from trade sources and possibly company visits. When quantitative information is available the analyst can correlate the expenditures on Research and Development against future returns. In a few cases useful relationships will be established which will aid the forecasting process. In the majority of cases, however, the associations will be difficult to quantify and the analyst will have to use judgment based on the expenditures incurred, prior performance of the company, company visits and scientific and trade journals. The analyst should recognise that Research and Development does lead to a greater flow of new products although profit relationships are very difficult to establish[9]. Other things being equal (i.e. profits and assets) a company which spends more on research is likely to be more profitable in the future than other, similar industry firms.

### Trade cycle

In forecasting sales and profits the analyst will need to be aware of trade cycles and how to interpret them. Many companies are in highly cyclical industries and find themselves ineluctably associated with it. Thus, the analysis of which phase the particular industry cycle is in, and its duration and length is of vital importance in forecasting. The methods used to measure the industrial cycle were mentioned in the paragraphs on the forecasting of sales. It is here worth briefly describing the causes of cyclical movements.

As the economy expands, strains appear in the system with rapidly expanding inflation, shortages of labour and supplies, increases in imports and decreases in exports as resources are devoted to the highly profitable home market. The Government then steps in to correct the position with deflationary strategies. These can consist of prices and incomes controls, interest rate adjustments, tax increases and credit restrictions. The impact of the deflationary measures is first felt in retail stores and consumer goods sectors. As these companies see their sales growth falling they cut back on capital projects and so the capital goods industry cycle then starts to turn down. When the restrictions are lifted and the economy starts to expand it is the retail distributors and consumer goods companies which benefit first, with the recovery in capital goods sectors coming several months later.

## Capital goods cycle

The capital goods cycle is far stronger than the retail and consumer durable and non-durable cycles. This is due to their demand being very reliant on the change in consumer goods companies' sales and because of build-ups and run-downs of stocks. The simplified example shows up the relationship between the two cycles (Table 4.3). The important

### Table 4.3

The capital goods cycle

| Year | 1 | 2 | 3 | 4 | 5 | 6 | 7 | 8 |
|---|---|---|---|---|---|---|---|---|
| Retail sales | 1,000 | 1,050 | 1,150 | 1,400 | 1,420 | 1,420 | 1,370 | 1,250 |
| Percent change from previous year | | +5.0 | +9.5 | +21.7 | +1.4 | 0 | −4.5 | −8.8 |
| Capital assets required* | 3,000 | 3,150 | 3,450 | 4,200 | 4,260 | 4,260 | 4,110 | 3,750 |
| New investment required | | 150 | 300 | 750 | 60 | 0 | 0 (−150) | 0 (−360) |
| Replacement of existing assets† | | 300 | 315 | 345 | 420 | 426 | 426 | 411 |
| Total investment required° | | 450 | 615 | 1,095 | 480 | 426 | 426 (276) | 411 (51) |
| Percent change | | | +36.7 | +78.0 | −56.2 | −11.2 | 0 (−35.2) | −3.5 (−81.5) |

*Assuming a capital to sales ratio of 3:1
†Assuming replacement of existing assets takes place at the rate 10% of previous year's capital stock
°Assumes no lagging in orders
The figures in brackets represent the capital assets actively being used by the company

statistic here, of course, is the capital needed to generate £1 of sales. If the ratio falls to below 1 then the capital goods cycle would, *ceteris paribus*, have less fluctuations than consumer goods. In practice, most companies have a ratio above 1 and hence the greater variability in the capital goods cycle. The absolute and percentage change figures for retail sales show a much lower fluctuation than the manufacturing turnover. The former's sales vary from a maximum increase of 21.7 per cent over the previous year to a maximum decrease of −8.8 per cent. The corresponding figures for manufacturers' sales are +78.0 per cent and −56.2 per cent. The figures in brackets represent the total capital investment actually being used by the retailer (the figures of −150 and −360 are excess capacity). They cannot sell the excess capacity but it may cause management to defer replacement of assets and so further reduce capital goods manufacturers' output.

The impact of stockholding on the cycle is shown in Table 4.4. As the retailer experiences a fall in sales he also cuts back on his stocks because he thinks the trend may continue and he does not want to be left with

**Table 4.4**

Stockholding and the trade cycle

| Year | 1 | 2 |
|------|------|------|
| | Units | |
| Retail sales | 500 | 450 |
| Retail stocks | 50 | 30 |
| Wholesale sales | 500 | 430 |
| Wholesale stocks | 50 | 30 |
| Manufacturers' sales | 500 | 410 |
| Manufacturers' stocks | 50 | 10 |
| Metal stockists' sales | 500 | 370 |

Example of calculation involved:

Wholesalers' sales in Year 2 = Purchases of retailers = sales of retailers in Year 2 (450) minus opening stock (50) plus closing stock (30) = 430.

unsaleable commodities on his hands. Thus, the fall in sales is magnified by the decrease in stocks and the wholesaler's turnover falls by 14 per cent. The wholesaler likewise reduces his stocks and so the manufacturers' sales fall by 18 per cent and the metal stockists' turnover falls by the even greater percentage of 26 per cent. When the economy is on the upturn the build-up of stocks by retailers and wholesalers will magnify the trend of increased sales. Stocks and percentage change in demand are two major determinants of the highly cyclical capital goods industry and the techniques mentioned earlier in the chapter will have to be used in analysing the cycle.

The recent history of the capital goods cycle in the UK has revealed a time lag of around one year between profits and capital expenditure. Figure 4.7 shows the time lag between the turning points in corporate profitability and the turning points in expenditure on plant and machinery. The behaviour of the pattern can be possibly explained in that companies get more confident of the future as their current operations become more profitable. This leads to an increase in capital commitments but these require time to plan, time to order and time for suppliers to meet demand. The graph shows the aggregate figures for capital expenditure and there are obviously significant variances for specific types of capital goods. Analysts should therefore construct similar analyses on specific types of capital goods and, if stable relationships exist, then this may aid the earnings forecasts of

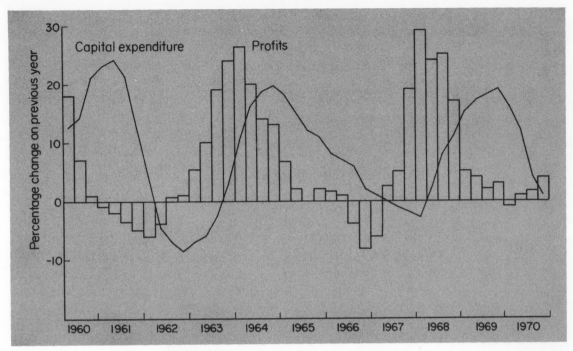

**Figure 4.7**

The relationship between corporate profitability and capital expenditure

capital-goods producers. It should be noted that the one-year time lag described above is broadly recognised by the market and the analyst will therefore either have to predict turning points in corporate earnings further ahead of other analysts or derive a more sophisticated relationship which perhaps also shows the magnitude of the cycle.

**Long-term company forecasting**

The intrinsic value method of share selection requires forecasts of dividends and earnings for as far ahead as is feasible. Thereafter one or more growth rates are applied to the terminal dividend or earnings estimate. The P/E models and other computer-based models also require growth rate forecasts. Much of the detailed analysis described in this chapter will not be very practical in assessing the longer-term prospects and growth rates of companies and the methodologies have to be adapted somewhat.

In longer-term forecasting the analyst will probably project sales revenues using statistical measures of growth allied to the necessarily subjective estimates of new-product development, technical obsolescence, competitive pressures and so on. Profit margins attributable to the sales will be based on the existing trends with adjustments made according to subjective judgments. Any breakdown of costs into fixed, semi-variable and variable expenses that has been made should be projected into the future and will greatly add to the forecasting accuracy. The impact of financial gearing assuming a continuation of the present asset structure can be readily measured and various assumptions about the requirements for capital raising can be incorporated. The analyst will use forecasts prepared by trade associations as they have considerable detailed information on their industry. Such forecasts, however, are often biased to some degree especially as regards competition from alternative industries. Competitive factors within industries will depend largely on the capital required and the managerial ability of individual companies, although analysts should be wary of companies being able to maintain a well above average return on capital employed. The resources needed to manufacture many products are so enormous that there is likely to be little 'new' competition (e.g. chemical firms or heavy engineering companies). For other industries, such as clothing or leisure, new firms and products are continually arising. Management is a difficult item to assess, the best measurement probably being prior performance of the company. Long-term forecasting will be helped if the constraints to growth can be recognised and if it is known whether the management has the skill to diversify successfully. In many cases the main growth constraint will be market demand although in the medium term, labour, management and supplies could all be constraining factors. There has been a fair amount of discussion recently about raw materials and energy supplies becoming limiting factors to long-term growth towards the end of the century. Some projections that have been made suggest that the vast annual usage of physical resources could bankrupt the world by the turn of the century. It is, of course, very difficult to forecast that far into the future with any great accuracy but it is perhaps worth recognising that some major companies are already planning up to the year 2000 and devising diversification strategies to protect themselves from the possible exhaustion of some raw materials.

There are certain general qualitative factors which the analyst can consider in longer-term evaluations. One example is to examine current consumer habits in the US as from past experience many of these consumer preferences will eventually materialise with the British public. Such analyses may: (1) indicate completely new marketing opportunities in the UK; and (2) help quantify some areas of longer-term growth. A similar factor is that of imputing the current behavioural tastes of the wealthier section of the community to be the future tastes of the poorer sections of the British population. Another general factor which should be considered is the increasing proportion of consumers' spending which is devoted to non-essentials. Thus, growth in food consumption is likely to rise only with the growth rate of the population* whereas growth in aggregate leisure pursuits is likely to grow at a much faster rate. Simple extrapolations of past consumer

---

*Obviously, inflation and desires for more expensive foods may increase the money value of food consumption well ahead of any rise in the population.

spending on essentials – non-essentials and of growth in leisure time may afford some useful guidelines as to the future expenditures on these factors. Having established probabilities of growth in non-essential spending, the analyst will, however, be left with the difficult problem of forecasting consumer non-essential spending preferences.

The above outline indicates methods which can be pursued in long-term forecasting although the analyst must recognise the difficulties involved. Some companies are far easier to forecast on a long-term basis than others. These will be the well managed companies with sound asset backing. The prime examples are property companies whose asset values are derived by surveyors using discounting techniques on future rental income.

## Management assessment

An important item in profits forecasting is the appraisal of management. For a management team that has been in existence over a longish period the company's financial performance will give a guide as to their ability. When new management is brought in, the analyst should examine the success in prior jobs of the individuals concerned although this in most cases will be impossible to establish with any great accuracy. Company visits and the news media will be found helpful in estimating managements' attitudes and views. The analyst should examine the scope for improvements in the business and when allied to his opinion of the new management he should be able to obtain a good idea of the direction, at least, of the company's fortunes. The various operating and efficiency ratios described in Chapter 3 will provide an important basis in assessing managerial ability. Management is exceptionally important in determining a company's profitability but it is perhaps one of the most difficult factors to evaluate and quantify.

## Company visits

Most companies recognise the need for a fair, or better than fair rating for their shares. This will enable them to deter unwanted takeover bids, or at least to obtain a substantial price if acquired, make acquisitions financed by equity issues cheaper, give greater confidence to bankers, and creditors, and to satisfy the various status reasons attached to a successful company. Many companies will therefore be prepared to arrange a meeting with investment analysts from institutional funds and from stockbrokers. These company visits usually entail discussions with senior management and public relations departments and visits to factories and operating divisions. During these various brochures and information sheets will usually be handed out. The type of information that can be gained includes:

1   Details of products, markets to which the company sells, new-product ventures, unprofitable lines and the relevant industry statistics appropriate to the firm.

2 Constraints to growth, factors of production and their constraints, financing constraints, competition.

3 Long-term objectives and plans.

4 Research and Development projects and the nearness of commercial application.

5 Management structure.

6 Importance of external factors such as Government legislation, supplies from abroad, revaluation of currencies.

7 Discussion of past performance, the reasons therefore and comparisons with the analyst's projections.

8 Discussion of accounting policies.

9 Discussion of the analyst's forecasts. Certain 'hypothetical' questions can be put to management who may indicate areas of probability for the outcomes of certain variables.

As can be seen, the type of information obtained can be very substantial for both near- and long-term forecasting. In order to get the best results from the company visit, the analyst should do as much preparatory work on the firm and its industry as possible. This will enable him to ask more relevant questions and management will be more ready to respond to somebody who has obviously put a fair amount of effort in. If the analyst has a pro-forma forecast ready he may find that management will discuss this and the assumptions behind the figures.

Hopefully, the analyst will be able to arrange regular meetings with the company and build up substantial goodwill. The continual assessment and feedback from company visits will readily build up the analyst's expertise on the firm.

### Quantitative techniques in forecasting

So far the chapter has described the projecting of revenues and cost structures from economic data. These have then been used to calculate EPS. There are, however, several quantitative techniques which can be used: (1) to make better use of the basic projections that have been done; and, (2) to help in making the projections. The remainder of the chapter describes these techniques and their practical feasibility. Although they have not gained much more than a toehold at present there is little doubt that these sophisticated techniques will eventually become a pre-requisite to any serious investment analysis.

### Probabilistic forecasting

This technique allows the analyst to incorporate numerous values for the items he is forecasting and probabilities are attached to these factors. From this data a number of EPS figures will be derived each with a probability of occurrence and thus a clearer picture of the company's earnings risk profile is shown. The value of this approach is that in forecasting sales and the various costs, the analyst is likely to come up with a range of estimates depending on various economic, political and market assumptions and the probabilistic model allows him to incorporate all these factors in an objective manner. By using a single point estimate, the analyst will have to discard a lot of information which he has collected and eventually this may influence the analyst to only consider certain variables. The single point forecast is likely to be a subjectively based median value although there is the great danger that an extreme value may be taken. This is very easily done if the analyst starts out with a biased view.

Probabilistic forecasting is especially useful in long-term projections where assumptions have to be made about growth rates, political stability, consumer demand, etc. The model allows various estimates to be used and, as seen later, more sophisticated adaptions incorporate sensitivity analyses which measure the impact on earnings of changing economic assumptions. The technique is also useful when there is a high degree of uncertainty about earnings and its component items. If the analyst feels that the disparity between his high and low estimates of earnings is great, then the probabilistic approach becomes very relevant.

## Probabilistic forecasting as an aid in investment decision making

In using the various EPS figures the analyst will derive a number of intrinsic share price values. Although the investor will be faced with the difficulty of determining his own risk preferences it is surely better to have too much information than too little. The full range of forecasts can be usefully broken down into high, low and the mean or expected value. It is also possible to obtain a computer print-out showing the distribution of earnings in the form of a graph and in the form of a probability distribution. These classifications and visual aids can readily help analysts and investors to get a quick insight of the possible outcomes. By disclosing the array of possible EPS figures or the classifications thereof, the investor will be able to assess more accurately the risks and returns involved. For example, the expected EPS of company A may be 7p but there may be a one-in-a-hundred chance that a high loss could occur which would wipe out the firm's reserves. Such occurrences could be caused by expropriation of foreign assets or a natural catastrophe to a civil engineering project. The investor seeing these odds may not take up the investment whereas if only the single point estimate of 7p were given he might have purchased the share in question. Thus, probabilistic forecasting greatly aids the decision making of investors where they have strong risk aversion and where the EPS are highly uncertain.

## Evaluating possible outcomes

The technique involves assessing the various factors which affect profitability as discussed in the previous part of the chapter but, instead of allocating single figures to the items, the analyst includes all the outcomes he feels are possible. This allows different assumptions to be incorporated. For example, sales of a scrap-metal merchant might be projected as £10 million by the methods previously described (using the most likely outcome). However, the analyst may feel that there is a chance of a boom in capital expenditure by manufacturing industry and that sales could rise to £11 million. To this figure he will attach a probability of occurrence, say, 0.1. He may further think that there is a probability of 0.15 that sterling could be devalued in which case exports would increase by a total of £1 million. Other variables can easily be thought of and incorporated in the model. These various estimates can be represented in the form shown in Figure 4.8. The expected value in

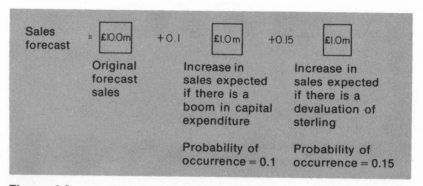

**Figure 4.8**

Simple probabilistic sales forecast model

this simplified situation comes to £10.25 million, i.e. projected sales (£10 million) plus capital expenditure boom (0.1 × £1 million) plus exports increase due to currency realignment (0.15 × £1 million). Analysts will rarely be able to put precise figures to the above factors and so further probabilities will be attached. For example, if there was a devaluation of, say, 10 per cent the increased exports might be £1 million with a probability of 0.7 and £1.5 million with a probability of 0.3. A devaluation of 20 per cent might lead the analyst to expect an increase in sales of £1.5 million with a probability of occurrence of 0.4, £2 million with a probability of 0.4 and £2.5 million with a probability of 0.2. Further, the probabilities of a devaluation of 10 and 20 per cent might be 0.06 and 0.04 respectively and it may be that only one can occur in a year. Figure 4.9 represents the more complex relationship and Figure 4.10 shows the data in the form of a probability tree[10].

**Probability trees**

The tree shows the various possible outcomes, i.e. the maximum sales revenue expected is £13.5 million which occurs if there is a capital expenditure boom and a devaluation of 20 per cent leading to an increase in exports of £2.5 million; the minimum receipts occur if there is no capital expenditure boom and no devaluation, i.e. £10 million. The various branches of the tree also show the probabilities of the

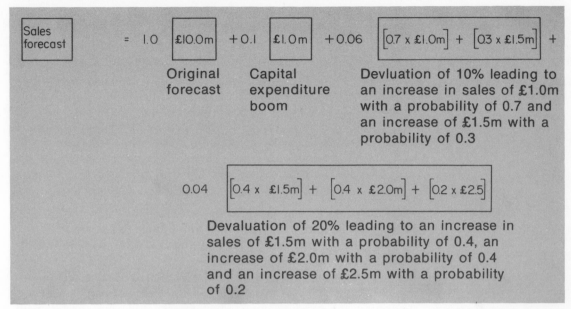

**Figure 4.9**

A more complex probabilistic sales forecast model

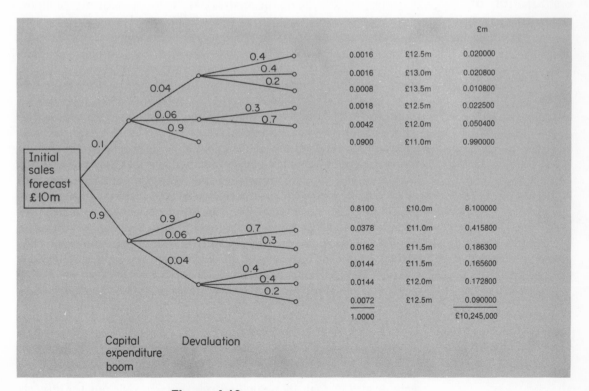

**Figure 4.10**

Probability tree

various returns. These are computed by multiplying the probabilities together (i.e. $0.9 \times 0.04 \times 0.2 = 0.0072$). The total of the probabilities comes to 1. The multiplication of the probabilities by the sales revenues gives the expected value of each possibility and the total of these gives the expected value of £10,245,000[11]. The probability model has therefore shown the expected value (£10,245,000) but also gives the probabilities of other outcomes. The tree shown in Figure 4.10 has twelve outcomes and the reader can readily appreciate how these numbers can grow. The analyst will now make various forecasts of costs and attach probabilities thereto. These will be incorporated into the sales forecasts tree described above. The computational work will now be enormous but this can easily be handled by a computer.

## Event forks and decision forks

Probability networks are a technique often used by company management in deciding upon courses of action to take. Here there are two types of branches in the tree: (1) an event fork which shows the possible outcomes (uncontrolled variables); and, (2) a decision fork showing possible courses of action (controlled variables). The expected monetary values (or utilities) are calculated for each event fork and this determines the decision action to be taken (i.e. following the fork with the highest expected monetary value). For security analysis, however, the only branches are event forks as shown in Figure 4.10.

## Calculation of probabilities

A major problem facing the analyst is the calculation of probabilities. For rare occurrences, such as political upheavals or natural catastrophes, a nominal probability will suffice. This admits the possibility of an event and is shown up in an analysis of high, low and median estimates. The low estimate may indicate the bankruptcy of the company. More common occurrences can be weighted according to past experience, e.g. excessive rainfall affecting crops (or sales of umbrellas!) or labour strikes in, say, Chile, affecting copper supplies. It is apparent, then, that a good deal of judgment has to be exercised in determining weights but the discipline in doing so will ensure that all possible avenues of analysis will be pursued and that personal bias will be minimised. One method that has been used in reducing the workload is to formulate just three estimates for each factor contributing towards the EPS prediction. The estimates would represent the high, low and median or mean values. The median value is that one which is halfway between the high and low whilst the mean figure is the expected value (all outcomes multiplied by their probabilities). If there is a very minute chance of an enormous profit or loss then the use of high and low values may lead to unwarranted optimism or pessimism (the median value would also be affected). In such cases the quartile values could be used* and a note taken of the extreme high and low

---

*This statistic divides the number of items into quarters and the value of that item is the value of the quartile. The first quartile represents the number of items divided by four, the second quartile represents the number of items divided by two (this is the median) and the third quartile is the number of items multiplied by three-quarters.

values. A simplified form of probabilistic EPS model is shown in Figure 4.11. The EPS forecast will be represented by a distribution of values for each year such as shown in Figure 4.12. Here, actual EPS are shown up to 1972 and then the distribution of forecast outcomes are shown up to the year 1977. The mean values are shown as a line through the hump of the distribution, the shaded areas represent the upper and lower quartile ranges and the median is the distance one-half the way along the distribution. The distribution of forecasts could show other statistics such as the standard deviation, i.e. shading the areas outside one standard deviation from the mean.

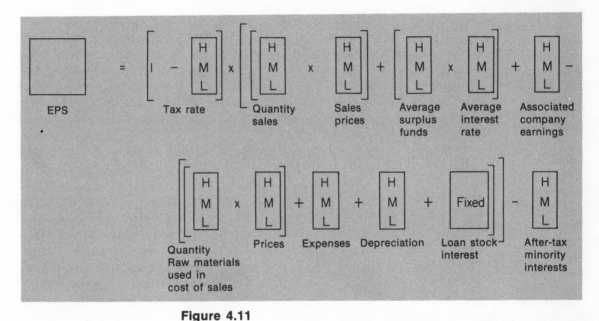

**Figure 4.11**

High, Low and Median outcome probabilistic model

**Computers in probabilistic forecasting**

The number of computations required for building the probabilistic models are very large and a computer is required if there is going to be much application of this technique. Once the model has been built the analyst can easily update his forecasts by using different probabilities and by varying the assumptions. This will provide better information and provide it much more quickly than the single point estimates which have to be worked out longhand. Computers can also facilitate sensitivity analyses which measure the impact on sales, costs, EPS or other dependent variable of changes in one or more of the assumptions or independent variables. There are 'risk analysis' programs available which, whilst built initially for capital expenditure project selection, can be adapted for security analysis. Risk analysis is a sophisticated version of probabilistic forecasting[12].

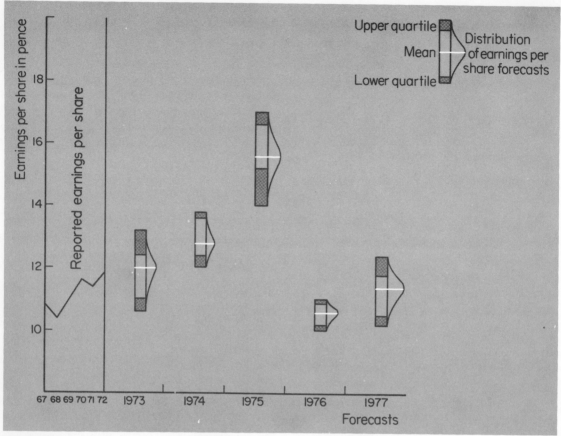

**Figure 4.12**

Probabilistic forecasts of earnings per share

## Benefits from probabilistic forecasting

The advantages of probabilistic forecasting are that it incorporates all data in an objective manner, is relatively free from personal bias, shows all possible outcomes and, perhaps, makes the analyst think that much harder about collecting basic information and its relevance to EPS. The technique will also be helpful in pinpointing where and how the analyst's forecast differed from actual events. Whilst the setting up of the model will be fairly costly, the ease of revising forecasts and the additional information gained will more than compensate for the effort.

## Conditional forecasts

A variant on probabilistic models is the use of conditional forecasting. This analysis derives a relationship between a company's earnings and that of another variable. This, for instance, could be the earnings of the market as a whole and, thus, given a figure of aggregate profits the analyst will be able to derive a figure for the individual firm. One advantage of this model is that it allows different analysts to do various parts of the forecasts, i.e. one analyst can derive an equation for the relationship whilst the economist may forecast the independent variable, the aggregate profits. However, probabilistic forecasts can also utilise several analysts' talents for different parts of the analysis and the various estimates of independent variables, such as aggregate levels of profits, can be incorporated in the model.

The conditional forecast model may take the form:

$A = x + yB$

where *A* could equal company earnings, and *B* equal aggregate earnings with *x* and *y* as coefficients found by regression analysis on past data. Or *A* could be company sales and *B* industry sales. This type of relationship can also be used to compute the marginal rate of return, e.g. for a given increase in (say) sales, gross profit margins will increase by a certain amount. It can therefore take account of the gearing impact of fixed expenses. The expression is, of course, a linear relationship but can accurately represent many real-life business operations. A similar formula could be derived to show, say, the return on capital employed. Thus, for a 10 per cent increase in capital employed the return thereon may increase by 15 per cent. Thus, by examining capital employed at the beginning of the year a guide to likely profits may be given by the equation. The analyst should then examine the reasons why this return has materialised (e.g. new-product lines, closing down of unprofitable divisions, changes in pricing policies). If such conditional forecasts are found to give quite accurate approximations, then the relationships could be used as an initial step in the analysis before the detailed forecasting begins. The formulas can be a lot more complex than this and can take the form of econometric models. Whilst the simple model above is used in individual company share price evaluations, being a relationship of market yields, it is perhaps of little use in profits forecasting. Its main usefulness is where an immediate assessment is needed of a lot of companies and where there is insufficient time for completing the detailed analyses described previously in the chapter.

**Computer models**

Besides making the probabilistic and conditional models described earlier viable, the computer also makes tenable the use of econometric and simulation models. These models can be used to predict both the factors making up the forecast, the most common being turnover, and corporate profits. Simulation involves testing models that have been derived to explain certain processes. The feedback from the simulation is used to correct the model so that it eventually represents as near reality as possible. Simulation involves large amounts of computation and, hence, the need for high-speed computers. The technique is not in great use by analysts because they do not have sufficient data on the company with which to build sophisticated models. In time, however, this approach may well become more viable and the greater detailed breakdown of company activities by the analyst will speed this day.

## Econometrics

Econometrics involves building models and uses statistical regression analyses in the derivation of the weights attached to factors. Regression analysis is described in Chapter 10 and the reader can turn to this chapter now if he wishes to understand the basics of the technique.

The model can include predictor variables, predictor variables and estimates, or solely estimates. Predictor variables are factors which are known in advance of the dependent variable (e.g. the item being forecast, such as, sales or profits). These predictor variables are usually trade or economic indices which are published, say, monthly or three-monthly. Thus, the model expresses the relationship between, say, sales and published data relating to relevant industrial factors. The error term in the model describes the unexplained variance in the model. Estimates are independent factors which are estimated, i.e. they are not known ahead of the dependent variable. Such estimates are, of course, only used where the analyst finds it considerably easier to estimate these factors than the dependent variable itself. There will be very few regression models which use estimated independent variables solely; however, many models, and perhaps the best models, incorporate some estimates.

The advantages of using regression models are that they express mathematical relationships, exclude personal bias of the analyst, can be updated quickly and sensitivity analysis can be carried out easily. However, any estimated variables are usually single-figure forecasts and so the technique is perhaps not as wide ranging a method as probabilistic models (very sophisticated econometric models can incorporate risk analysis).

## Building models

The analyst is likely to derive the important factors for the inclusion in the model and will provide any estimates. These will probably be similar to the details described for probabilistic models. The statistician and computer programmer will write programs and derive the regression coefficients and test the models. After the initial evaluation of weights and the testing thereof, the analyst will be consulted for feedback until a successful model has been achieved.

### Summary

The chapter has outlined the methodologies and particular techniques of forecasting company profits. It makes use of all available public knowledge about the company and derives relationships to interpret this basic data. The analyst commences by looking at past financial data to obtain measures of performance and then examines the business factors which determined that profitability. The main growth constraints to the business and the important profit determinant factors can often be obtained at this stage. The deriving and testing of leading indicators (usually trade statistics) will then be made and after experimentation a number of indicators will probably be found that can help forecast profits of the company with reasonable accuracy.

From the indicators, and from half-yearly reports and news about the specific company, the analyst will derive current year profits. Future years' profits can then be estimated, obviously with less accuracy, by using similar techniques and incorporating industry reviews of long-term forecasts. The analyst will use specific techniques which will enable him to improve the results from the above data. Regression models can be built for forecasting the various factors contributing to the Profit and Loss Account and these can incorporate quite sophisticated relationships. Probabilistic models give ranges of earnings depending on different assumptions and estimates made about the various factors. These estimates are given probabilities of occurrence by the analyst. Thus an investor can examine the different likely outcomes, the assumptions behind each, and can evaluate whether he is prepared to take the risk involved. Computers have made the above techniques feasible and along with sensitivity testing have allowed the implications of new information to be quickly evaluated. However, a lot of work is needed before a model can be built and thus the regression and probabilistic techniques have not gained very much acceptance up to the present. However, once built, the updating and adaptation of the models will be very quick, much quicker than evaluating data in the traditional way.

The analyst will find that his forecasts may be very wrong on some occasions but he should use this positively and examine his original assumptions[13]. Experience will give greater insight into business behaviour and make profits forecasts more accurate. The forecasting of company profits and future prospects, although very difficult, forms the basis of most investment decision making and is vitally important in economic planning.

### Appendix

This appendix references some of the more usual sources of industry and economic statistics[14]. The analyst specialising in particular sectors will be able to considerably augment this list. For young analysts who have not specialised very long in a sector the references should prove useful and he will be able to improve on it in time.

### *Economic*

1  Annual Abstract of Statistics

2  National Income and Expenditure (Blue Book)

These annual publications are supplemented during the year by

1  Monthly Digest of Statistics (Green Book)

2  Financial Statistics

3  Economic Trends

4  DTI Journal

Further Government publications include White Papers produced by the Treasury and Statistics on Incomes, Prices, Employment and Production.

To these can be added forecasts and statistics of the economy prepared by various independent groups such as the National Institute of Economic and Social Research (published quarterly in the *Economic Review*), Confederation of British Industries (*Industrial Trends*), The Bank of England (*Quarterly Bulletin*), London Graduate School of Business Studies business forecasts published in the *Sunday Times*. Other useful publications include *Framework Forecasts, Business Forecasts, Business Ratios, The Economist, Management Today* and *Times Review of Industry*.

### Industrial

1   Census of Production Reports which are produced every few years, the last being in 1968. Smaller censuses carried out on samples of firms are made in the intervening years. The census divides the respondents into industrial classifications and provides data on numbers of employees and their wages, raw materials purchased, value of manufactured goods bought, transport costs, analyses of stocks, capital expenditure, total production, and sales. A major drawback to the data is that it is not published until two or three years after the year to which it relates.

2   Reports by the National Economic Development Council. There are various committees for different industries and they produce reports giving financial statistics and publishing constraints and prospects relevant to that industry.

3   Reports of the Monopolies Commission.

4   Trade journals. These are varied in nature and content and the analyst can build up a lengthy reading list. The journals can range from those that give statistics and forecasts of future performance at the industry or at individual firm level, to those that just discuss various items of technical interest to the trade. The analyst will soon discover which information sources give the best data and those that need only be skimmed through.

The major industrial trade journals include the following.

| Industry | Journal |
| --- | --- |
| Aircraft | *Flight* |
| | *Flying Review International* |
| Banks | *Banker* |
| | *Bankers' Magazine* |
| Breweries | *Brewing Trade Review* |
| Building | *Building* |
| | *Build International* |

| Industry | Journal |
|---|---|
| | *Construction News* |
| | *Construction Trends* |
| | *Development & Materials Bulletin* (GLC) |
| | *House Builder and Estate Developer* |
| | *Housing & Planning Review* |
| | *Housing Review* |
| | *Housing Statistics* |
| | *Monthly Bulletin of Construction Statistics* |
| | *National Builder* |
| Chemicals | *Chemical Age* |
| | *European Chemical News* |
| Electronics & computers | *Computer Survey* |
| | *Data Processing* |
| Engineering & machine tools | *Machine Tool Review* |
| | *Machine Tool Engineering* |
| | *Metalworking Production* |
| Food | *Food World* |
| | *Grocer* |
| Heavy electricals | *Electrical Review* |
| Hire purchase | *Credit* |
| Insurance | *Bests Review* |
| | *Policy Holder* |
| Investment trusts and unit trusts | *Money Management* |
| Mining & commodities | *Investors' Guardian* |
| | *Mining Journal* |
| | *Mining Magazine* |
| | *Optima* |
| | *Platinum Metals Review* |
| | *World Metal Statistics* |
| Motors | *Monthly Statistical Review* (Society of Motor Manufacturers Trades) |
| Office equipment | *Business Equipment Buyers Guide* |
| Oil | *Oil and Gas International* |
| | *Petroleum Press Service* |
| | *Petroleum Review* |
| | *Petroleum Times* |
| Paper | *World's Paper Trade Review* |
| Property | *Estates Gazette* |
| Rubber manufacturing | *Rubber Statistical Bulletin* |
| Shipbuilding | *Shipbuilding and Shipping Record* |
| Shipping | *Lloyds Register of Shipping* |
| | *Shipping World and Shipbuilder* |
| Stores | *Retail Business* |
| | *Which?* |

*Investment analysis*

| Industry | Journal |
|----------|---------|
| Textile, clothing and footwear | *Footwear Industry Statistical Review* |
| | *Textile Monthly* |
| Tobacco | *Wool Year Book* |
| | *Tobacco* |
| | *Tobacco Intelligence* |
| | *World Tobacco* |

The major sources of financial statistics relating to individual companies are those services run by Exchange Telegraph (Extel) and by Moodies Services Ltd. These present summarised breakdowns of profits, assets and performance ratios for each company over a number of years. The Stock Exchange Official Year Book summarises financial data and the capital structures of companies quoted on the Stock Exchange. Some agencies provide press-cutting services on individual companies. There are various business publications which are helpful to the analyst, e.g. the 'Directory of Directors' which gives the names of company directors and their directorships, 'Who Owns Whom' which lists parent companies and their subsidiaries, and 'Kompass' and 'Key to British Enterprises' which are directories of trade and industry categorisation.

Companies have to provide the following statutory information under the Companies Acts.

1   Memorandum of Association.

2   Articles of Association.

3   Prospectus.

4   Register of Mortgages and Charges.

5   Register of Directors and Secretaries.

6   Register of Directors' Shareholdings.

7   Register of Members (Shareholders).

8   Register of Debenture Holders.

9   Annual Return.

10   Annual Report and Accounts.

For a description of these items see a text on Company Law[15]. However, it is only the Annual Reports and Accounts which are likely to provide substantial information to the analyst. The Stock Exchange also makes certain requirements by which quoted companies must abide. The most important is the publication of half-yearly interim accounts; other requirements are mainly to do with disclosure of certain facts in the Annual Accounts (e.g. subsidiary company details, the activities of the company, substantial shareholdings) and these are generally extensions to Company Law provisions.

## References

**1** Little, I. M. D., 'Higgledy Piggledy Growth', *Bulletin of the Oxford Institute of Statistics*, Oxford, Vol. 24, No. 2, November 1962. Little, I. M. D. and Rayner, A. C., 'Higgledy Piggledy Growth Again', Oxford, Blackwell, 1966. Similar studies conducted on America data also derived the same conclusions; see, for example, Lintner, J. and Glauber, R., 'Further Observations on Higgledy Piggledy Growth', paper presented to the Seminar on the Analysis of Security Prices, University of Chicago, May 1969.

**2** For a description of time series analysis see: 'Smoothing, Forecasting and Prediction of Discrete Time Series', Brown, R. G., Englewood Cliffs, Prentice Hall, 1963, or: 'Applied General Statistics', Croxton F. E. and Cowden, D. J., Englewood Cliffs, Prentice Hall, 1955.

**3** For example, Box, G. E. P. and Jenkins, G. M., 'Time Series Analysis Forecasting and Control', Holden-Day, 1970.

**4** For empirical proof see: Lintner, J., 'Distribution of incomes of corporations among dividends, retained earnings and taxes', *American Economic Review*, May 1956, and Michaelson, J. B., 'The Determinants of Dividend Policies: a theoretical and empirical study', PhD. dissertation, University of Chicago, 1961.

**5** The empirical evidence here is not so clear-cut as with yearly earnings changes. Green and Segall investigated the predictive usefulness of using quarterly earnings data for full year results and found them to be of no use; Green, D. and Segall, J., 'The predictive power of first-quarter earnings reports', *Journal of Business*, Vol. 40, No. 1, January 1967. However, similar research by Brown and Niederhoffer drew opposite findings and they concluded that quarterly data was useful in predicting annual results; Brown, P. and Niederhoffer, V., 'The predictive content of quarterly earnings', *Journal of Business*, Vol. 41, No. 4, October 1968. There have been no similar studies on UK data although if there were, half-yearly results are all that could be used at present as few companies give quarterly data.

**6** See: Nightingale, R. D., 'Money supply and the stock market', *The Investment Analyst*, No. 23, June 1969.

**7** See, for example, McMahon, C., 'The Techniques of Economic Forecasting', OECD (HMSO), 'The Analysis and Forecasting of the British Economy', Surrey, M. J. C., Cambridge University Press, 1971.

**8** For a description of industrial life-cycles see: 'Exploit the product life cycle', Levitt, T., *Harvard Business Review*, Nov. – Dec. 1965, and: 'Growth Patterns in Industry: a re-examination', Gaston, J. F., New York National Industrial Conference Board, 1961.

**9** See: Mansfield, E., 'Rates of return from industrial Research and Development', *American Economic Review*, May 1965, and Zinbarg, E. D., 'Research and Development – the stockholder's view', *Financial Executive*, July 1965.

**10** For an example of the construction of probability trees see: 'Decision trees for decision making', Magee, J. F., *Harvard Business Review*, Jul. – Aug. 1964.

**11** For a description of probability theory see: 'Probability and Statistics for Business Decisions', Schlaifer, R., McGraw-Hill, 1959, or: 'An Introduction to Probability Theory and its Applications', Feller, W., John Wiley & Sons, 1957.

**12** For a good description of risk analysis see: 'Risk analysis in capital investment', Hertz, D. B., *Harvard Business Review*, 42, Jan. – Feb. 1964. The article deals with project selection but the reader will easily see its use in security analysis.

**13** There has been very little published research on the performance of analysts' earnings forecasts and similarly there has been little research on the forecasting methods used. Cragg and Malkiel in the major piece of research published to date found that their sample of analysts' forecasts made in 1962 and 1963 did not fare much better than those made by using simple extrapolations of past data; see: 'The consensus and accuracy of some predictions of the growth of corporate earnings', *Journal of Finance*, Mar. 1968. For a more positive conclusion on the ability of the market to forecast earnings see: Ball, R. and Brown, P., 'An empirical evaluation of accounting income numbers', *Journal of Accounting Research*, Autumn 1968. They found that most of the information in an earnings announcement had already been anticipated by the market.

**14** For a summary of business and economic statistics see: Edwards, B., 'Sources of Economic and Business Statistics', Heinemann, London 1972.

**15** For example, Gower, L. C. B., 'The Principles of Modern Company Law', Stevens and Sons, 1969.

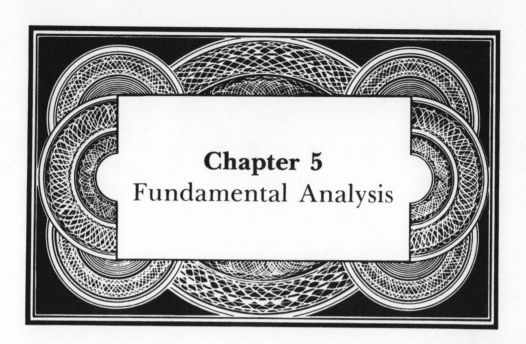

# Chapter 5
## Fundamental Analysis

We have now progressed to the stage where we have studied the company's past performance and made estimates of future earnings and dividend potential. This data has now to be translated into its meaning for share prices and cash dividends, the assessment of which is the *raison d'etre* of investment analysis. The analyst is concerned with forecasting the total return to the shareholders which is made up of cash dividends and movements in the share prices. Investment advisors and portfolio managers will also have to give consideration to the tax considerations and risk aversion requirements of their clients. It is the share price component of an investor's total return that provides the variability in the return – it provides the greatest annual gains and can produce annual losses (there are no negative cash dividends). Table 5.1 shows the percentage differences between the 'highs' and 'lows' in the market indices of the major stock exchanges in the ten years 1963 to 1972. This clearly shows the magnitude of changes in share price movements and highlights the importance of investment timing. Figure 5.1 shows the movement of the FTA Ordinary Share Index from May 1962 to 1973* and Figure 5.2 shows the percentage quarterly changes in the FTA All Share Index. These more detailed analyses again show the significant variability in Stock Market levels. All this does not mean that dividends do not count in investment appraisal for, as will be described later, the growth rate of dividends forms the main basis of many share price evaluation models. Thus,

*Figure 5.1 has been drawn on log scale which shows the proportionate movements.

**Table 5.1**

Percentage annual change in national Stock Market indices

| | 1963 % | 1964 % | 1965 % | 1966 % | 1967 % | 1968 % | 1969 % | 1970 % | 1971 % | 1972 % | 10-year total % |
|---|---|---|---|---|---|---|---|---|---|---|---|
| US | 19.7 | 12.8 | 9.5 | −12.6 | 12.3 | 10.4 | −13.3 | −2.5 | 12.3 | 14.3 | 34.5 |
| Canada | 10.7 | 20.7* | 1.7 | −12.4 | 9.9 | 15.0 | −0.2 | −6.4 | 12.6 | 23.1 | 94.8 |
| UK | 17.6 | −9.5 | 6.7 | −7.7 | 10.8 | 46.0* | −15.8 | −9.8 | 42.6 | 0.6 | 61.6 |
| Germany | 11.1 | 1.6 | −15.7 | −18.7 | 45.9 | 10.2 | 19.8 | −26.7 | 19.6 | 14.6 | 49.7 |
| France | −16.3 | −3.7 | −7.0 | −11.8 | −4.1 | 9.7 | 14.4 | −8.7 | −2.7 | 20.0 | −15.2 |
| Netherlands | 14.1 | 6.0 | −11.5 | −20.0 | 33.0 | 32.7 | −8.0 | −10.8 | −3.2 | 23.6 | 48.4 |
| Belgium | 13.7 | 4.1 | −6.5 | −25.0 | 16.8 | 6.6 | 1.1 | 1.8* | 16.4 | 26.5 | 56.6 |
| Italy | −16.1 | −29.8 | 24.4* | 4.9* | −6.5 | −0.2 | 11.2 | −20.3 | −14.8 | 11.5 | −39.6 |
| Australia | 22.6* | 3.1 | 11.7 | 2.5 | 61.5* | 23.8 | 15.8 | −21.1 | −4.7 | 17.8 | 196.8 |
| Japan | 4.4 | 5.6 | 15.4 | 4.8 | −8.9 | 21.3 | 28.6* | −15.6 | 48.6* | 121.2* | 425.6 |

*Best performing market in each year
Source: Capital International SA
Capital international indices, adjusted for exchange fluctuations relative to US dollar

dividend expectations influence share prices even though the cash receipt may form only a small part of the return for a given year. There are two quite distinct methods of forecasting future share price performances. One is fundamental analysis which utilises the earnings and dividends forecasts which were described in Chapter 4. The other is technical analysis which relies on patterns in share prices or on mechanical strategies. This chapter concentrates on fundamental analysis whilst technical analysis is covered in Chapter 6.

## Fundamental analysis in share selection

There are a number of 'fundamental' techniques which can be used by analysts in selecting shares. Firstly, the analyst can estimate the 'intrinsic worth' of a share and then compare it against the market price. He will then buy, sell or do neither depending on whether the intrinsic value is above, below or the same as the current market price. This is based on the assumption that the market will eventually come to the same view of the value of the share as the analyst. Secondly, the analyst can compare his estimates of earnings and dividend potential against what he believes the market is anticipating and accordingly buys, sells or does neither[1]. This does not involve deriving a 'right' share price. The method is based on the assumption that the existing share prices represent average market opinion of the company's prospects, and share purchase recommendations will be made when the analyst is forecasting better results than the market is expecting. This method is prevalent when the analyst has no firm idea of which way the market as a whole is going or if he does not feel confident about interpreting earnings and dividend figures into share price equivalents. The analyst therefore has to forecast company profits and to estimate what the market is expecting (the 'market' being average

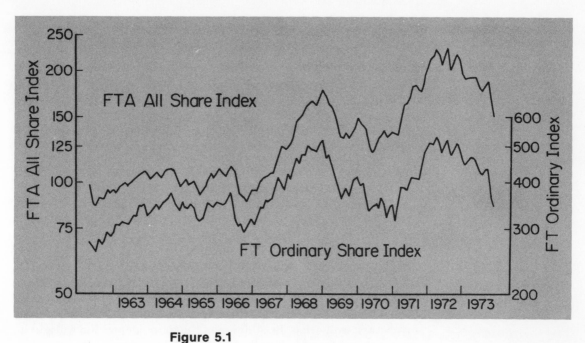

**Figure 5.1**

Movement of the FTA all share index and the FT ordinary share index from May 1962 to December 1973

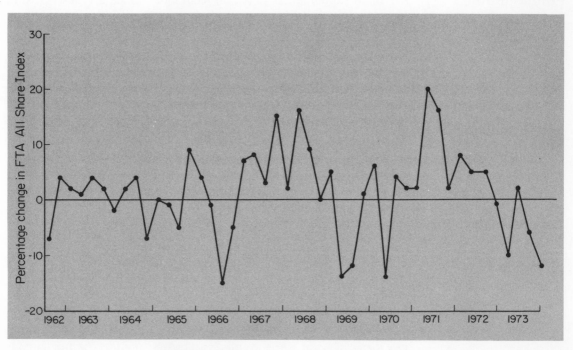

**Figure 5.2**

Percentage quarterly changes in the FTA all share index

opinion). Thirdly, the analyst can rank companies as to which offer the best growth prospects in terms of dividends and share prices and select those which appear to be the most undervalued. Although this is a ranking method it is not a mechanical strategy as it relies on fundamental forecasting and not on purely historical data. This type of evaluation is again prevalent when the analyst has no firm view of what the market as a whole is likely to do. Additionally, it is a useful analysis when the analyst places little reliance on any longer-term forecasting and therefore the compilation of intrinsic values.

In practice an analyst probably uses all of the above methods either in total or in part. For example, any intrinsic values would probably be stated in the form of a range, i.e. 'worth at least 100p'; if this value was well above the market price the analyst would consider making a purchase. However, before doing so, he will check on what grounds and premises the market was evaluating the company and reappraise his own forecasts. Additionally, the analyst will rank the shares by cheapness and by risk and select accordingly. The above fundamental approaches have considered one share but investment managers need to have regard to the portfolio characteristics of the security. This will involve assessing what the addition of the share in question will add in terms of return and risk to the portfolio. These assessments may well fall to the analyst. Chapter 7 describes portfolio building and discusses theoretical and practical considerations.

## Fundamental valuation techniques

The main fundamental valuation techniques which are described in this chapter and which are explicitly and implicitly in practical use can be classified as follows:

1   The intrinsic value approach which treats stock selection as a discounting operation in the same manner as capital expenditure project selection. The purchase of a share is a present capital expenditure which gives the right to a stream of future dividends and to a terminal liquidation payment.

2   The evaluation of a market yield that can be given to a company and applying this to the forecast dividends and earnings. The most common yield used in such methods is the price/earnings (P/E) ratio. These methods involve establishing relationships between yields, earnings and dividends and their growth rates.

3   Modelling approaches. These vary in sophistication from those giving a simple linear relationship to those incorporating many variables. The models attempt to establish relationships between share prices and various 'predictor variables'. The variables used will include historical data as well as forecasted factors. The approach is based on being able to determine the important factors affecting share price movements and on being able to forecast them.

The techniques all rely heavily on estimates of future earnings and dividends and the forecasting of such is an enormously important part of the analyst's job. If a company appears cheap, the investor will buy on the assumption that the market will come to the same view (partly or completely). The time taken for the price to adjust towards the analyst's value, assuming he is correct, may take up to a year. This is because the models are based on forecasts of future profitability and it may be up to one year before the investing public can measure the analyst's success in predicting the first year's earnings and dividends (most models are heavily weighted on the next year's figures). Before the analyst's value is reached the share price may be expected to vary roughly in line with the appropriate industrial share price index. Models have been built to explain the relationships between individual prices and market indices and these can be useful in predicting short-term share price behaviour. These models are described later.

## Valuation of convertible loan stocks

An equity analyst may also have to make evaluations of the worth of convertible loan stocks for the companies he specialises in. The major factor in determining the price of a convertible is, of course, the market price of the equity into which the loan stock can be eventually converted. Other influences in the price behaviour include: (1) the income differential between the loan stock yield and the dividend yield; (2) the safety of the convertible compared with the equity. This involves looking at the 'gearing' ratios described in Chapter 3; (3) the number of opportunities available for conversion. Typically, the loan stock is convertible into ordinary shares during one month in a number of stated years; (4) the time before the first opportunity for conversion. The further away the conversion date the less attractive the loan stock will be. A number of models have been derived which have measured both the theoretical and actual price performance of convertibles against existing equities. These have produced some strong correlations but in order to predict the future performance a correct forecast of equity prices will be required. The interested reader should refer to the specialist papers on this subject[2].

## Warrants

Models also exist for the pricing of warrants[3], which are the most volatile of equity issues. Basically, these are an option to purchase shares at a given price. A number of British companies have made such issues although they have been small in size. Theoretically and in practice (to date) a case can be made for investors not exercising their warrant options to buy the shares and thus they are an interest free capital issue by the company. The theoretical value of a warrant is given by the expression

$$\text{Theoretical value} = \left(\begin{array}{c}\text{market price of} \\ \text{ordinary shares}\end{array} - \begin{array}{c}\text{option} \\ \text{price}\end{array}\right) \times \begin{array}{c}\text{No. of shares} \\ \text{each warrant} \\ \text{entitles owner} \\ \text{to purchase}\end{array}$$

In practice, warrants sell above the theoretical values and thus they will not be exercised by investors. The reasons for the warrants being priced above the theoretical value is because of the speculative appeal of high personal gearing.

The valuation of convertibles and warrants is a specialised area but one which relies heavily on the price of the associated equity shares. Thus, the correction valuation of equities will be the main requirement for profitable investment in convertibles and warrants. Neither of these two securities, however, figure very prominently in the British Stock Market.

### The normative value of a share

When an investor buys a share he expects to receive in the future cash dividends, usually on an annual or semi-annual basis, and a cash receipt from any sale of the security. The purchaser of his share will likewise expect to receive cash dividends plus the proceeds of any subsequent sale. If the shareholder does not sell his shares during his lifetime, a deemed disposal will arise when he dies and the market value of the share will form the basis of the valuation[4]. Sometimes companies are taken over and investors receive cash or securities of the bidding company in exchange. More rarely, limited companies are wound up and as long as they are not insolvent the shareholders will receive a cash payment. From all this it can be seen that the financial rewards of holding a share are represented by the right to receive all future dividends until the share is sold plus the proceeds of the sale. The purchase of a share is thus a capital expenditure decision involving an initial outlay and the receipt of a future stream of income represented by dividends and proceeds of sale.

## Return on an investment

When an investor buys a share he will be of the opinion that the future cash inflows will be greater than his outlay by an amount to at least give him the necessary reward he requires. After having bought the share the process is similar: the analyst evaluating future benefits against the current share price which is the cash equivalent he can realise. The return on investment is shown thus:

$$MP_0 = D_1(1+i)^{-1} + D_2(1+i)^{-2} + D_3(1+i)^{-3} \ldots + D_n(1+i)^{-n}$$
$$+ MP_n(1+i)^{-n} \qquad 1$$

which reduces to $MP_0 = \dfrac{D(1-(1+i)^{-n})}{i} + MP_n(1+i)^{-n} \qquad 2$

IF $D_1 = D_2 = D_3 \ldots$

$MP_0$ = market price paid for share

$D_{1,2,3}$ = dividend for each year

$MP_n$ = sale proceeds of share at year $n$ (or final liquidation or takeover payment)

$i$ = yield (the return on investment expressed as a percentage).

When the sale proceeds equals the cost ($MP_n = MP_0$) and $D_1 = D_2 = D_3 \ldots$, expression 2 becomes $MP_0 = D/i$ or $i = D/MP_0$ which is the dividend yield. In practice, of course, dividends change with time and the second expression is normally only seen in relation to fixed-interest stocks. The figure for $i$ is calculated from the formula and represents the return to the investor on his original expenditure expressed usually as a percentage per year*. If $i$ is below the rate of return he expects from that share the investor will not purchase it. If the investor already owns the share he should substitute the current market price for the cost price (i.e. $CMP_0$ for $MP_0$) and re-evaluate $i$. If $i$ is still too small the investor should sell; if $i$ is greater than the return the investor expects from this sort of investment and offers a better return than other forms of investment, he should buy more. The return, $i$, which an investor requires, varies according to the individual's preference as regards risk and the alternative uses he could put the money to. It ought, however, to be above the riskless rate of interest which is given by the current yields on gilt-edged Government stocks.

## Present value approach

Another way of assessing a share's value is to measure its 'present value' (PV). This involves deriving estimates of future cash inflows (dividends and sale proceeds) and discounting them back to the present day†. Thus, the present value is a capitalisation of future cash flows. PV is notationally described as follows:

$$PV = \frac{D_1}{(1+r)^1} + \frac{D_2}{(1+r)^2} + \frac{D_3}{(1+r)^3} + \cdots \frac{D_n}{(1+r)^n} + \frac{P_n}{(1+r)^n} \qquad 3$$

where $D_{1,2,3}$ = dividends in each year

$r$ = discount rate. These can vary from year to year, i.e. $r_1$, $r_2$, $r_3$

$P_n$ = sale proceeds or any terminal receipt

The PV figure is compared against the current market value and if greater, a purchase is implied; if below, a sale is implied. The discount rate used will be that which represents an adequate return to the investor for his risk taking (it will be the yardstick against which $i$ was measured in expressions 1 and 2 above). Formula 3 is similar to formula 1 but instead of $i$ being calculated, it is the present value PV which is being derived°. If $i$ is substituted for $r$ in equation 3 the PV will equal $CMP_0$, i.e. the current market price. The present value gives an absolute figure for profit, whilst $i$ gives the profit in the form of an annual rate of return.

The normative models above give precise and correct answers if future dividends and share prices are known with certainty and if the investor

---

*This is known as the internal rate of return method and it assumes that dividends can be reinvested at the internal rate of return.

†The technique of discounting is dealt with in Chapter 10.

°Note $(1+i)^{-n} = \dfrac{1}{(1+i)^n}$. Therefore, equation 3 could be written:

$$PV = D(1+r)^{-1} + D_2(1+r)^{-2} \ldots$$

has well defined risk preferences. The only requirements for these models are knowledge of future dividends, takeover bids, share prices and discount rates (the latter being determined to some extent by returns from other investments)! The following methods provide the practical approaches to fundamental security analysis. The intrinsic value technique is broadly similar to the normative models described above. The model does not usually have any estimate of terminal share prices within it and discounts long-term dividends or dividend growth rates. The P/E models involve deriving relationships between yields, earnings and dividends and attaching them to future profits forecasts. Computer models establish associations between various factors and share price performance. In practice, the techniques borrow certain facets from other models and often an analyst will use several methods and compare the differences.

## Taxation

Nothing yet has been said about taxation on dividends and capital gains even though this has a considerable impact on the returns to the investor. It is the investment adviser or portfolio manager who will have to appraise the effects of taxation on the investor; the analyst will concentrate on forecasting the gross returns although he may, if he has the requisite knowledge, advise on taxation. Chapter 9 will give an outline of the tax liabilities of different funds. Pension funds, for example, do not generally bear taxation of any form, investment and unit trusts bear capital gains tax of 15 per cent, whilst private individuals are taxed at the rate of 30 per cent for capital gains and 33 per cent for dividend income (1974/5). The investment adviser or portfolio manager should examine the after tax returns to the investor. However, analysts, specialising in particular shares, will be engaged in determining share prices before any capital gains tax, and forecasting dividends either gross or net of standard rate income tax.

### Intrinsic value[5]

The intrinsic value approach to investment analysis involves deriving an absolute price or a range of prices for a share by discounting future dividends. It does not rank against other shares and does not involve estimating the level of the market, although these factors can be incorporated. The intrinsic value is compared against the current market quotation and investment decisions made accordingly.

## Discounting of dividends

The Intrinsic Value Theory states that the true value of a share is the present value of all future receipts received by the shareholder. The technique is therefore very similar in concept to the normative models described earlier although the variables are forecasts. Instead of forecasting terminal share prices the analyst discounts all future dividends or, in practice, dividend growth rates. Share prices are in fact determined by dividend expectations and so, instead of trying to estimate terminal share prices which can fluctuate considerably within short time periods, the analyst forecasts the perhaps more stable dividend prospects. There are a number of variants used in the intrinsic value technique and these will be discussed later.

The intrinsic value formula is very similar to expression 3 except that there is no terminal share price. Thus:

$$V = \frac{D_1}{(1+r_a)^1} + \frac{D_2}{(1+r_b)^2} + \frac{D_3}{(1+r_c)^3} \cdots + \frac{D_n}{(1+r_z)^n} \qquad 4$$

where $V$ = intrinsic value

$D_{1,2,3,\ldots,n}$ = dividend in each year, per share

$r_{a,b,c,\ldots,z}$ = discount rate which may vary from year to year (This will be discussed later.)

As can be seen $V = $ PV in equation 3.

**Use of growth rates**

Equation 4 requires analysts' forecasts of all future dividends which are derived via the processes described in Chapter 4. It is obviously impractical to make detailed analyses of the longer term and so the analyst reverts to estimating growth rates. These greatly simplify the calculations involved and allow the analyst to easily measure the impact of using different growth rates and discount rate assumptions. The intrinsic value of a share whose current dividend is $D$ and which is expected to grow at rate $g$ per annum compound and whose discount rate is $r$ for all years is given by:

$$V = \frac{D}{1+r} + \frac{D(1+g)}{(1+r)^2} + \frac{D(1+g)^2}{(1+r)^3} \cdots \qquad 5$$

This reduces to:

$$V = \frac{D}{r-g} \quad \text{or} \quad r = \frac{D}{V} + g \qquad 6$$

Thus, given the constant growth and discount rates this says the yield on a share to infinity is its current dividend yield plus the growth rate*. This 'true' yield is compared against other investment alternatives.

*Example* A company's share price is 80p and its current dividend is 12p per share. The analyst regards the dividend as not being abnormal and forecasts a growth rate to infinity of 6 per cent. The forecast yield on the share is therefore:

$$r = \frac{D}{V} + g$$

$$r = \frac{12}{80} + 0.06$$

$$r = 0.15 + 0.06$$

$$r = 0.21 \text{ or } 21\%$$

*The formula will only yield meaningful results if $r$ is greater than $g$. If not, there is no upper limit to the intrinsic value. In everyday terms if a company grew faster than the discount rate for ever, it would eventually control the world's resources.

The constant growth rate equation shown above is often shown in a form incorporating continuous compounding of $g$ and $r$, such that the intrinsic value is the integral:

$$V = D \int_o^\alpha \exp(gt) \exp(-rt) \, dt \qquad\qquad 7$$

Thus, the intrinsic value is equal to current dividends $D$ growing at rate $g$ and discounted by the rate $r$ over infinitely small time periods $dt$. This formula when integrated or infinitely summed reduces to the form $V = D/(r - g)$ which has already been met above (equation 6).

## Calculation of growth rates

The analyst should forecast individual dividends and earnings as far ahead as possible. If these become very tenuous they can be used as the basis for calculating growth rates. The long-term forecasting procedures outlined in Chapter 4 will also provide data for growth rate assumptions. In practice, historical growth rates are often projected into the future for a number of years. At the end of this period an industry or economic growth average will be assumed. This especially applies where the company's historical growth rate has been greater than that of the economy.

## Possible problems in use of constant growth rates

When using constant growth rates it is important to use normalised 'dividends', otherwise no matter how accurate the growth rate projections are, the results will go badly astray*. This does not matter with the model of the form of equation 4 as growth rates are not used and dividends at all stages of the industrial cycle are taken account of. Other problems that can arise with the use of growth rates are that it may make analysts shirk from making explicit forecasts when these are feasible, and the method does not reveal specific bad years which affect short-term prices and risk factors.

## A practical approach to intrinsic value

The recommended intrinsic value approach is to use a combination of individual years' forecasts as in equation 4 and the use of a terminal growth rate as in equation 6 or 7. The analyst's individual year projections will be used for as long as he feels he can forecast with reasonable accuracy and then a growth rate is added to the final projection. The final projection to which the growth rate is applied should be a 'normalised' dividend for the reasons just discussed. In practice this may involve taking the average of the last, say, three years' figures. The expression for the intrinsic value would now look like:

$$V = \frac{D_1}{(1+r_a)^1} + \frac{D_2}{(1+r_b)^2} + \frac{D_3}{(1+r_c)^3} + \frac{D_4}{(1+r_d)^4} + \frac{\dfrac{D_4}{r_d - g}}{(1+r_d)^4} \qquad 8$$

The first four terms of the right-hand side of the equation are of the form of formula 4 and the final term gives the intrinsic value of the share at the end of year 4 ($D_4/r_d - g$ as in equation 6), discounted to today's value (i.e. divided by $(1+r_d)^4$). Thus, the analyst has made

*Additionally, the analyst will have to consider the impact on dividends of any convertible loan stocks which the company has outstanding.

Fundamental analysis

individual forecasts for each of the next four years and has then forecasted a terminal growth rate.

*Example*   The forecast dividends for the next five years of XYZ LTD are as follows: 10p, 10p, 11p, 10p, 14p. The terminal growth rate is 9 per cent and the discount rate is a constant 12 per cent*. Substituting into the equation, the intrinsic value is given as:

$$V = \frac{10.0p}{1+0.12} + \frac{10.0}{(1+0.12)^2} + \frac{11.0}{(1+0.12)^3} + \frac{10.5}{(1+0.12)^4} + \frac{14.0}{(1+0.12)^5}$$

$$+ \frac{\dfrac{14.0}{0.12-0.09}}{(1+0.12)^5}$$

$$V = 8.93 + 7.97 + 7.83 + 6.68 + 7.94 + 264.6$$

$$V = 303.95$$

The investor should purchase shares in XYZ LTD if the market price is below 304p. In practice, of course, the investor will have to assess the costs involved and the time and effort spent. He may therefore only buy if the price is below say, 290p.

**The use of several growth rates**

The analyst may feel that he can estimate an above average growth rate over the next few years but that after this period he can only forecast growth at some historic industrial average. Thus, the intrinsic value model will incorporate more than one growth rate. The following expression shows a model which is made up of individual year's dividends for four years ($D_1$, $D_2$, $D_3$ and $D_4$), then a growth rate of $g_1$ projected on $D_4$ for five years, then a growth rate of $g_2$ projected on the dividend value in year 9 for five years, plus a final growth rate $g_3$ projected on the dividend value in year 14. The discount rate $r$ can vary from year to year (i.e. $r_a$, $r_b$ etc.) although in practice it is often taken to be constant.

$$V = \frac{D_1}{1+r} + \frac{D_2}{(1+r_a)^2} \cdots \frac{D_4}{(1+r_c)^4} + \frac{D_4(1+g_1)}{(1+r_d)^5} + \frac{D_4(1+g_1)^2}{(1+r_e)^6} \cdots$$

$$+ \frac{D_4(1+g_1)^5}{(1+r_h)^9} + \frac{D_4(1+g_1)^5(1+g_2)}{(1+r_i)^{10}} + \frac{D_4(1+g_1)^5(1+g_2)^2}{(1+r_j)^{11}}$$

$$\cdots + \frac{D_4(1+g_1)^5(1+g_2)^5}{(1+r_m)^{14}} + \frac{\dfrac{D_4(1+g_1)^5(1+g_2)^5}{r_m - g_3}}{(1+r_m)^{14}} \qquad 9$$

It is quite simple to incorporate more growth rates – each new rate is projected on the final dividend at the previous growth rate and the final term is that of equation 6 discounted to today's value. As in any growth rate projection the factor $D$ to be projected ($D_4$ above) should be normalised. The reader can substitute various estimates for the factors $D_1$, $D_2$, $D_3$, $D_4$, $g_1$, $g_2$, $g_3$, and $r$, $r \ldots r_m$ to evaluate the intrinsic

*The discount rate is the minimum rate of return the investor requires from the share to meet his selection criterion. The choice of the discount rate is dealt with later.

value[6]. As time progresses the intrinsic value as given by the expression $V = D/r - g$ will increase (if dividends increase). This is intuitively obvious as $r - g$ stays constant whilst the numerator, $D$, increases.

## Incorporating terminal share prices in models

An alternative to using a terminal growth rate is to estimate the share price at this date. The model is the same as in equation 9 except that the final term is replaced by the forecast share price discounted back to today's values. The terminal share price is usually derived as some multiple of the last dividend or earnings forecast. These multiples are often based on growth rates and thus the same assumptions and forecasts are required as those required in using equation 6. The derivation of market yields applicable to a company is given in the section on P/E models.

## Discounting of earnings

Instead of discounting dividends some analysts discount earnings. The advantages of this are: (1) dividends are an appropriation of earnings and so any forecast of dividends implicitly requires a projection of earnings; (2) dividends tend to rise in steps and the analyst will find these difficult to forecast as they require not only information on profitability but also managerial attitudes to dividends; (3) if a company is expanding quickly it may not increase its dividends for a number of years and this would not represent the true growth in the assets or earning power of the company. The analyst who was not aware of the nature and extent of the circumstances may automatically project dividends per share without any adjustments. Additionally, some companies do not pay dividends at all and so earnings have to be used.

The earnings that are used in the model are often multiplied by a forecast of the payout ratio*. This, of course, gives an estimated dividend, i.e. if the analyst forecasts EPS for the succeeding five years as 12p, 12.5p, 15p, 16p and 20p, and the payout ratio is estimated as 0.6, then the intrinsic value formula becomes

$$V = \frac{12 \times 0.6}{1 + r} + \frac{12.5 \times 0.6}{(1 + r)^2} + \frac{15 \times 0.6}{(1 + r)^3} + \frac{16 \times 0.6}{(1 + r)^4} + \frac{20 \times 0.6}{(1 + r)^5} + \frac{\dfrac{20 \times 0.6}{r - g}}{(1 + r)^5}$$

Some models, however, do not make this adjustment, although the analyst will use a higher discount rate or make some adjustment to the computed intrinsic value. Because of the high rates of inflation, earnings are needed to replace existing production capacity (i.e. maintain real earnings) and so the real growth is hidden. For this reason growth in dividends is often regarded as a better surrogate of a company's growth and so a payout ratio is attached to the earnings

*This ratio was described in Chapter 3. It represents the percentage of earnings paid out as dividends. The introduction of the imputation system has created different 'versions' of EPS and therefore different payout ratios. The analyst should be aware of the differences and use the method which gives the best forecasting results. The definition adopted in Chapter 3 was that of the maximum dividend that could be paid but the actual payout ratio may be the more appropriate statistic in the modelling approach.

forecast. However, as described above, high growth companies may retain substantial earnings and in these cases the use of payout ratios in the model may well be spurious[7]. The methods of forecasting payout ratios were given in Chapter 4.

## Discounting inflation-adjusted earnings

From 1974 quoted companies have been recommended to prepare and publish a supplementary set of accounts which take account of inflation. The earnings of the company under the CPP method will be the historical accounts figure plus the impact of inflation on the firm's assets and liabilities. If CPP earnings are used in the discounting process then this will allow for the replacement of assets such that the company can maintain its physical output (strictly this will be represented by 'replacement accounting' earnings but CPP figures should give, in most cases, a reasonable approximation). The analyst thus has the choice of using CPP earnings in the numerators of his formula and these will represent the 'real' rate of growth after allowing for inflation in assets and liabilities (again recognising the caveat of using CPP as a surrogate for the individual rates of inflation appropriate to specific assets). The analyst, in using CPP earnings, can apply a rate of growth and a discount rate to the dividends (or earnings times a payout ratio) and the final term in the model will be the value of the assets (i.e. today's CPP assets compounded by the growth expected in the index of retail prices). That is, using equation 6:

$$V = \frac{E(\text{CPP}) \times P}{r - g} + \frac{\text{Net assets (CPP)}}{r - g_1}$$

where  $P$ = the payout ratio

$r$ = discount rate

$g$ = real rate of growth in earnings

$g_1$ = growth in assets due to inflation (CPP inflation)

*Note:* The various items making up the net assets will have to be disaggregated and the inflation index applied to each.

The above model assumes no real increase in assets; adjustments could, however, be made to account for this.

## Practical application of intrinsic value

The intrinsic value approach is very applicable when the analyst feels he can make accurate long-term predictions of dividends, earnings and their subsequent growth rates[8]. Because of their relative cost and asset structures, property companies are particularly amenable to this method of evaluation. Similarly, mining companies are commonly evaluated by discounting methods although the assumptions used regarding future mineral prices and costs are usually varied significantly to give the analyst an idea of the different possible outcomes. This is an example of the use of probabilistic forecasting where the various earnings/dividends per share figures produce different intrinsic values. When the appropriate probabilities are attached to the intrinsic values the investor will have a good view of the possible returns from the investment.

## Intrinsic value approach as a check on assumptions inherent in share price forecasts

The intrinsic value technique is also used as a checking technique for other methods of evaluation. If the analyst derives a 'true' share price via, say, computer modelling, he can incorporate this as the intrinsic value and by using a specified discount rate he can derive what growth rate assumptions are implicit in the forecast[9]. He can then reflect on whether those rates are feasible. The same process can be used in determining what growth rates the current market price is expecting. The following shows a very simplified but quick assessment of growth rate assumptions in a current market quotation: company *A* has a dividend yield of 8 per cent. The current yield on gilt-edged stocks (risk free) is 10 per cent. The market may require a premium over the risk free rate of return of 2 per cent for *A*'s stock*. From this the analyst can deduce that the market is expecting the dividend growth of *A* to be 4 per cent, i.e. the required rate of return = risk free rate (10 per cent) plus risk premium (2 per cent) = 12 per cent.

$$\text{Required rate of return} = \text{Dividend yield} \frac{\text{(dividend)}}{\text{(market price)}}$$
$$+ \text{growth rate}$$
$$12\% = 8\% + 4\%$$

The analyst can then assess whether this rate of growth to infinity is likely. He may decide that inflation will grow at 10 per cent and that dividends will grow by a like amount:

i.e. Prospective return = Dividend yield (8%) + Growth rate (10%)

The yield of 18 per cent compares with a required rate of 12 per cent and the share price should therefore be 50 per cent higher (i.e. $18/12 \times$ current price). This assumes the real value of the company's assets is maintained such that it can continue to sustain this rate of growth.

## Intrinsic value of the company in its present state

An alternative approach to valuing a company is to measure the present value of its future net cash flows over the life of the firm plus the present value of the assets at the end of its life. The difference between this and previous approaches is that it assumes some terminal point for the company's existence and does not require determining growth rates to infinity†. This, of course, is an unrealistic picture of most companies' operations as:

1 They continue indefinitely.

2 They expand their assets in areas where they expect to make at least an adequate return.

*Two per cent extra return on market value, not 2 per cent of 10 per cent.

†This approach is therefore directly comparable with the net present value analyses of capital expenditure projects.

**3** The 'real assets' of the company will include intangibles such as consumer and brand loyalty and management expertise which may be reflected in, say, earning above average returns.

However, an analyst may find the model useful in the following circumstances: (1) where a company does have a definite life. This relates mainly to mining companies exploiting just one ore field; (2) comparing two similar companies which can be expected to have the same growth potential; (3) as a check on the previously described models to see what the impact of an indefinite life and the physical growth in a company's operations has over the present value of the company in its current state. The method involves discounting the future net cash flows of the company back to today's value. (This is similar to the discounting of CPP earnings. The growth rates are only applied over the remaining life of the assets, however.) The future cash flows will consist of those generated from the company's trading operations, and those generated from the terminal sale value of the company's assets. The future cash flows will be measured over the average remaining life of the company's assets; the method of deriving this figure was described in Chapter 4, *viz.*:

$$\frac{\text{Gross book value of assets}}{\text{Depreciation charge for the year}} = \text{average expected life of assets}$$

$$\frac{\text{Accumulated depreciation}}{\text{Depreciation charge for the year}} = \text{average expired life of assets}$$

The difference between the two figures gives the average remaining life of the assets. The future cash flows over the remaining life of the company may be compounded at various rates, i.e. cash flows from trading operations (i.e. profits plus depreciation) growing at $g$ per annum; property assets growing at $g_1$ per annum; other capital assets = some scrap value; working capital assets growing at $g_2$ per annum†.

A derivative of this method is to measure the rate of return as if the company's assets were new. Here the cash flows are calculated over the average life of the assets (as opposed to just the average remaining life) and are measured against the replacement values of the current physical assets. (As described in Chapter 4. The CPP accounts will give surrogates for replacement values.)

These approaches to share evaluation can be modified to include growth factors at the end of the average asset life and to include other assumptions. This makes them more realistic although they become more and more like the previously described models. In their basic form the models are mainly useful as a check on the intrinsic value approaches.

---

†A deduction will have to be made representing the present value cost of the future increments required to finance the growth in the working capital.

## Discount rate

The discount rate which reduces future cash inflows to current day values is the time value of money. This is the value investors attach to not being able to spend their money for various periods of time. This value is partly made up of the inconvenience of not having the money to spend, the productive value of the money and partly to inflation which makes goods more expensive to buy. It is the latter factor which causes most of the variability in interest rates. Some texts separate these factors but for all practical purposes the analyst need not go to these lengths. The time factor of money is generally referred to as the risk-free interest rate. There are a number of surrogates used for this rate, notably the yields on gilt-edged securities, deposit account rates, Bank rates, short-term loan rates and long-term loan rates. Unfortunately, these rates vary slightly between one another and assuming the investor does not give his preference the analyst will be left to decide which is the appropriate rate. The rate that is most often used is the average yield on Government gilt-edged securities and this is the yardstick that is recommended for most uses. The dividends and earnings can also be discounted by what is known as a risk premium. This is an additional rate of return the investor requires because of the risk involved. In practice this premium is added to the time value of money factor to produce the overall discounting factor of $r$. Risk and uncertainty are dealt with in the following paragraphs.

## Risk and uncertainty

In addition to the time value of money, investors will expect to receive additional returns from equity investments. This will be because the future returns from a share are not known and the forecasts of such are subject to error. Investors are, in the main, risk averters and, given two similar returns, they will prefer the one which is guaranteed to the one which is only a forecast. The risk or uncertainty* of the return to the investor is made up of imperfect knowledge of all future dividends and share prices which are partly a function of the accuracy of the forecasting of earnings and dividends. Although the investor may be very confident of his estimation of the intrinsic value he cannot be so sure that the market will come quickly to the same opinion at all times. Thus the intrinsic value forecast may be correct but it may take some

---

*Strictly speaking, risk relates to different possible outcomes which have probabilities of occurrence, whilst uncertainty is an event which is unpredictable. Thus, betting on cards or dice is subject to risk as the probabilities are known and the event can be repeated. The return from a share is uncertain as there is no objective probability distribution (past distributions can give valuable information when building subjective risk profiles) and the event cannot be repeated in exactly the same situation (i.e. economic backgrounds change). However, risk and uncertainty are often used synonymously with risk being the prevalent description. This usage will be kept throughout the chapter.

time before the market recognises this and the investor, if he requires the funds for other uses immediately, will have to take a low price. Equity investments are therefore more risky to investors whose surplus funds are not necessarily long term.

The problem now exists of determining how the risk is to be accounted for. One method involves increasing the discount rate so that it includes a risk premium. Another involves deriving subjective probability intrinsic value models, i.e. obtaining a number of intrinsic values, based on different dividends and earnings assumptions, and possibly attaching probabilities thereto. The latter method could give high, mean, median and low estimates of the share prices or a more detailed probability distribution of outcomes. The techniques are similar to the probabilistic forecasting methods described in Chapter 4. It is then up to the investor to decide which investment gives him the best return for the degree of risk he is prepared to accept[10]. A similar approach using certainty equivalents can be adopted. This is a factor which is multiplied to the individual dividend forecasts and represents the amount of cash that an investor would require with certainty to make him indifferent between this certain sum and the uncertain future dividend. The certainty equivalents are derived from the analyst's or the investor's utility functions.

*Example*    An analyst may forecast future dividends of 10p, 15p, 18p and 20p for the next four years. The figures are multiplied by the certainty equivalents and then discounted. The expression may now look like:

$$V = \frac{10 \times 0.8}{1 + r^1} + \frac{15 \times 0.75}{(1 + r)^2} + \frac{18 \times 0.6}{(1 + r)^3} + \frac{20 \times 0.5}{(1 + r)^4} + \text{Terminal value}$$

Here, the certainty equivalent factors change across time as the further the forecasting period is away, the greater the uncertainty.

## Risk premium

The assessment of a risk premium is the extra return investors expect to receive from holding that particular investment. Unfortunately, it is not feasible to ask individual investors for this figure and indeed few could give an explicit answer. The approach that can be adopted is to estimate the risk premium on the average equity investment on the Stock Exchange. A subjective adjustment is then made to allow for the specific characteristics of the particular share. This can include the historic return earned by investors in the particular stock.

## Estimation of average expected returns

The general method of calculating the average expected return on equity investment is to determine the average rate of return earned by investors from dividends and share price increases over some period of time[11]. The assumption here is that investors are expecting these returns to continue. The analyst can adjust this historic rate of return to take account of: (1) current market opinions of the growth in GNP and the share attributable to corporate profits; (2) projections of historic trends in the variability of returns; (3) specific adjustments made for individual industry rates of return, and if possible, for the specific stock. The risk premium is given by the excess of this expected rate of return over the riskless rate of interest. This technique assumes that investors have, over the period used in determining the rate of return, been successful in predicting share prices! The returns that have been earned would appear to be 'within reason' and so the technique is plausible.

**Portfolio risk**

The subjective risk premium allocated to a particular share will depend partly on its historical volatility and predictability. However, the greatest determinant of the premium is likely to be the portfolio risk characteristics. Most active purchasers of investments have portfolios of several shares and in adding to these they will be interested in not only the additional return but also the change in the riskiness of the portfolio. A share which on its own is quite volatile but which tends to rise when the market falls and vice versa, is likely to be very attractive to an investor as it will reduce portfolio risk. This attraction will tend towards investors giving it a smaller risk premium than would otherwise have been the case. Chapter 7 describes portfolio risk more fully, it being sufficient at this stage to realise that it is an influence in the discount rate used in the intrinsic value formula. As a rough guide, shares whose prices vary very little with changes in the market index are likely to have low portfolio risk.

### Price/Earnings models

The computation of the P/E ratio (or PER) was explained in Chapter 3 and is defined as the number of years' purchase of earnings based on the 'net' method (or 'nil' method for companies with large overseas interests). When the earnings for the year are multiplied by the P/E ratio this gives the market capitalisation (equivalent to the total number of shares multiplied by the share price). The P/E ratio is, along with the dividend yield, the most popular measurement yardstick used in share comparisons. The main use of P/E ratios in investment analysis takes two forms. One is the derivation of a P/E ratio applicable to a particular company and attaching it to historical or to the forecast of current year profits. Example – if current earnings are forecast at 12p per share and the assessed P/E ratio for the firm is 15, this implies the share is worth 180p. The second form ranks P/E ratios against an average (market, industrial or the company's historical average) and the shares are assessed accordingly.

**The use of P/E ratios in calculating share values**

The use of an estimated P/E ratio is one method of deriving the terminal value in the intrinsic value model. Here, instead of earnings in year $n$ being multiplied by a constant growth factor, they are multiplied by the P/E figure and discounted to today's value. However, the main methodology is to forecast earnings for the current year and to multiply by the computed P/E ratio. The last year's earnings figure or the average of the last few year's earnings are sometimes used as the earnings factor. The 'advantage' of this technique is that it is simple to calculate, although this does not necessarily make the forecast any the better and, indeed, it generally requires less detailed analysis than the intrinsic value approach.

## Normalised earnings

It is very important to use 'normalised' earnings in the P/E model and this is why an average of the last few year's figures are sometimes used. Thus, if current year profits were expected to be abnormally low due to, say, exceptional stock losses or to shortages of components, it would be unrealistic to apply the normal P/E factor estimated for that share to this figure. Apart from exceptional profits or losses, the normal trade cycle can cause considerable variations in profits especially for capital goods companies. If the earnings were at a peak or a trough of the cycle the application of the derived P/E ratio would result in a too high or too low an estimate of the share price. The analyst, if he realises that the earnings figure is not normal, could adjust the P/E ratio he has estimated for the company. However, the normal procedure is to adjust the earnings. This can be done on a subjective basis or can be a statistical average of past earnings. Obviously, for a company with an erratic but non-cyclical earnings pattern, it will be difficult to establish a 'normal' earnings figure. In addition to the normalised earnings approach the analyst can calculate the abnormal earnings times P/E factor as this may help explain what is influencing the market.

In the ranking of shares by relative P/E ratios the analyst should likewise take care to use 'normalised' earnings. This is especially important as some investors may automatically use the P/E ratios which appear in the news media. The *Financial Times*, for instance, uses historical earnings for some shares whilst for others they use company forecasts. A published 'high' P/E ratio may be the result of the above-average earnings potential of the company or it could be due to the earnings being exceptionally low for the particular year. Similarly, a low P/E ratio may be due to poor prospects for the company or to it being calculated on abnormally high earnings.

## Determining the appropriate P/E ratio

The difficult aspect of the P/E model, of course, is the establishment of the appropriate P/E ratio. It entails looking at all the various factors which the market uses in evaluating stocks. These factors include past and future projections of earnings and dividends, share price and P/E ratio performance and volatility, managerial ability and the yields from other forms of investment[12]. In practice, the assessment of the P/E ratio is often a subjective opinion based on descriptive evaluations of the various factors and so it is difficult to describe the methodologies in use. However, a growing number of analysts are now evolving more analytical approaches to ascertaining the P/E ratio and these are generally based on forecast growth rates. From what has been said earlier it is fairly obvious that future forecasts of dividends and earnings and their growth rates are the most important determinant of share price performance and, hence, greater weight should be given to the more analytical P/E ratio models. The forecasting of growth rates is conducted along the same lines as described in the section on the intrinsic value approach and in Chapter 4. Different growth rates can be assumed for different periods (i.e. high initial growth rate for, say, five years followed by a market average rate) and tables can be constructed to show the appropriate P/E level for the various required rates of growth[9]. Such tables are often used as a means of highlighting the growth rate assumptions inherent in the P/E ratio. Thus, the analyst can arrive at a P/E ratio from a subjective assessment of the company and by looking at the growth tables he can see the growth assumptions which are implicit in his estimate. Although the use of growth rates can be common to both intrinsic value and the P/E technique, the latter places greater weight on the near term as it is the current, or possibly the past year's profits which are being extrapolated. In addition, the perhaps more vigorous forecasting techniques used in assessing intrinsic values gives greater preference to long-term growth possibilities, whilst the P/E model generally relies more heavily on the evidence of past growth rates.

**Ranking P/E ratios**

The other main method of assessing shares by the P/E ratio is that of relative ranking. This does not involve assessing an absolute ratio for the company but instead evaluates the company against its past average or against an industrial or overall market index. One technique is to assess the high and low P/E ratios in each of the last few years and this acts as a guide to the current estimate and to future events. Other techniques measure the historical P/E against the historical market or industrial average to obtain a relative coefficient, i.e. a company may have had a P/E ratio which over a number of years has averaged around 0.8 of the industrial or market index. If in the future the relative moves to 0.6 this would imply a good purchasing opportunity. The relationship is of the form: $Y = a + bX$

where $Y$ = company P/E

$a$ = constant

$b$ = coefficient, (i.e. 0.8)

$X$ = market average P/E

The P/E models can, of course, incorporate such relationships and the extra work involved in deriving the terms for $a$ and $b$ is not too great*. This technique used on its own is a form of mechanical strategy which does not require any forecasting of earnings but instead relies on a continual assessment of the relative to see whether it alters significantly from the historical relative. When this happens a purchase or sale signal is given. This technique is therefore a type of technical analysis which forms the content of Chapter 6. In fundamental analysis, however, the P/E relative can be used as a check against the subjectively appraised P/E ratio.

Both the methods of P/E ranking models offer broad guidelines to the subjective assessment of the figure applicable to a particular company.

*These are obtained from regression analysis which is described in Chapter 10.

They are based on prior information and trends and cannot take account of any significant changes in circumstances such as substantial new-product development, changes in management, increased competition, etc. These factors are a matter of subjective assessment although the use of growth tables may reveal the assumptions that are inherent therein.

Whilst the analysis that goes into P/E assessments is perhaps less detailed than the intrinsic value approach, the method does allow quicker evaluations of companies which may be important for analysts who have a lot of shares to look at. Additionally, the P/E ratio acts as a screening device in some mechanical rules and can also be used as a check against the intrinsic values found for various companies. P/E ratios are often used in computer models and sometimes act as the dependent variables. These methods are described next. The reader should appreciate that the P/E ratio is not the only market yield that can be used. Similar analyses can be carried out on dividends and earnings yields.

### Computer-based stock selection methods

These can be split into two groups, one being the use of financial models, and two, data screening. The first uses statistical regression analysis and the second analyses vast masses of data to extract certain financial characteristics and ratios. This latter type usually investigates for certain sets of historical data which are of interest to the analyst*. Examples include determining those companies with the highest P/E ratios relative to the market, and deriving ratios of past earnings growth divided by current P/E ratios. These analyses are based on historical data and so are a form of trading rule, the most common of which are described in Chapter 6. The computer is very necessary in these screening processes due to its capacity to handle large masses of data and to perform arithmetical calculations.

The model-building approaches include the intrinsic value and P/E ratio techniques as well as econometric models. The former have been described earlier and the rest of this section will introduce the fairly sophisticated regression models.

The importance of the computer is that it can deal with large masses of data and handle the mathematical relationships required. Most stockbrokers have computers or access to computers and these are universally used in the administration and paperwork attached to the business. A few brokers and institutional investors are now using their computing resources to evolve economic, company sector and occasionally company models for forecasting purposes and for stock selection. There are numerous standard statistical packages available

---

*There are a number of central computer-based systems which are available to analysts. One is SCAN LTD which provides a number of services ranging from portfolio administration to financial statistics of quoted companies.

for building regression models although the analyst may decide he can obtain better results by writing his own programs.

**Model building**

The model-building approach involves the ascertaining of the vital factors affecting share prices and deriving the weights the market attaches to these variables. The methodology can be split into three parts:

1 The ascertainment of the factors. This is usually subjective at first with many being very obvious (i.e. growth rates in dividends and earnings). Various factors and combinations of factors can be tried in models so as to obtain the best forecasting tool.

2 Some of the factors will be forecasts and therefore the work from Chapter 4 will be required. The main forecasts used will be of growth rates and expectations of share price movements in general. For models that do not rely on future forecasts the model will be a form of technical rule with the computer screening company data.

3 The derivation of the weights for the factors described above. This involves the use of multiple regression analysis using least squares. This is briefly outlined in Chapter 10. The weights appropriate to each factor represent the importance of the factor within the model in describing the share price and therefore its relevance in the model. If the weight (or coefficient) is very small then the analyst may decide to leave the variable out of the model altogether[13]. The derivation of the important factors is therefore partly determined by the weighting process.

The model takes the form of an equation thus:

Theoretical yield $= a + by + cx - dz + e$

The theoretical yield is the item being forecasted (the dependent variable)*. It is theoretical in that it is the yield that ought to exist. The yield is often the P/E ratio but it could be any other yardstick. $y$, $x$ and $z$ are the various 'important' factors, called independent variables and $b$, $c$ and $d$ are the coefficients of each. The computer can handle vast numbers of factors and so the analyst can incorporate as many variables as he can think of. Some variables will be minus terms showing that investors do not like that particular factor. $e$ is the error term and the reduction of $e^2$ to as low a value as possible forms the criterion of deciding which is the best explanatory model of prior share price movements.

The technique gives the contribution within the model of each factor, to historical yields or share prices and the $e$ term gives the unexplained variance, which can be thought of as all the other variables which influence prices. The method relies on these relative contributions continuing into the near-term future. The theoretical P/E ratio is

*Absolute share prices can be used for models built specially for one particular company.

compared against the actual price earnings and if above, a purchase is implied, if below, a sale implied. This is on the assumption that the market price is temporarily out of place and will tend toward the price indicated by the model.

## Types of regression model

Models can be constructed for individual companies but this is not often met with in practice. This is partly due to the cost and partly that there is insufficient data. Regression analyses involve taking numerous observations of independent variables and the model becomes more accurate the greater the number of these observations. The only way to obtain numerous observations on an individual company is to go back over time. This, however, is not all that satisfactory as investors' preferences and economic conditions can change significantly over, say, a five-year period. The more usual technique is to build a model to explain share price performance in general. Thus, various factors and yields are taken for, say, a hundred companies and these form a hundred sets of observations. The computer will derive the weights for each factor such that the error term $e^2$ is as small as possible*. The analyst will now have quantitative data on the coefficients. He will then use the individual company's factor estimates and derive the theoretical yield. This technique will be more appropriate for some companies and sectors than for others. For example, the model will give the average market coefficient attached to historical earnings growth but this weight may not be correct for certain industries, i.e. property companies where past earnings growth may count for little. In this case, asset values are likely to be an important determinant of property share prices but they would account for very little in the share prices of industrial companies. One answer to the problem is to construct a model for individual sectors or ultimately individual companies (the disadvantages of which have just been mentioned). An alternative is to incorporate in the model a factor which represents the constant under- and over-valuation of the share by the model.

## Factors

The first stage is for the analyst to decide which dependent variable is to be forecasted. Usually this is the P/E ratio or the dividend yield. Occasionally absolute share prices are forecasted but this requires an individual model for the particular company. Share prices are, of course, easily derived from the particular market yield that is computed for the company and the analyst should use that yield which is most easily predictable.

The initial derivation of the independent variables will be subjectively based and the impact of these is assessed by testing the model. The most usual factors met with are past earnings and dividend performance, future forecasts of dividends and earnings growth rates, past share price volatility† against the market index and past variability in

*The criterion is to minimise the sum of the squares of the residuals, i.e. $e^2$.

†Defined as the percentage change in the share price for a one percentage change in the market index.

share prices. Many other factors can be incorporated although the above variables will probably account for most of the explained movement. Examples of other factors include marketability of the shares, quality of management, size of company, asset values and geographical location. Some will be quality variables and the analyst will have to ascribe some sort of rank to the factors. If the major variables mentioned above account for most of the share price movement the analyst need not spend too much time on other factors. The forecasts of future growth will have already been made in accordance with Chapter 4 whilst the past performances will be derived from historical data. The analyst can experiment with forecasts for various periods, i.e. if he has a long-term growth forecast this may not be as good an explanatory variable as a shorter-term projection as the market places a heavy weight on near-term earnings. Variability and volatility are important determinants of share prices as they represent risk. Few analysts make estimates of future volatility and variability and therefore historical relationships are generally used.

When the model is tested some factors will have small coefficients attached to them even though they would appear to be very important. This will probably be because the impact of the particular factor is already reflected in another variable. Such interdependence or, in statistical terms, multicollinearity between factors might be evidenced in, say, past earnings performance which will in fact be largely taken account of in future forecasts. Another example will be dividend and earnings growth rates as the former is a function of the latter. Therefore, either dividend or earnings growth is likely to have a lowish coefficient as it will have been accounted for in the other factor. The factor with a low coefficient is not necessarily useless to the model as it was required to see which factors best explained price performance and, indeed, in later testing it may assume the major importance.

## Regression

Regression analysis is a method of estimating relationships between a dependent variable and other, independent variables. The actual technique of obtaining the regression coefficients is known as least squares and is dealt with in Chapter 10*. As explained previously the regression coefficients are obtained from using data on a number of companies which are representative of companies in general or representative of a specific industry. The coefficients obtained are those which best explain the relationship between past share yield behaviour and the independent variable factors. The feedback from comparing the forecasts against actual results may indicate trends which are not fully accounted for in the weights. Such feedback should be used to revise the factors and the coefficients used. The criterion for finding the best explanatory model, or the line of 'best fit' is the reduction of $e^2$, the error term, to as low a figure as possible. Models

*Chapter 10 also describes measures of the explanatory powers of a regression model. If the explanatory power is poor then little reliance can be placed on its forecasts.

should be constantly revised to allow for changing shareholder preferences regarding share prices which are evidenced by the coefficients. Similarly, models should be revised to allow for new additional factors which may arise. The regression analysis will automatically adjust the position of the variables to obtain the best model. This will involve some intrinsically important factors being given low weights because their impact has been reflected in another, preceding variable. When comparing actual results with the forecasts it may be found that some companies are continually being under- or over-valued by the model. This will be because the market coefficients are not so applicable to the particular company or that there are additional, important factors which were not significant in the market model. Examples might include asset values for property and mining companies or a qualitative geographical/political factor for firms with large overseas interests.

## Advantages of using regression models

The main advantages of modelling systems are that:

1 Once constructed they can be used in evaluating hundreds of shares. Care has to be taken, however, to update the model.

2 It is objective, unbiased and consistent.

3 The assumptions are fairly explicit.

Against the technique the regression coefficients are those for the market or an industry as a whole and are not necessarily relevant to the individual company. Investor preferences and business conditions can change quite dramatically in short periods of time and the analyst needs to continually re-appraise the model. A further possible disadvantage is that it is easy to use estimates of growth rates which have a poor foundation and indeed the model may give substantial weight to past performance and little to the projected future prospects. Additionally the models may have poorish explanatory powers and the analyst may over-rely on the model's 'answers'.

## Computer models in use

The use of computer models for individual share price forecasting has begun to grow with the emphasis coming from America. A number of articles and reports have been published describing the techniques employed, their derivations and their success in forecasting. Amongst the foremost is Whitbeck and Kisor's theoretical P/E model[14]. The independent variables were earnings growth rate forecasts obtained from professional analysts, the dividend payout ratio and the standard deviation in the growth rate (as a surrogate for risk). The coefficients were derived from a regression of the above factors of 135 shares as at June 1962 against the P/E ratio. The model evolved was:

Theoretical P/E ratio = 8.2 + 1.5 (earnings growth %) + 6.7 (dividend payout %) − 0.2 (standard deviation in growth rate %)

The risk was a negative factor as may have been expected. The individual factors for each company are incorporated into the model and a theoretical P/E ratio obtained. When they tested the model, Whitbeck and Kisor found that it provided profitable investment decisions especially when the actual P/E ratio was below 85 per cent of the theoretical P/E ratio or when more than 114 per cent of the computed ratio[15].

Weaver and Hall described a model used by their firm in share selection[16]. The model was of the form:

$$\log dz = a + b \log y + c \log x + d \log w + e \log v + f \log u$$

where $z$ = mean dividend yield

$y$ = mean dividend payout ratio

$x$ = forecast short-term earnings growth rate

$w$ = forecast long-term dividend growth rate

$v$ = historical earnings variability

$u$ = historical earnings growth rate

The coefficients for dividend and earnings growth rates $(c, d, f)$ were negative.

Their paper detailed the derivation of the model and should be read by interested readers.

In a more recent paper[17] Hall described a new model which expressed the relationship of the P/E ratio of the market index to measures of pre-tax profits, money supply, capital investment, dividend cover and Bank Rate. The model derived was expressed thus:

$$\text{Log}_{10} \text{ P/E} = -9.5519$$
$$+ 1.8153 \log_{10} (\% \text{ change in pre-tax profits})$$
$$+ 3.1192 \log_{10} (\% \text{ change in excess money})$$
$$+ 1.3294 \log_{10} (\text{investment/GDP})$$
$$- 0.8988 \log_{10} (\text{cover})$$
$$- 0.1726 \log_{10} (\% \text{ change in Bank Rate})$$

Percentage explained = 97%

Standard error of equation = 4%

The derivation of the independent variables is explained in Hall's paper and this should be referred to by the interested reader. The percentage change in pre-tax profits relates to the change in quarterly profits from those four quarters (one year) earlier.

The model provided a good explanation of the actual movement in the P/E ratio of the FTA 500 Index: the percentage of variance in the market P/E index explained was 97 per cent.

To date, regression models have not fared terribly well in forecasting share prices and have thus given poor returns for the costs involved. The major difficulty experienced by the models has been to obtain accurate forecasts of future earnings and dividends and their growth rates: thus the comments by Keenan in the article referred to previously. A secondary difficulty is that the relationships expressed by the models are historical and some forecasting errors are caused by investors changing their preferences as regards fundamental factors. Another problem in evaluating individual securities is that the market relationships, or any modification of such, just do not hold up for individual shares.

There have been many models based on historical data and these have received considerable statistical testing by academics. In general, most of these rules have not been found to be profitable on future data and such results have provided the base for the claims of the efficient market protagonists. Some of the more well known technical models will be described in Chapter 6 whilst Chapter 11 will review the empirical testing of such.

**Market model forecasts**

Another computer model, which can be used for making quick assessments of a lot of shares, is to measure the volatility of the share price against the market or industry index. Thus the analyst forecasts the market index and can then derive estimated share prices for all those companies for whom he has derived a volatility relationship. Any discrepancy between the computed and actual prices provides buy and sell decisions.

The usual form of the relationship is:

Movement in share price of company $= a + b \times$ movement in market index $+ e$

where $a$ = constant

$b$ = regression coefficient

$e$ = error term (which is to be minimised)

The figures for $a$ and $b$ are obtained by regressing the share price against the market or industrial index. This is done by taking many share prices of the company and market indexes, collected on the same days. If the coefficient, $b$, is 1 then the share price moves in a constant relationship to the market index. If $b$ is below 1 then it means that the share price is relatively stable against the market, whilst if $b$ is greater than 1 this represents a share whose value is significantly affected by the index. Figure 5.3 shows the graph of a share whose volatility relationship is equal to $5 + 1.5$ times the change in the market index. The coefficient 1.5 says that the share price changes by a greater amount (50 per cent more) than the market index and the figure 5 means that given no change in the index the share price will move up by 5 per cent. In the scale used in the graph, a line at 45 degrees equals a '$b$' coefficient of 1 whilst a flatter line gives a coefficient of under 1. The straight line represents the theoretical values of share prices given the market index for the particular relationship.

The method assumes that the relationship so derived will hold for future periods of time. This has been the subject of a fair amount of

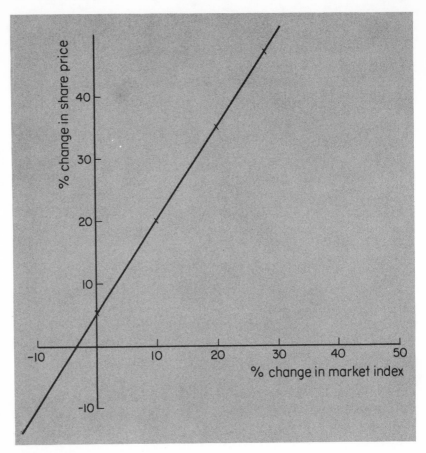

**Figure 5.3**

Share price volatility index

research and it would appear that there is some statistically significant association between market indices and individual share prices over short periods of time[18]. The technique relies on the analyst forecasting the market index successfully. Once the forecast has been made the various individual share prices for which a relationship has been derived can be easily obtained. The errors in the system include both forecasting difficulties in predicting the market index and those contained in the assumption that the relationship is sufficiently precise and stable. A further disadvantage is that dividends are ignored. However, this can be overcome by measuring returns instead of share price movements (i.e. share price changes plus dividends). It is possible to use the model without forecasting the market although this is a form of technical analysis. The analyst uses the present market index to compute the theoretical market price. Any discrepancy between this and the actual price is assumed to be due to the share price being temporarily out of place and so buy and sell decisions are made accordingly.

## The market model for short term forecasts

Besides its use in being able to establish share prices for many companies from one forecast of the market index, the volatility approach is also used for short-term predictions of price behaviour. It may take some time before the share price approaches the intrinsic value and in-between times the returns could be very poor. Thus, an assessment of near future share prices is required, especially for short-term investors. As there is some evidence to support the contention that the volatility model is stable over short periods the technique can be used to estimate shorter-term share prices. This can be done by either estimating the future market index or by using the existing index; the latter approach however, is really a mechanical rule. The forecasting of the market index will include estimating company and economic news in the near future, the yields on alternative investments, cash positions and borrowing facilities and 'market sentiment'. This latter qualitative item may be made up partly from Press comment and from feedback from institutional investors as to what they think the market will do (it is, after all, the institutional investors who eventually make the market prices).

## Market models in performance measurement

An additional use of the volatility model is that of evaluating portfolio performance. This will be dealt with in greater detail in Chapter 8. Returns on shares should be measured against the market index to obtain relative performance and it is necessary to incorporate dividends in the model (i.e. use total returns as opposed to share prices solely). One way is to use a constant relationship.

*Example*
Share price 100p, market index 250. If the share price rises to 150p and the market index to 300, the relative performance is given by the statistic $\frac{150}{300} \div \frac{100}{250} = 1.25$. Thus, the price has risen by 125 per cent of the market average (for simplicity's sake dividends have been ignored).

However, this measurement does not take account of the risk in the portfolio and is therefore only properly applicable when funds having the same riskiness are compared. Some academics have suggested that the volatility index provides an adequate risk-adjusted performance measure and this has received a fair amount of acceptance. This method of performance assessment is very widely adopted in academic research both for studies on individual securities and for portfolios.

*Example*   The volatility index for a share might be:

Movement in share price $= 0.6 + 0.9 \times$ movement in market index $+ e$ (error term)

The coefficient 0.9 indicates the slope of the line is below 45 degrees (1 = 45 degrees) and the share price is therefore comparatively stable against the market index. If the market index rose by 20 per cent the expected rise in the share price would be:

$0.6 + 0.9 \times 20 = 18.6\%$

**177**

If the actual price rose by, say, 15 per cent then the share will be shown to have performed poorly. The model can also be interpreted in that the share price is temporarily out of place and that it will tend to drift towards the theoretical price.

The volatility index is therefore useful for making quick evaluations of many shares and for short-term forecasting. Additionally, it has found an important role in performance assessment, a role in which it has had little competition to date.

## Suggested methodology

A number of models have just been described which attempt to forecast share prices. All have merits and can provide valuable feedback and guidelines for the other methods. Thus, if the analyst has sufficient resources he should attempt all the methodologies and compare the results. Once he has done the detailed analyses required for the intrinsic value approach the analyst will have all the necessary forecast data for computing the P/E growth rates and for the 'future' variables in econometric models. The remaining factors in the model building approaches can be obtained from past data. The computational work in deriving models will be time consuming but once in operation the main work of the analyst will be in making the forecasts of future growth rates.

If the analyst is reasonably certain of his detailed forecasts over say, the following five years the intrinsic value approach may offer the most successful technique. It will disclose individual years' dividends and earnings which should help the analyst understand any seemingly odd price movements. The terminal growth rates forecasts for the model can be incorporated into the P/E and regression models and these will provide guidelines especially in the short-term which is perhaps the weak point of intrinsic analysis. It is important to acknowledge the growth rates implicit in the various forecasts as these may show up some predictions as being clearly unrealistic. Another important factor in all the models is to analyse the accuracy of the forecasts. This can give valuable insight into the important factors affecting the business and, in the case of model building, may indicate areas of continual under- or overvaluation by the model. Although there is some doubt about the stability of the weights, the volatility index can be used as a device for forecasting short-term price movements, the success of which should be regularly screened.

Chapter 11 describes the efficient markets hypothesis and its ramifications for investment analysis. The theory says that, given a reasonably efficient market place, no further investment analysis will, in general, be worth while. This is based on many competing analysts working on much the same original data. The hypothesis however, acknowledges that it is the detailed analyses of the analysts that make the market 'efficient' and therefore a more perfect allocator of resources and of their ownership.

## References

1 This forecasting of what the market average is expecting has been succinctly described by Keynes who said, 'We have reached the third degree where we devote our intelligences to anticipating what average opinion expects the average opinion to be. And there are some, I believe, who practise the fourth and fifth and higher degrees', Keynes, J. M., *General Theory of Employment, Interest and Money*, Macmillan, 1936.

2 Skerratt, L. C. L., 'The price determination of convertible loan stock: a UK model', *Journal of Business Finance and Accounting*, No. 3, 1974; Weil, R. L. Segall, J. E. and Green, D., 'Premiums on convertible bonds', *Journal of Finance*, Jun. 1968; Baumol, W. J. Malkiel, B. G. and Quandt, R. E., 'The valuation of convertible securities', *Quarterly Journal of Economics*, Vol. LXXX, No. 1, Feb. 1966.

3 Samuelson, P. A., 'Rational theory of warrant pricing', *Industrial Management Review*, VI, Spring, 1965; Shelton, J. P., 'The relation of the price of a warrant to the price of its associated stock', *Financial Analysts' Journal*, XXIII, May–Jun. 1967 and July–Aug. 1967.

4 The provisions of estate duty taxation allow valuations of shares to be based on other than the market value on the day the investor dies. See, for example, 'Estate Duty Planning', Farringdon Publishing Company, 1973.

5 This methodology is largely associated with the name of Williams, J. B., whose book 'The Theory of Investment Value' published in 1938 (Harvard University Press) extensively covered the use and applications of this approach. There are also numerous other works describing the application of the intrinsic value method, although many add little to Williams' work. Major texts that can be consulted include Gordon, M. J., 'The Investment, Financing, and Valuation of the Corporation', Irwin, 1962; Lerner, E. and Carleton, W., 'A Theory of Financial Analysis', Harcourt Brace & World Inc., 1966. Additionally, there are numerous articles on the subject and reference should be made to the *Financial Analysts Journal* for many of these.

6 Tables can be constructed which show present values of a number of growth rates running in series. See, for example, 'Growth Yields on Common Stock: theory and tables', Revised Edition, Soldofsky, R. M. and Murphy, J. T., Ames, Iowa, State University of Iowa, Bureau of Business and Economic Research, 1963.

7 For a discussion of the contention between discounting earnings and discounting dividends see: Lorie and Hamilton, 'The Stock Market: theories and evidence', Irwin, 1973, Chapter 6.

8 For a description of the intrinsic value approach in actual use see: Peck, L. G., 'The Goldman, Sachs & Co. Valuation Model', manuscript, Goldman, Sachs & Co., New York.

9 For an interesting article on this subject see: Holt, C. C., 'The influence of growth duration on share prices', *Journal of Finance*, Sept. 1962.

**10**  This is determined by the investor's utility function which, in practice, is usually a subjective assessment and, for private investors, often unconsciously made. For a description of utility see: Friedman, M. and Savage, L. J., 'The utility analysis of choices involving risk', *The Journal of Political Economy*, Vol. VI, No. 4, Aug. 1948.

**11**  These returns can vary slightly depending on the time period looked at. Fisher and Lorie found that the average rate of return for all stocks listed on the New York Stock Exchange for all holding periods between 1926 and 1965 was approximately 9 per cent, 'Rates of return on investments in common stock: the year by year record 1926–1965', *Journal of Business*, XL, Jul. 1968. The average compound growth rate per annum of dividends in the UK since 1920 has been $4\frac{1}{4}$ per cent and the total after tax return to investors, including capital appreciation, has averaged $8\frac{1}{4}$ per cent.

**12**  For an interesting 'quantification' of these factors see: Cohen and Zinbarg, 'Investment Analysis and Portfolio Management', Irwin, 1967, pp. 246–247.

**13**  There are various statistical tests which examine the significance of variables in explaining share price or price/earnings movements. These form the criteria for accepting or rejecting the factors in the model; see: Kane, 'Economic Statistics and Econometrics', Harper & Row, 1968.

**14**  Whitbeck, V. S. and Kisor, M. Jr, 'A new tool in investment decision making', *Financial Analysts' Journal*, May–Jun. 1963. The reader might also look at an article by Keenan, M., 'Models of equity valuation: the great serm bubble', *Journal of Finance*, May 1970. This reviewed some of the model building approaches and criticised their performance. Keenan recommended that analysts should devote their resources more to detailed analyses than to building sophisticated models.

**15**  Several adaptions of the Whitbeck and Kisor model have been made. These have included both different estimates of the Whitbeck and Kisor variables and different factors. Major studies have been reported by Ahlers, D. M., 'SEM: a security evaluation model' in Cohen, K. J. and Hammer, F. S. (Eds), 'Analytical Methods in Banking', Irwin, 1966; Fischer Black, 'Yes, Virginia, There Is Hope: tests of the value line ranking system', Paper prepared for the Seminar on the Analysis of Security Prices, University of Chicago, May 1971; and Bower, R. S. and Bower, D. H., 'Risk and the valuation of common stock', *Journal of Political Economy*, May–Jun. 1969.

**16**  Weaver, D. and Hall, M. G., 'The evaluation of ordinary shares using a computer', *Journal of the Institute of Actuaries*, Vol. 93, Sept. 1967.

**17**  Hall, M. G., 'Forecasting movements in the UK equity market' in 'Mathematics in the Stock Exchange', The Institute of Mathematics and its Applications, 1972.

**18**  See Chapter 7 for a fuller description of the market model and its validity. Tests on the stability of the regression coefficients on UK data appear to be reasonably good. See: Cunningham, S. W., 'The sensitivities of individual share prices to changes in an index', in 'Mathematics in the Stock Exchange', The Institute of Mathematics and its Applications, 1972 and his 'The predictability of British Stock Market prices', *Applied Statistics*, Vol. 22, No. 3, 1973.

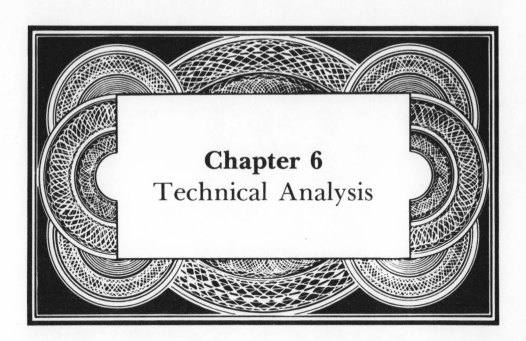

# Chapter 6
# Technical Analysis

Technical analysis is the name given to forecasting techniques which are derived from measuring historical patterns of share price behaviour and from measuring historical characteristics of other financial data. Analysts then examine present-day share price data to see if any of the established patterns are applicable and, if so, extrapolations can be made. The rationale behind technical analysis is that share price behaviour repeats itself over time and so attempts have been made to derive methods to predict such repetition.

Share prices are determined by the demand/supply relationship and the 'intrinsic value' is but one factor of this complex function. Other influences, many of which are psychologically based, are present and these are reflected in share prices. The protagonists of technical analysis therefore state that Stock Market price formation is not subject solely to scientific analysis and that knowledge of investor behaviour is needed. The share price performance reflects this behaviour and, although it may be irrational, the technical analysts claim it is predictable.

**The Efficient Markets Theory and technical analysis**

The Efficient Markets Theory contends that the market is sufficiently well endowed with numerous expert analysts specialising in individual stocks that all publicly available information is discounted immediately and that share prices represent the best estimate of the true worth. The theory therefore says that any additional fundamental analysis would not be warranted and indeed that some present analysis may be

183

redundant*. The technical analysts have used such a description of Stock Market processes to back their own techniques. They say that as the market is efficient there is no need for any more fundamental analysis, but there is a need to look at psychological factors and therefore the rules of technical analysis. Chapter 11 describes the efficient market arguments and summarises many of the empirical findings. Briefly, however, extensive tests of technical analysis rules have been made but no evidence has been found of their being of any value. Thus, the efficient market theorists reject the conclusions drawn by the technical analysts on the implication of the Efficient Markets Theory for technical analysis.

## Categorisation of technical analysis

Technical analysis is traditionally divided into the techniques which look at visual patterns on charts of share prices and those which rely upon the application of mechanical investment strategies. The chartists plot share price movements on charts and attempt to read a pattern into it. The 'pattern' is then compared with previous patterns to see if there are any similarities. The analyst will then project future price performance in accordance with the pattern. Mechanical trading rules do not require the construction of charts but rely on buy or sell indicators given by ratios or control limits. The ratios and limits are set by the analyst and are usually derived from past data. The more popular technical rules are described later although the reader should look at the recommended references to obtain a wider spectrum of the methods and the interpretations.

## Claims made for technical analysis

Analysts make varying claims for their techniques. Some use only their methods and disregard fundamental analysis altogether. In this form the analyst need not even know the name of the share; they just look at the chart patterns or the numerical data. Indeed, such purist technical analysts decry the knowledge of the name of the company they are looking at, saying it only induces bias. Other analysts will, perhaps, use a number of technical analyses and may well use fundamental data as well. Claims of success vary also. Most technical analysts acknowledge their methods do not 'work' every time but that, taken as a whole, the returns are significantly positive. An investor would therefore need sufficient resources to accept one or two failures (this is no severe criticism really as this applies to all forecasting methods). Others, however, claim 100 per cent success. These must be treated with scepticism. It should be noted that some rules and charts are interpreted to show only the direction of price movement whilst others claim they can predict levels that will be reached.

## A short term forecasting method

Technical analysis is usually a short-term forecasting method although as the world markets show, the year-to-year fluctuations are substantial and correct prediction of these can result in far greater returns than could be made through long-term forecasts. There are various charts

*Some authors say that a fundamental analyst whose views about a major company differ significantly from the market's evaluations should be very wary of his forecasts, i.e. that the market is correct.

and rules which can predict the market index and from this individual share prices can be forecast. However, the majority of charts and mechanical rules are used in predicting the returns from individual stocks no matter what the market is expected to do. Technical analysis can, of course, be used in conjunction with fundamental analysis. For example, positive signals from both methods may be required before a purchase is made. Another frequent combination is that of share selection being made from fundamental analysis, but the timing of purchases being determined by technical analysis.

## Self-fulfillment

A comment frequently made about technical analysis is that it is self-fulfilling in that if a pattern appears which suggests a certain future price performance, and if enough analysts believe in the pattern, then they will all make the same purchase or sell action and continue until the price is pushed to the theoretical level. Any technical pattern which is widely believed-in will therefore be self-fulfilling to some extent. This will result in analysts attempting to anticipate a pattern before it is completely established, and this process will continue as other analysts follow suit. Eventually the pattern will never be formed. This latter process of competing analysts driving away profit potential from technical patterns helps create an efficient market.

## The need to understand major technical theories

The Efficient Markets Theory is presented in Chapter 11 and some of the empirical testing of it is summarised there. The theory says that all publicly available information is discounted in share prices immediately and that the present price is the best forecast of 'true value'. The implication for technical analysis is that it has no predictive value*. Many technical theories, especially the mechanical rules, have been statistically tested and in general no evidence of their having better than average performance has been found. Thus the techniques that have been publicised are under an academic cloud although they still have many protagonists especially in the USA. The extensive use which is made of technical analysis in share selection demands a description of the techniques in use, in an investment analysis text, for two reasons: firstly, despite the academics' findings there may be some validity in the techniques which have escaped empirical testing to date; secondly, even if technical analysis does not have any predictive value, the particular chart patterns and mechanical rules do influence buying and selling decisions of many investors and thus the fundamental analyst has to acknowledge these as an influencing factor in share price determination.

### Chart analysis

The most well known form of technical analysis is chartism. The analyst plots in various ways the movements of share prices and

*It also implies that further fundamental analysis is of no value unless the investor has access to inside knowledge.

attempts to establish patterns which are extrapolated to give a forecast of future prices. Chart analysis is also applied to other statistics, notably trading volume, in order to predict prices. The principle behind the use of charts is that share price behaviour repeats itself over time and the analyst examines present price patterns and trends to see if they fit in with established relationships derived from past data.

## Chart construction

There are three types of chart in use: line, bar, and point and figure. Line charts are the simplest to construct – entries are made usually at closing prices (in the UK the *Financial Times'* data will almost invariably be used) and a line is drawn between the points. The price scale is normally shown on the vertical axis and the horizontal axis is the time scale of the recordings (usually daily, weekly or, for long-term charts, monthly). Volume statistics can be constructed similarly although they are often incorporated on the price-line chart (See Figure 6.1a). Line

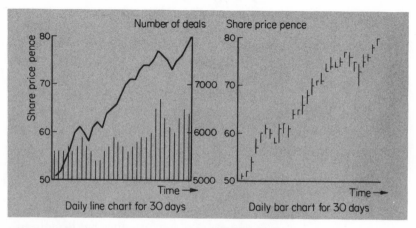

**Figure 6.1a**

Line chart

**Figure 6.1b**

Bar chart

charts are their least sophisticated form and in America they are often only used for recording long-term performance indices or long-term individual share prices. Line charts are, however, used fairly extensively in the UK as data relating to daily highs and lows, which is required for bar charts, is difficult to obtain.

## Data requirements

Most UK analysts will use data collected from the recordings given in the *Financial Times* or in the Official Lists. The Official Lists will have to be used when there is no FT quote for a particular security. The *Financial Times* quotations are taken from jobbers and represent closing prices. Thus, they do not show data which is sufficient to draw bar charts but the information is adequate for the more popular point and figure charts.

## Volume of business

Volume statistics are not available in the UK and so chart patterns and mechanical investment strategies utilising such data are not relevant in the analysis of UK shares. In future, however, these statistics may be given. The major indicator of volume in the UK is probably the share price itself with relatively large price movements indicating increased volume*. An indication of volume can also be given by the number of bargains marked in a stock. The bargains record the various prices at which deals are done on the London Stock Exchange although no indication is given of whether the bargain represents a sale or a purchase. Only one bargain at each price is recorded, i.e. if a stock has twenty dealings in it at a sale price of 30p then only one bargain is recorded. Stock Exchange members do not have to mark bargains except in special cases, and the list cannot, therefore, be regarded as a complete record of prices at which business was done. A bargain is made for a specific price with no regard to the number of shares involved and thus one bargain may represent a transaction to the value of £100 whilst another in the same stock may represent £250,000. Nevertheless, the recordings do give the best indication available of the activity of dealings in a particular stock and are frequently quoted as such in the financial press. (The *Financial Times* gives a table listing the most active stocks each day. This list is compiled from the number of bargains reproduced in the Official List.)

Individual brokers will of course have a better idea than most of the volume of trading and this can be utilised. In general, however, the British Stock Market does not provide adequate data for the construction of volume charts and the best use of such data as there is, is as a broad indicator of dealing activity.

**Bar charts**

Bar charts are similar to line charts in the terms of scales but they record the high and low price range for the day (or other period) and the close price is marked with a horizontal bar. Figure 6.1(b) shows a typical bar chart. High and low price data and the exact closing prices are difficult to establish in the UK and even if considerable effort is made, the figures may be somewhat tenuous. Thus, although bar charts provide fairly sophisticated information for the analyst, their usefulness in analysing British equities is restricted because of the lack of adequate data. The price scale is sometimes constructed on semi-logarithmic paper as this shows the percentage moves, i.e. equal distances on the chart represent equal proportionate changes. An investor is interested in his return on capital and the semilog scale gives this statistic. For chart patterns, however, whichever scale gives the best patterns (i.e. those that provide the most accurate forecasts of future prices) is the one to use. For pictorial presentations of performance the log scale is perhaps the best intercompany comparison although it should be noted that most practising investment advisers use arithmetic scales. The differences in chart patterns between the two types of scale are of course very significant and add ammunition to the disbelievers' arguments. The choice of the scales (both price and time) also vary the pattern formation and when allied to the frequent different interpretations given by analysts to one particular chart, one

*Relative to the market average.

can understand why there is a considerable anti-chartist school. The scale will depend somewhat on the activity of the share and its marketability. The analyst will probably prepare more than one chart so as to find the scale that is sensitive enough to indicate the important changes, but which excludes small changes which do not indicate major trend reversals or congestion breakouts. Chart scales should be reviewed from time to time especially if there has been a major move to a new price area.

## Point and figure charts

Point and figure charts show price movements which increase (sequences) or decrease (reversals) by some predetermined amount, the objective being to show a compressed picture of significant price changes. Prices are recorded on the vertical scale. The horizontal axis is not a time scale but represents a reversal from a previous trend. The construction of a point and figure chart is best explained with an example. The following closing prices on successive days were recorded*:

120, 125, 127, 128, 131, 140, 137, 140, 151, 145, 130, 130,

140, 140, 160, 145, 147, 145, 140, 130

Price increases are recorded on the chart as in Figure 6.2 at the appropriate square, with an 'x'. Thus, in the example an x is placed at 120 on the 5p scale chart (this means only prices in 5p increases from base zero are shown). The choice of scale is up to the analyst – the larger the scale the less sensitive it becomes but, conversely, it only records major changes and thus changes in trends. An x is marked for the following price of 125p as it is an increase of 5p. The prices 127p and 128p are not recorded as they have not moved into a new price region. A recording is made at 130p for the price of 131p. Two crosses are entered for the next price (140p) as it crosses two scale intervals (135 and 140p). 137p is not recorded as the change is too small and the same applies for 140p. Two crosses are entered at 151p. The next price is 145p but as this is a decrease the x is made in the column to the right of the previous column. This is because an x has previously been made in the column at this point. Reversals are only recorded if they are of 5p or more. The next recording is 130p and three further marks are made on the graph. If the next price recording had been 150 instead of 130 and thus an increase, we would not move to another column but would record it above the x at 145p. This is done as, if we did move a column, it would create a misleading pattern of great width, showing a movement for every price change of a minimum scale. Thus every column will have at least two entries and a new column is needed when the square required is already occupied in the current column. The remaining price recordings are plotted as in Figure 6.2.

## Point and figure variants

The above describes the basic method of compiling point and figure charts. These however can be modified by analysts. One common

*In the US intra-day prices are used by the serious point and figure analysts; however, such data is not readily available in the UK.

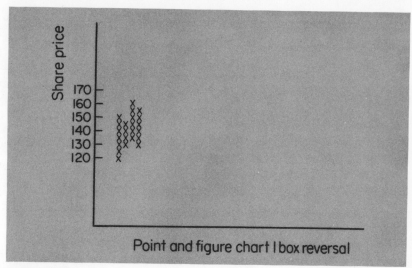

**Figure 6.2**

Point and figure chart

variant is a three-box reversal (or other numbered box reversal) chart where sequences are recorded for each movement of 5p but a reversal is not recorded until a price drops by 15p (three boxes of 5p). A reversal of up to 15p would not be recorded at all. To help differentiate rises and falls the analyst usually records the rises with x's and falls with o's. In general, arithmetic scales are used in point and figure charts as semi-log scales are said to distort the 'congestion areas'. Time is recognised in point and figure charts usually by putting the month number (1 through to 12) instead of an x or o for the first transaction of the month. This data can be useful as it indicates sudden surges of activity. This is compared against the ordinary fixed time scale bar and line charts which give equal weighting to time (although activity can be noted visually). Point and figure charts are perhaps more popular than bar charts as they show only the changes in prices (sequences and reversals) whilst time scale charts often tend to obscure patterns and trends. The horizontal scale on point and figure charts are reversals and these, say the analysts, are the important items in congestion area resistance. Volume data, if known, is not incorporated on the point and figure chart as there is no time scale. However, point and figure charts are used in conjunction with volume data line charts.

**The interpretation of charts**

From the point and figure and the bar and line charts the analyst attempts to form patterns or trend lines or, if there is no pattern or trend, to ascertain the breakouts of congestion areas. A point and figure chart is used in the main. This is because congestion areas of several months duration can be shown succinctly on a point and figure chart – bar and line charts would stretch over a large distance and make the patterns less obvious. A congestion area of a point and figure chart is depicted in Figure 6.3. There is no upward or downward trend and

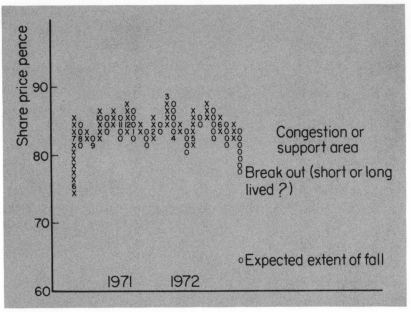

**Figure 6.3**

Point and figure conjestion area

no established pattern. The share price has in fact traded in the range 80 to 90p for twelve months. The analyst will attempt to predict the breakout from the congestion area. The breakout should be long enough and far enough to enable the investor to make an adequate return, i.e. breakouts of 1 or 2 per cent for a couple of days (before returning into the congestion area) are false and investors following such patterns would lose money. Analysts are less concerned with predicting prices within narrowish congestion areas as quite apart from the forecasting accuracy, the returns, even if analysis is entirely correct, will be small.

**Congestion areas**

Congestion areas arise when the market has a fairly clear opinion of the price of the share and the supply and demand functions are even. Built into this is the market psychology of investors who, having bought shares at, say, 83 will only sell if they show a profit, and investors who having sold at say 87 will buy only if the price is below this selling price. This tends to keep the price in the region of 80 to 90p. The efficient market theorists will argue, of course, that the 80 to 90 price range reflects the intrinsic value of the company and that one would expect shares to trade in this range.

**Congestion area breakouts**

Predicting an outbreak is very difficult and the techniques used by analysts are not always explicit. The methods used usually involve looking for a break from the area as in Figure 6.3. This break could be false in that the price can quickly revert into the congestion area or could be real, in which case it could be completed very quickly. Thus, an analyst will have to predict the breakouts at an early stage. This may involve predicting many breakouts which are eventually recognised as being false breaks. Some analysts employ cut-off techniques where a breakout has to reach a certain percentage before the analyst will react.

## Extent of a breakout

Having predicted the trend or direction of change in price the analyst will also try to forecast the amount of change, i.e. to predict the new price level to which the share is headed. There are numerous rules by which chartists can measure the extent of price change, although the most popular technique involves counting the number of columns covered by the band of congestion or the neckline of a head and shoulders formation. This measure is then added to the breakout of the congestion or neckline area and the resultant price is said to be the level which is expected. Thus, in Figure 6.3 the rule would indicate that the price will fall to a level of between 60 and 70p. There are, of course, numerous modifications which can and are made to this rule and the analyst will probably experiment to find the best techniques.

## Trend lines

Frequently the charts produce patterns which appear in an upward or downward trend. The chartists explain this behaviour pattern in terms of market psychology where investors get carried away with the initial share price rise and 'jump on the bandwagon' hoping to obtain profits. This often forces the prices too 'high'. The analysts also explain the price action in that fundamental news of dividend and earnings expectations takes time to be recognised and evaluated by investors, and so price patterns appear in trends.

Trend lines on charts that are moving up should be drawn connecting the bottoms (e.g. line *AB* in Figure 6.4). Figure 6.4 shows price sequences in multiples of 1p and reversals of 3p. Down-trend lines should be drawn connecting the tops (see line *EF* in Figure 6.4). Trend lines are formed from the initial data but as time goes on the line so formed will be found to be inappropriate for the later price behaviour. Thus the trend line will be modified with the old trend lines still being kept so as to show the minor variances within the major trend. Depending on the length of the trend and its visual linearity, the analyst will decide whether the share will remain within the trend. This gives a quick predictive device.

## Trend reversals

The analyst will have to use his judgment and skill, possibly using pre-determined action limits, to determine major reversals of trends. The chart will show breaks from the trend line and the analyst will have to decide whether it is a legitimate break or a false reaction. Obviously, time will tell which it is but by then the analyst will not be needed. If the analyst's judgment is wrong the false trend reversals will prove very expensive to the investor both in losses in investment value and from transaction costs. A frequent method used by analysts is to use a percentage break from the trend line. Thus, the analyst may wait until the highs fall, say, 10 per cent from the trend line before taking action. The extent of a reaction is largely a matter of judgment on the part of the analyst as few explicit techniques exist. Obviously the extent of the original trend will give some indication of the amount of the reaction.

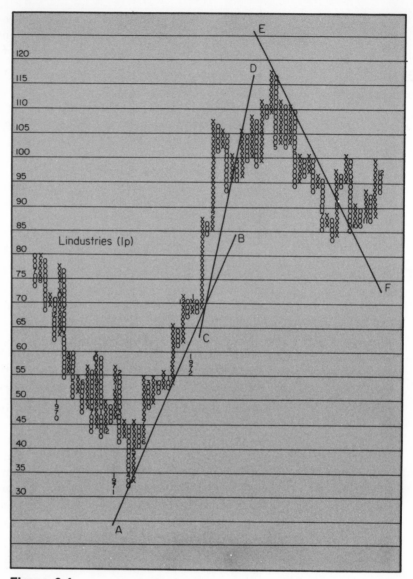

**Figure 6.4**

Point and figure trend lines

**Channels**

Trend lines can also be drawn as channels if the data is adequate. Here the tops of the up trend are connected as are the bottoms. Similar lines are drawn for the down-trend patterns. Figure 6.5 shows a three-box reversal point and figure chart for Hanson Trust. Lines *AB* which join the tops of the up trend and lines *CD* which join the bottoms of the up trend give the uptrend channel. Likewise, lines *EF* and *GH* give the down-trend channel.

The channels give additional guidelines to the analyst as he can see which of the lines are being tested the most, i.e. *AB* or *CD*. In Figure

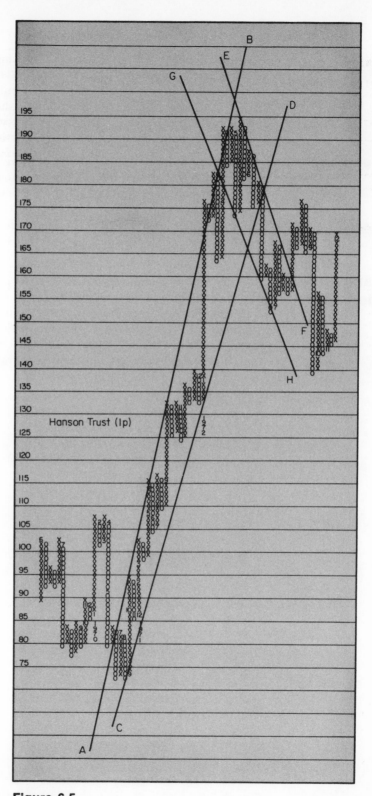

**Figure 6.5**

Point and figure channel pattern

193

6.5 *AB* is being tested more than *CD* and indicates a continued rise which in fact materialised. In the down-trend it was still the upper line, *EF*, which was being tested the most. This might suggest a purchase. The price did rise but it was smallish and short-lived, and so a false indication has been given. Thus, in common with other chart patterns it is no easy matter to interpret charts consistently and accurately.

**Complex patterns**

Apart from price trends and channels there exist more complicated patterns which analysts look for. These patterns give signals of major price reversals. They are explained by analysts as occurring due to market psychology with investors over-reacting to good performance and driving the price further upwards and over-reacting to price reactions where investors drive it down fast once disenchantment sets in.

**Head and shoulders**

The most well known of the reversal formations is the head and shoulders pattern. This is shown in Figure 6.6. Here the share price soars upwards on buying pressure which is further backed by investors 'jumping on the bandwagon'. Thus, a major top (*A*) is formed. A reaction sets in as the purchasers relax and a minor reversal to point *B* ensues. The theory claims that another upsurge takes place as the share

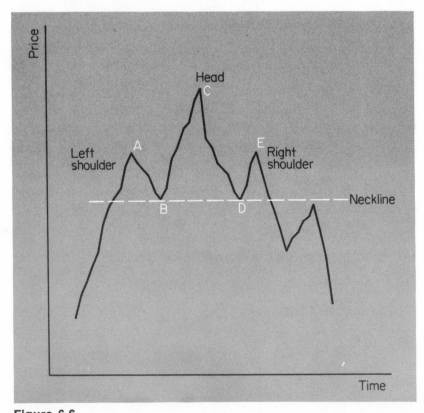

**Figure 6.6**

Head and shoulders pattern

is still a favourite and still very much in the limelight, and thus a new high top *C* is formed. Once again, the buying support is exhausted and the share price begins to drift lower. Technical analysts say that the area of the previous reaction low, *B*, should provide a resistance level (*D*) and a new, but lower than *C*, peak arises, *E*. From here the share price falls. It has no more buyers to attract and the price falls at a rapid rate. Once it has passed the line drawn through the points *B* and *D* (called the neckline) support is violated and the head and shoulders pattern completed. The break through the neckline is often followed by a substantial fall in price and any subsequent upward price trend is likely to find resistance at the head and shoulders neckline. Head and shoulder patterns also occur in an inverted form. The head and shoulders formation can have a number of tops and reversals although three is the number that analysts look for first and which occur most frequently. The neckline may not be horizontal but could slope upwards or downwards, the important factor being the breakthrough of a trend. The major cut-off point for analysts is when the neckline is broken; of course there can be very slight breaks below a trend line and so the analyst will have to form his own guidelines as to when the breakouts are 'real'.

The extent of declines depends partly, of course, on the degree of increase that occurred prior to the head and shoulder top. The extent of the top across the neckline is one method some analysts use in determining the subsequent fall. The larger the degree of prior increase and the greater the top formation the more likely that the subsequent fall will be greater. Figure 6.7 shows a three-box reversal pattern for European Ferries. The left shoulder is formed by a strong rise from 175p during December 1971. Two left shoulders are clearly visible before the top is eventually reached at 215p. The neckline is formed by drawing a line across the bottoms formed by the price reversals. This slopes upwards, therefore, giving an early selling signal. The right shoulder was formed during May 1972 and the price subsequently dropped to 170p before a period of congestion was formed. Note the break of the neckline at 200p indicated a sale and in this case the head and shoulder pattern gave a correct prediction. However, the appearance of two left shoulders could have deceived some analysts into an early sale before the peak top. This again emphasises the considerable skill and judgment required in interpreting charts.

## Triangles or flags

Other patterns include triangles or flags. Where the price movement has been erratic with a fair degree of movement between highs and lows a situation can occur such as in Figure 6.8. A triangle (flag) can be formed by constructing a line through the highs and lows of the series. The analyst interprets an upwards break out of the triangle as indicating that a purchase should be made and a downward break indicates a sale. The example shows a downward break from the triangle. Like all chart patterns the analyst will have to use judgment in deciding whether a break is real or not.

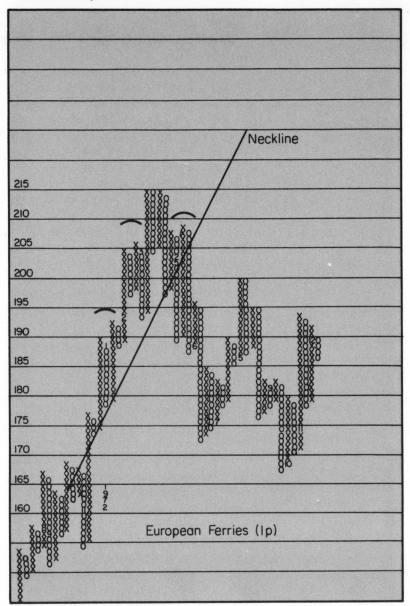

**Figure 6.7**

Head and shoulders pattern: An example

## Other patterns

There are other chart patterns which are in use and the reader is referred to the recommended texts at the end of the chapter for descriptions of these. These references also describe the use of charts and mechanical rules in conjunction with one another. For example, some analysts follow what is called a 'contrary' opinion theory. This says that if the market is optimistic then this is the time to sell, and vice versa. The logic here is that a bull market always over-reaches itself and the subsequent reaction is considerable. Of course, the method

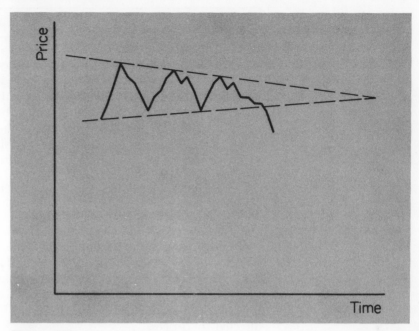

**Figure 6.8**

Triangle or flag pattern

requires knowing when the optimistic market becomes over-bullish as a sale could be made at the beginning or half-way through a bull market.

**Differing interpretations of charts**

Unlike the mechanical investment strategies charts need interpreting and thus experience and skill is needed. The varying conclusions drawn by practising analysts from the same chart is disturbing in that the technique is shown to be subjective and therefore difficult for a neophyte analyst to learn. However, the different conclusions drawn from the same pattern do reject one argument of the efficient market theory that, with a large number of chartists, any profit potential should be discounted away. However, it also points out that investors need to determine who is a good chartist as the different interpretations imply that some analysts are going to be completely wrong, whilst others may do little better than the market average.

**Practical chart analysis**

Experience in interpreting charts is also needed as chart patterns in practice are usually only vague impressions of the traditional textbook head and shoulders, triangle and trend line patterns. Thus the analyst will need skill in deciding when a pattern has been formed and even more to forecast the future direction and magnitude of prices. Obviously, profits are potentially the greatest when the analyst can determine patterns at an early stage. This requires considerable judgment, however, as many 'reversals' are spurious and to assidu-ously follow each one will result in large losses. Consistently correct interpretations of charts leads to significant profits and the fluctuations of the market indicate that the ability to decide when to buy and sell is potentially more profitable than knowing what to buy and sell. The evidence would seem to point out, however, that the average chartist is not all that successful.

**Use of computers in chart analysis**

Computers can be used in constructing charts and for serious technical analysts they may soon become a normal tool of the trade. Initially, computers can be used to build charts from data banks of share prices. Different scales can be used thus enabling the analyst to decide which produces the best predictive patterns. The computer can also be programmed to construct trend lines, measure deviations, count the extent of breakouts and highlight other patterns. The advantages of the computer are that it can handle masses of data very quickly and can act as a data retrieval system when there is a library of many thousand charts.

**Visual aid**

Besides behavioural patterns, charts are useful for the analyst as a visual aid in seeing what has happened to the price. It is also very useful in monitoring investment performance as the user can see at a glance the general overall picture. Charts also highlight the peaks and troughs of prices and an analyst new to the particular share therefore has reference points, i.e. he can look at the fundamental news which affected the prices.

### Mechanical investment strategies

The second major type of technical analysis does not make use of chart patterns but employs mechanical selection techniques. These rules use stock prices and other data (volume, for instance) and instead of plotting them on charts they are arranged into arithmetical formulae and ratios. At certain instances the rules will require that action be taken (buy or sell). Many of the rules are ranking methods which give relative forecasts and these are often short-term predictions. Numerous strategies have been devised and the major ones are described below. Some of these are not applicable to the UK at present because of data limitations and so will be described very briefly.

**Formulating strategies**

Many of the rules are derived from existing strategies with some modification, often relating to different action limits. Typically these rules are established on past data which showed profitable results. Following the technical analyst's claims that patterns exist, these mechanical rules which work on past data are assumed to work, at least more often than not, on future data. Such trading rules are very exact, unlike chartism which requires skill and judgment in interpreting the patterns. For this reason the random walk investigators have concentrated on investigating mechanical rules in their testing of market 'efficiency'.

### Volume of trading

As mentioned previously, volume data does not exist in the UK (apart from the marking of bargains which is a very rough indicator) but in the US it is used for a number of rules. One such strategy says that the end of a bear market can be signified by there being an increase in volume even though prices are low and possibly still falling. Similarly, in a bull market where the volume starts to drop this is an indicator of a pending fall. Many technical analysts believe that if the volume of trading increases on the days when a price rises and falls off when prices temporarily recede, the overall pattern is bullish. If, however, volume rises when the price falls, and falls when price rises, the pattern is bearish.

**Prediction of turning points**

Whilst major movements may be accompanied by changes in volume the problem arises of knowing when the volume statistics represent major turning points. Many of the volume statistics so obtained will give false indicators which will result in missing continuing up trends and also result in substantial costs. Conversely, if the investor waits a long time before acting, i.e. waiting for volume changes to consolidate themselves, he may miss the profitable opportunities; others act ahead and adjust the prices. Few explicit techniques have been publicised for calculating when the statistics represent genuine turning points. Most analysts will have cut-off points beyond which they will act, e.g. rising volume for seven days accompanied by price rises of at least 1 per cent in each day (giving a purchase signal).

Until volume data is made available in the UK little use can be made of the above techniques although brokers will be in a slightly advantageous position in that they will have certain knowledge of their volume transactions and of orders placed by investors. However, the trading rules really require very detailed and accurate information for them to be of any use.

**Indicators**

There is a substantial amount of technical analysis based on 'leading indicators' i.e. statistics which are in a lagged relationship to share prices. These data are used for predicting both market indices and individual share prices. Of course, once these relationships become well known one would expect them to be discounted immediately and for investors to start anticipating the indicators such that the market might tend towards 'efficiency'. Technical theorists counter this by saying that the indicators need interpreting (i.e. subjective expertise) and that they have better anticipatory skills. The most popular methods are summarised below although it must be realised that many are not applicable in the UK because of lack of data.

**Short sales**

Short sales are sales by investors of stock they do not own as they expect prices to fall. However, eventually they must cover their positions and buy stock and so substantial purchase demand will be built up in order to cover positions. The New York Stock Exchange (NYSE) and the American Stock Exchange (Amex) make public monthly the amount of short interest (uncovered stock) for stocks when such interest has showed significant increases since the prior month. The analyst computes the ratio of short interest to average daily trading volume of the stock. If, for instance, the ratio rises dramatically it signifies that a larger percentage of future trading activity is likely to be anxious buyers covering short positions (of course significant short selling also indicates impending bad news, thus the technical investor will want to keep his positions very short).

## Application in UK

The existence of bear covering (covering of short sales) is a frequently-cited reason for price movements in some UK shares. However, only the brokers may know of the position, and then it will only be for their own clients. Thus the extent of short sales in the UK is largely a subjective estimate based on market rumours. As investors have to cover their positions by certain dates (the account date) the technical analysts will start buying two or three days before the end of the Account (as more technical investors come in the further back the buying date will have to go). This process will be abrogated by individuals and institutions who do not have to work within the Account. Thus, only investors actually in the market will have any data on which to make evaluations and these will be tenuous anyway.

## Credit balance accounts analysis

Similar analyses can be made by examining credit balances in Brokers' Customer Accounts. The statistics relating to these are published monthly in the US. When the credits rise it indicates that a strong buying potential exists. That is, investors are not investing their cash in fixed interest stocks or in any other commodity but are waiting for early share purchasing opportunities. Such statistics do not exist in the UK although brokers themselves may have opinions of the weight of liquid money awaiting investment. Further, few British investors leave surplus monies with their brokers.

## Dow Theory

Probably the best known mechanical rule is the Dow Theory which predicts the market level as a whole. The theory consists of measuring when a series of tops and bottoms in a price series emerges as a major upward or downward trend and not just another minor oscillation. The Dow Theory considers that a major reversal has taken place when the chart pattern has occurred in both the industrial and railroad averages. Variations of the theory using different indexes have been made subsequently by analysts. This type of analysis can be conducted in the UK where there are adequate industry indices. For instance the 'breadth of market' analysis can be constructed. This measures the advance/decline statistics and compares the figures of the daily cumulation of the number of share prices advancing and declining against the Market Index. The net difference is calculated and cumulated thus:

| | No. of bargains recorded | Advances | Declines | No change | Net advances or declines |
|---|---|---|---|---|---|
| Monday | 1200 | 430 | 370 | 400 | 60 |
| Tuesday | 1250 | 435 | 485 | 330 | −50 |
| Wednesday | 1220 | 480 | 505 | 235 | −25 |
| Thursday | 1150 | 460 | 450 | 240 | 10 |
| Friday | 1200 | 510 | 330 | 360 | 180 |

**Cumulative total**

| | |
|---|---|
| Monday | +60 |
| Tuesday | +10 |
| Wednesday | −15 |
| Thursday | −5 |
| Friday | +175 |

The numbers so obtained are then plotted against the market average such as the FT Ordinary Share Index. Normally they will move in tandem but when significant divergences appear this indicates that a significant number of issues are, say, falling whilst the blue chips (the constituent stocks of the FT Ordinary Share Index) are rising. The analyst then has to decide whether the blue chips will adjust or whether it is the secondary issues which will alter. In most cases the FT Ordinary Share Index will be expected to adjust. Of course this type of analysis could be obviated by the use of the FTA All Share Index. Because of the FTA All Share Index's wide spread it should move very closely with the advance/decline statistics. There are no published results showing that any of the FTA indices or the FT Ordinary Share Index can be forecast from advance/decline statistics. The theory has its advocates, however, and the interested investor can test this and similar strategies.

## Odd-lot trading

Odd-lot trading is the name given to bargains made by the small, private investor who makes transactions of less than a hundred shares (odd lots). According to the theory these investors make the wrong decisions at turning points in share prices or market levels. The sales to purchases ratio of odd-lot investors, statistics which are available daily in the US, is compared with the market average as a whole and the degree of divergence noted. Analysts have different limits when they think the divergence has gone far enough to warrant action. Again, this analysis cannot be conducted in the UK.

### Relative strength

A number of rules have been devised based on the premise that a share that has had a good performance will continue that performance in the near future. Obviously this will not hold true for ever. However, its protagonists claim it works consistently enough to provide worth while profits. The criteria of good performance depends upon the rule and upon the analyst in particular.

One common analysis is to compare the share's performance against its moving average. The moving average is the average price of the stock over the preceding $x$ number of days. The rule requires buying the stock when it moves above its moving average or when it moves above by at least, say, 5 per cent, or by some other percentage. Similar filter tests have been devised based on buying or selling shares when they have moved $x$ per cent above or below previous highs or lows*.

Another test that is frequently used and publicised is to rank the relative strength ratios, calculated as above, and to purchase those securities in, say, the top 10 per cent of the list. The list is amended at regular intervals and stocks that have fallen so far from the top 10 per cent are sold and purchases made of new entrants in the top 10 per cent. These rules have been subject to considerable testing by statisticians and the profit potentials appear to be non-existent. However, the reader may like to derive similar tests with his own control limits. They may work for certain periods but it is unlikely to be a very consistent rule. The whole basis behind these analyses is that good performance will be followed by good performance. The interpretation being that news of a company's 'worth' is only slowly disseminated and therefore there is a gradual price adjustment. This is in serious contention with the efficient market hypothesis which contends that fundamental news is immediately reflected in share prices.

### Formula plans

There exist a number of mechanical rules which give formula plans for the timing of investment purchases and which make no attempt to predict the market level. The aim is to reduce the average purchase price to as low a figure as possible. The techniques do not attempt, therefore, to beat the market. It is used primarily by investors who expect the returns from the Stock Market over long periods of time to be significantly profitable but who cannot or will not try to measure shorter-term share price movements. In some respects this reason is entirely plausible for although the Stock Market averages are expected to be higher in, say, twenty years from now, the various statistical studies have shown that predicting the market for shorter-term fluctuations is very difficult.

**Pound averaging**    The most common method is that of pound averaging where an investor selects a stock or group of stocks and invests an equal pound amount at equal time intervals, regardless of the level of the market. The Stock Market will be going up and down within a long-term upward trend and so by the pound-averaging method the investor will be buying more shares when the prices are low than when the prices are

*One such test is known as the Hatch System.

high (this is contrasted to the method of buying equal numbers of shares).

*Example*

| | Period | 1 Market price of stock p | 2 No. of shares bought with £1,000 | 3 Cumul- ative total no. of shares owned | 4 Total invest- ment £ | 5 Value of shares held (2 × 4) £ | 6 Avg. cost per share (5 ÷ 4) p | 7 Avg. market price p | 8 Profit or loss (6–5) £ |
|---|---|---|---|---|---|---|---|---|---|
| Stable share price | 1 | 50 | 2,000 | 2,000 | 1,000 | 1,000 | 50 | 50 | 0 |
| | 2 | 45 | 2,222 | 4,222 | 2,000 | 1,900 | 47.4 | 47.5 | −100 |
| | 3 | 55 | 1,818 | 6,040 | 3,000 | 3,322 | 49.7 | 50 | +322 |
| | 4 | 50 | 2,000 | 8,040 | 4,000 | 4,020 | 49.7 | 50 | +20 |
| Buy and hold strategy at period 1 | | 50 | 8,000 | | 4,000 | 4,000* | | | 0 |
| Share price with high volatility | 1 | 50 | 2,000 | 2,000 | 1,000 | 1,000 | 50 | 50 | 0 |
| | 2 | 30 | 3,333 | 5,333 | 2,000 | 1,599 | 37.5 | 40 | −401 |
| | 3 | 65 | 1,538 | 6,871 | 3,000 | 4,466 | 43.7 | 48.3 | +1,466 |
| | 4 | 60 | 1,667 | 8,538 | 4,000 | 5,123 | 46.8 | 51.2 | +1,123 |
| Buy and hold strategy at period 1 | | 50 | 8,000 | | 4,000 | 4,800† | | | 800 |

*8,000 shares at 50p (Period 4)
†8,000 shares at 60p (Period 4)

The example shows the performance of the averaging formula against a buy and hold policy. The impact of using the policy on a share with a volatile price behaviour is similarly shown. Similar pound averaging can be conducted in buying the index although this is likely to be done via a widely spread unit trust. The results are similar to those produced by ordinary stocks.

## Practical modifications to pound averaging

The pound-averaging formula can be modified to incorporate certain items and perhaps to incorporate specific alterations where the investor feels he has good knowledge. This may take the form of having inside information on the prospects of one security and he may invest all his money in that stock thus ending (temporarily) his averaging rule. Or it may take the form of him having a confident view of what the market is going to do. Again, he may modify his rule to allow him to invest more money when the Stock Market average is (say) below the long-term trend of prices he has projected. For example, the investor's plan may consist of investing, say, an average amount of £1,000 for a period of twenty years in a stock. However, the modified plan would allow him to accelerate or decelerate the pace at which investments are made, depending on whether the market is below or above a projected trend line.

## Ratio plans

Another type of investment formula is that of ratio plans where a certain proportion of a portfolio is to be kept in fixed interest stocks, i.e. an investor may want an annual income whilst at the same time wanting to have a hedge against inflation. If the investor cannot predict the short-term fluctuations of the Stock Market the portfolio can adopt a ratio plan. This devotes a proportion of funds to equities, the remainder being in fixed-interest stocks. After a period the investor examines the values and proportions of the portfolio and if (say) the equity content had risen significantly above its stated proportion a sale would be made and the funds invested in fixed-interest stocks to bring back the original proportion. The proportion settled on is often a rising trend, i.e. a 75 per cent equity content initially, and changes are made only if this value increases beyond 80 per cent in five years, 85 per cent in ten years. This is done because the capital value of the equity shares are expected to grow in time. The fixed-interest stocks provide the security and the annual income.

## Guidelines in pound averaging policies

The following points should be noted by analysts advocating a pound-averaging policy as any deviations may ruin the whole idea of such policies.

1  The share prices should be fairly volatile.

2  The investor should obviously be confident that over the longer period share prices will show substantial growth.

3  The strategy should be employed for a fair period of time (say ten to twenty years). This will straddle a number of bear and bull markets and thus produce a low average cost per share. This means an investor should be fairly sure he will not need to liquidate his investment at short notice, at least one year, which would prevent, say, selling in a (very apparent) bear market.

4  The fixed investment should be made at consistent intervals at, say, three-, six- or, at most, twelve-monthly intervals. If consistent dates are not used then this brings in the subjective timing judgment of the investor – i.e. it no longer is a purely mechanical rule. The interval between investing should not be too long as bear cycles could be missed and these are the best times to buy.

For the investor who does not think he can successfully predict the short- and medium-term movements of the market the pound-averaging plan may, whilst he accumulates capital, give the best strategy. For the investor who starts off with a large sum of capital he may be better off investing all of it immediately. If, however, the investor thinks the market will fluctuate considerably (without knowing when) and that the current time is not recognised as being particularly cheap, then pound averaging may afford a solution.

**Assumptions in formula plans**

Although the formulae do not require a knowledge of the fluctuations of the Stock Market, they do require assumptions of investments providing long-term growth over the analyst's time horizon and more specifically for estimates of the trend of Stock Market levels (for ratio plans). Such estimates of the trend will need to be fairly accurate for the plan to work successfully. In summary, the formula plans offer a formal investment framework. However, it assumes that any investment analysis available to the investor is not worth while.

**Combining technical rules**

One method used by technical analysts is to use a number of mechanical rules and chart patterns in evaluating securities. If there is a strong majority in favour of a purchase or sale then the projection is followed. This composite method is commonly used in evaluating the market as a whole although individual shares can also be forecast in the same way. This method makes especial use of the leading indicator type of mechanical rule.

This section has described the more commonly-used mechanical rules although there are numerous others that have been devised and indeed readers may readily think of original relationships. As can be seen different action limits may be set by analysts, these often being determined by testing on historical data. An important factor in the analyst's appraisal of a rule is that the more active the control limits, the greater the expenses involved and the greater the chance that the indicator is wrong. A major 'advantage' of the rules is that they are quite explicit and do not require any judgment on the part of the investor. Some of the rules that have been described arose in the US and are not applicable in UK at the present time due to lack of data. This, however, may change in time as the demand for greater disclosure grows.

**The use of computers in mechanical investment strategies**

The computer has an important role in these mechanical selection techniques because of the voluminous calculations necessary in deriving rules and in the selection of cut-off points. The computer enables the analyst to test any number of rules using various action limits and it is an easy matter to examine the sensitivity of the rules and to 'update' historical data. Whilst chart analysis requires substantial individual judgment, mechanical trading rules are tailor-made for data banks of share prices and for the arithmetic function of a high-speed digital computer.

**Conclusion**

Technical analysis has come in for considerable criticism from the proponents of the Efficient Markets Theory and this has applied especially to the explicit mechanical trading rules. The main defence to this argument is that any truly profitable rule won't have been publicised and therefore not statistically tested (the investigations have generally been on published rules). The existence of firms engaged in technical analysis shows that many investors have faith in the methods of technical analysis and this may be based on a successful record.

Chart patterns require skilful subjective judgment from the analyst and because of the lack of conceptual backing the techniques maintain an air of mystery. Mechanical rules on the other hand have been proved to work on historical data and indeed this is how they are usually derived. However, the very mechanical nature of the rules allows any investor to obtain the same results and so a widely accepted strategy would discount and rule out any profitable opportunities. Neither chartism nor mechanical rules have the logical 'correctness' of fundamental analysis although in the efficient market the success rate of the various techniques would be the same. If the market is 'efficient' this may explain why no one method of analysis has taken complete preference over the others.

Technical analysis has gained a fair amount of acceptance as a short-term forecasting method and as a timing strategy for purchasing securities selected by fundamental analysis. This has gained weight from the self-fulfilment of prophesies of the better known technical rules. Technical strategies certainly play a part in determining share prices and so the analyst will at least have to have an appreciation of the techniques that are in use. Conversely, technical analysts often incorporate fundamental data in their forecasts. Although lacking in conceptual backing, technical theories certainly determine the investment strategies of many investors. Within the framework of fundamental analysis and a Stock Market with many competing analysts it may be that technical strategies provide the best forecasting device. It will be up to the individual analyst to derive and test various mechanical rules and to assess chart patterns. If these are successful the analyst will obviously follow them up, the only caveat being to constantly re-appraise the methods.

**References**

The following represent the major texts on chart analysis and mechanical trading strategies. They give detailed descriptions of the various techniques they advocate.

Barnes, L., 'Your Investments', American Research Council, 1967.
Drew, G. A., 'New Methods for Profit in the Stock Market', Fraser Publishing Co., 1966.
Edwards, R. D. and Magee, J., 'Technical Analysis of Stock Market Trends', John Magee, Springfield, Mass.: 1964.
Ellinger, A. G., 'The Art of Investment', Bowes and Bowes, 1971.
Gordon, W., 'The Stock Market Indicators', Investors' Press Inc., Larchmont N.Y.
Granville, J. E., 'New Key to Stock Market Profits', Englewood Cliffs, 1963.
Investors Intelligence Inc., 'Encyclopaedia of Stock Market Techniques, Section I, Technical Patterns and Indicators', Larchmont N.Y., 1965.
Seligman, D., 'Playing the market with charts', *Fortune*, Feb. 1962.

*Technical analysis*

Seligman, D., 'The mystique of point and figure', *Fortune*, Mar. 1962.

Tomlinson, L., 'Practical Formulas for Successful Investing', New York: William Funk, 1953.

Wheelan, A. H., 'Study Helps in Point and Figure Technique', Morgan, Rogers and Roberts, US, 1957.

There have been many empirical examinations of the validity of mechanical investment strategies and these are usually described as Efficient Market Theory studies. Summaries of the major studies in this field are contained in the reference books by Brealey 'An Introduction to Risk and Return from Common Stocks', MIT Press, 1969, and 'Security Prices in a Competitive Market', MIT Press, 1971, and by Granger and Morgenstern, 'Predictability of Stock Market Prices', Heath Lexington, 1970. Research covering the technical theories discussed in this chapter include the following.

### Indicators

Homa, K. E. and Jaffee, D. M., 'The supply of money and common stock prices', *Journal of Finance*, XXVI, Dec. 1971, No. 5.

Pinches, G. E., 'The random walk hypothesis and technical analysis', *Financial Analysts Journal*, Mar.–Apr. 1970.

Seelenfreund, A., Parker, G. G. C. and Van Horne, J. C., 'Stock price behaviour and trading', *Journal of Financial and Quantitative Analysis*, Special Issue, Sept. 1968.

### Breadth of market

Drzycimski, E. F., 'Testing the Breadth-of-Market Theory', *Business Perspectives*, Vol. 5, No. 4, Summer, 1969.

### Filter tests

Alexander, S. S., 'Price movements in speculative markets: trends or random walks', *Industrial Management Review*, 2 May 1961.

Alexander, S. S., 'Price movements in speculative markets: trends or random walks no. 2', *Industrial Management Review*, 5, Spring, 1964.

Dryden, M. M., 'Filter tests of UK share prices', *Applied Economics*, Vol. I, No. 4 January 1970.

Fama, E. and Blume, M., 'Filter rules and Stock Market trading profits', *Journal of Business*, 39 (Special Supplement), Jan. 1966.

### Moving averages

Cootner, P., 'Stock prices: random *vs.* systematic changes', *Industrial Management Review*, 3, Spring, 1962.

James, F. E., 'Monthly moving averages – an effective investment tool', *Journal of Financial and Quantitative Analysis*, Sept. 1968.

Van Horne, J. C. and Parker, G. G. C., 'The Random Walk Theory: an empirical test', *Financial Analysts Journal*, Nov. – Dec. 1967.

### Relative strength

Jensen, M. C. and Bennington, G. A., 'Random walks and technical theories: some additional evidence', *Journal of Finance*, 25, May 1970.

Levy, R. A., 'An Evaluation of Selected Applications of Stock Market Timing Techniques, Trading Tactics and Trend Analysis', Unpublished Ph.D dissertation, The American University, 1966.

Levy, R. A., 'Relative strength as a criterion for investment selection', *Journal of Finance*, 22, Dec. 1967.

Weisman, B. B., 'An Empirical Study of 21 Investment Criteria Employed in Common Stock Selection', Ph.D thesis, New York University, 1970.

### Fixed proportion investment strategies

Cheng, P. L. and Deets, M. K., 'Portfolio returns and the Random Walk Theory', *Journal of Finance*, Mar. 1971.

Evans, J. L., 'An Analysis of Portfolio Maintenance Strategies', *Journal of Finance*, Jun. 1970.

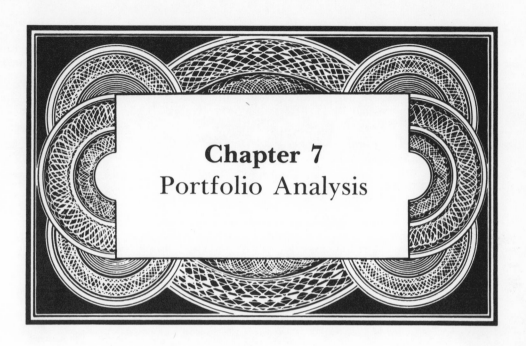

# Chapter 7
Portfolio Analysis

So far, the book has described techniques with which to value individual shares, and these values are then compared against the existing market price to give the cheapness or dearness of the security. A rational investor in the certain world would purchase the cheapest security until the market price increased such that another share becomes the cheapest. However, the relative rankings of shares are not certain as are virtually all forecasts of the future. This risk or uncertainty* can be defined as the unpredictability of the return from an investment. In portfolio theory the risk profile of an analyst's forecast or a share's past performance is used as a surrogate for the unknown probability distribution of future returns. Although the analyst has made a detailed forecast of the company's earnings position and its intrinsic value there is still the possibility that the firm could become bankrupt and so leave the shares valueless. For instance, the expropriation of assets held abroad, some natural calamity or an outbreak of war could all make nonsense of the most careful evaluation. A much more common occurrence is that of the analyst's evaluations of share prices and market movements being inaccurate to varying degrees. Thus, whilst not going into liquidation, the investor could find share prices falling by 10 per cent against an expected increase of 10 per cent. A further risk is that of predicting short-term price movements for investors who have short-term surplus funds. Here the analyst has to forecast the intrinsic value and additionally he has to assess when the market is likely to come to the same opinion.

*Strictly this is a case of uncertainty. However, risk and uncertainty are usually used synonymously in investment literature.

## Reduction of risk

The main method used to reduce the level of risk in equity returns is for the investor to purchase shares in more than one company. For example, the chance of an oil company having its assets expropriated and thus going into liquidation may be 0.01. Thus there is one chance in a hundred of the investor losing all his money. If the investor puts half his money into an engineering concern which has no overseas assets then the most the investor will lose because of political instability will be one-half of his investment. As long as the various shares the investor owns are not dependent on exactly the same external events then diversification acts to reduce risk. The term 'portfolio' is given to the case where an investor makes a number of investments and 'portfolio management' refers to the building and administration of such groups of investments*.

## Number of shares needed in a portfolio

In general, the greater the number of investments up to a total of twenty or so, the greater the diversification and the less the risk†. Many investment and unit trusts have followed a very diversified portfolio policy and their annual returns over many years show very little difference from the market average. However, in practice a carefully selected portfolio of around twenty stocks can provide virtually as much risk aversion as buying the 'market'. Such portfolios may be much cheaper to administer and may offer greater returns. Thus portfolio management is not just a matter of picking the 'cheapest' stocks or of buying the 'market'. As will be described later the relationships between securities often contribute more to the characteristics of a portfolio than does the relative cheapness of the securities involved. It is the derivation of the relationships between returns from shares that has evoked considerable quantitative research to portfolio planning.

The chapter will begin by examining why portfolios are built; it will then describe the methods employed and the problems involved in fund management and, finally, briefly introduce some of the more recent quantitative approaches to building optimal portfolios.

## Riskiness of shares

The risk in holding shares and portfolios of shares is the uncertainty of future returns. Additionally, there is the uncertainty of future returns from other forms of investment an investor could have made. This is the risk of opportunities foregone, such as increases in property values or increases in fixed-interest securities. The investor normally says how much money he is willing to put into equities and it is then up to the portfolio manager to reduce risk and increase expected returns. There are a growing number of services, however, which now look at the complete financial requirements of their clients, and they apportion the funds between various investments.

## Risk aversion

Before examining how risk can be reduced it is relevant to assess why

*In this chapter we are concerned solely with shares. It should be recognised that a portfolio can consist wholly or partially of other assets.

†This will be expanded upon later. It is very possible for a group of twenty stocks to be less risky than a randomly selected group of, say, fifty securities.

investors want to reduce risk. Most investors can be classified as risk avertors, i.e. for a given level of return they prefer less risk[1]. Quantification of an investor's attitude to risk can be obtained by asking them how much return they would expect for given levels of risk. As there is usually a point beyond which increasing returns yield a lesser increase in investor satisfaction the relationship between risk and return is of the form shown in Figure 7.1. This is a concave relationship showing the risk aversion preference (known as an indifference curve). For gamblers, the function will be convex showing the investor's preference for higher and higher possible returns. In practice, of course, it is not feasible to ask all investors what their risk preferences are and this will be partly because they will not know themselves.

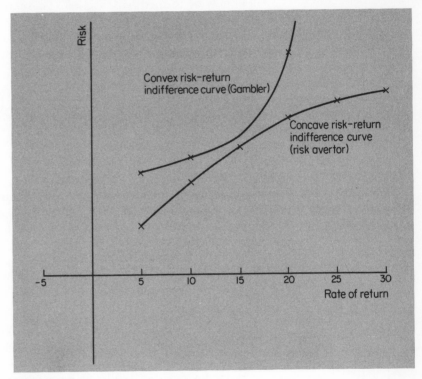

**Figure 7.1**

Risk-return indifference curves

**Factors in an investor's risk preferences**

The extent of an investor's risk aversion will depend on a number of factors, all of which will need to be assessed by the portfolio manager. The main factors are:

1  The investor's financial circumstances, i.e. his wealth, annual income, and financial commitments. Investments in stocks and shares should be for investors who can afford to lock away their funds for two or three years. Whilst, historically, the Stock Market indices have risen there have been individual years when large negative returns have been made. Short-term investors will therefore be looking for a very wide coverage of shares if they are interested at all in Stock Exchange equity

investment. Investors whose funds represent savings for their old age will obviously prefer less risk and they are usually attracted by a portfolio consisting of the more traditional 'safe' shares.

2 The strength of an investor's belief in the shares he buys. If, for example, he has inside knowledge of a company's prospects or inside knowledge of, say, a takeover bid, he may decide to invest all his money in one share. In this case the investor has reduced his risk by having superior knowledge of the future.

3 The personal objectives and characteristics of the investor. There are investors who have funds which they want to increase substantially and which they are prepared to lose completely in this quest. This can definitely be termed 'risk' capital. There are a fair number of these 'fortune seekers' and they have a significant impact on the market prices of shares they invest in. Many of these individuals invest in the more volatile areas of Stock Market activity such as warrants and options.

4 Various portfolios have legal obligations to which the portfolio manager must adhere. In some cases these consist of limitations to the amount of risk that can be taken. Typical examples include not being able to invest more than 5 per cent of total funds in one particular stock or not investing in shares which have not paid dividends in every one of the last ten years.

## Measuring investors' risk preferences

In managing private clients' portfolios the investment manager will have to assess how much risk the investor wants to bear. This will be difficult to establish exactly but the skilled manager should be able to obtain an approximate idea. He will be helped by knowing the investor's total financial position and his general objectives in life. These together with the tax position of the investor should give some criteria for a suitable portfolio to be built.

## The work of investment managers

The investment manager may be charged with the complete management of an investor's resources, in which case he will have to consider all the various investment alternatives. This chapter, however, assumes that the portfolio manager's brief is to look after Stock Exchange investments and specifically ordinary stocks and shares. His job will entail the choosing of stocks and the evaluation of their impact on the expected returns and the risk of the portfolio, and the administration of such. His decisions will include deciding whether to invest at all or whether to dis-invest at various stages. This involves judgment of what the market as a whole is likely to do and the practical problems in building and liquidating portfolios.

## Correlation in returns between shares

The expected return from a portfolio is the weighted return of the constituent shares. The risk of the portfolio is, however, a more complex matter. In some cases diversification does little in the way of reducing risk: e.g. dividing funds into two and investing half in one oil company and the other half in another oil company may achieve little in reducing risk. Both companies would be subject to the same political and economic conditions and these are likely to be the important factors in determining their worth. If one company had its assets expropriated then so, probably, would the other, assuming they have their oilwells in the same country. Similarly, their sales patterns are likely to be affected more by economic conditions such as import or Customs' and Excise duties and these are common to all oil companies; the movement in market share is not likely to be as big a determinant of profitability in periods of, say, one year. The share prices of the two oil companies would therefore be highly correlated and the risk of the two stock portfolio would be very similar to those of the shares individually. Hence, the reduction of risk is better facilitated by diversifying into shares in different industries, and the impact can be quite dramatic, i.e. one portfolio consisting of ten motor distributors may be far more risky than one portfolio consisting of three stocks, one being in the motor industry, one in the building industry and the third being in insurance. It will be quite obvious that diversification into other forms of assets or into foreign stocks and shares will further reduce risk as the returns from these investments are poorly correlated with share price movements in the UK. It must be recognised, however, that risk cannot be diversified away completely in an equity portfolio. This is partly because all share prices are correlated to some extent with the market average, and the various industrial indices are correlated to some degree with each other. Some American research based on multiple regression and factor analysis has shown that on average 31 per cent of a share's price behaviour was attributable to the market factor, 12 per cent explained by the industrial index, 37 per cent to other groupings and 20 per cent to the particular characteristics of the individual stock[2]. Although this study was conducted on American data in the period 1927 to 1960 it might well be that the market and industrial indices have a similar impact in the UK.

**Optimising diversification policies**

Portfolio managers have been aware of the importance of spreading portfolio stocks over several industries for a long time. This, however, has been done on an intuitive basis with few managers statistically evaluating the correlation between stocks and the portfolio or assessing the relationships between variables. Since the early 1950s however, significant strides have been made in quantifying the relationships between share prices and the impact on portfolio risk. There is now a significant body of knowledge concerning portfolio theory and the basic ideas will be outlined later. Unfortunately as yet much of the theory is inapplicable to the practical problems of portfolio management and this is because of a number of reasons which will be discussed later.

**Marketability and liquidity constraints**

Apart from the quantification of risk and return the portfolio manager is usually faced with various constraints, the most common being liquidity and marketability, the tax position and statutory law. The ease of liquidating a portfolio is especially important for short-term investors who cannot afford to adopt a disinvestment policy lasting several weeks. Commercial companies and banking institutions may have short-term surplus funds which they wish to invest in the Stock Market but as these funds may be required very quickly for working capital requirements, or to meet demand liabilities in the case of a bank, the investments must be easily liquidated. Further, the liquidation process should not drive the market price too low. In practice this will mean the manager will have to invest in the medium to large companies as smaller concerns tend to have poorer marketability. Also, large positions should not be taken in companies when liquidity and marketability are essential. Thus not more than, say, 1 per cent of a company's equity should be acquired as any excess may be difficult to liquidate conveniently. In the US there exists a fairly efficient market in the placing of large blocks of stock: this is not the case in the UK however, and so large holdings are undesirable for portfolios which have to be very marketable.

**Longer-term portfolios**

Some portfolios such as pension funds and investment trusts do not have to be particularly marketable and large positions can be taken in various investments. Thus pension funds are quite often invested in private companies who have no market for their shares and in other longer-term investments.

**Tax liability**

This chapter later describes the taxation of certain institutions who have obtained exemptions and variations on the normal rates of tax. The manager will need to be fully aware of the tax liability of the fund he is managing as the impact can be quite large. The general rule is to use after-tax returns to the fund. This can easily be applied to dealing in bonds and fixed interest investments when the annual interest and amounts payable on redemption are known precisely. The process is more difficult in the case of equities as dividend income is an estimate and capital gains are an even more tenuous forecast. The portfolio manager will often have to estimate what form the returns are likely to be in, i.e. income or capital appreciation. For example, a wealthy individual will prefer capital gains as opposed to the higher taxed dividend income. It will therefore be advisable for him to buy the low-yielding, high-growth share the main return of which will be in the form of a capital gain. Thus the portfolio manager will have to determine the tax liabilities of the funds he is administering and plan accordingly.

**Statutory law and trust deed constraints**

The construction of portfolios may be subject to various constraints imposed by law or by specific trust deeds. These usually refer to the types of shares held and the amounts that can be held in any one security. The principal rules and regulations governing the main categories of portfolios will be discussed below. Trust deeds which set out the administration and investment policies of charitable foundations or bequeathals can impose many varied conditions. For example, some trust deeds prevent investment in brewery shares or in South African companies whilst some may insist that an investment is kept in, say, a family company. Many of these trust deeds were drawn up many years ago and, whilst some of the conditions are no longer relevant, they still have to be adhered to. The portfolio manager must acknowledge the various legal requirements governing the investing of the funds under his care and set out to maximise the return and minimise risk within the constraints set out.

**Trustee Investments Act**

Where a trust fund is established with no guidelines as to how it is to be invested the Trustee Investments Act 1961 will apply. This empowers a trustee to obtain a valuation of the trust fund whereupon he can divide the portfolio into two equal parts, one of which will consist of 'narrower-range investments' and the other 'wider-range investments'. Narrower-range investments are made up of various fixed-interest securities. The wider-range investments include fully-paid shares issued and registered in the UK by a company incorporated in the UK whose issued and paid-up share capital totals at least £1 million and which has paid a dividend on all of its issued shares in each of the preceding five years.

**Unit trusts**

The majority of the country's population do not have sufficient resources to diversify their investments or to manage them properly on a day-to-day basis. To cater for these needs, unit trusts have been set up which enable small investors to purchase a stake in a large number of equities. The unit trust will sell units representing a proportion of the trust's total assets to an individual at a specified price. This price is governed by the underlying value of the fund. The unit trust will buy back units from investors who want to sell, at a price determined by the underlying value of the fund. It is possible for unit trusts to be making greater repayments than it is obtaining in new money and therefore there needs to be a fair sprinkling of easily liquidatable investments. Authorised unit trusts are governed by a trust deed and by the Prevention of Fraud (Investments) Act 1958. The provisions of this Act are administered by the Department of Trade and Industry. The trust deed often lays down regulations as to what shares can be bought for the fund as well as giving details of amounts that can be invested in any one share and details of liquidity requirements. For example, many unit trusts can only invest in certain sectors of the market such as gold shares or exporting companies. The trust deed is enforced by the trustees who are often a well-respected bank or insurance company.

**Unit trust taxation**

Authorised unit trusts pay no tax on their franked income and make no income tax deduction from distributions to unit holders. They pay corporation tax on unfranked income net of allowable expenses in respect of management and interest charges. From 6 April 1972 unit trusts have paid capital gains tax at 15 per cent. Individual taxpayers are then taxed at 30 per cent on the gains made on disposals of the units but this is reduced by a credit of 15 per cent of the gain. The net effect is that investors are taxed at 15 per cent. Certain exemptions are given as regards capital gains when the withdrawals from a trust exceed the inflows and for certain trusts whose holders are charities or approved pension funds.

**Investment trusts**

Investment trusts are limited liability companies, the shares of which

215

are bought and sold like any other stock. The capital is fixed and investors participate by owning shares in the company. The function of an investment trust is to invest in stocks and shares and it is the value of these funds which determine the price of the trust shares. Investment trust share prices are usually at a discount to the asset value partly because of the expenses in running the trust and partly because of the lower dividend yield. Under the provisions of the 1965 Finance Act* there are a number of requirements which must be satisfied in order for the company to qualify for tax treatment as an investment trust. The major items of the Act affecting portfolio management are that not more than 15 per cent of the portfolio may be invested in any one security, that dividends paid by the investment trust must amount to at least 85 per cent of income and that the income is derived wholly or mainly from stocks and shares.

## Investment policies of investment trusts

Investment trusts can raise fixed-interest capital which enables investors to obtain the benefits and the risks of gearing. Some investment trusts specialise in certain sectors of the market and such conditions are written into their articles. A large number of trusts have capital structures which allow for capital shares and income shares. The capital shares entitle their owners to all the capital gain of the fund over a certain amount whilst the income shares are entitled to all the annual income over a certain sum or, in some cases, the entire income. These financial structures are referred to as 'split-level trusts'. Investment trusts are allowed to invest in unquoted companies and mortgages; any restrictions will appear in the articles of association[3]. Because investment trusts are assumed to have an infinite life, i.e. unless the articles state otherwise, they are not necessarily regarded as short-term investors. However, they do have a market price and so management cannot ignore short-term performance altogether.

## Investment trust taxation

The tax liabilities on investments in an investment trust are the same as for authorised unit trusts. This only applies to the companies which are designated investment trusts by the 1965 Finance Act and by subsequent Finance Acts.

## Pension funds

Pension funds typically increase with time as new contributions outweigh pensions being paid out. As there is no limit to the life of pension funds the investments can be long-term. This is strengthened by the fact that the pension fund performance is not published and indeed its measurement would be difficult anyway. Thus, there is little pressure on the investment manager to achieve a good return over the short period. Obviously, there needs to be some liquidity in the case of unusual events and in the few cases of there being a declining pension fund. Pension funds are allowed to be invested in unquoted companies and various other assets. Approved pension funds are generally free from all taxation on dividends and capital gains. Thus, they can reclaim income tax deducted from dividend receipts.

*As modified by subsequent Finance Acts.

**Assurance companies**

Assurance companies invest large sums of money in the Stock Market and these are often of a long-term nature. As with pension funds, assurance premiums are expected to outweigh any outgoings. Again like pension funds, assurance companies rely on acturial valuations to describe probable liquidity needs.

**Application of portfolio theory**

Up to the present portfolio managers have not made much use of portfolio theory, this being due to both implementation problems and to problems in the assessment of risk. In practice, portfolio managers have devoted most of their time in assessing market trends, examining the prospects of individual shares and in the administration of the fund. Considerably less effort has been spent on the efficient reduction of risk by diversification of investments. Many a manager's criterion here has been to invest in a large number of stocks regardless of their inter-relationships and thus even many of the smaller portfolios consist of over fifty stocks. Whilst this will reduce risk it has been done on an arbitrary basis and a well chosen portfolio of ten to twenty stocks may provide greater expected returns for a similar level of risk.

**Forecasting returns on investments**

In a large fund the investment manager will have access to a lot of share price forecasts from either his own analysts or from outside stockbrokers. From all this data the manager will be in as good a position to judge the overall future market movements as any. Added to the analysts' forecasts will be the manager's own knowledge of particular companies. For funds which do not have access to substantial research facilities the manager will be forced into relying upon the various statistical services which, whilst not giving profits and share price forecasts, do give a summary of a company's financial position and past performance. In these cases the manager can also determine the conditional forecast of a company's price from its relationship to the market index. This was described in Chapter 5 and it provides a method of analysing a lot of shares without requiring detailed investigation. It does, of course, require success in predicting the market movements.

**The evaluation of risk**

If the share price forecasts have been made in the form of probability distributions this will greatly help the manager in his evaluation of portfolio risk. Thus simulation and risk analysis programs could be run to produce an expected return probability distribution for various sets of portfolios. If such probabilities were reasonably accurate a considerable reduction in risk could be gained and with the application of portfolio theory significant benefits would accrue to investors. However, probabilistic forecasting has not been developed greatly in investment analysis and so the portfolio manager will have to rely on other methods in measuring uncertainty. The main method used is to measure the historical variation in returns and to measure the covariances in returns between shares.

**Diversification categories**

The main diversification within UK ordinary shares is by industry grouping. Share prices are largely determined by profits and companies within the same industry tend to have similar earnings positions.

This especially applies to those sectors which are very cyclical and clearly defined. Thus, industrial grouping provides an easy reference for diversification policies. The industrial classification adopted by UK managers is usually the *Financial Times* Actuaries industrial subgroups (FTA). The following table lists the groups and the constituent number of stocks as at 1 May 1974; the names of the constituent companies can be obtained from the *Financial Times.*

## Equity Groups

### Groups and Subsections

Figures in parentheses show number of stocks per section

1   CAPITAL GOODS (183)
2   Building materials (29)
3   Contracting construction (22)
4   Electricals (16)
5   Engineering (heavy) (16)
6   Engineering (general) (62)
7   Machine and other tools (13)
8   Miscellaneous (25)
9   CONSUMER GOODS (DURABLE) (61)
10  Light electronics, radio, television (15)
11  Household goods (16)
12  Motors and distributors (30)
13  CONSUMER GOODS (NON-DURABLE) (168)
14  Breweries (16)
15  Wines and spirits (8)
16  Entertainment, catering (16)
17  Food manufacturing (23)
18  Food retailing (18)
19  Newspapers, publishing (16)
20  Packaging and paper (14)
21  Stores (28)
22  Textiles (20)
23  Tobacco (3)
24  Toys and games (6)

### Other Groups

25  Chemicals (22)
26  Office equipment (10)
27  Shipping (10)
28  Miscellaneous (42)

---

29  INDUSTRIAL GROUP (496)

---

30  Oil (4)

---

31  500 SHARE INDEX

---

32  FINANCIAL GROUP (101)
33  Banks (6)
34  Discount houses (8)
35  Hire purchase (5)
36  Insurance (life) (9)
37  Insurance (composite) (8)
38  Insurance (brokers) (8)
39  Merchant banks (18)
40  Property (29)
41  Miscellaneous (10)

---

42  Investment trust group (50)

---

43  ALL-SHARE INDEX (651)

---

COMMODITY GROUPS
(Not included in 500 or
All-Share indices)
44  Rubbers (10)
45  Teas (10)
46  Coppers (3)
47  Mining finance (11)
48  Tins (8)

---

FIXED INTEREST

---

1  Consols $2\frac{1}{2}$% yield
2  20-yr Govt stocks (6)
3  20-yr Red. Deb. and Loans (15)
4  Investment trusts prefs (15)
5  Coml. and indl. prefs (20)

---

## Financial Times-Actuaries indices

All the indexes are weighted by market capitalisations and so the composite indices are not the arithmetic average of the component indexes. Because of their heavy capitalisations, the four oil stocks account for a substantial portion of the All-Share and the 500 Index and so the industrial index is perhaps the best indicator of industrial share price performance.

The indices cover the major UK-quoted ordinary shares; any other stocks can be allocated to a particular grouping so as to obtain an appropriate index. The FTA grouping has a number of weaknesses, specifically: (1) it has a large number of stocks in the miscellaneous groups which cover a multitude of activities. The manager may want to disaggregate these miscellaneous sectors; (2) many companies straddle a number of industries and no one grouping is particularly appropriate; (3) companies can change their products and marketing outlets sufficiently to alter their industrial grouping. This may not be recorded by the FTA indices for some time. The manager may therefore want to allocate a more appropriate index for the share. If the manager has the available resources he can re-group the FTA classifications and can even build new indices\*. The FTA industrial indices represent the changing values of a portfolio of investments held in the same proportions as the market capitalisations. In total, the All-Share Index accounts for the major part of the total market capitalisation of UK ordinary stocks quoted on the United Stock Exchange.

**Efficiency of FTA classifications**

One test of how well the FTA Industrial Indices separate the importantly different types of activity is to measure the covariance between the indices†. The results can then be compared against any other classification, and the industry grouping showing the least covariance with other combinations of individual groups is the most appropriate in risk reduction. If the covariance was very strong between all possible combinations of groups then there would be minimal reduction of risk by diversifying according to the FTA classifications.

**Use of industrial groupings in a diversification policy**

In reducing risk the manager will be looking to combine shares whose covariance with other stocks is low. As the computations will be enormous a practical solution is to measure the correlation between the various industrial subgroups. The manager will therefore make up his portfolio with stocks from groups which show little covariance in their returns. As share price behaviour and economic conditions change over time it will be necessary for the manager to periodically evaluate the relationships between the various indices. Russell and Taylor[4] have shown that there is significant correlation between many of the FTA indices and so the portfolio manager will have to make detailed analyses to obtain useful data.

**Time horizons of portfolios**

Portfolio managers will select shares showing the expected highest returns and will diversify across industry groupings. An additional consideration may be the time horizons adopted by, or relevant to, the portfolio. Analysts' evaluations of shares are sometimes couched in terms regarding time periods such as 'good long-term prospects' or 'good over the short term'. Thus the expected returns may be expected to accrue over a long period or not to accrue until after a longish period. Other recommendations may be very short-term forecasts with the analyst having little idea of the longer term. Such evaluations of short-term performance are often made by analysts and managers as they make judgments of market movements over the next six to twelve months. For funds which need to have a good shorter-term performance the near future returns are particularly important, whilst the longer time horizon funds can afford to stand several bad annual performances in making a large long-term return. Funds with short-term horizons include unit trusts where there are detailed monthly performance statistics and where bad performance will lead to withdrawals exceeding new money coming in. Similarly, private

\*At least one firm of London Stockbrokers have built their own index.

†Another check is to measure the covariance between shares within a particular group. If the covariances are high it is evidence that the companies are in the right grouping.

portfolios being managed by merchant banks or investment counsellors will be concerned with short-term performance as they may not have time to await the potentially greater long-term benefits. For pension funds and charities short-term performance is relatively insignificant, and they can afford to wait for longer-term capital gains. Neither are usually under any pressure from members or contributors and the financial news media do not have access to performance statistics. Investment trusts come in between the short- and long-term classifications: they do not suffer from withdrawals and there is no limit to their life. However, they have a share price and they are subject to takeovers, management can be removed by shareholders and performance statistics are made public.

## Short- and long-term investing

Short-term price forecasts are especially useful when a fund is small and can therefore divest itself and subsequently fully invest. Larger funds which often have long time horizons will find it impossible to sell all their securities without reducing the existing share price. Similarly, large funds will be unable to invest substantial sums of money without sending share prices significantly upwards. Thus the larger funds will rarely be sellers of shares; if conditions look poor they will keep any cash liquid but will not dis-invest. This is, of course, one reason why they often end up holding large stakes in quoted companies. Smaller portfolios can, however, trade in and out of yearly market movements quite easily. Additionally, a smaller fund can sell short and buy long on proportionately greater scales*. Short sales are sales of stock which the investor does not own; he will be of the opinion that the price of the share will fall and that he can buy at the lower price before he has to deliver. Long buying involves buying shares without having the money to pay for them; he will be of the opinion that the share price will rise and that he can sell before he has to pay. Selling short and buying long is usually only undertaken when the investor is extremely confident of his forecasts and when he has special facilities for payment or for delivering stock. The advantages of smaller funds in being able to liquidate and invest completely can be outweighed if the market movements are forecasted incorrectly. An additional factor which has to be taken into account in such investment policies is the large broking cost involved.

## Switching shares

The manager will be constantly re-evaluating the portfolio and he will probably decide to add or switch various shares. This will be because of greater expected returns and, or, reduction of risk. In doing so the manager must be aware of the costs of transactions. There have been a number of studies in the us[5] which have found that the more active investment funds have had the poorest performance, and this is partly due to the greater costs they have incurred. Switching stocks can occur as the manager may feel that one sector is particularly undervalued, i.e. the portfolio may switch out of consumer durables stocks into capital goods stocks, on, say, the upsurge of the business cycle. Another type of

*Large funds can engage in such activities but these are not likely to be as large in proportion terms.

switching occurs when the management decides to invest specific proportions in different sectors. In time the market values of these proportions will change as some industrial sectors do better than others. Stocks are then switched so as to obtain the original balance. Switching stocks incurs considerable expenses and any projected benefits should cover these. As the main component of price changes is the market index itself the manager should beware of a too-active policy of switching stocks.

## Large blocks of shares and investment timing

The manager will also have to deal with the practical problems of building the portfolio. One constraint he will be faced with is picking up large amounts of stock in a particular company. The portfolio plan may include buying substantial stakes in certain companies but in effecting this the manager may find that the share price soars. Thus the portfolio plan has to be amended; it is difficult to judge the impact of large share transactions on market prices and so few plans attempt to incorporate such constraints. Similarly, sales of large blocks of stock have to be carefully planned and a below market price may have to be accepted. Another factor the manager will have to deal with is timing. Many analyst's recommendations make share price forecasts which they do not necessarily expect to accrue for up to one year hence. In-between times the market price can fluctuate widely offering cheaper buying opportunities. The only feasible way to estimate the short-term price performances is to forecast the market movement as a whole and base individual price behaviour on this. As the manager will be receiving considerable volumes of research data and picking up the views of institutional investors and estimating the weight of liquid money waiting to be invested, he will probably have some ideas on the movement of share prices in the near term.

## Improving portfolio performance

The more important factors in improving portfolio performance include:

1   Increasing the accuracy of the share price and dividend forecasts. This includes both obtaining more accurate expected values and in reducing the overall variability between expected values and actual results.

2   Assessing short-term market performance. If the manager can forecast with some degree of success then this will provide bases for investment timing. As explained earlier, the market factor is a major determinant of share prices especially in the periods between pieces of fundamental news being released by the companies.

3   Reduction of risk. This is probably the least developed of the factors influencing portfolio performance. In general, funds have diversified extremely widely and this has possibly detracted from its total return without much reduction in risk. An efficiently diversified portfolio of a few stocks may reduce the risk as much as a randomly diversified portfolio of over a hundred shares. Thus, greater research and analysis of the covariances between industrial sectors will lead to more efficient risk diversification. Portfolio theory is still not very applicable in

practice and the benefits of the considerable resources spent on developing it may be some years off.

4 The formulation of analysts' estimates in the form of probability distributions may provide good measures of risk. Unfortunately, little research has been done in this area yet, although the increasing sophistication of investment analysis may soon incorporate probabilistic forecasting.

5 There could be greater thought given to the objectives of investment portfolios and these should be disclosed to the public. Thus potential investors could choose between various funds according to their particular investment objectives.

### Portfolio theory

Fund managers have traditionally diversified portfolios across various industries to reduce the risk or future variability of returns. However, this has been done on an intuitive basis with no real knowledge of the extent of risk reduction gained. Since the 1950s, however, a body of knowledge has been built up which quantifies the expected return and riskiness of portfolios and these studies have been termed 'portfolio theory'. The methods involve deriving what are termed efficient portfolios which are the portfolios giving the best expected return for given levels of risk. At present the theory has received little application by existing portfolio managers in the UK, this being due to both lack of knowledge and resources on the behalf of the managers and to practical difficulties in implementing the theory.

**Efficient portfolios**     To find the efficient set of portfolios the manager will need to know the expected returns and the risk of those returns for the various individual securities. Additionally the covariances between a stock and all other combinations of the remaining stocks will be required. From this he can calculate the expected return and risk of the possible portfolios. The expected return of the fund is the weighted average of the expected returns of the individual securities. However, the variance of a portfolio is a more complex affair as we need to know the covariance* of the component stocks. If the risk of an actual return differing from the expected return of a stock, is different in some respect from the risk of another stock, then the risk of a portfolio invested equally in both stocks will be less than the weighted average of the risks of the component stocks. For example, the risk attached to the return from an engineering share might be dependent upon the movement in the capital goods cycle, raw material prices and inflationary wage demands, whilst a property share's value will be affected by Government legislation on office development permits and fixed interest rates applicable to the company's gearing. These particular factors affecting the two shares are not dependent on each other and

*The statistical terms appearing in the remainder of the chapter will be explained in Chapter 10.

the chances of both shares suffering adverse factors at the same time are slim. Thus a portfolio consisting of an engineering share and a property share would have a risk measurement far below that of the two constituent stocks. We have previously discussed, however, that combining shares which have their risks dependent on the same outcomes does little to reduce portfolio risk (this is the case of the two oil shares).

**Portfolio risk**

The reduction of the risk in a portfolio is very dependent upon the covariances between the various combinations of the total stocks available for selection. It can be quite easily shown that the major determinants in reducing portfolio risk are: (1) the riskiness of each individual component share; and, (2) the covariance between those stocks. The numbers of stocks invested in is not very relevant in reducing risk as long as there are around ten to twenty component stocks in the portfolio. Thus there are funds in existence which have about ten or twenty constituent stocks and, because the individual riskiness of each was low and the covariance low, they have a lower portfolio variance than many funds with a hundred stocks.

**The efficient frontier**

The early development of portfolio theory is largely associated with the work of Markowitz[6]. He set out to determine the portfolio which gave the maximum level of return for a given level of risk. Figure 7.2 depicts

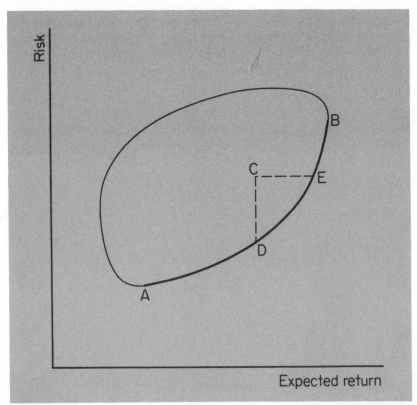

**Figure 7.2**
Markowitz's model

all the possible outcomes from various combinations of securities and the line AB gives the efficient frontier (also known as the efficient set), i.e. the maximum return for given levels of risk. Portfolio *C* is not efficient as an equal expected return is available from portfolio *D* and the risk is less. Similarly, portfolio *E* has the same risk as *C* but offers a greater expected return. The measurement of expected returns is fairly straightforward as the fund manager will have the various analysts' forecasts. The risk or uncertainty of future returns is, however, a more contentious measurement. One method is to use the probability distribution of future returns prepared by the analysts. Unfortunately, few analysts prepare detailed probability profiles of possible outcome and so risk is generally measured by using the variation in past returns. Some managers may in fact measure the variation in actual returns from the expected returns as computed by individual analysts. This, however, is more difficult to calculate, partly because analysts move jobs and so little long-term data may be available. The general measures of historical share price variation used are the standard deviation, variance, semi-standard deviation and semi-variance. The use of the semi-deviations is advocated by some authors as it is the variation below the expected return which represents the undesirable risk to an investor. Markowitz used the semi-variance as his measurement of risk and these are computed for all the individual stocks in his solution.

## Expected return

The expected return from a portfolio is the weighted average of the returns on the constituent shares. This is described notationally as:

$$R_p = X_1R_1 + X_2R_2 + X_3R_3 \cdots X_NR_N$$

$$= \sum_{i=1}^{N} X_iR_i$$

where $R_p$ = return on portfolio

$\quad X_i$ = the amount invested in share $i$

$\quad R_i$ = the return from share $i$

*Example*

£1,000 is used to construct a portfolio of four shares, *A*, *B*, *C* and *D*. The money is allocated to the shares in the proportion 0.1, 0.4, 0.3, 0.2 respectively. The returns on these individual shares are 15, 10, 20 and 25 per cent respectively. The return on the portfolio is:

$$R_p = X_1R_1 + X_2R_2 + X_3R_3 + X_4R_4$$

$$R_p = 0.1 \times 0.15 + 0.4 \times 0.10 + 0.3 \times 0.20 + 0.2 \times 0.25$$

$$R_p = 0.165$$

$$R_p = 16.5\%$$

Figure 7.2 shows the expected returns derived from the formula along the horizontal axis.

## Portfolio variance

The risk of a portfolio consists of the riskiness of the individual securities and the covariance between the returns of the securities amongst all possible combinations of them. The risk of a portfolio consisting of two shares, $A$ and $B$, is expressed thus*:

$$\sigma_p^2 = X_A^2\sigma_A^2 + X_B^2\sigma_B^2 + 2X_AX_B\text{Cov}_{AB}$$

where    $\sigma_p^2 = $ variance of portfolio

        $X_A = $ proportion invested in share $A$

        $X_B = $ proportion invested in share $B$

        $\sigma_A^2 = $ variance of the rate of return on share $A$

        $\sigma_B^2 = $ variance of the rate of return on share $B$

    $\text{Cov}_{AB} = $ the covariance between the rates of return on shares $A$ and $B$

The expression is easily extended to the $n$ share case.

The covariance term expresses the relationship between the movements in the rates of return from share $A$ and share $B$. It is derived from the statistic:

$$\text{Cov}_{AB} = p_{AB}\sigma_A\sigma_B$$

This is the correlation between $A$ and $B$ (the $p_{AB}$ term) times the standard deviation of $A$ times the standard deviation of $B$.

*Example*

A sum of money is invested equally in two shares $X$ and $Y$ which are expected to earn returns of 8 and 6 per cent respectively. The variances of $X$ and $Y$ are 2 per cent each and the correlation of the rates of return between $X$ and $Y$ is zero (i.e. $p = 0$).

The expected return $= X_xR_x + X_yR_y$

$$= (0.5)(0.08) + (0.5)(0.06)$$
$$= (0.04) + (0.03)$$
$$= 0.07 \text{ or } 7\%$$

The portfolio risk    $= X_x^2\sigma_x^2 + X_y^2\sigma_y^2 + 2X_xX_yp_{xy}\sigma_x\sigma_y$

$$= (0.25)(0.02) + (0.25)(0.02)$$
$$\quad + 2(0.5)(0.5)0(\sqrt{0.02})(\sqrt{0.02})$$
$$= (0.25)(0.02) + (0.25)(0.02) + 0$$
$$= 0.005 + 0.005$$
$$= 0.01$$

By purchasing equal amounts of the two shares the rates of return of which are not correlated at all, the risk of the portfolio is half that had all the portfolio money been invested in $X$ or $Y$ solely. The portfolio risk is shown on the vertical axis in Figure 7.2.

**Computational workload**

When there are many shares in consideration for inclusion in the portfolio the covariance of each security with every other security and combination of securities has to be measured. As can be imagined, the computations become enormous, and thus high-speed digital compu-

*Using variance as the measure of risk. Other definitions can be substituted.

ters become a prerequisite to any portfolio analysis. For example, if there were 1,000 shares available to a particular portfolio, 1,000 estimates of expected returns would be needed, 1,000 variances and 499,500 covariances!

## Examination of the covariance term

In the above example the covariance was nil and in the particular circumstances the portfolio risk was halved from what it would have been had all the portfolio money been invested in $X$ or $Y$ solely. There are two general rules which hold in both asset cases. If there is perfect positive correlation ($p = +1$) then there will be no risk reduction by diversification, as long as the proportion $X_x$ invested in the portfolio is set equal to $\frac{\sigma_y^2}{\sigma_x^2 + \sigma_y^2}$, i.e. in the example:

$$\sigma_p^2 = (0.25)(0.02) + (0.25)(0.02) + 2(0.5)(0.5)1(\sqrt{0.02})(\sqrt{0.02})$$
$$= (0.005) + (0.005) + (0.5)1(0.02)$$
$$= 0.01 + 0.01$$
$$= 0.02 = 2\%$$

This is the same as the individual variances on shares $X$ and $Y$. If there is perfect negative correlation ($p = -1$) then there will be no portfolio risk, again, as long as the proportion $X_x$ invested in the portfolio is equivalent to the expression $\frac{\sigma_y^2}{\sigma_x^2 + \sigma_y^2}$, i.e.:

$$\sigma_p^2 = (0.25)(0.02) + (0.25)(0.02) + 2(0.5)(0.5)(-1)(\sqrt{0.02})(\sqrt{0.02})$$
$$= (0.005) + (0.005) + (0.5)(-1)(0.02)$$
$$= 0.01 - 0.01$$
$$= 0$$

As long as the correlation between the rates of return of shares is less than +1, combining them will reduce the variance of the portfolio: and the nearer the correlation is to −1 the less the risk will be. In practice, most shares have a correlation of less than +1 but greater than 0.

## Selection of an efficient portfolio

Figure 7.2 shows the various possible efficient portfolios (line $AB$) available to the investor. The investor now has to decide which efficient portfolio is optimum for himself. This requires knowledge of the investor's risk-return indifference function or risk aversion profile which was described earlier in the chapter. Figure 7.1 showed an investor's indifference curve where risk was traded off against return. An investor will of course have numerous risk-return indifference curves each expressing combinations of risk and return to which he will be indifferent. Figure 7.3 shows a set of indifferences curves for an investor. Curve 1 will obviously be preferred to curve 2 as the return is greater for an identical level of risk. Curve 2 will be preferred to curve 3 and curve 3 preferred to curve 4, and so on.

An investor is now able to select his optimum portfolio from the efficient set. This portfolio will be the one at the point of tangency between an indifference curve and the efficient frontier. Figure 7.4

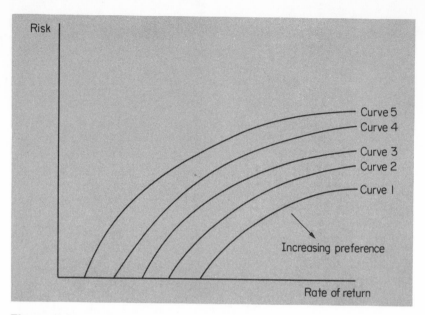

**Figure 7.3**

An individual's risk-return indifference curves

shows the set of efficient portfolios available to the investor (line *AB*) and a specific investor's risk-return indifference curves (curves 1 to 4). Portfolio *C* is optimum for this particular investor as no other portfolio is on as high an indifference curve. The portfolio manager will have to specify indifference curves for the particular fund under considera-

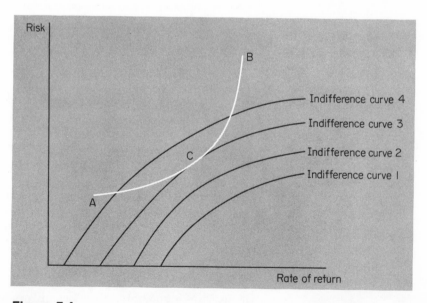

**Figure 7.4**

Selection of an efficient portfolio

tion. This will almost certainly involve some subjective judgment and the factors mentioned earlier in the chapter will provide a framework for this.

There are some conceptual question marks in using an investor's risk-return indifference curve of the form portrayed in Figure 7.3. These curves can be represented by a quadratic expression which means that utility can be measured solely in terms of expected return and variance. Unfortunately it also means that eventually an investor will require more risk for a given increase in expected returns! This of course cannot be justified in economic or real world terms.

There are other formulae which represent the concave indifference curves of Figure 7.3 but they cannot be expressed solely in terms of expected returns and variance. Thus they are not satisfactory for the Markowitz analysis.

To date, there has been no resolution of the expression(s) that represent investors' utility curves. In building risk-return indifference curves economists never reach a point where they consider that returns fall as risk increases and so the 'quadratic' problem is ignored in practice. Another problem is that the results obtained by this method may be in conflict with the results of Baumol's model which is described later. This model rejects certain 'efficient' portfolios and reduces the efficient set. Instead of an investor's utility function being given, the investor expresses confidence limits to the distribution of expected returns which he is prepared to accept. Given the assumptions in Baumol's analysis his method is conceptually sound but the results can reject the optimum portfolio selected by the Markowitz solution. There has been no reconciliation between Baumol's use of confidence limits and the use of indifference curves and so any discrepancies in the results will have to be dealt with subjectively (possibly by seeing how confident the investor is in his stated confidence limits and in his stated indifference curves).

## Markowitz solution

Markowitz derived the efficient set by using quadratic programming to solve the expression:

$$z = \lambda R_p - (1 - \lambda)\sigma_p^2$$
$$= \lambda \sum_{i=1}^{N} X_i R_i - (1 - \lambda) \sum_{i=1}^{N} \sum_{j=1}^{N} X_i X_j \, \text{Cov}_{ij}$$

for all values of $\lambda$ from 0 to 1. $\lambda$ represents an investor's risk-return preferences. The solution is subject to the constraint that the portfolio is fully invested, i.e.

$$\sum_{i=1}^{N} X_i = 1$$

and to the constraint that there are no short sales, i.e. $X_i \geq 0$ for all $i$.

## Borrowing and lending

Adaptations have been made to Markowitz's solution which incorporate lending and borrowing cash and this gets rid of the non real-world

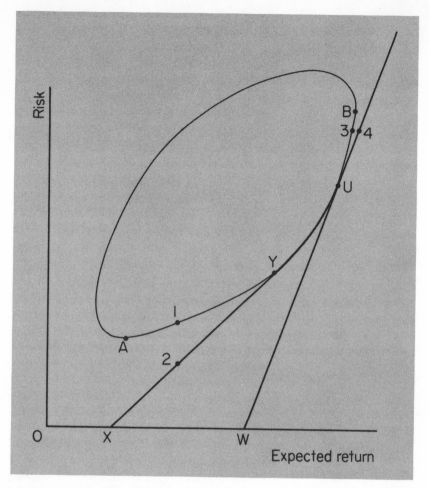

**Figure 7.5**

Sharpe's model

constraints of being fully invested and of making no long buying or short sales. An additional advantage is that the computational workload is significantly reduced. The pioneering work in this field was led by Sharpe[7], and his solution is shown diagrammatically in Figure 7.5. The efficient set is shown by the line *AB* and is computed by the methods previously described. If an individual invests his money in a risk-free bank deposit account his risk return profile would be the point *X*. Thus he would be incurring no risk and earning a return of *OX*. If he invested half his money in ordinary shares the risk of the portfolio is only half the risk if all the money was invested in ordinary shares. The line *XY* is established by drawing a straight line from *X* at a tangent to the efficient set, *AB*. The risk return combinations that are available from investing varying amounts in portfolio *Y* and the risk-free investment *X* lie along the line *XY*. The expected returns from a portfolio consisting of risk-free securities and a portfolio of shares, *Y*, is the weighted average of the returns of the components, i.e.:

$$R_p = X_1 R_1 + X_2 R_2$$

where the symbols have the same meaning as before: $R_1$ is the risk-free rate of return and $R_2$ is the return on the assets at *Y*. The variance of the portfolio is given by

$$\sigma_p^2 = X_1^2 \sigma_1^2 + X_2^2 \sigma_2^2 + 2X_1 X_2 p \sigma_1 \sigma_2$$

$X_1$ represents the proportion invested in the risk-free asset. This asset has a standard deviation of zero (it being free of risk) and so the first and third terms on the right-hand side of the equation are zero. The variance of a portfolio lying along the line *XY* is therefore entirely dependent upon the proportion of the portfolio invested in the assets at *Y*. The line *XY* represents different proportions of money invested in risk-free investments and the portfolio combination at *Y*. Any portfolio along the line *XY* will be preferable to any along the line *AY*. For example, portfolio 2 offers the same return as portfolio 1 but its risk is far less. With the incorporation of lending the efficient set becomes the line *XB* and the line *AY* is inefficient. The manager now only has to consider the portfolios along the line *YB* and the amount of cash to invest in the stocks represented by point *Y* (often known as the lending portfolio; *X* is the lending rate).

A similar analysis can be carried out with relation to the borrowing of money to invest in securities. Assume *W* is the rate at which money can be borrowed. The next step is to draw a line from *W* so that it touches the efficient set at a tangent *U* and extend the line beyond this point. The risk return combinations available to the investor by borrowing funds to invest in *U* lie on the line above *U*. If there is no constraint on borrowing, the line above *U* has no limit. Portfolio 4 represents the risk return combination of borrowing funds from the bank and together with the investor's original cash purchasing the shares that make up the portfolio *U*. Thus the line above *U* becomes part of the efficient set. Portfolio 4 is clearly preferable to portfolio 3 for whilst it has the same risk it offers a greater expected return. The programming load will now be reduced to discovering the portfolios which lie along the line *UY*. This reduction in programming is very significant in practical terms and makes portfolio analysis more feasible from a cost point of view. The manager will now have to choose between the various portfolios in the efficient set *UY*. Additionally, if he chooses those stocks representing the points *U* and *Y* he will have to decide how much to invest and how much to lend or borrow. The choice of lending along the line *XY* or borrowing along the line extending above *U* depends on the individual investor's attitude towards risk.

**Borrowing and lending interest rates equal**

If the borrowing rate is the same as the lending rate then only one combination of shares will be efficient. The manager's work will then just involve deciding whether to lend completely, lend and purchase in portfolio *A*, invest all his money in *A* or to borrow and invest in

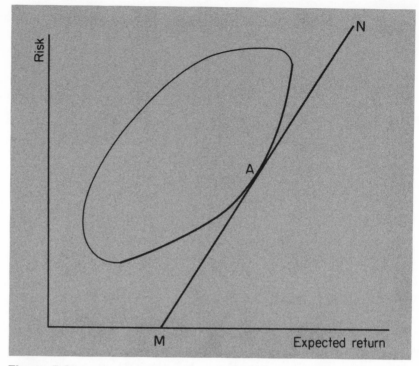

**Figure 7.6**

Sharpe's model: borrowing and lending rates equal

portfolio *A*. This process is shown graphically in Figure 7.6. It must be noted that borrowing rates are rarely the same as lending rates and so a single efficient portfolio such as *A* will rarely be found. Additionally, if just one combination of stocks was efficient and enough managers recognised this, then one would expect that the buying pressure would alter the expected returns such that the efficient set changed very quickly. Although the lending and borrowing rates are rarely similar some authors have contended that they are so close that there are only a smallish number of 'efficient' combinations of stocks. These same authorities say that the question of how much to invest in shares should be completely separate from the problem of which shares to purchase, i.e. there is only one combination of shares which is efficient, and the only choice left to the investor is to decide their risk attitudes as regards lending or borrowing funds.

**Capital asset pricing model**

The above conditions were extended in a famous article by Sharpe who proposed a general theory of the pricing of stocks and shares[8]. This is based upon a number of assumptions; namely, identical time horizons and risk-return expectations for each share by all investors, no transaction costs or taxes and identical borrowing and lending rates. Figure 7.6 shows that when the above conditions are present the investor has the opportunity to invest anywhere along the line *MN* (which is called the capital market line by Sharpe). As investors' expectations are identical the line will be stable and the portfolio of risky assets, *A*, must be the market portfolio, i.e. it contains all the shares available in proportion to their market capitalisations. If this were not the case then shares not in portfolio would not be desired by any investor (investors' expectations being identical*) and so their prices would fall until the returns became large enough for them to be included in the portfolio. Sharpe's capital market line is expressed thus:

$$E(R_p) = R_i + \frac{[E(R_M) - R_i]}{\sigma_M} \sigma_p$$

where $E(R_p)$ = expected return on the portfolio

$R_i$ = riskless rate of interest

$E(R_M)$ = expected return on the market portfolio

$\sigma_M$ = standard deviation of the market return

$\sigma_p$ = standard deviation of the portfolio return

The slope of the line *MN* gives the relationship between an increase in return and the increase in risk. The capital asset pricing model argues that the only decision an investor has to make is to decide whether and how much to borrow or lend: the choice of risky shares is in fact the market portfolio. This theory supports or uses the Efficient Markets Theory when it assumes that all investors' expectations are identical. Although the presence of transaction costs makes buying the 'market' a very expensive operation it has been shown that a well selected small number of shares can reduce the risk very near to the market average, and these can therefore provide 'optimum' portfolios. The model is entirely plausible in an efficient and equilibrium market and its applicability to actual stock markets depends greatly on the efficiency assumptions†.

**Baumol's model**

Baumol[9] has suggested a method for helping an investor decide between the various portfolios making up the efficient set. This method involves the investor establishing confidence limits for the expected returns and relies on the distribution of returns from the portfolios being normal. For example, there is less than a 100:16 chance that the return from a portfolio will be more than one standard deviation below its expected value and a less than 100:1 chance that the return will be more than three standard deviations below the expected value. If the expected value minus one standard deviation is above the expected value plus one standard deviation of another portfolio, *A*, in the efficient set and if this level of confidence is satisfactory to the investor, portfolio *A* can be discarded from the efficient set. Once an investor has detailed his level of confidence, the efficient set can be reduced in

*Investors are also assumed to be risk-averse and rational.

†The efficient market hypothesis is examined in Chapter 11. In general most empirical studies support a weaker definition of efficiency but this does not include all investors' expectations being identical.

accordance with the above procedure. In the example below, Baumol argues that no investor would choose portfolio *A* as its best realistic return (10 per cent) is lower than the worst realistic return (11 per cent) for portfolio *B*. The confidence limit set in the example is one standard deviation and this quantifies the word 'realistic'.

|            | *A* | *B* |
|------------|-----|-----|
| E          | 8   | 15  |
| $\sigma$   | 2   | 4   |
| E + $\sigma$ | 10  | 19  |
| E − $\sigma$ | 6   | 11  |

where E = expected return.

$\sigma$ = standard deviation.

Additional characteristics in the rates of return have been suggested as being desired by investors. Arditti[10], for example, argued that investors may prefer distributions which are skewed to the right, i.e. for portfolios with similar expected returns and similar risk an investor will prefer the one the distribution of which is skewed to the right (offering small chances of very large returns).

## Reducing the computational workload

One of the main practical problems in implementing portfolio theory is the enormous data preparation and the computational loads. This is especially important, as to gain the best possible results the portfolio needs to be reviewed regularly to take account of changing expected values. For example, a constituent share of an efficient portfolio may rise by say 30 per cent and its future expected return might then be nil. In such a case the share would almost certainly not be present in an updated efficient set. To update the efficient set even once a month would involve an enormous amount of work. The introduction of lending and borrowing rates has significantly reduced the efficient set and the computations involved but even so the workload is still considerable. Further reductions in the computational problems have been made possible by the development of single- and multi-index models. These use the relationship between a share's rate of return and the rate of return from a market or industrial index (indices). The relationships are used as surrogates for the full covariance matrix.

## Single-index model

Sharpe[11] studied the use of a single-index model in portfolio management. It is based upon a relationship which has been seen before:

$$R = a + bI + c$$

where $R$ = rate of return from the share

$I$ = rate of return on the index

$c$ = variability not attributable to the market index
$a$ and $b$ are regression coefficients.

The term $c$ is assumed to have an expected value of zero and a variance of $Zi$. The return from the portfolio requires knowledge of the regression coefficients $a$ and $b$ and the expected return from the index $E(I)$. The risk from the portfolio is obtained from the variance $Zi$ for each stock and from $ZM$. $ZM$ is the variance in the index rate of return i.e.

$$I = E(I) + C$$

where $I$ = rate of return on the index

$\quad E(I)$ = expected rate of return on the index

$\quad\quad C$ = random variable with a mean of zero and a variance $ZM$.

From the above data the calculation of the efficient set is computed by using quadratic programming techniques.

The technique cuts down the computer costs but more significantly it substantially reduces the amount of data required from the analyst. Thus, instead of requiring expected returns, risk measures and covariances for every available security, only a forecast of the market rate of return is required. The relationship between the market rate of return and the individual security's rate of return will probably be based on historical data which should be updated at regular intervals. As long as the market index relationship is relatively stable the technique should give similar answers to the Markowitz full covariance matrix approach[12]. A simplification of the single-index model has been developed by Sharpe[13] and is known as the linear model. This method only requires knowledge of the regression coefficients $a$ and $b$ and the market index. Sharpe's article also explains a graphical solution to the formulation of efficient portfolios from the index model.

## Multi-index models

Multi-index models are in the continuum between the single-index model and the full covariance Markowitz analysis. Thus a share's rate of return may be related to a number of indices such as the market index, an industrial index and maybe, say, a geographical index. Multi-index models are expected to give more accurate results than the single-index model and, although they obviously involve more computational work, there should still be a significant workload advantage over the Markowitz solution.

## The empirical testing of portfolio models

There have been a number of studies which have investigated the ability of the models to predict actual behaviour. Farrar's[14] study looked at the composition of mutual funds (unit trusts and investment trusts) and compared their risk-return combination against the efficient portfolios as constructed by the Markowitz model. He found the risk-return combinations of the actual and the theoretical portfolios to be fairly similar. Further, he found that the mutual funds which described themselves as being fairly risky had portfolios which were similar to the high risk efficient portfolios.

Cohen and Pogue[15] produced a comprehensive assessment of the Markowitz, single-index and multi-index models, looking at both ex ante, and ex post performance. The portfolios were built on 75 and 150 security universes for the periods 1947–57 (ex ante) and 1958–64 (ex post). The ex-post performance was measured against randomly selected portfolios and the actual performance of a group of seventy-eight ordinary share mutual funds. Cohen and Pogue found that both the market models and the mutual funds performed better, ex post, than the randomly generated portfolios. For larger returns the models outperformed the actual experiences of mutual funds although for returns below 15 per cent this was not the case. The more sophisticated Markowitz model proved to perform slightly better than either of the index models. Surprisingly, however, the multi-index model did not perform as well as the single-index model in the ex-ante investigation. In contrast, other researchers following on from this study have found that multi-index models have outperformed the single-index model[16]. There is now a fairly heavy stream of research investigating the applicability of formalised models in portfolio planning. The portfolio manager should therefore keep abreast of these reports and of developments in portfolio theory.

**Problems in applying portfolio theory**

The major problem that exists in portfolio theory is the measurement of the risk or uncertainty of future returns. Variability of past returns has been used as a surrogate for the risk mainly because of the existence of large masses of past data. The errors of an analyst's predictions from actual returns would provide, perhaps, a better measure of risk but in practice there is usually insufficient data available to undertake this. Probabilistic forecasting can offer substantial scope for risk reduction but this technique has received little application. This is probably due to the immense amount of detailed analyses needed. In time, however, the measurement of risk along the above lines may become more tenable.

From the practical angle there are a number of problems to the applicability of portfolio theory. Firstly, there is the enormous quantity of data that has to be made by analysts. Secondly, there is the computational workload. Although computers can handle the necessary calculations the costs can be very great if the portfolio is to be kept updated. This updating means additional work for the analysts as well as for the computing facilities. If the efficient portfolio is not kept updated any significant movement in share prices can make the 'efficient' portfolio very suboptimal.

The use of index models has significantly improved the computational process and especially reduced the analysts' workload. However, the models still represent a fair amount of work. There are also the various legal and administrative constraints such as availability of stocks, liquidity requirements etc. which have to be taken into account. It is very difficult, if not impossible, to incorporate these in the programming solutions and so the 'optimum' portfolio may have no real world meaning.

As a final word it is worth noting that many managers say that until analyst's forecasting abilities improve, further development of portfolio theory or its application is not warranted. The contention is that the resources spent on portfolio theory would be better expended on improving forecasting techniques and on the formation of probability distributions.

**References**

1    Quantitative studies have shown that higher returns are expected, and indeed earned, for higher levels of risk: see US Congress, 'Institutional Investor Study Report of the Securities and Exchange Commission', Vol. 2, 92nd Cong., 1st sess., 1971, H. Doc. No. 92 – 64, Part 2.

2    King, B. F., 'Market and industry factors in stock price behaviour', *Journal of Business*, 39, Jan. 1966.

3    For a description of the investment policies of unit and investment trusts see: Burton, H. and Corner, D. C., 'Investment and Unit Trusts in Britain and America', Elek Books, 1968.

4    Russell, A. and Taylor, B., 'Investment uncertainty and British equities', *Investment Analyst*, Dec. 1968. The study covered the period from January 1963 to June 1967.

5    See: Sharpe, W. F., 'Mutual fund performance', *Journal of Business*, 39, Jan. 1966.

6    Markowitz, H., 'Portfolio selection', *Journal of Finance*, XII, Mar. 1952, and: 'Portfolio Selection: efficient diversification of investments', John Wiley, 1959. For a later text on portfolio theory see: Sharpe, W. F., 'Portfolio Theory and Capital Markets', McGraw-Hill, 1970.

7    Sharpe, W. F., 'A simplified model for portfolio analysis', *Management Science*, IX, Jan. 1963.

8    Sharpe, W. F., 'Capital asset prices: a theory of market equilibrium under conditions of risk', *Journal of Finance*, Vol. 19, No. 3, Sept. 1964. His book 'Portfolio Theory and Capital Markets', McGraw-Hill, 1970, updates and extends the capital asset pricing model.

9    Baumol, W. J., 'An expected gain-confidence limit criterion for portfolio selection', *Management Science*, Oct. 1963.

10   Arditti, F. D., 'Risk and the required return on equity', *Journal of Finance*, 22, Mar. 1967.

11   Sharpe, W. F., 'A simplified model for portfolio analysis', *Management Science*, IX, Jan. 1963.

12   Cunningham in the UK and Jensen in the US have found the regression coefficients to be fairly stable; Cunningham, S. W., 'The predictability of British Stock Market prices', *Applied Statistics*, Vol. 22, No. 3, 1973; Jensen, M. C., 'Risk, the pricing of capital assets, and the evaluation of investment portfolios', *Journal of Business*, Vol. 42, No. 2, Apr. 1969.

**13**   Sharpe, W. F., 'A linear programming algorithm for mutual fund portfolio selection, *Management Science*, XIII, Mar. 1967.

**14**   Farrar, D. E., 'The Investment Decision Under Uncertainty', Prentice-Hall, 1965.

**15**   Cohen, K. J. and Pogue, J. A., 'An empirical evaluation of alternative portfolio selection models', *Journal of Business*, Apr. 1967.

**16**   See, for example, Wallingford, B. A., 'A survey and comparison of portfolio selection models', *Journal of Financial and Quantitative Analysis*, Jun. 1967.

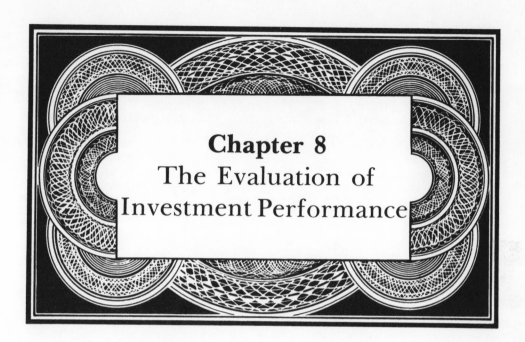

**Chapter 8**
The Evaluation of
Investment Performance

Chapter 5 described the evaluation of shares and Chapter 7 gave an outline of portfolio management. It is readily apparent that the performance of analysts and managers needs to be assessed both for internal feedback purposes and for potential investors. The measurement of performance is, however, a good deal more complicated than may be realised at first sight and considerable effort has been spent on devising appropriate yardsticks of evaluation. The chapter will commence by looking more closely at the need for performance statistics and then discuss various measurement problems. Finally some time will be spent on describing various methodologies for measuring performance.

## Benefits from performance appraisal

Performance evaluation should help towards an efficient market in that it will influence investment funds to be channelled to the successful managers. These are defined as being successful by their ability to correctly value stocks and shares. Specifically the advantages of performance testing include the following:

1   Improves competition amongst analysts and portfolio managers. The increased exposure of their performance is the best antidote to lethargy. This will speed the acceptance of new techniques and will highlight new managerial talent.

2   Indicates the superior analysts and managers so that existing and new funds can be given to their care. The more efficient market which ensues is likely to induce further investment by private individuals and thus help meet the enormous amounts of capital monies required by businesses.

239

3 Investors require information on the stewardship of the funds they have entrusted to the care of the portfolio managers.

## Problems in performance measurement

It is therefore very important to assess performance, and the measurement of this will ultimately involve comparative evaluation. The measurement, however, is not at all straightforward and the incorporation of the risk element probably means that there is no exactly 'right' evaluation technique; all existing methods are thus surrogates of varying efficiency, of a true performance measurement. The following represent some of the major problems facing performance measurement.

## Constraints on Investment policies

1 Portfolios often have various constraints and limitations applied to their investment policies and so comparative performance is only directly applicable with similarly constrained funds. The most common limitations that apply in the investment policies of portfolios were mentioned in Chapter 7 and these constraints are enforced by statutory law or by the trust deeds or articles of association governing the fund. Apart from statutory limitations there are also certain operating constraints that may be applied by a manager. For example, unit trusts may only want to invest in relatively marketable stocks. Another example is the charitable foundation, which often has restrictions which only allows the income of a fund to be spent for charitable purposes, the capital staying intact. In such cases income is often defined as dividends and interest but not capital gains. Whilst such definitions were probably well conceived at the initiation of the charity they are no longer appropriate as investment returns are now largely made up of capital movements. However such restrictions are quite prevalent and it may influence a manager into, say, forsaking capital gains for income, even though the capital gains are greater. Such restrictions are very difficult to quantify and any allowance for them will probably involve subjective judgment. Care should be taken not to allow managers to invent non-applicable constraints as excuses for their poor performance. Thus the evaluation should only acknowledge real constraints.

In evaluating the 'constrained' portfolios comparisons should be made with funds with similar limitations. However, it may well be that there are very few or perhaps no exactly similar portfolios, in which case comparative appraisal is impossible. Similarly market comparisons, using a share price index or a portfolio index are inappropriate yardsticks. The evaluation will, in such cases, determine the relative return from the portfolio and investors will have to use their judgment in allowing for the particular constraints. In most cases there will be broadly similar portfolios to use as yardsticks. The measurement of a specific fund against a market average and against a more appropriate index will show both the relative performance given the specific conditions and the impact of the constraints. If the limitations in investment policy are not statutory, it might well be that they will be amended if it can be seen that they were responsible for the poor performance.

**Risk**    2    Performance evaluation commonly measures returns over periods of one year. However, this performance can change from one year to another for a given fund and so an investor will require some measure of the predictability of returns. The main basis used in estimating the uncertainty is the past risk profile of the fund's performance. This, however, may be inappropriate especially if the management team is changed, and in practice research has shown that portfolio success is often followed by poor performance. Techniques for accounting for risk will be described later although the description of risk and uncertainty in portfolio returns in Chapter 7 is directly relevant.

**New monies**    3    Where funds receive new capital monies during the year such as unit trusts it is no longer possible to measure performance by looking at the increase in wealth over a period of one year. The returns need to be measured each time new money comes in and this brings in practical computational difficulties as well as conceptual problems. In evaluating the performance of the new investment monies there are two possible dates to look at; one is to measure the returns from when the new money was received, the other from the date the new money was invested in securities.

Another decision that has to be made is whether to weight the returns by the value of money or not. For example, one fund's performance may be exactly the same as another's in terms of its investments but because the cash inflows into the second fund were, say, greater, the overall monetary value may be better or worse but rarely the same. If we are measuring the performance of the fund manager only, it is contended that money weighting is spurious and that only the time-weighted return should be used.

In making sophisticated evaluations, similar problems to the above occur when internally generated funds, usually net dividends, are received. In different portfolios dividend income may occur at significantly different times and these may or may not be distributed. Problems also exist when monies are withdrawn from portfolios such as in the case of unit trusts or pension funds.

The methods of calculating the rate of returns from investment portfolios, including cases of incoming and outgoing monies, is described later. These add considerably to the computation processes and the solutions often rely upon estimates.

**Size and time horizon**    4    Other problems include the size and time horizon of the fund. Many commentators argue that it is only the smaller funds that can outperform the market averages and therefore large funds should only be compared against other large portfolios. Assuming this description of investment success is correct the answer would seem to be to split the large fund up into smaller portfolios and hence gain superior performance. Size of portfolios under the above assumption would therefore be considered a spurious constraint. Experience has shown that large funds don't figure greatly in the leading 'performers' and neither do they figure much in the 'laggards': large funds, whilst not obtaining the best returns, generally offer lower risk. The size of a portfolio is therefore not generally a relevant constraint although its impact may be felt in the risk factor.

In general, the differentiation of funds into their time horizons does not give rise to the use of different yardsticks although cases for doing so can be made out. Longer-term portfolios may for instance say that they don't mind bad short-term performance as they are building up substantial stakes in major growth companies whose share price potential may take a few years to achieve. Similarly, unit trusts may say they are forced to speculate in order to have a chance of achieving a satisfactory return (this applies to trusts going through a bad patch).

As the long-term is an amalgam of all the short terms the differentiation of funds on the basis of time horizons may be spurious. However, if a long-term portfolio, such as a pension fund, is wishing to build up a very substantial stake in a company (say 20 per cent of that company's shares) the buying policy will take some time and it may involve making purchases when the share price performance is poor. In general any such matters are handled subjectively as opposed to attempting to construct differing yardsticks which hide poor performance.

As for problems associated with 'short-term' portfolios only the constraint of needing to be invested solely in very marketable stocks has any standing. In such cases the portfolios should perhaps be evaluated against other similarly constrained portfolios and against the *Financial Times* Ordinary Share Index which is made up of thirty of the most marketable stocks (this index is not weighted by market capitalisation).

**Other assets**  5  Problems also arise when there are assets other than ordinary shares in the portfolio. For example, property and fixed interest securities are quite popular components of many pension funds. The funds should be split into the various assets covered and each sector evaluated separately. This will give feedback on the manager's ability in assessing the value of various assets. Unless the portfolio specifically requires investments of certain monies to be made in particular assets, the fund should also be evaluated against the returns that could have been made from an all equity, all gilt-edged or all property portfolios. This will measure the manager's success in determining which are the best sectors to be in: the previous methods measured the manager's ability to select stocks within specific sectors. In measuring returns from different assets the impact of risk aversion comes into play. The techniques described in the remainder of the chapter refer solely to equity investment. Property performance is the realm of another discipline and is not relevant here*.

**Analysts'**  6  The criteria by which investment analysts' performance is measured
**forecasts**      can take several forms. The obvious basis is to evaluate the analyst's

---

*It must be recognised however that in analysing the results of a portfolio, the risk reduction obtained from buying different types of assets has to be taken into account.

ability to predict share prices but this needs a more specific definition. For example, should risk be incorporated in the evaluation? Analysts who recommend small speculative stocks stand a much better chance of having an exceptionally good performance in some years but this is often more than offset by exceptionally bad returns from other periods. As the occurrence of good and bad years cannot be predicted, the performance evaluation should possibly take some account of the risk or uncertainty in returns. Another problem is that of analysts' time horizons within which they forecast share prices. Some analysts may recommend a share because they think the price will do well over the next three years. Therefore to measure annual performance might not be an adequate criterion. Fortunately, most analysts predict share price performance over shortish periods and so comparative evaluation is feasible.

In analysing the analyst's recommendations comparisons should be made against an industry index where the analyst is confined to looking at specific sectors. In such cases the incorporation of risk becomes less necessary as the risk profile of an industrial sector will not be too different from the risk profiles of the individual component shares. Comparisons of the performance of industry specialists should also be made against the market index as whilst the prior statistic showed his ability at selecting stocks within a sector, the latter test shows the impact of restricting investment recommendations to particular industries. Any other constraints placed on an analyst's recommendations also needs to be acknowledged in the evaluation process. Examples might include only looking at companies with capitalisations of over, say, £50 million, thereby preventing the analyst from recommending smaller growth stocks which might have shown a superior return and still have been reasonably marketable. If an analyst ranks his recommendations in order of preference then this can be acknowledged, probably subjectively, in his ability 'evaluation'.

A factor which needs to be taken account of is the usefulness of an analyst's forecast as opposed to his accuracy. For example, one analyst may have a very good success rate in predicting the price behaviour of very small companies whilst another analyst may have a reasonable ability to forecast prices of large companies. Whilst the former's success rate is higher, the latter analyst may be of far more use to a portfolio. This is because large sums of monies can be invested in the larger companies whereas it may be difficult to invest more than a few thousand pounds in a poor marketability stock, without forcing up the price. Thus investment analysts' abilities might need to be measured with respect to their contributions towards the portfolio. This will obviously incorporate recommendations made by analysts which were not taken up by the portfolio manager.

Some difficulty will be encountered where the analyst recommends selling short, i.e. selling shares the portfolio does not own. In this case the risk involved is fairly considerable and some managers might contend that it is so great that the ordinary measures of risk are inappropriate and separate yardsticks should be used.

One more difficulty in making comparative evaluations is that some analysts give specific share price forecasts, some give ranges and some only forecast relative performance, i.e. ranking shares in order of cheapness. Performance in these cases may be difficult to establish and subjective appraisals of what the analyst's forecasts 'really meant' may need to be made.

Apart from the feedback available from a performance evaluation of the analyst's recommendations the data can also be used as a measure of risk in portfolio theory. Thus by measuring the variability of the analyst's projections from the actual rates of return a surrogate for risk can be obtained. As the expected rate of return from a share is an analyst's forecast it is perhaps appropriate that the variability of his success is used as the measure of risk. Up to present this has received no practical application but with greater data available from performance testing this measure of risk may become more feasible*.

Another performance measurement which is needed is the accuracy of the analyst's forecasts of company profitability. If an analyst was very accurate in predicting earnings but his share price evaluations were poor the portfolio could employ the analyst solely for his profits forecasts and let another analyst interpret the results in their meaning for share prices. In determining the analyst's ability to predict profits, various problems, similar to those above arise, i.e. the risk factor, some companies and sectors are easier to predict, the time scale, the time between the forecast and the actual results, and comparing results where some analysts give specific forecasts and others, ranges of outcome.

## Rate of return

For investment portfolios which have no new capital monies coming in, have no capital repayments and receive no dividend income during a year, the computation of the rate of return is straightforward. It is, in fact, the difference between the opening and closing valuations of the portfolio divided by the opening value. If dividend income is received and is immediately paid out to the owners of the fund these should be added to the return. In a very sophisticated performance evaluation these dividends should be weighted by their timing, i.e. an investor who receives a dividend from a portfolio at the beginning of the year is better off than an investor who receives the same dividend at the end of the year as he could have invested his dividend receipt. Thus an assumed level of interest, say bank deposit rate, is sometimes applied to the dividend receipt received early in the year from a portfolio.

*There is the problem, of course, that analysts change jobs and so it may be difficult to obtain sufficient data to measure statistical variability.

*Example*

| Portfolio | A | B |
|---|---|---|
| Increase in capital appreciation from 1.1.70 to 31.12.70 | £5,000 | £5,050 |
| Dividend paid out 1.1.70 | £1,000 | |
| Dividend paid out 31.12.70 | | £1,000 |
| Assumed interest earned by investor on dividend (10%) | £ 100 | – |
| Total return | £6,100 | £6,050 |

The example shows how portfolio *A* was in fact superior to portfolio *B*, something not apparent from looking at the increase in capital appreciation. In practice few evaluations would be so clear-cut and the use of the above analysis is rarely met. Where the dividends are maintained inside the fund they will go towards increasing the capital value.

When it comes to analysing portfolios which receive new capital monies or make capital repayments the computation of the rate of return becomes more complex. This is because allowance has to be made for the fact that the new money has only been available for part of the period being looked at. Sometimes dividend income is treated in the same way but here the investment manager does have power to switch into shares which pay dividends early or more often and this decision-making process should therefore be included in the rate of return.

**Time and money weighted return**

The methodology used to calculate the return from a fund receiving new monies during the year is to calculate the internal rate of return. This is given by solving $r$ in the following expression:

$$MVS(1+r)^1 + NMp_1(1+r)^{1-p_1} + NMp_2(1+r)^{1-p_2} + \cdots = MVE$$

where $MVS$ = market value of portfolio at the start of the period

$NMp_1$, $NMp_2$, etc. = new monies received at time period $p_1$, $p_2$, etc.

$MVE$ = market value of portfolio at the end of the period

Solving for $r$ gives the rate of interest at which the opening portfolio value and the net new money would have to be invested in order to attain the market value at the end of the period. Derivations of the internal rate of return formula give the rates of return for funds which suffer withdrawals in excess of incomes. Strictly, the ordinary transaction costs of investing the new monies should be deducted from the capital amounts as these are unavoidable costs. Obviously, if a specific asset acquired demanded extraordinarily heavy transaction expenses then this would have to be dealt with in the performance appraisal. Expenses incurred in switching between different shares and assets are an avoidable cost (i.e. a static investment policy could be adopted) and so should be included in the investment performance. The performance should be measured before deduction of management fees for the purposes of evaluating and diagnosing investment policies and skill. The investor will then measure the returns after management fees to determine the increase in his own wealth.

## Time weighted returns

The above rate of return is referred to as the time and money weighted return of a portfolio. This statistic, however, is inappropriate in measuring the performance of the investment manager. As the portfolio is likely to be performing at different rates during the year, the occurrence and the amount of new money will affect the performance. As the managers have no direct influence on the net cash inflows or outflows it is not relevant to money-weight the returns. The method for measuring the ability of the fund managers involves knowing what the value of the portfolio was on each date new money came in or when existing capital monies were repaid. Thus, rates of return for each period bordered by the receipt of new money are calculated and the geometric addition gives the annual rate of return.

*Example*   The following information is obtained from a portfolio:

| | £ |
|---|---|
| Market value of fund 1.1.73 | 2,000,000 |
| New money in on 1.1.73 | 200,000 |
| Total funds at market value (*MV*) 1.1.73 | 2,200,000 |
| Market value at 31.3.73 | 2,600,000 |
| New money in on 31.3.73 | 400,000 |
| Total funds at *MV* 31.3.73 | 3,000,000 |
| Market value at 30.6.73 | 3,500,000 |
| New money in on 30.6.73 | 300,000 |
| Total funds at *MV* 30.6.73 | 3,800,000 |
| Market value at 30.9.73 | 3,600,000 |
| New money in on 30.9.73 | 300,000 |
| Total funds at *MV* 30.9.73 | 3,900,000 |
| Market value at 31.12.73 | 4,200,000 |

The rates of return for each period are:

$$1.1.73 \text{ to } 31.3.73 = \frac{2,600,000}{2,200,000} = 1.1818$$

$$1.4.73 \text{ to } 30.6.73 = \frac{3,500,000}{3,000,000} = 1.1667$$

$$1.7.73 \text{ to } 31.9.73 = \frac{3,600,000}{3,800,000} = 0.9474$$

$$1.10.73 \text{ to } 31.12.73 = \frac{4,200,000}{3,900,000} = 1.0769$$

The geometric average is $(1+r)^4 = (1.1818)(1.1667)(0.9474)(1.0769)$

$$(1+r)^4 = 1.4067$$

$$r = 8.8\%$$

Thus the return obtained by the manager is 8.8 per cent per quarter or 35 per cent per year.

## An estimated value of rates of return

The method requires a knowledge of the market value of the portfolio at every date when new money is received or is paid out. This can pose quite an administrative problem especially for pension funds. Unit trusts normally revalue their portfolios each day and so no additional work is required. Fisher has derived a method which gives an estimate of the rate of return for a fund and this relieves the very heavy workload associated with revaluing a portfolio every day which can be necessary in investment management evaluation[1]. The technique estimates the rate of return of a portfolio from the return on the market index and the characteristic line of the fund*. As the market index is calculated every day and the characteristic line is known, an approximate rate of return for the fund can be calculated. Fisher testing his model found it worked comparatively well. Summarising, the geometric average rate of return is used in evaluating the investment manager's performance whilst the internal rate of return is used to measure the portfolio's performance.

## The date of new monies

A further problem in assessing the manager's ability is that at what date should the new monies be assumed to be received? There is the actual date of receipt or the date of investment of the new cash inflows. For example, a manager may not want to invest at one particular stage in the year and if he receives funds during this period they will lie idle. Additionally, if large cash inflows occur it may take some time to invest them. Thus there is a case for only analysing the manager's performance from the date of investing the monies. In practice this is only done if the new inflows are substantial. Similar differentiations can occur when there are large-scale repayments and the manager has to dis-invest over a period of several weeks.

## Notional portfolio performance indicators

Many quick evaluations are made by comparing the rate of return from a portfolio against a return from a notional portfolio made up of all the stocks in the market. This method does not take account of risk although the relative performance could be classified or plotted against the historical variability of returns. In the UK the *Financial Times* Actuaries All-Share Index is generally used as the market average. The opening value of the portfolio is divided by the market index to obtain the number of 'units' in the fund. Each time new money accrues it is divided by the market index to give the number of additional 'units' created. The new money should be net of normal broking transactions as these are unavoidable costs. At the end of the period the total number of 'units' multiplied by the market index gives the value of the notional portfolio. This is then compared against the value of the actual portfolio. Portfolios can be ranked in this fashion although as stated earlier no account of risk is taken. The method is similar to the calculation of unit trust prices where they use the fund's value per unit instead of the market index to derive the number of units created. An adjustment that has to be made to the FTA index is to include a figure for notional dividend income and this goes towards buying further units. One measure of notional dividend income can be obtained by

*This is described later.

using the market yield. The market yield multiplied by the market index gives the annual income. If monthly recordings are taken the mean of the two months' market yields is calculated. This figure divided by twelve gives a figure for monthly income. This method of computing dividend income assumes dividends are received equally over the period of the year. Yet another problem in the evaluation is that realised investment profits have to pay capital gains tax whilst the market index does not reflect this. An adjustment therefore has to be made and this normally takes the form of showing a cash outflow when the tax is paid.

*Example* £300,000 was invested in a portfolio at the end of January and additional new capital money is introduced as in column 7. The performance of the fund (which re-invests or accumulates any dividend income) is compared against the notional market portfolio. This portfolio is constructed by buying the index when new monies come in. The terminal value of the notional portfolio is the number of 'units' purchased times the index, plus any uninvested cash (i.e. dividends received in June). The actual portfolio performance is measured against £361,919, the market portfolio value. The example is fairly simple and has not been complicated by taxes, transaction costs and other factors but it shows the basic principles.

| Month end | 1 Market index | 2 Money invested* £ | 3 'Units' pur-chased | 4 Total 'Units' pur-chased | 5 Dividend per 'unit'† | 6 Dividend amount‡ £ | 7 New money £ | 8 Dividends and new money £ |
|---|---|---|---|---|---|---|---|---|
| January | 150 | 300,000 | 2,000 | 2,000 | 0.5 | 1,000 | 300,000 | |
| February | 146 | 51,500 | 353 | 2,353 | 0.5 | 1,176 | 50,500 | 51,500 |
| March | 142 | 31,176 | 220 | 2,573 | 0.5 | 1,286 | 30,000 | 31,176 |
| April | 139 | 21,286 | 153 | 2,726 | 0.52 | 1,417 | 20,000 | 21,286 |
| May | 124 | 31,417 | 253 | 2,979 | 0.49 | 1,460 | 30,000 | 31,417 |
| June | 121 | | | | | | | 1,460 |

$$\text{Notional market portfolio value, 30 June} = (2,979 \text{ units} \times 121) + \text{uninvested cash}$$
$$= £360,459 + £1,460$$
$$= £361,919$$

*The split up between capital monies and dividends is given in the final three columns
†This figure is derived by multiplying the market yield by the index and then dividing by twelve to obtain a monthly recording (the figures in column 5 are given)
‡Received at the end of the period; available for investing in the succeeding period

## Tax differences

If comparisons have to be made between funds with different tax structures then before-tax returns should be used. For similar tax status funds it is the after-tax returns which should be compared. Difficulties arise in deciding how to treat potential capital gains tax on unrealised investment profits. In general these should be deducted from the market value of the portfolio. However, the postponement of paying capital gains tax gives the fund a larger base on which to grow and this should be recognised. The deduction of the potential capital gains tax will show the impact of this over time. Portfolio managers should bear in mind the benefits of delaying payment of capital gains tax and any switching of securities should more than compensate the benefits foregone.

### Risk

Apart from the rate of return the other main measure of portfolio performance is the risk factor. This represents the estimate of the future unpredictability of returns. The historical rate of return from a fund is often used as a measure for estimating future performance. However, this simple extrapolation is subject to significant errors as some funds' performances can change from being enormously successful to being a drastic failure within a year. Similarly a medium above-average performance may be followed by a below-average return. The long-term investor can afford to ride out poor performances and so he may select the portfolio offering the highest return over the longer-term future. However, shorter-term investors will need to assess, if possible, the risk in future estimated returns. For example, one portfolio may offer a high expected return of 30 per cent per annum. If, however, there is a 10 per cent chance that the return could show a loss of 40 per cent, short-term investors who may have to dis-invest within a matter of weeks, may decide that this risk is too great.

Chapter 7 described possible methods for estimating the risk profile of future returns from portfolios and revealed that the past variability of returns is the most common measure. The use of variability in returns has been adopted by several official financial bodies and by academics in deriving a number of risk measures. These range from standard statistical deviations to relationships based on regression analyses. The major techniques are described below.

### Treynor Index

The variability of a fund's performance can be split into three component parts; one is the degree of variability against the market average, another the degree of variability in the market average and, finally, there is the independent variability peculiar to the particular share. The first measure can be a significant component of the total variability and the analysis of this was used by Treynor in his method of measuring performance[2]. Treynor's method involved plotting the rates of return of a fund against the rates of return from the market index* as shown in Figure 8.1. A straight line XY is then drawn through the points either by visual means or by regression analysis. This was termed the portfolio's 'characteristic line' by Treynor. If no

*This includes capital appreciation and dividends.

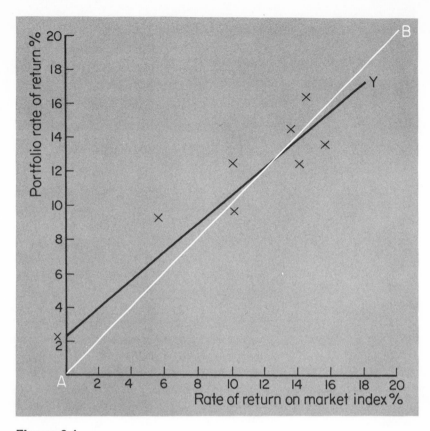

**Figure 8.1**

Treynor's characteristic line

straight line can be constructed then the method becomes impracticable. The further the points lie from the straight line the less reliance can be placed on the volatility relationship; volatility being described as the change in a portfolio's value for a given change in the market index. The steeper the slope of the line the greater the volatility of the fund, that is the greater the rate of change in the portfolio value for a given movement in the market index. The line *AB* in Figure 8.1 represents the market average rate of return and is at an angle of 45 deg. and passes through the origin. Where the characteristic line cuts through the vertical axis this represents the rate of return from a portfolio for a nil change in the market average.

**Comparing portfolios**

Plotting the volatility relationships of several funds on one graph can show the relative performance as in Figure 8.2. Here portfolio 2 is clearly preferable to portfolio 1 as it has the same degree of volatility (the slope of the line is the same) but always offers a higher return. Similarly, portfolio 4 is preferable to portfolio 3. In order to determine the relative performance of portfolios 2 and 4 Treynor derived an analysis which involved using a risk-free investment rate. Figure 8.3 shows the characteristic lines for portfolios 2 and 4 and additionally

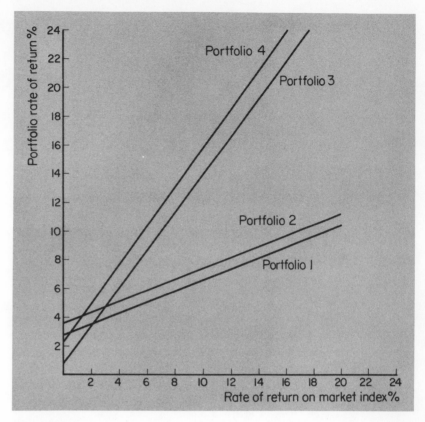

**Figure 8.2**

Comparing similar risk portfolios

gives a horizontal line representing a risk-free investment. In this case the risk-free rate is assumed to be 6 per cent. As portfolio 4's characteristic line cuts the risk-free interest line before portfolio 2 the former has the better performance. It can be demonstrated that by investing part of a portfolio's resources in portfolio 4 and lending the remainder at the interest-free rate that a portfolio, $XY$, can be constructed parallel to portfolio 2 but above it. This is shown by the line $XY$. Thus the portfolio $XY$ has the same volatility (risk) as portfolio 2 but offers a greater return. An investor would prefer portfolio 4, for even if he preferred the risk profile of portfolio 2 it is possible to construct a portfolio of fund 4 plus lending which offers a higher return for the same risk, i.e. $XY$. The distance $OP$ and the distance $OQ$ is referred to as the Treynor Index for the portfolios 4 and 2. This gives the level of the market index at which a portfolio will produce the same return as that obtained from a riskless asset. The smaller the index the better the fund. It is tedious to evaluate many portfolios using graphical methods and so simple computer programs have been written to handle the computations. These usually include a regression analysis to obtain the characteristic line.

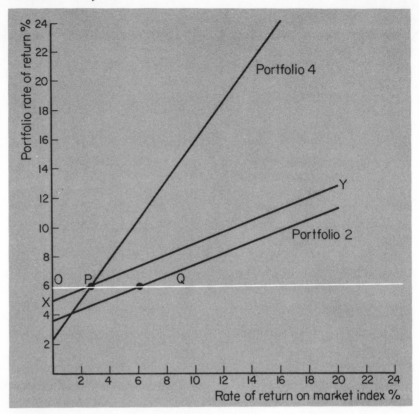

**Figure 8.3**

Treynor Index

## Comparison of portfolio performance against the market average

The Treynor Index is also used in measuring the performance of a fund against a market average. The market index is represented by a line drawn at an angle of 45 deg. through the origin and if this cuts through the interest-free rate of return later than the portfolio's characteristic line, *AB*, as in Figure 8.4, the portfolio has outperformed the market average. It can be shown along the lines previously described that a portfolio constructed of all securities compiling the index* and a risk-free security can have a characteristic line lying parallel to *AB* but below it. This is shown as line *XY*. Thus portfolio *XY* has the same volatility as portfolio *AB* but does not offer as high a return. The distance *PQ* measures the superiority of the fund over the market average, per unit of volatility whilst the vertical distance *QO* gives the superiority in returns at the particular volatility of the portfolio.

### Sharpe Method

W. F. Sharpe derived a technique for ranking portfolio performance incorporating risk[3] and his surrogate for the unpredictability of future

*And weighted by capitalisations if this is how the market average is constructed.

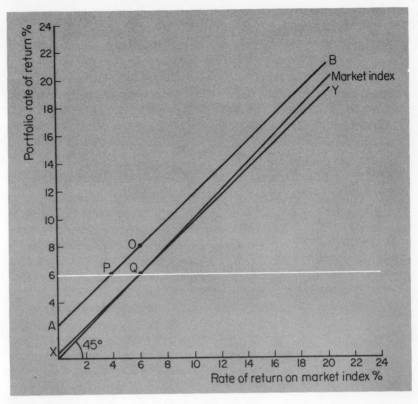

**Figure 8.4**

Treynor Index: performance relative to market average

returns is the standard deviation of historical returns. The average rate of return and the standard deviation for each fund under investigation is plotted on the graph as shown in Figure 8.5. The risk-free rate of return is designated X. Sharpe's method involves deriving a reward to variability ratio (*RV*) which is given by the following expression:

$$RV = \frac{(A - X)}{\sigma}$$

where $A$ = the average rate of return

$X$ = risk-free interest rate

$\sigma$ = standard deviation of the portfolio's returns

The higher the ratio the better the fund for a given level of variability, thus portfolio 1 is superior to portfolio 2 in Figure 8.5.

Sharpe demonstrated that as long as there was a lending opportunity, in this case X, an investor who found the variability of portfolio A too great, could still optimise his wealth by investing in portfolio A and by lending some of his funds at the risk-free rate. The line XA will represent the various combinations of this optimum portfolio for different levels of risk.

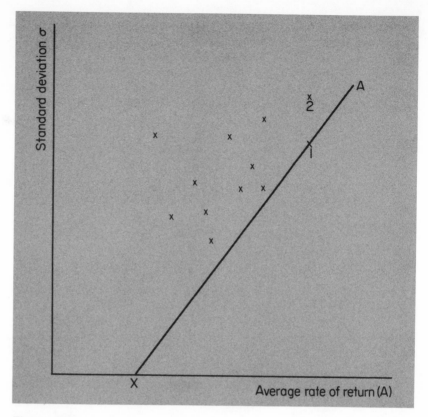

**Figure 8.5**

Sharpe's performance model

## Sharpe and Treynor methods compared

Sharpe's methodology is similar to Treynor's but he uses a different risk measurement. If the Treynor Index for a portfolio is deducted from the interest-free rate this will give a reward to volatility ratio. The two measures can in fact be drawn together on the same graph with the rate of return being plotted against the volatility index and the relative variability. If the volatility and variability recordings are close together this indicates little 'independent variability' whereas if they are far apart this means the fund or share price is relatively unaffected by market movements.

Treynor acknowledged the existence of the independent variability in a share's rate of return. He suggested, however, that this could be diversified away by analytical portfolio management. Whether this happens in practice is doubtful even though Treynor's empirical research showed that for fifty-four mutual funds in the years 1954 to 1963 the deviations of observations lay very near the characteristic line. Subsequent research and knowledge of the slow application of portfolio theory suggests that the independent variability for many portfolios is significant. The time period over which the historical data is taken can throw up different 'characteristic lines' and so care may be required in the analysis.

## Difficulties in applying the techniques

The Treynor and Sharpe models and their derivative techniques have been applied fairly extensively to the American mutual fund industry although little has been done in the UK[4]. There are a number of weaknesses in the methods which need to be acknowledged. Firstly, there is the problem that it may be impossible to fit a straight line to the data and comparisons of curves of various funds becomes more or less impossible. Secondly, a fair body of data is required and possibly only unit trusts and investment trusts could satisfy the requirements. This shortcoming is, however, relevant to most measures of performance. Thirdly, there is the determination of the risk-free rate of interest. Not only are there several rates that could be used* but these change over time. A change in the rate may easily alter the rankings of performance. Another factor in the Treynor and Sharpe evaluations of performance is that they take yearly data and, whilst this is satisfactory for short-term funds, it may not be so relevant for long-term portfolios such as pension funds. The latter can afford to ride out bad years and so performance measures incorporating annual recordings of variability or volatility are inappropriate. The models could be adapted to show recordings taken over longer periods, say five years, but the relationships may turn out to be very poor. The techniques discussed are not appropriate for the evaluation of other types of assets and so difficulties will arise in the appraisal of portfolios which can be invested in different types of investments. Market average returns of other forms of assets will have to be worked out over various periods so as to derive performance yardsticks which allow switching of investments during the period under review. To cover all the possible 'averages' will be an enormous task and so various aggregate yardsticks will have to be used.

The main use of evaluating portfolio performance is to estimate future returns. There have been a number of studies examining the predictive ability of the Treynor Index and Sharpe's model. The authors themselves found their methods gave reliable data but subsequent independent tests have found the predictive ability tenuous[5].

## Mean absolute deviation as a measure of risk

The use of the mean absolute deviation as a measure of risk has been suggested by the influential research report, published by the Bank Administration Institute[6]. They defined this as the time weighted average of quarterly absolute deviations (that is the mean deviation disregarding the sign + or −) between the quarterly time weighted returns from the fund and the time-weighted return of the fund for the whole period. The mean absolute deviation is used as a measure of variability of returns in the place of the standard deviation or other risk measurement. Thus Sharpe's model described earlier can use the absolute deviation as the measure of risk. The advantage of using the mean absolute deviation is that it is more stable through time than the standard deviation and is therefore a more reliable surrogate for risk.

*See the possibilities mentioned in Chapter 5.

**Probabilistic and simulation approaches**

Another method of accounting for risk uses probabilistic or simulation modelling. This involves estimating an expected rate of return for the fund and a measure of variability, usually the standard deviation or variance. In practice this method is used for longer-term portfolios and is considered by its protagonists to be more appropriate than the Treynor and Sharpe approaches. The estimated rate of return may consist, for example, of an extrapolation of historical performance and the variability will usually be computed from past data as well. In this case it is possible to use the variability of actual returns from forecasted expected returns; this is as opposed to the more usual process of measuring the variability of actual returns around a mean. Probabilities of the possible outcomes using the expected rate of return and variability can then be obtained for particular time horizons by using simulation or probabilistic models. Various factors such as withdrawals or accretions to the portfolio can be included in the model. It should be readily apparent that the figures obtained can only serve as a rough guide: the outcomes derived are dependent on the estimates used and the time horizon assumed. Sensitivity analysis can be applied to the results to show the impact of varying growth rates, measures of variability and time horizons. Whilst the results are tenuous, based as they are on long-term assumptions, they do provide a good measure for predicting the likely performance of portfolios that do not have to liquidate within a short period of time.

**The role of performance measurement**

The main role of measuring investment performance is in helping derive better returns in the future. This is achieved by highlighting the major reasons for good performance, often the quality of management, and by forecasting possible future rates of return and their likelihood of occurrence. Measurement of returns should be time weighted when analysing the management performance and money time weighted when evaluating fund performance. In comparing performances against other portfolios or against market averages or random portfolios* care should be taken to account for differences in constraints and objectives placed on the portfolio. In general this will mean comparing the results with similar funds or otherwise making a subjective allowance for the limitations imposed on particular portfolios.

The above analyses make no allowance for risk and so it is important to measure performance over a longish period. The chapter has described a number of methods of incorporating past variability into the ranking methods. There has been little application of these measures in the UK due in some part to the lack of data needed to compute the figures. Apart from unit trusts and investment trusts there is little published information available with which to work.

**Determination of performance**

Apart from measuring overall performance it will be vitally important to determine the reasons for the results achieved. Thus analyses can be constructed to see: (1) whether the market timing was correct; (2)

*Portfolios constructed randomly from a list of securities.

whether the correct industry sectors were chosen; (3) within the industry sector, were the best performing shares bought?; (4) if gearing was allowed, how much was used and how much did it add or detract from overall performance?; (5) were the correct assets bought?; i.e. although the equity shares bought outperformed the market index they might not have done as well as having invested the resources into property. Other breakdowns of performance returns and various classifications of such will shed greater light on the factors determining the success of portfolio management. Similar analyses can be applied to individual share recommendations made by analysts.

## Performance statistics in the UK

Because of the lack of data there has been little published evidence on the performance of investment analysts and financial institutions in the UK. Research on investment advice given by stockbrokers and investment counsellors indicates that this has not outperformed the market although the evidence is sparse and subject to various biases in data collection. Data on the performance of pension funds and charitable foundations is virtually non-existent and these types of funds are complicated by the holding of other forms of assets. In contrast, however, there are substantial performance statistics available for the unit trust industry and some lesser figures are available for investment trust evaluation. The *Money Management* magazine publishes monthly performance statistics for the major British unit trusts and these are quoted as a major reference by most authors. The statistics measure the rates of return given by the portfolios and give ranking tables. In the US the mutual fund industry has been evaluated as in the UK but some studies have been published incorporating the Sharpe and Treynor analyses. Whilst both Sharpe and Treynor found their measures were fairly consistent, subsequent studies found they were not too good at predicting future performance. Both Sharpe and Jensen have made comprehensive studies of the mutual fund industry in the US and little evidence was found of any superior predictive ability on their parts[7]. This and later evidence on mutual fund performance has thus supported the efficient market hypothesis.

### References

1  Fisher, L., 'Measuring the Investment Performance of Pension Funds for the Purpose of Inter-Firm Comparison', Bank Administration Institute, 1968.

2  Treynor, J. L., 'How to rate management of investment funds', *Harvard Business Review*, XLIII, 1, Jan. – Feb. 1965.

3  Sharpe, W. F., 'Mutual fund performance', *Journal of Business*, XXXIX, Jan. 1966.

4  For a fuller description of the use of formal methods in performance appraisal, see: Bower, R. S. and Wippern, D. F., 'Risk-return measurement in portfolio selection and performance appraisal

models: progress report', *Journal of Financial and Quantitative Analysis*, Vol. 4, No. 4, Dec. 1969. See also: Fama, E. F., 'Components of investment performance', *Journal of Finance*, Vol. XXVII, No. 3, Jun. 1972.

5   The application of the Treynor model to UK data has been used by Russell and Taylor in an article titled: 'Investment uncertainty and British equities', *The Investment Analyst*, No. 22, 1968. They found the model's relationships were consistent for a group of unit trusts over a period of five years.

6   'Measuring the Investment Performance of Pension Funds for the Purpose of Inter-Firm Comparison', Bank Administration Institute, 1968.

7   Sharpe, W. F., 'Mutual fund performance', *Journal of Business*, XXXIX, Jan. 1966. Jensen, M. C., 'The performance of mutual funds in the period of 1945 – 1964, *The Journal of Finance*, XXIII, May 1968.

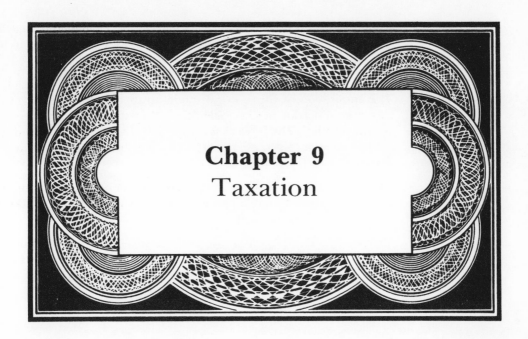

# Chapter 9
Taxation

## Current taxation structure

With effect from 1973 Parliament has altered the rules relating to both corporate taxation and personal taxation. As from 6 April 1973 company profits will be assessed to the imputation system of corporation tax. In general the rules relating to the determination of company profits assessable to corporation tax are the same for both the pre-imputation and the imputation systems. These profits are then taxed at the appropriate rates. Under the imputation system, however, capital gains are effectively taxed at a different rate to trading profits; under the pre-imputation system both were taxed at the same rate. The major difference between the methods, however, lies in the treatment of dividends. Under the pre-imputation system income tax at the standard rate was deducted from the dividend by the company and handed to the Inland Revenue (Schedule F tax). As income tax up to the fiscal year 1972 (i.e. 1972/3) was at a higher rate than capital gains tax this meant distributed profits bore heavier tax than retained earnings. Under the imputation system, however, a tax credit is given to shareholders, which at the present rates, means there is no income tax payable at the basic rate* on dividends. Under the imputation system a new tax called 'advance corporation tax', or ACT for short, has become payable when dividends are distributed. There was no similar item, pre-imputation. The advent of ACT has complicated the calculation of earnings per share (EPS) and the resultant yields. The different definitions were itemised in Chapter 3.

*In the reorganisation of personal taxation the standard rate is re-termed the basic rate.

259

**Personal taxation**

From 1 April 1973 the system of personal taxation has undergone a significant change as regards the computation of tax liability and as regards administration. The new method of personal taxation is known as the unified system. The taxation of dividends and capital gains from investments pre and post 1 April 1973 will be described.

The chapter commences with an outline of the computation of company profits applicable to tax and describes possible reasons for seemingly odd tax charges. The pre- and post-imputation systems of taxation will then be described. This involves a discussion of the tax and accounting treatment of ACT. Finally, personal taxation as regards investments will be dealt with.

### Corporate taxation

The profits which are subject to corporation tax are rarely those which appear in the published Profit and Loss Account. The Inland Revenue have specific valuation processes for some expenses and certain items are taxed separately. Increases in the general provision for bad debts, for example, is not a deductible expense for corporate taxation and neither are entertainment expenses for UK-based customers. Depreciation as calculated by the company is similarly not a deductible expense although the Inland Revenue allow depreciation in the form of capital allowances to be deducted from the profits of the year. The capital allowances are often greater than the depreciation charged by the company and the difference is the major contributor to the item 'deferred taxation account' which appears in many Balance Sheets. The difference between the depreciation charge and the capital allowances is also usually the major reason for the variation between the actual tax charge from that produced by multiplying published profits by the prevailing tax rate. The major allowances given by the Inland Revenue for plant and machinery are: (1) a 'first-year allowance' which is given for the year in which the expenditure is incurred. The rate of allowance since 22 March 1972 has been 100 per cent of the capital expenditure. Between this date and 20 July 1971 first-year allowances were at a rate of 80 per cent: there was also a special rate of 100 per cent if the expenditure was on new plant for use in a development area or in Northern Ireland. The first-year allowance for expenditure incurred between 27 October 1970 and 19 July 1971 was 60 per cent, again with a special rate of 100 per cent for development areas and Northern Ireland. (2) A writing down allowance of 25 per cent. This is not given for plant which is entitled to a first-year allowance during that year. The allowance is calculated on the outstanding value of the asset after deduction of allowances already received. Thus, no writing down allowances will be available if the expenditure has been wholly relieved by a 100 per cent first-year allowance. The analyst will need to be aware of any changes in capital allowances as these can have a significant impact on profits and liquidity.

**Dividend income**

Another reason for the difference between the actual and the computed tax charge is the treatment of dividend income. Dividends received have been paid out of profits which have already been subject to corporation tax and they are not taxed again in the Accounts of the recipient company. Thus dividend income, or franked income as it is known, does not form part of the profits for company taxation. However, the recipient company will have included the dividend income, up until 5 April 1973 at its grossed-up amount, in its Profit and Loss Account. The accounting treatment of dividends, post imputation, will be discussed later.

**Unfranked income**

Other investment but non-dividend income is assessed to corporation tax. These receipts are known as unfranked investment income and are differentiated from dividend income as they have been paid out of pre-tax profits. Examples of unfranked investment income include debenture interest and loan interest.

As companies do not usually differentiate between unfranked and franked investment income in their accounts the analyst will not be able to determine the impact on the tax charge for the year. For many companies investment income is such a small part of their total profits that the split-up between franked and unfranked income is not terribly important. For investment trust companies, however, the differentiation is of much greater importance as investment income is the major revenue. An additional factor is that any unrelieved investment management charges of the investment trust can be offset against income tax borne on franked investment income and a repayment claimed.

**Capital gains**

Profits on the sales of investments and fixed assets are assessed to corporation tax. In certain cases the capital gains arising from substantial sales of fixed assets are taken direct to reserves or included in the Profit and Loss Account as an extraordinary item. In these cases the company taxation will be shown, explicitly or not, as a deduction from that credit, i.e. it will not be part of the tax charge separately stated after the 'profit before tax' figure. As capital gains do not necessarily have to be shown separately in published Accounts the analyst will find it difficult to measure the impact on the tax charge. If the capital gains are very large they may be disclosed as an exceptional item.

**Taxation of corporate capital gains**

Under the imputation system, capital gains are to be taxed at a lower rate than trading profits (for 1973 the rates are 30 per cent tax on capital gains and 52 per cent tax on trading profits). The exact procedure is that a portion of the gain is taxed at the corporation tax rate, i.e. in 1973/4 30/52 of the gain will be taxed at 52 per cent making the effective tax rate 30 per cent. The impact of the lower taxation of capital gains under the imputation system is reduced, however, as ACT cannot be set against the tax liability. This will be dealt with later in the chapter.

## Taxable profits

*Example*

A company's Profit and Loss Account may show a profit of £10,000 made up as follows:

| | £ | | £ |
|---|---|---|---|
| Expenses | 30,000 | Trading profit | 50,000 |
| Loan stock interest | 4,000 | Gross debenture | |
| Entertainment expenses | | interest received | 2,000 |
| for UK customers | 1,000 | Gross dividend income | |
| Depreciation | 12,000 | received | 5,000 |
| Net profit | 10,000 | | |
| | £57,000 | | £57,000 |

In computing the tax charge the profits chargeable would be:

| | £ | | £ |
|---|---|---|---|
| Expenses | 30,000 | Trading profit | 50,000 |
| Loan stock interest | 4,000 | Gross debenture | |
| Net profit | 18,000 | interest received | 2,000 |
| | £52,000 | | £52,000 |

From the net profit of £18,000 is deducted capital allowances. These might amount to, say, £14,000 and so the net profit would be £4,000.

If the tax charge is 52 per cent then the tax payable is £2,080 and this is the figure which appears in the Accounts. The above example shows why the tax charge on the reported profits may appear low (i.e. a charge of £2,080 is only 20.8 per cent of the reported £10,000 profits).

## Schedule F

Up to 5 April 1973 company profits were assessable to corporation tax at the particular rate relevant to the fiscal year. The after-tax profits formed the basis for calculating the earnings per share (EPS) figure and represented that year's funds out of which dividends could be paid. From the dividend declared for the year the company deducted income tax at the standard rate and paid this to the Inland Revenue (subject to offsets against franked investment income, the procedure for which is described below). The net amount was distributed to shareholders.

*Example*

| | £ |
|---|---|
| Pre-tax profits | 10,000 |
| Taxation (40%) | 4,000 |
| | 6,000* |
| Dividend gross | 5,000† |
| Retained earnings | 1,000 |

*Figure for calculating earnings per share (EPS)
†£3,500 paid to shareholders. £1,500 paid to Inland Revenue on behalf of shareholders, tax at 30%

Prior to 6 April 1973 the company will have received dividend income net of income tax. The income tax suffered can be offset against the income tax due to the Inland Revenue on the dividends paid out in the

*Taxation*

fiscal year of assessment (Schedule F payment). If the dividends received are greater than those paid during any one year the balance is carried forward and can be offset against future dividend payments. The excess can also be offset against certain management expenses, charges on income and trading losses incurred in the particular year. This will enable a repayment of income tax to be received.

*Example*
Dividend paid as in the previous example. Gross franked investment income is £1,000. Tax rate 30 per cent.

| | |
|---|---|
| Tax due to Inland Revenue on dividends paid | = £1,500 |
| Less tax borne on dividend receipt, £1,000 @ 30% = | 300 |
| Net payment to Inland Revenue | £1,200 |

If the tax borne on dividend receipts was greater than £1,500 and there were no management expenses, charges on income or trading losses during the year, then the excess is carried forward and is available against future dividend payments.

**Dividends paid: Imputation system**

The imputation tax continues the above system although instead of having had income tax deducted from the dividend it will have received a tax credit. This credit is added to the dividend receipt in arriving at franked investment income for offsetting against distributions in computing the amount of ACT due.

From 6 April 1973 companies are subject to a new form of corporation tax which is known as the imputation system. Basically this involves taxing profits at a corporation tax rate as under the old system but part of the tax on the distributed profits is available to be set as a credit against the shareholder's own tax liability and a repayment can be claimed by him in appropriate circumstances.

*Example*
A company makes a profit of £1 million pre-tax and pays the maximum dividend possible from the year's profits. If the tax rate is 52 per cent the maximum net dividend payable is £480,000 which is equivalent to a gross dividend of £716,418 less ACT of 33/67 of the net payment. (This is equivalent to a gross payment of £716,418 less income tax at 33 per cent – the rate for 1974/5.)

The figure of £716,418 is known as the franked payment.

| | £ |
|---|---|
| Profits | 1,000,000 |
| Tax 52% | 520,000 |
| Maximum net dividend | 480,000 |

Gross dividend (ACT 33/67ths) = $480,000 \times \dfrac{100}{67}$ = 716,418*

*Or, $(\frac{33}{67} \times £480,000) + £480,000 = £716,418$.

Under the old corporation tax system the maximum dividend would have been:

|  | £ |
|---|---|
| Profits | 1,000,000 |
| Tax 52% | 520,000 |
| Maximum gross dividend | 480,000 |

Net dividend (income tax 33%) $= \dfrac{67}{100} \times 480,000 = 321,600$

The new system encourages higher dividend payouts although this is currently being restricted by prices and incomes controls. Low dividend payouts are likely to be more expensive taxwise as corporation tax under imputation is likely to be higher than under the old system.

## Advance corporation tax (ACT)

In order to mitigate the impact of possibly having to wait longer to collect taxes and in order to prevent company profits being taxed at a lower rate than that imputed to the shareholder and to prevent a repayment of tax to a shareholder without any tax having first been paid, the Inland Revenue is to receive what is known as advance corporation tax (ACT). ACT will be collected from the company when it pays dividends and is currently at the rate of thirty-three sixty-sevenths (33/67) of the amount distributed. For one year from 1 April 1974, when companies pay their ACT on distributions they will also have to pay an additional payment of half that sum*. Thus during 1974/5 companies will have to pay to the Inland Revenue a sum equal to 99/134 of the dividend paid out. When the company comes to discharge the corporation tax due on its profits of an accounting period it will set off the ACT already paid (and the additional payment discussed above) and pay the difference to the Collector of Taxes†. There are, however, a number of limitations on the amount of ACT that can be set off against the corporation tax liability and these will be described in the following paragraph. In the above example the company will have paid ACT of £236,418 plus one half of this sum, £118,209, to the Inland Revenue when the dividend of £480,000 was paid to the shareholders. When the company comes to settle its corporation tax for the year it will pay £165,373, i.e. tax of £520,000 less ACT already paid, £354,627. The UK resident shareholder receiving a dividend will also receive a notice telling him he is entitled to a tax credit of 33/67s of the amount he has received. This will discharge any basic-rate income tax liability the shareholder may have and may form the basis of a repayment°.

*This will be payable when ACT is paid or on 1 September 1974, whichever is the later.

†This payment has become commonly known as 'mainstream corporation tax'. In the case of companies trading prior to 1965 this mainstream corporation tax will be paid on the 1 January at least twelve months hence (i.e. for a company year end of 30 September 1973 the mainstream tax will be due 1 January 1975).

°This is dealt with more fully later. The 33/67s of the dividend paid in ACT is

## Offset of ACT

Only the ACT paid in a particular accounting period is capable of being offset against the corporation tax payable on the profits of that accounting period, and not the dividends declared for that period but paid after the end of it. The limitations on the amount of ACT that can be offset against the corporation tax liability are:

1  ACT can only be offset against tax on the 'income' for an accounting period. The definition of 'income' excludes chargeable gains.

2  The offset of ACT is further restricted to the notional ACT on a theoretical maximum distribution out of the income for a particular period.

*Example*

| | | |
|---|---:|---:|
| Income for period | | £1,000,000 |
| | | |
| Tax (52%) | | 520,000 |
| Maximum dividend on profits earned in the period | 670,000 | |
| ACT thereon (33/67) | 330,000 | 330,000 |
| | £1,000,000 | |
| | | |
| Minimum mainstream corporation tax | £190,000 | |

Thus in practical terms the set-off of ACT cannot be used to reduce the mainstream corporation tax payable to below 19 per cent of taxable income. This minimum amount will of course alter if the rate of ACT or the rate of corporation tax changes.

3  ACT is only paid when the 'franked payments' exceed the 'franked investment income', this being a continuation of the old pre-imputation, Schedule F procedure*. Franked payments are the dividends paid plus the rate of ACT in force for the particular year, i.e. if a dividend of £67 is paid, the ACT thereon is £33 and the franked payment is equal to their sum, £100. Franked investment income is the actual dividend received plus the ACT borne. Thus, a UK resident company receiving a dividend of £67 will receive a 'tax credit' of £33, equal to the ACT borne.

*Example*

A company during an accounting period earns trading profits of £90,000 and receives dividends from other UK companies of £21,000. It pays a dividend of £28,000 during the period.

| Franked investment income: | £ |
|---|---:|
| Dividends received | 21,000 |
| Add tax credit | 10,343 |
| | £31,343 |

equivalent to 33 per cent of dividend paid plus the ACT thereon, i.e. a dividend paid of £67 will bear ACT of £33 and ACT is therefore 33 per cent of £67 plus £33.

*Claims will be for accounting periods and not years of assessment (as in the pre-imputation system).

| Franked payment: | £ |
|---|---|
| Dividend paid | 28,000 |
| ACT thereon | 13,791 |
| | £41,791 |

ACT payable = $(41,791 - 31,343) \times 33\% = £3,448$

The £3,448 will have been paid paid to the Inland Revenue during the accounting period and will be available against the corporation tax liability of £46,800 (52% of £90,000). The ACT payable could have been derived by taking thirty-three sixty-sevenths of the difference between the dividends paid out (£28,000) and dividends received (£21,000).

## Unrelieved ACT

Where a company has paid ACT during the accounting period but there is no corporation tax liability, the ACT is unrelieved in that period. If, in the above example, the company made no profits there would be unrelieved ACT of £3,448 which had been paid to the Inland Revenue at the time of the dividend distribution*. Unrelieved ACT can be carried back to reduce the corporation tax liabilities of accounting periods beginning in the two preceding years†. The company will then be able to claim a repayment in respect of these earlier periods. The set-off applies against the prior period profits which are still subject to the limitations previously described. Any ACT which cannot be utilised as a set-off in the period in which it occurred or in prior periods can be carried forward to subsequent time periods without time limit. The same restrictions relating to the set-off will apply to future income.

## Rates of ACT

The rate of ACT for the fiscal year 1973 was three-sevenths and 33/67s for 1974. It is the intention of Parliament to fix the rate annually and, whilst it would hopefully be fixed at the beginning of the year, it can in fact be fixed or varied in retrospect at the next budget. The ACT payable in the first instance is the rate in use at the time and this will have to be adjusted if the rate changes. Thus accounting problems might accrue if the rate of ACT is changed.

## Returns of ACT

Companies are required to make returns of ACT due for the periods ending 31 March, 30 June, 30 September and 31 December and, additionally, the last day of the accounting period if not one of the four above-mentioned dates. The return has to be made within fourteen days of the end of the period to which it relates and any tax due will be payable at the end of those fourteen days. When ACT has been paid for a particular three-month return period and subsequently during the accounting period, it is found there is an excess of franked investment income over franked payments, a repayment of ACT can be claimed.

*The additional payment of one half of the ACT will also be outstanding. This will be repaid by the Inland Revenue at the date when corporation tax would have been due had there been any liability.

†The later or latest period must be utilised first. ACT cannot, however, be carried back to a period before 1 April 1973; any accounting periods straddling this date will have to be apportioned.

**Exemptions and amendments in special cases**

There are numerous exemptions and amendments to the foregoing provisions, all of which will affect the tax charge. However, the analyst is unlikely to be able to determine the extent of these in specific companies. Amongst the main items are: (1) exemption from ACT on intercompany dividends and the transferring of ACT to subsidiaries in the case of groups of companies and consortia; (2) separate provisions relating to close companies. Few quoted companies come within the definition of being a close company; (3) where a company's profit does not exceed £25,000 the tax charge will be at a lower rate (currently 42 per cent, 1973). This includes very large companies who make small profits. There are tapering provisions for companies with profits between £25,000 and £40,000. Certain organisations such as industrial and provident societies, co-operative organisations, housing associations and building societies will also be taxed at lower rates (40 per cent for 1973); (4) there is an extension of 'overspill' relief available to companies with heavily taxed overseas income; (5) there are various transitional arrangements with the changeover to the imputation system.

**Accounting periods**

Both pre-imputation and imputational corporation tax rates are set for fiscal years which run from 1 April to 31 March. Companies, however, are charged tax in respect of their own accounting period and these profits are apportioned to the 1 April where there is a change in the tax rate.

*Example*

The corporation tax rate for the fiscal year 1970 is 40 per cent and the rate for 1971 is 45 per cent*. A company's profits for the year ended 31 December 1971 amounts to £100,000. The tax charge for the year appearing in the accounts would be:

|  | £ |
|---|---|
| Profits from 1.1.71 to 31.3.71 = 25,000 @ 40% = | 10,000 |
| Profits from 1.4.71 to 31.12.71 = 75,000 @ 45% = | 33,750 |
| Tax charge | £43,750 |

**Dates of tax payment**

In the case of companies who were trading when corporation tax was introduced in 1965 the tax charge is normally paid on the 1 January at least twelve months hence. In the above example the charge of £43,750 would be payable on 1 January 1973, i.e. one year after the year end. Some companies show the corporation tax on the profits for the year which is not due for over one year separately from the current liabilities. This is because the liability does not come within the strict definition, adopted by most companies, of being due within one year. As long as the analyst can recognise which is the current year's tax charge no confusion is caused. For companies incorporated since the advent of corporation tax, the payment date for corporate taxation is usually nine months after their year end. The same payment dates apply under the imputation

*The fiscal year 1970 runs from 1 April 1970 to 31 March 1971. The rate is not usually fixed until the budget in the year after i.e. the rate for the fiscal year 1970 is not usually announced until the 1971 Budget.

system of corporation tax although payments of ACT, currently equivalent to 33/67s of the dividend, are made when the dividends are distributed (as was income tax deducted from dividend payments under the pre-imputation system).

## Double taxation relief

Where a company has an overseas subsidiary which remits profits to Great Britain, UK corporation tax will be payable. The parent is, however, entitled to some relief against the taxation borne abroad and this relief is calculated according to particular arrangements made by the Inland Revenue with foreign countries*. If the overseas tax rate is less than the UK rate an additional charge is made by the Inland Revenue to bring the tax charge up to the British level. If the overseas rate is higher than the UK levy then there is no liability to British corporation tax. The company's profits, including the overseas income, is assessed to UK corporation tax and relief is given in respect of the foreign earnings to the extent of the foreign taxation incurred or the amount of British corporation tax, whichever is the lower.

*Example*
Foreign earnings remitted to the UK for two companies $A$ and $B$ are as follows:

|  |  | A £ |  | B £ |
|---|---|---|---|---|
| Profits |  | 1,000 |  | 1,000 |
| *Less*: foreign tax | 30% | 300 | 60% | 600 |
|  |  | 700 |  | 400 |
| *Less*: withholding tax | 10% | 70 | 10% | 40 |
| Profits remitted to UK |  | £630 |  | £360 |

| UK corporation tax charge | A £ | B £ |
|---|---|---|
| Gross profits | 1,000 | 1,000 |
| *Less*: corporation tax (52%) | 520 | 520 |
| Double taxation relief (at lower of foreign taxes* or UK corporation tax) | 370 | 520 |
| Net additional UK charge | 150 | — |

*Includes withholding tax.

Thus, relief in respect of $A$ is limited to overseas tax suffered whilst $B$'s double tax relief is limited to UK corporation tax. The accounts of $A$ and $B$ will record the tax charges as follows:

*The extent and scope of double tax relief depends upon the particular agreement reached with any country.

|                        | A<br>£ |       | B<br>£ |       |
|------------------------|--------|-------|--------|-------|
| Pre-tax profits        |        | 1,000 |        | 1,000 |
| Taxation:              |        |       |        |       |
|   UK corporation tax | 520 |       | 520 |       |
|   *Less*: double tax |     |       |     |       |
|     relief | 370 |       | 520 |       |
|                        | 150    |       | —   |       |
| Overseas tax           | 370    | 520   | 640 | 640   |
| Profits after tax      |        | 480   |     | 360   |

Double tax relief is still available on foreign taxes paid, under the imputation system. However, the credit for foreign tax will be offsetable against corporation tax as reduced by ACT. If, in the above example, companies *A* and *B* had ACT of £100 each, the corporation tax liabilities would be:

|                       | A<br>£ | B<br>£ |
|-----------------------|--------|--------|
| Gross profits         | 1,000  | 1,000  |
| Corporation tax thereon | 520  | 520    |
| *Less*: ACT set off   | 100    | 100    |
|                       | 420    | 420    |
| Double tax relief     | 370 limited to | 420 |
| Mainstream charge     | 50     |        |

Companies who derive most of their profits from abroad and which are taxed at high rates will find themselves at a significant disadvantage to companies with a similar level of profits which are derived from the UK.

**Deferred taxation**

In the charge for taxation shown in published accounts there often appears an amount termed 'transfer to deferred tax account' or 'transferred to tax equalisation account'. The main items making up this amount are the capital gains tax liability payable if the company's revalued assets were realized and the increased tax payable if the Inland Revenue used the company's depreciation charge instead of the capital allowances as a deduction from profits. The deferred tax account is in fact an accounting treatment to show a 'truer' financial position of the firm. The composition of the amounts involved was described in Chapter 2. The accounts of ABC LTD showed the disclosure requirements of the deferred taxation account.

**Accounting considerations**

The imputation system of corporation tax will result in some additional accounting considerations and some changes in recording practices from the pre-imputation era. These are occasioned principally by the advance corporation tax payments. The main changes are as follows:

**Dividends paid**

1 Dividend payments will be shown net of ACT i.e. at the actual cash payment figure. Pre-imputation dividends were shown gross. It is

expected that most companies will show, as an inset note, the amount or rate of tax credit attributable to the dividend when received by shareholders resident in the UK.

**Dividends proposed**

2 A proposed dividend will be shown net and the advance corporation tax relating to it will be shown as a current liability. If it is reasonably certain that this advance corporation tax is recoverable then it should be deducted from the deferred taxation account or, in the absence of such an account, it can be shown as a deferred asset: the ASSC recommends that the amounts should not be offset against each other.[1] If the recovery of ACT is not reasonably certain and foreseeable then it should be written off in the accounts in which the proposed dividend is provided. The amount should be separately disclosed with the tax charge in the accounts. Similarly any carry forward of unrelieved ACT whose recovery now seems uncertain should be written off and separately disclosed in the accounts.

*Example*
A company makes neither a profit nor a loss during a year but pays a dividend of £6,700 (out of prior years' profits). No profits were made in the accounting periods beginning within the two preceding years and no future profits are expected. Thus it appears unlikely that the ACT on the dividend amounting to £3,300 (i.e. $33/67 \times £6,700$) will be recoverable against future corporation tax liabilities. The £3,300 ACT will therefore appear as a tax charge in the accounts.

If a company is unable to offset ACT against current or prior year profits it can be utilised against future income. If in the above example future profits were expected and foreseeable then the ACT paid would be deducted from any deferred taxation account or, if no such account exists, it can be included as a deferred asset.

**Preference dividends**

3 The ASSC propose that the new rate of dividend on preference shares (under the imputation system) should be incorporated in the description of the shares in the balance sheet,

*Any dividend right established before 6 April 1973 at a gross rate or a gross amount was reduced by the Finance Act 1972, Schedule 23, paragraph 18\* to seven-tenths of its former rate or amount. Steps should therefore be taken to distinguish, for example a 10 per cent preference share issued before 6 April 1973 on which the dividend is now 7 per cent, from such a preference share issued after that date. A change in the basic rate of income tax and a corresponding change in the rate of ACT would not affect this once-for-all 'netting down'. Thus a former 10 per cent preference share may in the future yield, with related tax credit, either more or less than 10 per cent on nominal value. The new rate of dividend on preference shares (including participating preference and preferred ordinary shares where the former rate of dividend forms part of the title), should therefore be incorporated in the*

---

\*Subsequent changes in the rate of ACT have varied the rate of tax credit but not the amount of the cash dividend payable to shareholders.

*description of the shares in the balance sheet, e.g.:*

|  | Authorized | Issued |
|---|---|---|
| 100,000 10 per cent (now 7 per cent + Tax credit) Preference shares of £1 | £100,000 | £100,000 |

**Franked investment income**

4 Franked investment income was shown at its grossed up amount (i.e. net receipt plus the standard rate of income tax borne) up until April 1973. Under the imputation system, however, there are several ways of dealing with franked investment income. The two main methods of dealing with it are:

(*a*) to bring into the profit and loss account the cash amount received or receivable (i.e. excluding the tax credit); or
(*b*) to bring in the amount of the franked investment income (i.e. including the tax credit, an equivalent amount then being treated as part of the charge for taxation).

The ASSC in their statement of standard accounting practice recommend the use of the second method.[1] The ASSC argued the case thus:

*The first method would involve treating the income either as an item of profit before taxation, or as an addition to the profit after taxation – both alternatives are open to objection. The second method would allow recognition of the income both at the pre-tax and at the after-tax stage in a way which is consistent with other elements of profit, and is therefore adopted as the standard accounting practice.*

They are not adamant on this, however, and in part 3 (Standard Accounting Practice) of the statement, the ASSC said:

*Incoming dividends from United Kingdom resident companies should be included at the amount of cash received or receivable plus the tax credit.*

**Transitional period**

5 SSAP8 gave some guidance as to how to compare and interpret earnings and dividends pre and post the imputation system. The provisions are:

*The change to the imputation system destroyed the comparability, as between one period and another, of many of the figures in the historical records. For example, earnings were formerly available to cover gross dividends before deduction of income tax, but under the imputation system they are now available to cover the actual cash dividends payable to the preference or equity shareholders. Hence, in calculating earnings for equity under the imputation system, preference dividends should be deducted at the amount declared and payable to the shareholders – not at the former gross amount.*

*In general, it is likely to be either impracticable or unsatisfactory to attempt to adjust profits earned under one system of taxation to another tax system. Furthermore, if a company had been taxed differently, it might have taken different financial decisions. Most of the items in the historical summary should therefore be left as originally published.*

*Figures such as earnings and dividends based on the old system of taxation should, however, be carefully distinguished from those based on the new system. It may be helpful to describe dividends paid under the old system of taxation as 'gross dividends' to distinguish them from dividends paid under the new system. The transitional period, which may cover more than one accounting year, presents particular problems. It would usually be preferable (where practicable) to show an overlap with the figures calculated both ways for the straddling period, or alternatively to indicate in some other manner the points where comparability has been destroyed by a change in the system of taxation (i.e. 1965 and 1973). Figures relating to earlier periods can then be shown entirely on the old basis with subsequent figures being entirely on the new basis.*

*To calculate the gross dividends for the straddling year (for the purposes of historical summaries only) any dividends relating to that year paid on or after 6 April 1973 may be increased by the amount of the appropriate tax credits and added to any dividends paid before 6 April 1973. To calculate the equivalent 'new' dividends from gross dividends, the gross dividends may be reduced by 30 per cent.*

## Earnings per share

6  The 'net' basis should be adopted for calculating earnings per share and thus incorporating irrecoverable ACT and irrecoverable foreign tax arising from dividend payments. This method has been adopted by the Financial Times in their share price statistics. The three methods of calculating earnings per share, the nil, the net and the full distribution base, were discussed in Chapter 3.

### Personal taxation

Prior to 6 April 1973 Companies deducted income tax at the standard rate (38.75p for 1972/3) from the dividend. This was handed to the Inland Revenue and the remainder sent to the shareholders. If the investor was assessed to surtax he would incur an additional tax liability in respect of the dividend. If, however, the investor's other income is very small and is more than covered by the various reliefs he is entitled to, then a repayment of tax can be claimed for all or some part of the tax deducted on the dividend.

## Tax credits

From 6 April 1973 UK resident companies will not deduct tax from the dividend but will notify shareholders of their 'tax credit'. This tax credit is equivalent to the ACT borne on the distribution, which for 1973/4 was 3/7 of the dividend and 33/67 in 1974/5. The shareholder then grosses up his dividend by the amount of ACT borne and is taxed at his particular rate. The tax credit is then deducted from this liability to give the net tax position. The tax credit is not available to non-residents although it is expected that many double taxation agreements will have to be amended to afford some relief.

### Example

An individual receives a cash dividend of £70 in 1972/3 and 1973/4. The rate of tax applicable to his income is taken as 30 per cent for both 1972/3 and for 1973/4. He has used up all his reliefs on his other income.

|  | 1972/3 | Tax borne | 1973/4 |  |
|---|---|---|---|---|
|  |  | £ | £ |  |  |
| Dividend Gross | 100 | 30 | Dividend | 70 |
| Income tax @ 30% |  | 30 | Tax Credit | 30 |
|  |  | – |  | 100 |
|  |  |  | Income Tax @ 30% | 30 |
| Tax Payable |  | – | *Less*: tax credit |  |
|  |  |  | (equal to ACT) | 30 |
|  |  |  | Tax Payable | – |

If the investor's marginal tax rate is 40 per cent* the position would be:

|  | 1972/3 | Tax borne | 1973/4 |  |
|---|---|---|---|---|
| Dividend Gross | 100 | 30 | Dividend | 70 |
| Income tax @ 40% |  | 40 | Grossed Up | 30 |
| Tax Payable |  | 10 |  | 100 |
|  |  |  | Income Tax @ 40% | 40 |
|  |  |  | *Less*: tax credit |  |
|  |  |  | (equal to ACT) | 30 |
|  |  |  | Tax Payable | 10 |

*Note*: Up to 1972/3 individuals were assessed to Surtax above certain levels whereas from 1973/4 they are taxed at higher levels of income tax. Thus the tax position of a shareholder is not changed if he receives the same cash dividend. However, in most cases the company will have found it more expensive to pay a dividend of £70 pre-imputation as its tax charge was greater and its available profits lower.

## Investment surcharge

Under the unified system there will be an investment income surcharge where this income exceeds £2,000. The surcharge for 1973/4 is 15 per cent of the excess over £2,000. In the 1974 Budget the Chancellor proposed to tax investment income between £1,000 and £2,000 at a rate of 10 per cent. Above £2,000 the investment surcharge remains at 15 per cent. Personal allowances will be deducted first against earned income and then against investment income.

## Capital gains

There have been no major changes in the computation and taxation of capital gains and losses in the Unified System. A capital gain or loss arises upon a realisation of shares or other assets and this is deemed to include a sale, a deemed sale at death or a disposal by way of a gift. Gilt edged securities and National Savings Certificates are exempt from capital gains tax but ordinary shares come within the scope of the tax. Currently capital gains tax is at a rate of 30 per cent or the notional income tax on one half of the chargeable gains when these do not exceed £5,000 plus the excess over £5,000 when the total chargeable gains do exceed £5,000, whichever is the lower. The gain or loss on the realisation of shares is the difference between the actual cash cost and the sale proceeds. Thus the costs of purchasing and selling shares are allowed as an expense. When more than one

*This is used purely as an example.

273

purchase is made of a particular company's shares the amounts are aggregated and the average cost computed and this is the 'cost' figure used in determining gains and losses.

For investments held prior to 6 April 1965, the normal method of computing the chargeable gain is to take the market value of the securities on 6 April 1965 and to compare that with the actual or deemed proceeds of realisation. The actual cost of the securities is then ascertained and if comparison of this with the proceeds of sale shows a lower gain or lower loss the lower figure is taken. If one method shows a gain and the other a loss the disposal is treated as having given rise neither to a gain nor to a loss. The taxpayer may, however, elect that chargeable gains or allowable losses on all his disposals of quoted securities after 19 March 1968 should be computed on the basis that they were acquired on 6 April 1965 at their market value at that date. This election, which is irrevocable, applies to all the taxpayer's ordinary shares held at 6 April 1965.

When a company is taken over and shares in the acquiring company are received as consideration there is no deemed disposal. The new shares are assumed to have cost the same as the cost of the original shares. The recommended text should be looked at for detailed descriptions of the tax and the treatment of losses. The analyst will also need to keep abreast of changes in the scope and rates of tax and should consult the Inland Revenue pamphlets which are produced.

## Capital gains of unit trusts and investment trusts

There are different rules *re* the computation of capital gains on the realisation of units held in an authorised unit trust or the realisation of shares in an investment trust. Prior to 6 April 1972 unit trusts and investment trusts suffered capital gains tax at 30 per cent. This 'net gain' was apportioned between the unit or shareholders and notices were sent to them notifying them of the apportionment. Investors then added the apportioned net gains to the cost of their units or shares and this figure was compared against the sales proceeds in computing capital gains or losses. This eliminated the element of double taxation.

From 6 April 1972 unit trusts' and investment trusts'* capital gains have been taxed at 15 per cent. This was computed by taxing three-eighths of the gain at corporation tax rate (40 per cent for 1972/3). When the unit holder or investment-trust holder sells his units or shares he will be taxed at 30 per cent but this will be reduced by a credit of 15 per cent of

---

*The definition of an 'investment trust' has been made more stringent. The additional requirements include (1) the company must be resident in the UK; (2) holdings in two companies which are members of a group must be counted as one and where the investing company is a member of a group any money owing to it by another member of the group must be aggregated with the shares in that company so as to form one holding. These provisions are in respect of the requirement that no more than 15 per cent of the Trust's investments may be invested in one holding; (3) the investment trust's ordinary share capital must be quoted on a recognised Stock Exchange.

the gain. Thus the investor will only be charged to capital gains tax on profits on unit-trust and investment-trust disposals at a rate of 15 per cent. The Chancellor of the Exchequer, in his 1974 budget speech, said he proposed to keep the effective corporation tax rate on capital gains made by unit trusts and investment trusts at 15 per cent.

The chapter has briefly outlined company taxation under the old and new corporation tax systems. This should give the analyst an understanding of the basis of taxation and an explanation of the items appearing in published accounts. Without full knowledge of a company's accounts the analyst can only make estimates of the impact of taxation on future profitability. As disclosure requirements become greater and especially in the case of particular companies with unusual tax positions, a greater knowledge of corporate taxation will be needed. Analysts will therefore have to extend their basic knowledge by referring to specialist textbooks.

**References**

1    'The Treatment of Taxation under the Imputation System in the Accounts of Companies', SSAP8, Accounting Standards Steering Committee, September 1974.

The latest editions of tax books should be obtained such as those by:

Carmichael, K. S., 'Capital Gains Tax', HFL Publishers.
Carmichael, K. S., 'Corporation Tax', HFL Publishers.
Clark, H. M., 'Corporation Tax – the Imputation System', General Educational Trust, The Institute of Chartered Accountants in England and Wales, 1972.
Marcus, S., 'Company Taxation 1974/1975 – a practical guide', Financial Techniques Ltd., 1974.
The Inland Revenue issue booklets on taxation which are generally the most up-to-date publications available.

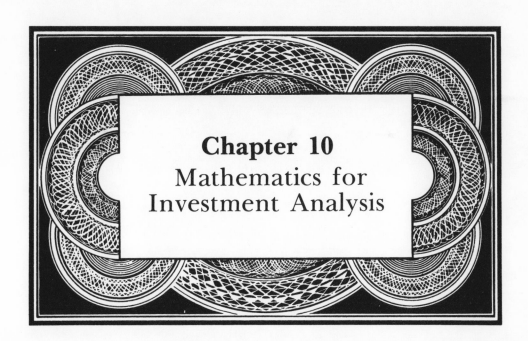

# Chapter 10
## Mathematics for Investment Analysis

This chapter briefly introduces and explains some of the mathematical and statistical techniques mentioned in the book. The relevant references should be used however for the more detailed applications and methodologies involved.

Investment analysis has been growing progressively more quantitative over the past decade and this trend is likely to accelerate. The growth in portfolio theory and the measurement of risk, both require a fair degree of mathematical knowledge. Further, the vast amounts of financial information now being collected have required investment institutions to build up efficient data retrieval systems and analysts need a knowledge of statistics in interpreting the various financial outputs. The analyst therefore needs at least a certain level of mathematical and statistical training if only to interpret the statistical analyses which will confront him. In time, however, even this level of competence is likely to be inadequate as the analyst is required to help devise sophisticated econometric models and in applying advanced statistical forecasting techniques to company data.

The chapter commences with the compound interest formulae which are used in the intrinsic-value models and in evaluating growth rates. Then averages and measures of variability are introduced and these will be remembered as being of importance in the assessment of risk in portfolio management. Finally, simple linear regression is explained and a reference is made to multiple regression. Regression equations were encountered in Chapter 5 in share price evaluation.

## Discounting

The concept of present value (PV) recognises that a given sum of money receivable at the present time is more valuable than the same amount receivable one year hence. This is the time value of money and represents the utility foregone in not having the use of the cash for the period, the effect of inflation and the productive capacity of money. One yardstick to measure this value is the interest that the sum of money could have earned in the year. Similarly, a given amount receivable one year hence is of greater value than the same amount received two years hence. From this it is obvious that to compare absolute sums of money receivable at different dates is invalid as it takes no account of the interest or return that could have been earned from the time of receipt*. For investment decisions the principle of discounting is important as the cash inflows are receivable for long into the future.

*Example*
A buys a share for £100 and received dividends of £8, £6, £8, £7 in one, two, three and four years hence. At the end of four years he sells the share for £110. His absolute cash position would be as follows:

$8 + 6 + 8 + 7 + 110 = £139$

*Less*: original

| | |
|---|---|
| payment | 100 |
| Profit | £39 |

This rate of return has omitted the interest that the investor would have earned on the dividends. The true cash return to the investor, assuming he invests his cash receipts in a bank deposit account which earns interest of 10 per cent would be:

| | £ |
|---|---|
| Dividend receipt at the end of year 1 | 8.00 |
| Receipt of interest on the above amount at the end of year 2 | 0.80 |
| | 8.80 |
| Dividend receipt at the end of year 2 | 6.00 |
| | 14.80 |
| Receipt of interest on the above amount at the end of year 3 | 1.48 |
| | 16.28 |
| Dividend receipt at the end of year 3 | 8.00 |
| | 24.28 |
| Receipt of interest on the above amount at the end of year 4 | 2.43 |
| | 26.71 |
| Dividend receipt at the end of year 4 | 7.00 |
| | 33.71 |
| Sale proceeds | 110.00 |
| | £143.71 |

*Other measures of the time value of money could be used but because of the difficulties of measurement, and in the interest of simplicity, the interest rate is used.

This produces a 'profit' of £43.71. In order to measure whether this return is adequate the investor would need to evaluate what were the alternative investment returns foregone and the risk involved. In the above example the investor would be able to use the interest rate (10 per cent) as a guide. Thus he could have put £100 in the bank at the beginning of year 1. His return would be:

|  |  | £ |
|---|---|---|
| Deposit at the beginning of year 1 |  | 100.00 |
| Interest at the end of year 1 |  | 10.00 |
|  | Balance *A* | 110.00 |
| Interest on balance *A* at the end of year 2 |  | 11.00 |
|  | Balance *B* | 121.00 |
| Interest on balance *B* at the end of year 3 |  | 12.10 |
|  | Balance *C* | 133.10 |
| Interest on balance *C* at the end of year 4 |  | 13.31 |
|  |  | £146.41 |

Clearly the investment in shares has not earned an adequate return; the investor could have made more money, with virtually no risk, by depositing his money in the bank. The investor ought to earn at least the risk-free rate of interest and increasing premiums are required the higher the risk. To work out investment decisions in this way takes a long time and mistakes can easily occur in handling so many figures.

## Present value

Another method of computing the returns has been devised. This involves discounting future cash flows by a rate of interest which represents an adequate return to the investor. The rate is likely to be the riskless rate of return (such as the market yields on Government gilt-edged securities) plus a premium for the risk involved*. The discounting operation reduces future cash inflows to present-day equivalents. This equivalent is known as the present value.

The general formula for PV is:

$$\text{PV} = \frac{\text{Cash flow}}{(1+i)^n} \text{ or, in an alternative form, } \text{PV} = \text{cash flow } (1+i)^{-n}$$

where $i$ = required rate of return (sometimes denoted as $r$).

   $n$ = the period between the outlay and the receipt of the cash flow.

In the case of a number of cash inflows, as is the case with dividends, the PV is given by:

$$\text{PV} = \frac{\text{Cash flow } A}{(1+i_A)^1} + \frac{\text{Cash flow } B}{(1+i_B)^2} + \frac{\text{Cash flow } C}{(1+i_C)^3} \dots$$

where $i$ can take various values ($A$, $B$, $C$). In practice, analysts usually use just one value.

In the example the present value is computed by substituting into the

*Risk, or uncertainty, can be dealt with in other ways although the adjustment to the discount rate is perhaps the most popular. See Chapter 5 (p. 164).

formula above:

$$PV = \frac{8}{(1+0.10)^1} + \frac{6}{(1+0.10)^2} + \frac{8}{(1+0.10)^3} + \frac{7}{(1+0.10)^4} + \frac{110}{(1+0.10)^4}$$

$$PV = \frac{8}{1.10} + \frac{6}{1.21} + \frac{8}{1.331} + \frac{7}{1.464} + \frac{110}{1.464}$$

$$PV = £98.16.*$$

The figures show that the return from the investment is inadequate, the minimum acceptable level is £100.

Note that the above figure is comparable with that produced by the previous method, i.e. $\frac{143.71}{146.41} = 98.16.*$

This method therefore produces the same answer as before but does so by jobbing backwards. The formula assumes as before that the dividends received can be re-invested at the bank interest rate from the date of receipt. As can be readily recognised, to work out the factor $(1 + i)^n$ will be very time consuming and subject to human errors in making calculations. Thus it would be no quicker than the procedure described originally. Fortunately, however, tables have been constructed showing the values of $1/(1 + i)^n$ for various rates of $i$ and for various time periods. Thus, from Table 10.1 we can look across the top row for the values of $i$ and down the left-hand column for the values of $n$. This gives the various values of $1/(1 + i)^n$, which when multiplied by the value of the numerator gives the present value of that cash flow†. Using the tables the PV is worked out as follows:

$$PV = 8 \times 0.909 + 6 \times 0.826 + 8 \times 0.751 + 7 \times 0.683 + 110 \times 0.683$$

$$PV = £98.147.$$

The table of present value factors are often headed with the symbol $Vn_i$.

In the evaluation of the intrinsic value of a share the forecast dividends and any terminal receipt are discounted back to today. If the PV is below the existing price, no purchase should be made. If the PV is above the existing price then a purchase should be made unless there is an even more attractive investment and funds are limited. This assumes the risk factor is solely accounted for in the discount rate, otherwise the investor may require a certain PV premium.

**Internal rate of return**

A different approach can be adopted in discounting and that is to calculate the rate of return. This determines what rate of interest is required to discount cash flows to produce a NPV$^\circ$ of zero. Thus, in

*To two decimal places.

†For example, the appropriate discounting factor for the dividend of £8 in year 3 is to look at the column of 10 per cent ($i = 10$ per cent) and go down three rows to $n = 3$ and the factor is shown as 0.751.

$^\circ$The net present value is the present value minus the current cost price of the share. If this is positive a purchase is implied.

**Table 10.1**
Future Worth to Present Worth, $Vn_i$ Present Worth of £1

| Year n | 1% | 2% | 3% | 4% | 5% | 6% | 7% | 8% | 9% | 10% | 12% |
|---|---|---|---|---|---|---|---|---|---|---|---|
| 1 | .990 | .980 | .971 | .962 | .952 | .943 | .935 | .926 | .917 | .909 | .893 |
| 2 | .980 | .961 | .943 | .925 | .907 | .890 | .873 | .857 | .842 | .826 | .797 |
| 3 | .971 | .942 | .915 | .889 | .864 | .840 | .816 | .794 | .772 | .751 | .712 |
| 4 | .961 | .924 | .889 | .855 | .823 | .792 | .763 | .735 | .708 | .683 | .636 |
| 5 | .951 | .906 | .863 | .822 | .784 | .747 | .713 | .681 | .650 | .621 | .567 |
| 6 | .942 | .888 | .838 | .790 | .746 | .705 | .666 | .630 | .596 | .564 | .507 |
| 7 | .933 | .871 | .813 | .760 | .711 | .665 | .623 | .583 | .547 | .513 | .452 |
| 8 | .923 | .853 | .789 | .731 | .677 | .627 | .582 | .540 | .502 | .467 | .404 |
| 9 | .914 | .837 | .766 | .703 | .645 | .592 | .544 | .500 | .460 | .424 | .361 |
| 10 | .905 | .820 | .744 | .676 | .614 | .558 | .508 | .463 | .422 | .386 | .322 |
| 11 | .896 | .804 | .722 | .650 | .585 | .527 | .475 | .429 | .388 | .350 | .287 |
| 12 | .887 | .788 | .701 | .625 | .557 | .497 | .444 | .397 | .356 | .319 | .257 |
| 13 | .879 | .773 | .681 | .601 | .530 | .469 | .415 | .368 | .326 | .290 | .229 |
| 14 | .870 | .758 | .661 | .577 | .505 | .442 | .388 | .340 | .299 | .263 | .205 |
| 15 | .861 | .743 | .642 | .555 | .481 | .417 | .362 | .315 | .275 | .239 | .183 |
| 16 | .853 | .728 | .623 | .534 | .458 | .394 | .339 | .292 | .252 | .218 | .163 |
| 17 | .844 | .714 | .605 | .513 | .436 | .371 | .317 | .270 | .231 | .198 | .146 |
| 18 | .836 | .700 | .587 | .494 | .416 | .350 | .296 | .250 | .212 | .180 | .130 |
| 19 | .828 | .686 | .570 | .475 | .396 | .331 | .276 | .232 | .194 | .164 | .116 |
| 20 | .820 | .673 | .554 | .456 | .377 | .319 | .258 | .215 | .178 | .149 | .104 |
| 25 | .780 | .610 | .478 | .375 | .295 | .233 | .184 | .146 | .116 | .092 | .059 |

| Year n | 14% | 15% | 16% | 18% | 20% | 24% | 28% | 32% | 36% | 40% |
|---|---|---|---|---|---|---|---|---|---|---|
| 1 | .877 | .870 | .862 | .847 | .833 | .806 | .781 | .758 | .735 | .714 |
| 2 | .769 | .756 | .743 | .718 | .694 | .650 | .610 | .574 | .541 | .510 |
| 3 | .675 | .658 | .641 | .609 | .579 | .524 | .477 | .435 | .398 | .364 |
| 4 | .592 | .572 | .552 | .516 | .482 | .423 | .373 | .329 | .292 | .260 |
| 5 | .519 | .497 | .476 | .437 | .402 | .341 | .291 | .250 | .215 | .186 |
| 6 | .456 | .432 | .410 | .370 | .335 | .275 | .227 | .189 | .158 | .133 |
| 7 | .400 | .376 | .354 | .314 | .279 | .222 | .178 | .143 | .116 | .095 |
| 8 | .351 | .327 | .305 | .266 | .233 | .179 | .139 | .108 | .085 | .068 |
| 9 | .308 | .284 | .263 | .226 | .194 | .144 | .108 | .082 | .063 | .048 |
| 10 | .270 | .247 | .227 | .191 | .162 | .116 | .085 | .062 | .046 | .035 |
| 11 | .237 | .215 | .195 | .162 | .135 | .094 | .066 | .047 | .034 | .025 |
| 12 | .208 | .187 | .168 | .137 | .112 | .076 | .052 | .036 | .025 | .018 |
| 13 | .182 | .163 | .145 | .116 | .093 | .061 | .040 | .027 | .018 | .013 |
| 14 | .160 | .141 | .125 | .099 | .078 | .049 | .032 | .021 | .014 | .009 |
| 15 | .140 | .123 | .108 | .084 | .065 | .040 | .025 | .016 | .010 | .006 |
| 16 | .123 | .107 | .093 | .071 | .054 | .032 | .019 | .012 | .007 | .005 |
| 17 | .108 | .093 | .080 | .060 | .045 | .026 | .015 | .009 | .005 | .003 |
| 18 | .095 | .081 | .069 | .051 | .038 | .021 | .012 | .007 | .004 | .002 |
| 19 | .083 | .070 | .060 | .043 | .031 | .017 | .009 | .005 | .003 | .002 |
| 20 | .073 | .061 | .051 | .037 | .026 | .014 | .007 | .004 | .002 | .001 |
| 25 | .038 | .030 | .024 | .016 | .010 | .005 | .002 | .001 | .000 | .000 |

our example:

$$0 = \frac{8}{(1+i)^1} + \frac{6}{(1+i)^2} + \frac{8}{(1+i)^3} + \frac{7}{(1+i)^4} + \frac{110}{(1+i)^4}$$

Unfortunately, $i$ has to be derived by trial and error and so is time consuming to calculate. It assumes that the cash dividends can be re-invested to produce the same return although such investment opportunities may not be available to the investor. The internal rate of return (IRR) is then computed against the required rate (10 per cent) and, if higher, a purchase is made. This method is rarely used in equity investment analysis because of the difficulty in calculating the return and because of the assumption of re-investing at the internal rate*. The PV method is therefore the recommended discounting technique.

Discounting formulae can be devised for different types of cash flows and appropriate tables of factors have been computed. The most popular of these are described below.

### Accumulation

This gives the eventual sum or amount of money $M$, invested at a rate of $i$ per period, will accumulate to after $n$ periods. This assumes the interest will be added to the principal ($M$) to form the opening balance for the following period. At the end of period 1 $M$ will have interest of $Mi$. Thus, $M + Mi$ or $M(1+i)$ will be the new principal for the following period. This amount will earn interest at a rate $i$ during the following period. At the end of period 2 the principal amount will be $M(1+i)^2$. This gives the general formula of:

$$S = M(1+i)^n$$

where $S$ = eventual sum of money

$M$ = initial outlay

$i$ = interest rate

From Table 10.2 it can be seen that £1 earning interest at 6 per cent for twelve years will accumulate to a total of £2.012. The factor 2.012 is multiplied by the amount of money ($M$) to obtain the accumulated total. Accumulation is equivalent to the compound interest plus principal and the tables of values are often denoted by the term $(1+i)^n$. Where interest is paid more than once a year the effective annual rate of interest is given by the formula:

$$S = M\left(1 + \frac{i}{K}\right)^{Kn}$$

where $S$ = eventual sum of money

$K$ = frequency of receipt of interest

$i$ = nominal rate of interest

*The method gives the same ranking and buy and sell decisions as the PV technique. If there are any negative cash flows there will be several IRR 'answers' and assumptions will have to be made in determining which is appropriate. This is unlikely to be met in practice, however.

**Table 10.2**
Present Worth to Future Worth, $(1+i)^n$. Compound Sum of £1

| Year n | 1% | 2% | 3% | 4% | 5% | 6% | 7% |
|---|---|---|---|---|---|---|---|
| 1 | 1.010 | 1.020 | 1.030 | 1.040 | 1.050 | 1.060 | 1.070 |
| 2 | 1.020 | 1.040 | 1.061 | 1.082 | 1.102 | 1.124 | 1.145 |
| 3 | 1.030 | 1.061 | 1.093 | 1.125 | 1.158 | 1.191 | 1.225 |
| 4 | 1.041 | 1.082 | 1.126 | 1.170 | 1.216 | 1.262 | 1.311 |
| 5 | 1.051 | 1.104 | 1.159 | 1.217 | 1.276 | 1.338 | 1.403 |
| 6 | 1.062 | 1.126 | 1.194 | 1.265 | 1.340 | 1.419 | 1.501 |
| 7 | 1.072 | 1.149 | 1.230 | 1.316 | 1.407 | 1.504 | 1.606 |
| 8 | 1.083 | 1.172 | 1.267 | 1.369 | 1.477 | 1.594 | 1.718 |
| 9 | 1.094 | 1.195 | 1.305 | 1.423 | 1.551 | 1.689 | 1.838 |
| 10 | 1.105 | 1.219 | 1.344 | 1.480 | 1.629 | 1.791 | 1.967 |
| 11 | 1.116 | 1.243 | 1.384 | 1.539 | 1.710 | 1.898 | 2.105 |
| 12 | 1.127 | 1.268 | 1.426 | 1.601 | 1.796 | 2.012 | 2.252 |
| 13 | 1.138 | 1.294 | 1.469 | 1.665 | 1.886 | 2.133 | 2.410 |
| 14 | 1.149 | 1.319 | 1.513 | 1.732 | 1.980 | 2.261 | 2.579 |
| 15 | 1.161 | 1.346 | 1.558 | 1.801 | 2.079 | 2.397 | 2.759 |
| 16 | 1.173 | 1.373 | 1.605 | 1.873 | 2.183 | 2.540 | 2.952 |
| 17 | 1.184 | 1.400 | 1.653 | 1.948 | 2.292 | 2.693 | 3.159 |
| 18 | 1.196 | 1.428 | 1.702 | 2.026 | 2.407 | 2.854 | 3.380 |
| 19 | 1.208 | 1.457 | 1.754 | 2.107 | 2.527 | 3.026 | 3.617 |
| 20 | 1.220 | 1.486 | 1.806 | 2.191 | 2.653 | 3.207 | 3.870 |
| 25 | 1.282 | 1.641 | 2.094 | 2.666 | 3.386 | 4.292 | 5.427 |

| Year n | 8% | 9% | 10% | 12% | 14% | 15% | 16% |
|---|---|---|---|---|---|---|---|
| 1 | 1.080 | 1.090 | 1.100 | 1.120 | 1.140 | 1.150 | 1.160 |
| 2 | 1.166 | 1.188 | 1.210 | 1.254 | 1.300 | 1.322 | 1.346 |
| 3 | 1.260 | 1.295 | 1.331 | 1.405 | 1.482 | 1.521 | 1.561 |
| 4 | 1.360 | 1.412 | 1.464 | 1.574 | 1.689 | 1.749 | 1.811 |
| 5 | 1.469 | 1.539 | 1.611 | 1.762 | 1.925 | 2.011 | 2.100 |
| 6 | 1.587 | 1.677 | 1.772 | 1.974 | 2.195 | 2.313 | 2.436 |
| 7 | 1.714 | 1.828 | 1.949 | 2.211 | 2.502 | 2.660 | 2.826 |
| 8 | 1.851 | 1.993 | 2.144 | 2.476 | 2.853 | 3.059 | 3.278 |
| 9 | 1.999 | 2.172 | 2.358 | 2.773 | 3.252 | 3.518 | 3.803 |
| 10 | 2.159 | 2.367 | 2.594 | 3.106 | 3.707 | 4.046 | 4.411 |
| 11 | 2.332 | 2.580 | 2.853 | 3.479 | 4.226 | 4.652 | 5.117 |
| 12 | 2.518 | 2.813 | 3.138 | 3.896 | 4.818 | 5.350 | 5.936 |
| 13 | 2.720 | 3.066 | 3.452 | 4.363 | 5.492 | 6.153 | 6.886 |
| 14 | 2.937 | 3.342 | 3.797 | 4.887 | 6.261 | 7.076 | 7.988 |
| 15 | 3.172 | 3.642 | 4.177 | 5.474 | 7.138 | 8.137 | 9.266 |
| 16 | 3.426 | 3.970 | 4.595 | 6.130 | 8.137 | 9.358 | 10.748 |
| 17 | 3.700 | 4.328 | 5.054 | 6.866 | 9.276 | 10.761 | 12.468 |
| 18 | 3.996 | 4.717 | 5.560 | 7.690 | 10.575 | 12.375 | 14.463 |
| 19 | 4.316 | 5.142 | 6.116 | 8.613 | 12.056 | 14.232 | 16.777 |
| 20 | 4.661 | 5.604 | 6.728 | 9.646 | 13.743 | 16.367 | 19.461 |
| 25 | 6.848 | 8.623 | 10.835 | 17.000 | 26.462 | 32.919 | 40.874 |

**Table 10.2** *(contd)*

| Year n | 18% | 20% | 24% | 28% | 32% | 36% | 40% |
|---|---|---|---|---|---|---|---|
| 1 | 1.180 | 1.200 | 1.240 | 1.280 | 1.320 | 1.360 | 1.400 |
| 2 | 1.392 | 1.440 | 1.538 | 1.638 | 1.742 | 1.850 | 1.960 |
| 3 | 1.643 | 1.728 | 1.907 | 2.067 | 2.300 | 2.515 | 2.744 |
| 4 | 1.939 | 2.074 | 2.364 | 2.684 | 3.036 | 3.421 | 3.842 |
| 5 | 2.288 | 2.488 | 2.932 | 3.326 | 4.007 | 4.653 | 5.378 |
| 6 | 2.700 | 2.986 | 3.635 | 4.398 | 5.290 | 6.328 | 7.530 |
| 7 | 3.185 | 3.583 | 4.508 | 5.629 | 6.983 | 8.605 | 10.541 |
| 8 | 3.759 | 4.300 | 5.590 | 7.206 | 9.217 | 11.703 | 14.758 |
| 9 | 4.435 | 5.160 | 6.931 | 9.223 | 12.166 | 15.917 | 20.661 |
| 10 | 5.234 | 6.192 | 8.594 | 11.806 | 16.060 | 21.647 | 28.925 |
| 11 | 6.176 | 7.430 | 10.657 | 15.112 | 21.199 | 29.439 | 40.496 |
| 12 | 7.288 | 8.916 | 13.215 | 19.343 | 27.983 | 40.037 | 56.694 |
| 13 | 8.599 | 10.699 | 16.386 | 24.759 | 36.937 | 54.451 | 79.372 |
| 14 | 10.147 | 12.839 | 20.319 | 31.691 | 48.757 | 74.053 | 111.120 |
| 15 | 11.974 | 15.407 | 25.196 | 40.565 | 64.359 | 100.712 | 155.568 |
| 16 | 14.129 | 18.488 | 31.243 | 51.923 | 84.954 | 136.970 | 217.795 |
| 17 | 16.672 | 22.186 | 38.741 | 66.461 | 112.140 | 186.280 | 304.914 |
| 18 | 19.673 | 26.623 | 48.039 | 85.071 | 148.020 | 253.340 | 426.879 |
| 19 | 23.214 | 31.948 | 59.568 | 108.890 | 195.390 | 344.540 | 597.630 |
| 20 | 27.393 | 38.338 | 73.864 | 139.380 | 257.920 | 468.570 | 836.683 |
| 25 | 62.669 | 95.396 | 216.542 | 478.900 | 1033.600 | 2180.100 | 4499.880 |

*Example*

If an investor receives interest of 6 per cent in monthly instalments of $\frac{1}{2}$ per cent for three years the eventual sum from an initial payment of £150 is:

$$S = 150\left(1 + \frac{0.06}{12}\right)^{12 \times 3}$$

$$S = £179.5$$

### Accumulation of an annuity

This gives the eventual sum of money which an annual amount invested at the end of each year which earns interest at the rate $i$ and which is re-invested, will accumulate to. Alternatively, it can be used to determine what sum of money invested annually at the rate of interest $i$ with re-investment of interest, will accumulate to a specific sum at year $n$.

A payment of $X$ invested at the rate $i$ at the end of 1961 would accumulate to $X(1 + i)^9$ by the end of 1970. This is explained by the simple accumulation formula above. An amount of $X$ invested at the same rate, $i$, in December 1962 would accumulate to $X(1 + i)^8$ by the end of 1970. This process is repeated for each year and the addition of the various amounts gives the eventual sum receivable.

$$X(1+i)^{n-1} + X(1+i)^{n-2} + X(1+i)^{n-3} \cdots + X(1+i) + X = \text{eventual}$$

$$\text{sum (S)}$$

In the example $n = 10$. The second to last payment only receives one year's interest whilst the last payment is made on the day of repayment and therefore accumulates no interest. The expression reduces to the form:

$$S = \frac{X((1+i)^n - 1)}{i}$$

The tables for various factors of $S$ are given in Table 10.3 and the conventional symbol used is $S_n i$. If £60 were invested at a rate of 7 per cent per annum in each of eight years the accumulated total would be

$$\frac{60((1+0.07)^8 - 1)}{0.07} = £615.6$$

which is the factor 10.260 multiplied by 60.

The formula for finding the annual amount that must be paid to

**Table 10.3**
Annuity to Future Worth, $S_n i$. Compound Sum of a £1 Annuity.

| Year $n$ | 1% | 2% | 3% | 4% | 5% | 6% | 7% |
|---|---|---|---|---|---|---|---|
| 1 | 1.000 | 1.000 | 1.000 | 1.000 | 1.000 | 1.000 | 1.000 |
| 2 | 2.010 | 2.020 | 2.030 | 2.040 | 2.050 | 2.060 | 2.070 |
| 3 | 3.030 | 3.060 | 3.091 | 3.122 | 3.152 | 3.184 | 3.215 |
| 4 | 4.060 | 4.122 | 4.184 | 4.246 | 4.310 | 4.375 | 4.440 |
| 5 | 5.101 | 5.204 | 5.309 | 5.416 | 5.526 | 5.637 | 5.751 |
| 6 | 6.152 | 6.308 | 6.468 | 6.633 | 6.802 | 6.975 | 7.153 |
| 7 | 7.214 | 7.434 | 7.662 | 7.898 | 8.142 | 8.394 | 8.654 |
| 8 | 8.286 | 8.583 | 8.892 | 9.214 | 9.549 | 9.897 | 10.260 |
| 9 | 9.369 | 9.755 | 10.159 | 10.583 | 11.027 | 11.491 | 11.978 |
| 10 | 10.462 | 10.950 | 11.464 | 12.006 | 12.578 | 13.181 | 13.816 |
| 11 | 11.567 | 12.169 | 12.808 | 13.486 | 14.207 | 14.972 | 15.784 |
| 12 | 12.683 | 13.412 | 14.192 | 15.026 | 15.917 | 16.870 | 17.888 |
| 13 | 13.809 | 14.680 | 15.618 | 16.627 | 17.713 | 18.882 | 20.141 |
| 14 | 14.947 | 15.974 | 17.086 | 18.292 | 19.599 | 21.051 | 22.550 |
| 15 | 16.097 | 17.293 | 18.599 | 20.024 | 21.579 | 23.276 | 25.129 |
| 16 | 17.258 | 18.639 | 20.157 | 21.825 | 23.657 | 25.673 | 27.888 |
| 17 | 18.430 | 20.012 | 21.762 | 23.698 | 25.840 | 28.213 | 30.840 |
| 18 | 19.615 | 21.412 | 23.414 | 25.645 | 28.132 | 30.906 | 33.999 |
| 19 | 20.811 | 22.841 | 25.117 | 27.671 | 30.539 | 33.760 | 37.379 |
| 20 | 22.019 | 24.297 | 26.870 | 29.778 | 33.066 | 36.786 | 40.995 |
| 25 | 28.243 | 32.030 | 36.459 | 41.646 | 47.727 | 54.865 | 63.249 |

## Table 10.3 (*contd*)

| Year n | 8% | 9% | 10% | 12% | 14% | 16% | 18% |
|---|---|---|---|---|---|---|---|
| 1 | 1.000 | 1.000 | 1.000 | 1.000 | 1.000 | 1.000 | |
| 2 | 2.080 | 2.090 | 2.100 | 2.120 | 2.140 | 2.160 | 2.180 |
| 3 | 3.246 | 3.278 | 3.310 | 3.374 | 3.440 | 3.506 | 3.572 |
| 4 | 4.506 | 4.573 | 4.641 | 4.770 | 4.921 | 5.066 | 5.215 |
| 5 | 5.867 | 5.985 | 6.105 | 6.353 | 6.610 | 6.877 | 7.154 |
| 6 | 7.336 | 7.523 | 7.716 | 8.115 | 8.536 | 8.977 | 9.442 |
| 7 | 8.923 | 9.200 | 9.487 | 10.089 | 10.730 | 11.414 | 12.142 |
| 8 | 10.637 | 11.028 | 11.436 | 12.300 | 13.233 | 14.240 | 15.327 |
| 9 | 12.488 | 13.021 | 13.579 | 14.776 | 16.085 | 17.518 | 19.086 |
| 10 | 14.487 | 15.193 | 15.937 | 17.549 | 19.337 | 21.321 | 23.521 |
| 11 | 16.645 | 17.560 | 18.531 | 20.655 | 23.044 | 25.733 | 28.755 |
| 12 | 18.977 | 20.141 | 21.384 | 24.133 | 27.271 | 30.850 | 34.931 |
| 13 | 21.495 | 22.953 | 24.523 | 28.029 | 32.089 | 36.786 | 42.219 |
| 14 | 24.215 | 26.019 | 27.975 | 32.393 | 37.581 | 43.672 | 50.818 |
| 15 | 27.152 | 29.361 | 31.772 | 37.280 | 43.842 | 51.660 | 60.965 |
| 16 | 30.324 | 33.003 | 35.950 | 42.753 | 50.980 | 60.925 | 72.939 |
| 17 | 33.750 | 36.974 | 40.545 | 48.884 | 59.118 | 71.673 | 87.068 |
| 18 | 37.450 | 41.301 | 45.599 | 55.750 | 68.394 | 84.141 | 103.740 |
| 19 | 41.446 | 46.018 | 51.159 | 63.440 | 78.969 | 98.603 | 123.414 |
| 20 | 45.762 | 51.160 | 57.275 | 72.052 | 91.025 | 115.380 | 146.628 |
| 25 | 73.106 | 84.701 | 98.347 | 133.334 | 181.871 | 249.214 | 342.603 |

| Year n | 20% | 24% | 28% | 32% | 36% | 40% |
|---|---|---|---|---|---|---|
| 1 | 1.000 | 1.000 | 1.000 | 1.000 | 1.000 | 1.000 |
| 2 | 2.200 | 2.240 | 2.280 | 2.320 | 2.360 | 2.400 |
| 3 | 3.640 | 3.778 | 3.918 | 4.062 | 4.210 | 4.360 |
| 4 | 5.368 | 5.684 | 6.016 | 6.362 | 6.725 | 7.104 |
| 5 | 7.442 | 8.048 | 8.700 | 9.398 | 10.146 | 10.846 |
| 6 | 9.930 | 10.980 | 12.136 | 13.406 | 14.799 | 16.324 |
| 7 | 12.916 | 14.615 | 16.534 | 18.696 | 21.126 | 23.853 |
| 8 | 16.499 | 19.123 | 22.163 | 25.678 | 29.732 | 34.395 |
| 9 | 20.799 | 24.712 | 29.369 | 34.895 | 41.435 | 49.153 |
| 10 | 25.959 | 31.643 | 38.592 | 47.062 | 57.352 | 69.814 |
| 11 | 32.150 | 40.238 | 50.399 | 63.122 | 78.998 | 98.739 |
| 12 | 39.580 | 50.985 | 65.510 | 84.320 | 108.437 | 139.235 |
| 13 | 48.497 | 64.110 | 84.853 | 112.303 | 148.475 | 195.929 |
| 14 | 59.196 | 80.496 | 109.612 | 149.240 | 202.926 | 275.300 |
| 15 | 72.035 | 100.815 | 141.303 | 197.997 | 276.979 | 386.420 |
| 16 | 87.442 | 126.011 | 181.870 | 262.360 | 377.690 | 541.990 |
| 17 | 105.931 | 157.253 | 233.790 | 347.310 | 514.660 | 759.780 |
| 18 | 128.117 | 195.994 | 300.250 | 459.450 | 700.940 | 1064.700 |
| 19 | 154.740 | 244.033 | 385.320 | 607.470 | 954.280 | 1491.600 |
| 20 | 186.688 | 303.601 | 494.210 | 802.860 | 1298.000 | 2089.200 |
| 25 | 471.981 | 898.092 | 1706.800 | 3226.800 | 6053.000 | 11247.000 |

produce an accumulated amount, $S$, is derived from above and is:

$$X = S\left(\frac{i}{(1+i)^n - 1}\right)$$

Tables exist for these values and they are usually headed:

$$\frac{1}{S_n} = \frac{i}{(1+i)^n - 1}$$

*Example*  If an investor requires a sum of £5,000 at the end of six years and the prevailing interest rate is 4 per cent, what is the annual amount that must be invested?

$$X = 5{,}000 \left(\frac{0.04}{(1+0.04)^6 - 1}\right)$$

From the appropriate tables the annual amount to be paid is $5{,}000 \times 0.1507 = £753.5$.

### Annuities receivable

The formula to determine the deposit that must be paid at the beginning of the period to be able to withdraw a fixed sum at the end of each of $n$ years and to end up with a nil balance whilst earning an interest of $i$ is:

$$C = P\left(\frac{1-(1+i)^{-n}}{i}\right)$$

Where $C$ is the present value of the annuity of £$P$ per period paid at the end of each period. Tables for the values of $(1-(1+i)^{-n})/i$ are usually designated $a_n i$.

*Example*  If an investor wanted to withdraw £200 for six years what sum would he have to originally invest, earning interest at 4 per cent, to end up with a nil balance?

$$C = 200 \left(\frac{1-(1+0.04)^{-6}}{0.04}\right)$$

From Table 10.4 the initial outlay is found to be $200 \times 5.242 = £1{,}048.4$.

From the above formula is derived the expression which tells us the payment $P$ received from a given present value, $C$.

Thus, $P = C(i/(1-(1+i)^{-n}))$. The appropriate tables are designated $1/a_n$.

*Example*  If an investor invests £4,000 earning interest at 4 per cent what annual amount can be withdrawn over five years to end up with a nil balance?

$$P = 4{,}000 \left(\frac{0.04}{1-(1+0.04)^{-5}}\right).$$

**Table 10.4**

Annuity to Present Worth, $a_{n}i$ Present Worth of a £1 Annuity

| Year n | 1% | 2% | 3% | 4% | 5% | 6% | 7% | 8% | 9% | 10% |
|---|---|---|---|---|---|---|---|---|---|---|
| 1 | 0.990 | 0.980 | 0.971 | 0.962 | 0.952 | 0.943 | 0.935 | 0.926 | 0.917 | 0.909 |
| 2 | 1.970 | 1.942 | 1.913 | 1.886 | 1.859 | 1.883 | 1.808 | 1.783 | 1.759 | 1.736 |
| 3 | 2.941 | 2.884 | 2.892 | 2.775 | 2.723 | 2.673 | 2.624 | 2.577 | 2.531 | 2.487 |
| 4 | 3.902 | 3.808 | 3.717 | 3.630 | 3.546 | 3.465 | 3.387 | 3.312 | 3.240 | 3.170 |
| 5 | 4.853 | 4.713 | 4.580 | 4.452 | 4.329 | 4.212 | 4.100 | 3.993 | 3.890 | 3.791 |
| 6 | 5.795 | 5.601 | 5.417 | 5.242 | 5.076 | 4.917 | 4.767 | 4.623 | 4.486 | 4.355 |
| 7 | 6.728 | 6.472 | 6.230 | 6.002 | 5.786 | 5.582 | 5.389 | 5.206 | 5.033 | 4.868 |
| 8 | 7.652 | 7.325 | 7.020 | 6.733 | 6.463 | 6.210 | 5.971 | 5.747 | 5.535 | 5.335 |
| 9 | 8.566 | 8.162 | 7.786 | 7.435 | 7.108 | 6.802 | 6.515 | 6.247 | 5.985 | 5.759 |
| 10 | 9.471 | 8.983 | 8.530 | 8.111 | 7.722 | 7.360 | 7.024 | 6.710 | 6.418 | 6.145 |
| 11 | 10.368 | 9.787 | 9.253 | 8.760 | 8.306 | 7.887 | 7.499 | 7.139 | 6.805 | 6.495 |
| 12 | 11.255 | 10.575 | 9.954 | 9.385 | 8.863 | 8.384 | 7.943 | 7.536 | 7.161 | 6.814 |
| 13 | 12.134 | 11.343 | 10.635 | 9.986 | 9.394 | 8.853 | 8.358 | 7.904 | 7.487 | 7.103 |
| 14 | 13.004 | 12.106 | 11.296 | 10.563 | 9.899 | 9.295 | 8.745 | 8.244 | 7.786 | 7.367 |
| 15 | 13.865 | 12.849 | 11.938 | 11.118 | 10.380 | 9.712 | 9.108 | 8.559 | 8.060 | 7.606 |
| 16 | 14.718 | 13.578 | 12.561 | 11.652 | 10.838 | 10.106 | 9.447 | 8.851 | 8.312 | 7.824 |
| 17 | 15.562 | 14.292 | 13.166 | 12.166 | 11.274 | 10.477 | 9.763 | 9.122 | 8.544 | 8.022 |
| 18 | 16.398 | 14.992 | 13.754 | 12.659 | 11.690 | 10.828 | 10.059 | 9.372 | 8.756 | 8.201 |
| 19 | 17.226 | 15.678 | 14.324 | 13.134 | 12.085 | 11.158 | 10.336 | 9.604 | 8.950 | 8.365 |
| 20 | 18.046 | 16.351 | 14.877 | 13.590 | 12.462 | 11.470 | 10.594 | 9.818 | 9.128 | 8.514 |
| 25 | 22.023 | 19.523 | 17.413 | 15.622 | 14.094 | 12.783 | 11.654 | 10.675 | 9.823 | 9.077 |

| Year n | 12% | 14% | 16% | 18% | 20% | 24% | 28% | 32% | 36% |
|---|---|---|---|---|---|---|---|---|---|
| 1 | 0.893 | 0.877 | 0.862 | 0.847 | 0.833 | 0.806 | 0.781 | 0.758 | 0.735 |
| 2 | 1.690 | 1.647 | 1.605 | 1.566 | 1.528 | 1.457 | 1.392 | 1.332 | 1.276 |
| 3 | 2.402 | 2.322 | 2.246 | 2.174 | 2.106 | 1.981 | 1.868 | 1.766 | 1.674 |
| 4 | 3.037 | 2.914 | 2.798 | 2.690 | 2.589 | 2.404 | 2.241 | 2.096 | 1.966 |
| 5 | 3.605 | 3.433 | 3.274 | 3.127 | 2.991 | 2.745 | 2.532 | 2.345 | 2.181 |
| 6 | 4.111 | 3.889 | 3.685 | 3.498 | 3.326 | 3.020 | 2.759 | 2.534 | 2.339 |
| 7 | 4.564 | 4.288 | 4.039 | 3.812 | 3.605 | 3.242 | 2.937 | 2.678 | 2.455 |
| 8 | 4.968 | 4.639 | 4.344 | 4.078 | 3.337 | 3.421 | 3.076 | 2.786 | 2.540 |
| 9 | 5.328 | 4.946 | 4.607 | 4.303 | 4.031 | 3.566 | 3.184 | 2.868 | 2.603 |
| 10 | 5.650 | 5.216 | 4.833 | 4.494 | 4.193 | 3.682 | 3.269 | 2.930 | 2.650 |
| 11 | 5.988 | 5.453 | 5.029 | 4.656 | 4.327 | 3.776 | 3.335 | 2.978 | 2.683 |
| 12 | 6.194 | 5.660 | 5.197 | 4.793 | 4.439 | 3.851 | 3.387 | 3.013 | 2.708 |
| 13 | 6.424 | 5.842 | 5.342 | 4.910 | 4.533 | 3.912 | 3.427 | 3.040 | 2.727 |
| 14 | 6.628 | 6.002 | 5.468 | 5.008 | 4.611 | 3.962 | 3.459 | 3.061 | 2.740 |
| 15 | 6.811 | 6.142 | 5.575 | 5.092 | 4.675 | 4.001 | 3.483 | 3.076 | 2.750 |
| 16 | 6.974 | 6.265 | 5.669 | 5.162 | 4.730 | 4.033 | 3.503 | 3.088 | 2.758 |
| 17 | 7.120 | 6.373 | 5.749 | 5.222 | 4.775 | 4.059 | 3.518 | 3.097 | 2.763 |
| 18 | 7.250 | 6.467 | 5.818 | 5.273 | 4.812 | 4.080 | 3.529 | 3.104 | 2.767 |
| 19 | 7.366 | 6.550 | 5.877 | 5.316 | 4.844 | 4.097 | 3.539 | 3.109 | 2.770 |
| 20 | 7.469 | 6.623 | 5.929 | 5.353 | 4.870 | 4.110 | 3.546 | 3.113 | 2.772 |
| 25 | 7.843 | 6.873 | 6.097 | 5.467 | 4.948 | 4.147 | 3.564 | 3.122 | 2.776 |

From the appropriate tables the annual receipt is given as $4,000 \times 0.2246 = £898.4$.

From the tables it is easy to calculate deferred annuities where the payments do not start until some way into the future.

### Averages

An average is a figure which is representative or typical of a group of data and because it lies centrally within that group of data averages are often called 'measures of central tendency'. The main types of average are the arithmetic mean, the geometric mean, the harmonic mean, the median and the mode. It is the first two which are referred to generally in investment matters although all will be described below:

### Arithmetic mean

This is given by the statistic:

$$\bar{X} = \frac{X_1 + X_2 + X_3 + \cdots X_N}{N} = \frac{\sum\limits_{j=1}^{N} X_j}{N} = \frac{\sum X}{N}$$

where $\bar{X}$ = the arithmetic mean.

*Example*    The arithmetic mean of the series $6, 8, 9, 12, 9, 13, 8, 9, 7, 9, 8$ is:

$$\bar{X} = \frac{6+8+9+12+9+13+8+9+7+9+8}{11} = \frac{98}{11}$$

$$\bar{X} = 8\frac{10}{11}.$$

The mean average is the 'expected' or the 'most likely' outcome.

### Geometric Mean

This is given by the statistic:

$$G = \sqrt[N]{X_1 X_2 X_3 \ldots X_N}$$

Thus the various values of $X$ are multiplied and the $N$th root taken.

*Example*    The geometric mean of 2, 4, 8 is:

$$G = \sqrt[3]{2 \times 4 \times 8} = \sqrt[3]{64} = 4.$$

The geometric average gives the compound yield, e.g. the compound rate of growth in a share price. The geometric average will equal the arithmetic mean only when the $X$'s are the same, otherwise the geometric average will always be lower.

*Investment analysis*

### Harmonic Mean

This is the reciprocal of the arithmetic mean of the reciprocals of the numbers and is given by the following expression:

$$H = \frac{1}{\frac{1}{N}\sum_{j=1}^{N}\frac{1}{X_j}} = \frac{N}{\sum\frac{1}{X}}.$$

*Example*  The harmonic mean of the numbers 2, 4, 8, 12 is:

$$H = \frac{4}{\frac{1}{2}+\frac{1}{4}+\frac{1}{8}+\frac{1}{12}} = \frac{4}{\frac{23}{24}} = 4.1739.$$

### The Median

This involves arranging a set of numbers into an array in the order of magnitude and the median is the middle value.

*Example*  The median of the numbers 12, 8, 15, 7, 9, 16, 5 is 9 as nine is the middle value in the array 5, 7, 8, 9, 12, 15, 16.

If there is an even number of numbers then the arithmetic average of the two middle values is taken.

*Example*  The median value of 11, 9, 7, 12, 5, 6 is 8 as this is the arithmetic average of the two middle values ((9 + 7)/2).

### The Mode

In a set of numbers the mode is the value which occurs most frequently.

*Example*  The mode of the figures 2, 3, 5, 3, 4, 6, 3 is 3 as it occurs more often than any other number. The mode may not exist (all the numbers may be different) and need not be unique (i.e. there may be two 'most popular' values).

### Variability

Besides knowing the average value of a set of data it is also useful to have some idea of its variability. The three main measures are the mean absolute deviation, the standard deviation and the variance.

### Mean absolute deviation

This is given by adding the deviations of a set of figures from its arithmetic average ($\bar{X}$) and dividing by the number of observations. The minus signs are ignored. The statistic is:

$$MAD = \frac{\sum_{j=1}^{N}(X_j - \bar{X})}{N} = \frac{\sum(X - \bar{X})}{N}$$

where $\bar{X}$ is the arithmetic average.

*Example*   The mean absolute deviation of the data 6, 12, 15, 9, 8 is 2.8.

$$\text{Arithmetic mean} = \frac{6 + 12 + 15 + 9 + 8}{5} = 10^5$$

$$\begin{aligned}\text{Mean absolute} \atop \text{deviation} &= \frac{(6-10) + (12-10) + (15-10) + (9-10) + (8-10)}{5} \\ &= \frac{(-4) + (2) + (5) + (-1) + (-2)}{5} \\ &= \frac{4 + 2 + 5 + 1 + 2}{5} = \frac{14}{5} = 2.8.\end{aligned}$$

## Standard deviation

This is the square root of the sum of the squares of the deviations from the average divided by the total number, or the total number minus one. As the data is squared minus signs disappear. Notationally it is described thus:

$$S = \sqrt{\frac{\sum\limits_{j=1}^{N} (Xj - \bar{X})^2}{N}} = \sqrt{\frac{\sum (X - \bar{X})^2}{N}}$$

*Example*   The standard deviation of the following data 9, 3, 8, 8, 9, 8, 9, 18 is 3.87.

$$\text{Arithmetic mean} = \frac{9 + 3 + 8 + 8 + 9 + 8 + 9 + 18}{8} = \frac{72}{8} = 9$$

$$S = \sqrt{\frac{\sum (X - \bar{X})^2}{N}}$$

$$S = \sqrt{\frac{(9-9)^2 + (3-9)^2 + (8-9)^2 + (8-9)^2 + (9-9)^2 + (8-9)^2 + (9-9)^2 + (18-9)^2}{8}}$$

$$S = \sqrt{15} = 3.87$$

If the data is a sample from a wider universe then the best estimate of the universe standard deviation is to use $N - 1$ in the denominator and not $N$. In the above example the corrected standard deviation is $\sqrt{17.14} = 4.14$.

The expression $S$ is generally given to the sample standard deviation whilst the sign $\sigma$ is given to the population standard deviation.

## Variance

This statistic is the square of the standard deviation and is denoted $S^2$ for the sample variance and $\sigma^2$ for the population variance. The variance in the above example would be 15 and 17.14 respectively.

The use of standard deviation and variance as measures of variability reaches significant importance in normal distributions. This is because tables exist which show the probability of an event being within a stated value of standard deviations from the mean. Thus in a normal distribution 68.27 per cent of cases are included between $\bar{X} - \sigma$ and $\bar{X} + \sigma$, 95.45 per cent of cases are included between $\bar{X} - 2\sigma$ and $\bar{X} + 2\sigma$ and 99.73 per cent of cases are included between $\bar{X} - 3\sigma$ and $\bar{X} + 3\sigma$. The tables give numerous values for $Z$ which is the number of standard deviations from the mean. For example, 95 per cent of the normal distribution's population is contained within 1.96 standard deviations on either side of the mean. This is shown graphically below.

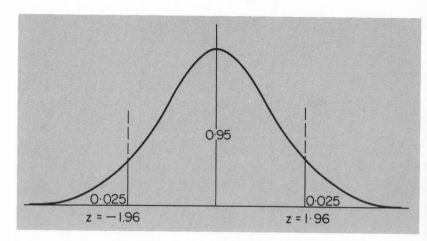

Many distributions are normal and those that are not, are often log normal*. The mean and standard distribution determine completely the shape of the normal distribution: a high standard deviation will give a squat distribution, whilst a low value will give a tall, pointed distribution. Much of the standard statistical theory is based on the normal distributions because of the availability of tables†. Most of the statistical evidence on the efficient market hypothesis has used tests which rely on normality in the change in share prices. This assumption has, however, been put in serious doubt recently and the currently prevailing opinion is that the distribution is not normal. Thus there are now significant doubts about the validity of the efficient market evidence. Whilst the statistical arguments about the validity of using standard statistical tests on non-normal data are outside the scope of the book it is worth noting that the problem is still wide open with many protagonists for both sides.

## Regression

Regression analysis is the technique which tells us the mathematical relationship between a dependent variable and a number of independent variables. It also tells us something about the accuracy of the relationship, i.e. the risk in predicting the dependent variable from the independent variables. The technique used in obtaining a regression

*This is the distribution of the logs of the various values.

†Tables could be constructed for some other distributions but each would be different.

equation is the 'least squares' method which is said to be the best linear unbiased estimator that has least variance between two or more variables. This computes the line of 'best fit' whose criterion is the minimisation of the squared deviations of observations from the line.

*Example* The following observations were taken for the price of a share and the industrial index for that company:

| Day | Share Y | Index X |
|-----|---------|---------|
| 1 | 68 | 65 |
| 2 | 66 | 63 |
| 3 | 68 | 67 |
| 4 | 65 | 64 |
| 5 | 69 | 68 |
| 6 | 66 | 62 |
| 7 | 68 | 70 |
| 8 | 65 | 66 |
| 9 | 71 | 68 |
| 10 | 67 | 67 |
| 11 | 68 | 69 |
| 12 | 70 | 71 |

These points are plotted in Figure 10.1.

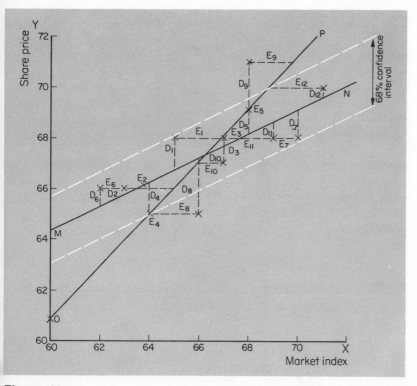

**Figure 10.1**

The straight line *MN* gives the line of 'best fit'. $D_1, D_2 \ldots D_{12}$ give the deviations of the observations from the line of best fit. The reader will find that the sum of the squared deviations from the line of best fit is the minimum amount possible, i.e.

$$D_1^2 + D_2^2 + D_3^2 \cdots + D_{12}^2 = \text{a minimum.}$$

Further it will be found that the line will pass through the arithmetic average or mean of the figures for $X$ and the figures for $Y$.

The line will be found exactly by calculating the regression equation and this will give various co-ordinates for $Y$ for given values of $X$. The equation of the least-squares line approximating the set of points $X_1 Y_1$ $X_2 Y_2 \ldots X_N Y_N$ is of the form:

$$Y = a + bX *$$

where the coefficients† are determined by solving the simultaneous equations:

$$\Sigma Y = aN + b \Sigma X$$
$$\Sigma XY = a \Sigma X + b \Sigma X^2$$

$N$ is the number of observations.

The coefficients $a$ and $b$ can also be found from the formulae:

$$a = \frac{(\Sigma Y)(\Sigma X^2) - (\Sigma X)(\Sigma XY)}{N \Sigma X^2 - (\Sigma X)^2}$$

$$b = \frac{N \Sigma XY - (\Sigma X)(\Sigma Y)}{N \Sigma X^2 - (\Sigma X)^2}$$

Using our example, the regression of $Y$ on $X$ is computed from the figures in Figure 10.2

$$811 = 12a + 800b$$

$$54{,}107 = 800a + 53{,}418b$$

The solution to the simultaneous equation gives a value for $a$ of 35.82 and a value for $b$ of 0.476°. Thus, the regression equation is $Y = 35.82 + 0.476X$ and the line $MN$ is constructed from this. If we wanted to compute a value for $Y$ for a given value of $X$ we can substitute into the formula, i.e. if $X = 80$ the value for $Y$ is given as:

$$35.82 + 0.476 \times 80 = Y = 73.9$$

*Note this is the simple form of model relating share prices to the market index as described in Chapter 5, p. 175.

†Often $a$ is referred to as the constant and $b$ as the regression coefficient. The coefficients express the importance of the independent variables in explaining the dependent variable. There are various tests which can be applied to the coefficients to see if they are statistically significant in explaining the relationships of the model. These significance tests involve using the $t$ distribution and are explained in the recommended texts which are referenced at the end of the chapter.

°The reader can check the results by using the alternative formulae.

| X | Y | $X^2$ | XY | $Y^2$ |
|---|---|---|---|---|
| 65 | 68 | 4,225 | 4,420 | 4,624 |
| 63 | 66 | 3,969 | 4,158 | 4,356 |
| 67 | 68 | 4,489 | 4,556 | 4,624 |
| 64 | 65 | 4,096 | 4,160 | 4,225 |
| 68 | 69 | 4,624 | 4,692 | 4,761 |
| 62 | 66 | 3,844 | 4,092 | 4,356 |
| 70 | 68 | 4,900 | 4,760 | 4,624 |
| 66 | 65 | 4,356 | 4,290 | 4,225 |
| 68 | 71 | 4,624 | 4,828 | 5,041 |
| 67 | 67 | 4,489 | 4,489 | 4,489 |
| 69 | 68 | 4,761 | 4,692 | 4,624 |
| 71 | 70 | 5,041 | 4,970 | 4,900 |

$\Sigma X = 800$   $\Sigma Y = 811$   $\Sigma X^2 = 53,418$   $\Sigma XY = 54,107$   $\Sigma Y^2 = 54,849$

**Figure 10.2**

The extrapolation of the line *MN* would pass through the coordinates 73.9($Y$) and 80($X$).

The regression of $X$ on $Y$ will only equal that of $Y$ on $X$ if there is perfect correlation between the variables, i.e. if all the observations lie on a straight line (i.e. no figures for $D$ or $E$). The equation for the regression of $X$ on $Y$ is given by:

$$X = c + dY$$

where $c$ and $d$ are obtained by:

$$\Sigma X = cN + d\Sigma Y$$

$$\Sigma XY = c\Sigma Y + d\Sigma Y^2$$

and

$$c = \frac{(\Sigma X)(\Sigma Y^2) - (\Sigma Y)(\Sigma XY)}{N \Sigma Y^2 - (\Sigma Y)^2}$$

$$d = \frac{N \Sigma XY - (\Sigma X)(\Sigma Y)}{N \Sigma Y^2 - (\Sigma Y)^2}$$

This formula gives a minimum for the squared deviations, $E$, i.e.:

$$E_1^2 + E_2^2 + E_3^2 + \cdots + E_{12}^2 = \text{a minimum}$$

This is shown by line *OP*. In the example the regression $X$ on $Y$ is:

$$X = -3.38 + 1.036Y$$

where $c$ and $d$ were derived from:

$$800 = 12c + 811d$$

$$54,107 = 811c + 54,849d$$

In using regression equations as a forecasting device we need to obtain some idea of the risk involved. That is, we would need to know how good the values of $a$ and $b$ are as approximators of $A$ and $B$ (the true coefficients) and the distance of a point from the true regression equation. The first difficulty is that the data we have is not that of the universe, i.e. we don't know future events but use past data as a sample of the universe. The second measure of risk is the measure of the scatter about the computed regression line. This is given by the standard error of the estimate. This is calculated by the formula:

$$Sy.x = \sqrt{\frac{\Sigma(Y - Ye)^2}{N}}$$

where $Ye$ represents the estimate of $Y$ from a given value of $X$.

If $Sy.x$ is only an estimate then the denominator is replaced by $(N - 2)$. This statistic is called the standard error of estimate of $Y$ on $X$. Figure 10.3 shows the workings required for calculating the standard error of estimate of $Y$ on $X$ in the above example.

| X | 65 | 63 | 67 | 64 | 68 | 62 | 70 | 66 | 68 | 67 | 68 | 71 |
|---|---|---|---|---|---|---|---|---|---|---|---|---|
| Y | 68 | 66 | 68 | 65 | 69 | 66 | 68 | 65 | 71 | 67 | 68 | 70 |
| Y est | 66.76 | 65.81 | 67.71 | 66.28 | 68.19 | 65.33 | 69.14 | 67.24 | 68.19 | 67.71 | 68.66 | 69.62 |
| Y − Y est | 1.24 | 0.19 | 0.29 | −1.28 | 0.81 | 0.67 | −1.14 | −2.24 | 2.81 | −0.71 | −0.66 | 0.38 |

**Figure 10.3**

From the table the statistic is computed:

$$Sy.x = \sqrt{\frac{\Sigma(Y - Ye)^2}{N}} = \sqrt{\frac{(1.24)^2 + (0.19)^2 + \cdots (0.38)^2}{12}}$$

$$= 1.28$$

If the points are normally distributed about the regression line, regression theory predicts that 68.27 per cent of the observations would be between the dotted lines in Figure 10.1 (i.e. ±1.28 either side of the line *MN*). Approximately 95 per cent and 99.7 per cent of observations would lie within $2Sy.x$ and $3Sy.x$ of the line, *MN*, respectively*.

The coefficient of determination gives a measure of the variability in $Y$ accounted for by movements in $X$. The formula for calculating the coefficient of determination is:

$$r^2 = \pm \frac{\text{explained variation}}{\text{total variation}} = \pm \frac{\Sigma(Ye - \bar{Y})^2}{\Sigma(Y - \bar{Y})^2}$$

where $\bar{Y}$ is the mean of the recordings for $Y$. In the example, $r^2 = 0.4938$.

Thus, the movement of $X$ explains 49 per cent of the movement in $Y$. The unexplained variance therefore equals 51 per cent.

*Another measure which is sometimes computed is the standard error of the forecast.

The regression equation $Y = a + bX$ was derived from sample data and there is a body of sampling theory which measures the relationships. These tests require the use of the $t$ distribution for which detailed tables exist. One such test involves ascertaining whether the regression coefficient $b$ is equal to a specified value $B$. The statistic is:

$$t = \frac{b - B}{Sy.x / Sx} \sqrt{N - 2}$$

Another test is to examine the hypothesis for predicted values. If $Y_J$ is the predicted value of $Y$ corresponding to $X = X_J$ as estimated from the sample regression equation $Y_J = a + bX_J$ and $Yk$ is the predicted value of $Y$ corresponding to $X = X_J$ corresponding to the population $(Y = A + BX)$ then the statistic

$$t = \frac{Y_J - Yk}{Sy.x \sqrt{N + 1 + (X_J - \bar{X})^2 / S^2x}} \sqrt{N - 2}$$

has a $t$ distribution. Confidence limits can be determined from this formula.

Confidence limits for the predicted mean population can be arrived at by the formula:

$$t = \frac{Y_J - \bar{Y}k}{Sy.x \sqrt{1 + (X_J - \bar{X})^2 / S^2 X}} \sqrt{N - 2}$$

where $\bar{Y}k$ is the predicted mean value of $Y$ corresponding to $X = X_J$ for the population. Confidence limits give the range of values in which we expect a mean to fall with a certain degree of probability. From the formulae we can determine a share price level given the market index. For example, if the market index is 70 we can be 95 per cent certain that the share price will be between 65.7 and 72.6 (these are the 95 per cent confidence limits).

The more complex share price models involve deriving share prices from a number of independent variables. The coefficients to the various factors are solved by multiple regression which again minimises the squared deviations. The techniques are thus similar to those described, although more complicated, and the arithmetic calculations are certainly longer. The various measures of errors, associations and variances and the calculation of confidence levels can be obtained from the analysis. Multicollinearity was briefly described in Chapter 5 and it represents the correlation between the various independent variables. Although this does not affect the predictive ability of the model the individual regression coefficients will not represent their individual impact on the share price.

This section has given a brief outline of simple regression analysis. The reader should look-up some of the standard texts to obtain a wider appreciation of the uses of regression analysis and the problems involved. The analyst should also be aware of statistical terminology, probability and statistical inference theory and time-series statistics.

## Correlation

This expresses the degree of relationship between variables and seeks to determine how well a linear equation explains the relationship between variables. Simple correlation, like simple regression, consists of just two variables. When more than two variables are considered we speak of multiple correlation.

The coefficient of correlation is the square root of the coefficient of determination. Thus, it is denoted:

$$r = \sqrt{\frac{\Sigma (Ye - \bar{Y})^2}{\Sigma (Y - \bar{Y})^2}}$$

where $\bar{Y}$ is the mean of the recordings for $Y$ and $Ye$ is the estimate of $Y$ from a given value of $X$.

If the relationship is linear, the coefficient of correlation can be described by:

$$r = \frac{\Sigma xy}{\sqrt{(\Sigma x^2)(\Sigma y^2)}}$$

where $x = X - \bar{X}$ and $y = Y - \bar{Y}$. This is known as the product moment formula. The standard deviation of the variables $X$ and $Y$ are denoted by $Sx = \sqrt{\frac{\Sigma x^2}{N}}$ and $Sy = \sqrt{\frac{\Sigma y^2}{N}}$. The term $Sx.y = \frac{\Sigma xy}{N}$ is the covariance of $X$ and $Y$ and can be written in the form $r = \frac{Sx.y}{SxSy}$. Covariance is equal to the expected value of the random deviations in each variable from its mean. It thus measures the degree by which variables vary jointly.

The product-moment formula can be written:

$$r = \frac{N \Sigma XY - (\Sigma X)(\Sigma Y)}{\sqrt{(N \Sigma X^2 - (\Sigma X)^2)(N \Sigma Y^2 - (\Sigma Y)^2)}}$$

In the example, the linear correlation coefficient is 0.7027. This is obtained by substituting the values in Figure 10.2 into the above expression, i.e.

$$r = \frac{(12)(54,107) - (800)(811)}{\sqrt{((12)(53,418) - (800)^2)((12)(54,849) - (811)^2)}}$$

$$r = 0.7027$$

This is the square root of the coefficient of determination described earlier, i.e. $\sqrt{0.4938}$. As with regression analysis there exists a substantial body of sampling theory where the sample correlation coefficient is compared against the population correlation coefficient. These and multiple correlation, rank correlation and curvilinear correlation are all excellently described in the references. The above, however, has given a brief introduction to the basics of correlation.

## References

### *Compound interest*

Soldofsky, R. M. and Murphy, J. T., 'Growth Yields on Common Stock: theory and tables', Revised ed., Ames, Iowa, State University of Iowa, Bureau of Business and Economic Research, 1963.

'Financial Compound Interest and Annuity Tables', Financial Publishing Company, Boston, Massachusetts.

### *Statistics*

Clark, C. T. and Schkade, L. L., 'Statistical Methods for Business Decisions', South-Western Publishing Co., 1969.

Ezekial, M. and Fox, K. A., 'Methods of Correlation and Regression Analysis', 3rd edition, Wiley, 1959.

Grayhill, F. A., 'An Introduction to Linear Statistical Models', McGraw-Hill, 1961.

Schlaifer, R., 'Probability and Statistics for Business Decisions', McGraw-Hill, 1959.

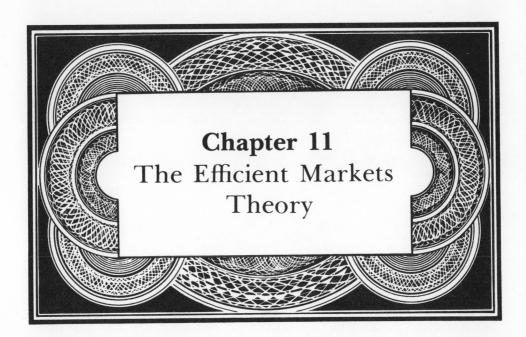

# Chapter 11
# The Efficient Markets Theory

An 'efficient' capital market is defined as one in which prices always 'fully reflect' available information. This implies that the complete body of knowledge of the company's prospects is publicly available and that such information is interpreted correctly in the share price. Although such a description does not fit the actual processes at work on the major Stock Exchanges of the world, some less strict definition may still warrant the 'efficient' title in that share prices provide reasonable values by which resource allocation can be 'optimised'. The protagonists of the Efficient Markets Theory argue that for the bigger company the competition between various investors produces a consensus of opinion which will, on average, be correct.

This weaker definition of an efficient market implies that investors without special information cannot make abnormal profits and that as new information becomes available it is quickly reflected in the security's price. As a consequence of the almost immediate adjustment of stock prices to new information, prices will follow a random walk or the concomitant stochastic process, the submartingale model.

### Models of share price behaviour

**Fair-game model**

The efficient markets hypothesis has been described in terms of an 'expected return' or 'fair-game' model by Fama[1]. In notational terms the 'expected return theories' are of the form:

$$E(V_{j, t+1}[X_t]) = (1 + E(r_{j, t+1}[X_t])) V_{jt}$$

301

where $E$ = expected value

$V_{jt}$ = price of security $j$ at time $t$

$V_{j, t+1}$ = price of security $j$ at time $t + 1$ with the re-investment of dividends

$r_{j, t+1}$ = percentage return for the period = $\dfrac{V_{jt+1} - V_{jt}}{V_{jt}}$

$[X_t]$ = set of information assumed to be fully reflected in the price at $t$

$V_{j, t+1}$ and $r_{j, t+1}$ are random variables at time $t$.

The formula implies that the information set $[X_t]$ is fully incorporated in the dynamic equilibrium model which produces the price at time $t$. The assumption of market equilibrium stated in terms of the information set $[X_t]$ only, rules out the possibility of trading strategies based on the information set $[X_t]$ earning returns greater than the market average.

Let $Y_{j, t+1} = V_{j, t+1} - E(V_{j, t+1}[X_t])$

If $[X_t]$ fully reflects the information on which the share price is based then:

$E(Y_{j, t+1}[X_t]) = 0$

and thus the process is a fair game with respect to the information sequence $[X_t]$. $Y_{j, t+1}$ represents the excess market value of security $j$ at time $t + 1$, the expectation of which at time $t$, is nil. Thus, let

$Z_{j, t+1} = r_{j, t+1} - E(r_{j, t+1}[X_t])$

then:

$E(Z_{j, t+1}[X_t]) = 0$

where $Z_{j, t+1}$ equals the excess return for the period, the expectation of which, at time $t$, is nothing. $Z_{j, t+1}$ is a random variable at time $t$.

**Fair-game model in portfolios**

The fair-game process for individual securities can be applied to portfolio trading strategies; thus a system, based on the information set, $(X_t)$, which tells the investor how much of his funds, $A_j$, are to be invested in each of the $n$ available securities can be described thus:

$A[X_t] = (A_1[X_t], A_2[X_t] \ldots, A_n[X_t])$

The total excess market value at time $t + 1$ given by such a system is:

$V_{t+1} = \sum_{j=1}^{n} A_j[X_t](r_{j, t+1} - E(r_{j, t+1}[X_t]))$

which has the expectation

$E(V_{t+1}[X_t]) = \sum_{j=1}^{n} A_j[X_t] E(Z_{j, t+1}[X_t]) = 0$

## Submartingale model

A somewhat similar process, the submartingale model, has been used as a description of share price behaviour and it appears to have superceded the random walk hypothesis as the prevailing theory. The model is described as follows:

$$E(V_{j,t+1}[X_t]) \geqslant V_{jt}$$

or, in terms of returns,

$$E(r_{j,t+1}[X_t]) \geqslant 0$$

Thus, the expected price at $t+1$ is equal to, or greater than that at $t$ (if the equation holds as an equality then the sequence follows a stochastic process known as a martingale). Such a process rules out the possibility of there being profitable 'one security and cash' mechanical trading strategies*. This means that 'one security and cash' rules cannot outperform a buy-and-hold policy as the expected returns are non-negative. The fair-game model, described earlier, does not rule out the profitability of 'one security and cash' trading strategy as the equilibrium-expected returns can be negative, and thus holding cash may lead to a higher expected return (there are likely to be few occasions when a security is bought and the expected return is negative. This could, however, arise in portfolio construction, i.e. a share whose returns on average move opposite to the general market is particularly valuable in reducing the dispersion of portfolio returns.)

## Random walk model

The random walk model which was popularly used as a description of the stochastic processes at work in stock prices implied that successive one period returns of a security are independent. It is often additionally assumed that the successive changes are identically distributed. Formally, the model can be stated as:

$$f(r_{j,t+1}[X_t]) = f(r_{j,t+1})$$

This states that the entire distribution of returns is independent of the information sequence, $[X_t]$; thus the sequence of the past returns is of no consequence in assessing distributions of future returns.

Most of the early empirical research was conducted into the dependence of price changes and thus directly tested the random walk hypothesis. Although many of the studies found that the random walk description did not fit exactly, they did show that the dependencies were so weak that no consistently profitable trading systems could be derived. The model may not be an exact description of share price behaviour but 'market efficiency' does not necessarily require successive one period price changes to be independent.

### Investment analysis and market efficiency

A perfect market would require share prices to be 'correctly valued' and this value is usually regarded as being the intrinsic worth.

*This type of rule gives signals when to buy, sell, or sell short a security at any time.

Fundamental analysts attempt to ascertain the intrinsic values and thus price securities at their 'true' worth. The Efficient Markets Theory argues that there are so many competing analysts that they will bring a share's price to its proper value. Thus the determination of share values may be said to be represented by a dynamic equilibrium model, i.e. the weighted mean of all investors' evaluations at that point in time. In fact, the theory contends that the price wanders randomly, within narrow limits, around the intrinsic value. Whilst fundamental analysis helps in the making of an efficient market, the efficient market hypothesis abrogates the claim of the technical analysts that their various strategies can outperform the market indices.

The random walk model states that successive one-period price differences are independent, that a series of price changes has no memory and that past history cannot predict the future in any profitable way. Both the random walk and submartingale models preclude earning returns in excess of a buy-and-hold policy by using charts and the various trading rules.

**Technical analysts' claims**

Technical analysts defend themselves from criticism coming from academic quarters by saying that the statistical tests employed in supporting the random walk hypothesis are not sophisticated enough and that they, the analysts, use longer time periods for their selection methods. Technical analysts can help market efficiency to the extent that if they publicise a profitable trading strategy they have devised then the Stock Market would react to discount such rules*.

*One might say that the random walk model is inevitable – if there were any other rule operating, then there would exist sure-fire investment strategies which, if used by a sufficient number of investors (speculators?) would just as inevitably wipe out the successful rule[2].*

**Changing intrinsic values**

The intrinsic value of a firm does, of course, change across time as a result of new information, actual, anticipated or putative. Share prices incorporating the new information will usually over- or under-adjust initially. The time taken for the share price to settle down to the new intrinsic value, after the receipt of additional data, is a stochastic variable: the process of adjustment is the reflection of the changing uncertainty remaining in the minds of investors. If there are many astute traders in the market, then, on average, the full effects of new information on the intrinsic value of a share will be reflected instantaneously; any under- and any over-adjustment and the time taken to adjust are randomly distributed and therefore no profitable trading rules can be based upon them.

**Non-random fluctuations**

If differences arise between intrinsic and actual prices owing to dependencies in the process generating new information or if disagreements over the intrinsic price are systematic, then knowledge of such would help analysts to outperform the market index. However,

---

*It is the various mechanical trading rules that have provided the main basis of the empirical testing of the efficient markets hypothesis.

the efficient market theorists say that there are so many rational market operators with sufficient resources who are able to take advantage of such profit opportunities, that they compete with each other until all non-random fluctuations about the intrinsic value become so small that they cannot be exploited for profit.

## Competitive investment analysis

To make an efficient market there needs to be a large number of analysts specialising in a particular security and the bulk of the value of market transactions in that security needs to come from investors who have the benefit of the analysts' advice. It is contended by many that for most of the larger quoted companies in the UK, there are sufficient numbers of analysts to create a competitive market. For smaller UK companies there are far fewer analysts evaluating share values and such securities may be priced incorrectly. American stocks are almost certainly more sophisticatedly analysed than their British counterparts and several authors have pointed out that the 'efficient markets' evidence compiled in the US may not be relevant in the UK because of the differences in shareholder behaviour and in the degree of investment analysis undertaken.

## The implications of the Efficient Markets Theory for investment analysis

One implication of an efficient market is that any additional analysis on top of that required to make the market efficient is superfluous. This is held especially to apply in the US where many hundreds of analysts compete in evaluating one specific stock*. Wallich[3] in taking this view, said:

*Incorrect pricing can produce serious disturbance. Here is the main social contribution of securities analysis. But approximately correct pricing could probably be obtained with a fraction of the manpower now employed in securities analysis. Once the best available judgment has put prices where they belong, there is no social benefit in duplicating the work . . . correct pricing of securities . . . is a public good available free to all, even though it costs money to produce. Anybody can get the benefit of the combined best judgment by simply accepting the prices set by the market.*

Analysts, especially those employed by advisory and management companies, will disagree with Wallich. Rinfret[4] said, 'In the market economy we live in, the ultimate test of anything is what the market will pay. The market pays for investment advice because investment advice is worth paying for.' The vast number of investment services, especially in America, gives testimony to Rinfret's comments. However, the success of investment services may be the result of investors' eternal hopes of earning spectacular returns, irrational though such hopes may be in light of the evidence to date.

The hypothesis implies that once a market is efficient then it does not pay to engage in any further analysis or, indeed, to engage in any

---

*Many analysts working for investment management companies actually spend their time analysing and evaluating brokers' research material and never go to the primary data themselves.

investment research at all. Stockbrokers probably disagree in public with this assertion and say that they have a special expertise in various stocks. However, the few empirical researches that have been done on analysts' abilities have not shown any consistently successful records. One hears of fewer complaints of duplicative analysts in London but criticisms could grow and already a number of institutions are cutting back on investment research staff and relying purely on stockbrokers' material.

The proponents of the efficient markets model argue that for the larger quoted company there are sufficient investment analysts with adequate expertise to ensure that new information is reflected in the share price quickly and accurately. Stockbrokers and the financial institutions no doubt would agree with the sentiment that they are helping to create and maintain a socially justifiable efficient market, but few would agree with the other implication of the hypothesis that any additional analysis is of no profitable use.

### Inefficiencies in the Stock Market

There are many potential and realised imperfections within even the most researched and regulated Stock Exchanges and much of the empirical academic research has been based on measuring the effect that the inefficiencies have on share prices. Major inefficiencies exist in the form of:

1  Transaction costs. These are, however, on a fixed, known scale and do represent service done.

2  Information that is not freely available. This is an obvious problem but the various regulatory bodies do have powers to act against known malpractises of using inside knowledge.

3  Differences among investors about the implications of given information. This can create a serious disturbance if certain investors can consistently interpret financial and economic data better than the average market operator.

**Ramifications of 'inefficient' markets**

Significant 'inefficiencies' will create a more volatile and speculative market which will deter many investors from holding ordinary shares. In more serious cases wholesale manipulation of share prices can take place and this will create an enormous crisis of confidence. Such an event would lead to non-optimal resource allocation and the withdrawal of substantial funds from the capital market. In order to reduce the occurrence of 'insider trading' various bodies and rules have been set up by many Governments and Stock Exchanges to regulate the market mechanism. In the UK the Stock Exchange and the Takeover Panel have formulated certain guidelines on the conduct of investment activity and have powers of investigation in certain cases. The Stock Exchange has the power to suspend members if they are found guilty of practices not in keeping with their position as agents on trusts. Of greater importance is the Stock Exchange's power to suspend the quote of companies if there are violent movements in share prices, or pending publication of important news as in the case of large acquisitions, or for leakage of news to specific investors. Suspension of an official quote is a very serious matter and acts as a real deterrent to the leakage of inside information.

## Takeover Panel

The Takeover Panel was set up partly to safeguard public investors during merger and takeover bids. Around the time of a bid there is often exceptional activity in a company's shares and certain outsiders (e.g. merchant banks), become privy to confidential financial information. It is in such circumstances that 'inside information' becomes very valuable. The Takeover Panel has formulated various rules[5] which require disclosure of investment holdings to the public during takeovers. Whilst such rules have no legal standing the various City institutions (including the Stock Exchange) abide by the terms and will support the Panel's rulings.

## Financial information disclosure

The Companies Acts and the accountancy bodies require public disclosure of financial information in stated formats. Such requirements lead to publication of minimum limits of financial data and impose certain time constraints and penalties for non conformity. The Department of Trade and Industry has certain rights to investigate companies if there are suspicious circumstances of illegal dealings in securities and have arbitrary powers in regulating certain investment bodies*.

## Securities and Exchange Commission

In America the various Stock Exchanges have a fair amount of authority over member firms and quoted corporations but the major regulatory force is the Securities and Exchange Commission. The SEC have sponsored several investigations and research reports into the efficiency of the Stock Market. The SEC and the major American Stock Exchanges require significantly greater disclosure of financial information by quoted companies than do British authorities. However, their main contribution to market efficiency has come from their rules which require disclosure of investment transactions by company officials, private investors and financial institutions. The publication of such information has given greater knowledge of investment demand and supply and has given greater confidence to the general public as transactions appear 'above board'. Additionally, academic research has pointed out areas where insider information is possible and where their findings imply the use thereof[6].

### Present state of research

There has been considerable dialectic over the past decade on the validity of the random walk and Efficient Markets Theory as a description of share price behaviour and reviews of the major studies

*For example, the Prevention of Frauds (Investments) Act 1958 which describes their powers in connection with licensed dealers in securities.

are contained in the bibliographical works of Brealey and Granger[7]. This has been occasioned by the increasing numbers of investors in their desire to find profitable trading strategies and by the advent of the computer and the computer data bank which enabled researchers to use sophisticated statistical methods to analyse large masses of data. Most of the work has been conducted in the US on their own stock price data. This is partly due to the size and therefore importance of American Stock Exchanges and partly to the emphasis the US has placed on financial and economic research.

## The interests of researchers

The American research has been undertaken from two different angles, one, the professional analysts and fund managers who try to formulate profitable strategies, or else to advertise their abilities, and second, the academics who were more concerned with the statistical processes at work and the implications for economic efficiency. As could be predicted the two types of researcher differed in their findings, with the professional analysts revealing numerous strategies for successful investment. The professional analysts have in the main based their findings on whether a particular strategy would have made profits in excess of the market average on given data; the academics have concentrated on using statistical techniques to obtain an understanding of the processes at work and to see if specific trading rules can work on future data.

## Differences in definitions of 'efficiency'

The research findings have in many cases shown similar results but the researchers involved have drawn different implications and conclusions. Some of the differences can be explained; e.g. some works refer to a strict statistical definition of random walk and efficient markets models and reject the hypothesis if the data does not fit exactly. Other researchers, however, do not reject the hypothesis of market efficiency unless particular rules are found to consistently beat a buy and hold policy by a significant margin. Other differences in conclusions are more difficult to explain and may reflect imperfections in the Stock Exchange. As regards market 'efficiency' it is contended that the strict statistical interpretations of the random walk and martingale models need not apply. The relevant practical yardstick should be whether profitable opportunities exist in a market. It is further argued that, even if some profitable strategies do arise, then as long as they are not consistently profitable over many years and do not involve enormous sums of money no serious economic disturbance will occur and the market for the major companies' shares will warrant the description 'efficient'. This definition describes a market where in general the larger companies, who own the majority of a countries' private economic assets, have their shares priced in a relatively 'perfect' market and where investors, both private and institutional, have confidence to invest. Thus, although insider information does arise and although particular trading rules may apply from time to time, the Stock Exchange in general is held to provide a market which reflects publicly available information on companies such that share prices provide accurate values for resource allocation. Many of the studies to date have measured the level of 'inefficiency' due to certain trading rules and then proceeded to interpret these on 'market efficiency' as a whole.

**Research methodologies**

Research into the efficient markets model can be classified into four types:

1   Statistical testing of the dependence of price changes. Such investigations involve assessing whether there is any statistical dependence between one-period returns; some techniques have looked at differently-spaced returns. A random walk model is in fact defined as a process where the one-period returns are independent. Much of the early literature concentrated on this type of test; the data and the length of periods investigated being different. As Fama has shown, the serial covariances of returns of a 'fair game' are zero and so investigations of statistical dependence are relevant for the expected return models. Although the statistical definition of 'random walk' requires linear independence of returns, the efficient markets hypothesis is not so strict; many of the empirical studies have revealed some statistical dependencies but they were so small that the researchers concluded the market to be efficient. Some supporters of the market efficiency hypothesis have in fact expressed surprise at the lack of linear dependence; thus Fama said,

*But it is perhaps equally surprising that, as we shall soon see, the evidence against the independence of returns over time is as weak as it is*[8].

and Van Horne and Parker said,

*. . . a small amount of dependence in a sequence of stock price changes does not negate the practical significance of their theory*[9].

Others have taken an opposite view thus, Smidt said,

*Persons . . . should be wary of interpreting a test that uncovered no dependencies as strong evidence supporting the random walk hypothesis. Rather such test results can often be interpreted more properly as indicating that the test was insufficiently powerful against relevant alternative hypotheses*[10].

2   Testing various trading rules used by technical analysts. Like the prior type this classification of research has been very popular. It is, however, a type of research which can be expanded as long as trading strategies can be derived. The research normally starts by describing the trading rule being examined and then testing it on a body of data. Many studies of particular strategies have been followed up by further research on the same rule but on different data and this has often produced opposite findings. Some of these disagreements arise because of the statistics used but the majority would seem to arise because the rule worked on one body of data but on no other and so was not a profitable trading rule in the proper sense*. Jensen and Bennington, in testing

---

*It is not consistent and cannot produce profits in the future but only on past data on which the rule was devised.

and refuting a claim by Levy that a 'relative strength' rule could outperform the market, said,

> ... *given enough computer time, we are sure that we can find a mechanical trading rule which 'works' on a table of random numbers – provided of course that we are allowed to test the rule on the same table of numbers which we used to discover the rule. We realise of course that the rule would prove useless on any other table of random numbers, and this is exactly the issue with Levy's results* [11].

Many of the academic studies have been in reply to particular strategies promulgated by various professional analysts although as many critics have pointed out the market professionals would only publicly disclose techniques which are no longer profitable. This is a possible bias, and probably the only way to assess its significance is to assess the performance of fund managers (although a concomitant problem arises in that if a strategy was very successful the operator of such would probably be working entirely on their own account and so no performance statistics would be available). Some investors eventually disclose their investment methods after they have made their fortunes and when either they no longer need further money or their strategies have become unprofitable [12].

3   Testing the ability of portfolio managers to outperform the market averages. The majority of this type of research has been conducted in America and mainly on mutual funds (unit trusts) which are the only data publicly available in large quantities. Lesser study has been completed on pension-fund performance and on the predictive ability of investment analysts. Apart from the statistical studies undertaken by various academics there are a number of financial service companies which give comparative performance data on unit trusts. *Money Management* gives monthly performance tables on British unit trusts and is a ready guide to the ability of particular investment managers. This research is of great value in the 'market efficiency' literature as the unit trusts they look at, control enormous sums of money and thus have a considerable impact on the economic capital markets system*. Although odd profitable trading rules may be found from time to time the amounts involved may be so small and are applicable for such short periods that they have little effect on the economic application of capital funds. Some of the investigations have involved looking at the various investments made by particular unit trusts. The remainder have employed statistical tests to measure overall performance over a longish period so as to ascertain any consistency of returns.

4   Testing whether share prices instantaneously and accurately adjust to new information. The main research in this area has looked at occurrences which have a precise, calculable, affect on share prices. These are then compared against actual price behaviour. For the less

---

*This includes the market for all types of capital, fixed interest as well as equity.

precise adjustments some researchers have adopted various regression-based equity valuation models to measure the share price movements. Such tests have included research on the adjustment of share prices to scrip and rights issues, annual and quarterly earnings and dividend announcements, Bank Rate changes, ex-dividend price behaviour, sales and production figures and secondary stock issues (large underwritten sale of stock by institutions). The investigators have in general tried to assess the amount of under- and over-adjustment of prices to new information and to measure the consistency (any significant relationships would throw up profitable trading strategies). This type of research is important in that if the adjustment of prices was poor, in the cases where it is possible to measure this with certainty, and was both numerous and consistent, then profitable strategies would arise and investor confidence wane as they realise that professional analysts cannot incorporate quantifiable data in share prices. Although a fair amount of work has been done on this aspect it does not compare with the previous three classifications. This is due to the fact that there is little information which has a mathematically correct effect on share prices and those that have are applicable over short periods of time only. Dividends and earnings which are the main determinants of share prices are not capable of having an 'exact effect' on prices although equity models have been used to estimate the relationships (such models have often been found to be tenuous and inconsistent).

In general, the 'academic' investigations have shown the American Stock Market to be reasonably efficient. Their approach has been more soundly statistically based than the studies reported by practising analysts and additionally the academic research has been applied on greater masses of data, both historical and future. Substantially, less research has been undertaken on the share price behaviour of other major capital markets and there is no reason to believe that the American results are exactly applicable elsewhere. Thus research on individual Stock Markets is needed in order to establish their efficiency in pricing shares. Research that has been conducted on the British Stock Market indicates similar behavioural traits to the US, although there are a number of individual instances of 'inside information' leakage. The initial impression therefore is that the British 'United Stock Exchange' does a 'reasonable' job in valuing shares and in providing a mechanism for dealing. 'Reasonable' is evidenced by the substantial funds which investors are prepared to put into Stock Exchange securities.

The techniques and analyses discussed in the book provide a sound framework with which to evaluate ordinary shares. Investor confidence gained from a more efficient market will produce greater sums of capital monies which industry will need in order to finance their way through the coming decades.

## References

1  Fama, E., 'Efficient capital markets: a review of theory and empirical work', *Journal of Finance*, 25, May 1970.

2  Granger, C. W. J., 'Empirical Studies of Capital Markets: a survey', in: 'Mathematical Methods in Investments and Finance', Szego, G. P. and Shell, K., (Eds) North Holland, 1972.

3  Wallich, H. C., 'What does the random walk hypothesis mean to security analysts?', *Financial Analysts Journal*, Mar.–Apr. 1968.

4  Rinfret, P. A., 'Investment managers are worth their keep', *Financial Analysts Journal*, Mar.–Apr. 1968.

5  See' 'The City Code on Takeovers and Mergers', available from the Issuing Houses Association, London.

6  See, for example, Scholes, M. S., 'The market for securities: substitution *vs* price pressure and the effects of information on share prices', *Journal of Business*, 45, Apr. 1972, and: Niederhoffer, V. and Osborne, M. F. M., 'Market making and reversal on the Stock Exchange', *Journal of the American Statistical Association*, 61, Dec. 1966.

7  Brealey, R. A., 'An Introduction to Risk and Return from Common Stocks', MIT Press, 1969. *Ibid*, 'Security Prices in a Competitive Market', MIT Press, 1971. Brealey, R. A. and Pyle, C., 'A Bibliography of Finance and Investment', Elek, 1973; Granger, C. W. J. and Morgenstern, O., 'Predictability of Stock Market Prices', Heath Lexington, 1970.

8  Fama, E., 'Efficient capital markets: a review of theory and empirical work', *Journal of Finance*, 25, May 1970.

9  Van Horne, J. C. and Parker, G. G. C., 'The random walk theory: an empirical test', *Financial Analysts Journal*, Nov.–Dec. 1967.

10  Smidt, S., 'A new look at the random walk hypothesis', *Journal of Financial and Quantitative Analysis*, Sept. 1968.

11  Jensen, M. C. and Bennington, G. A., 'Random walks and technical theories: some additional evidence', *Journal of Finance*, 25, May 1970. Levy, R. A., 'Relative strength as a criterion for investment selection', *Journal of Finance*, 22, Dec. 1967.

12  Owen, L., 'How Wall Street Doubles My Money Every Three Years', Bernard Geis Associates, New York, 1969. Mitchell, S., 'How to make Big Money in the Stock Market', George Allen & Unwin, 1970.

# Glossary of Terms

*Articles of Association*   These contain the rules and regulations for conducting the business of the company and define the rights of the members and the powers and duties of the directors.

ASSC   Accounting Standards Steering Committee.

*Audit*   This is the verification of a company's accounts by outside, independent accountants. Under the Companies Act 1948 auditors have to express a view as to whether the accounts show a 'true and fair view' of the company's state of affairs at the year end and of the profit for the year.

*Bear*   This is the description given to the Stock Market when share prices are falling and when the economic outlook is pessimistic.

*Bull*   This is the description given to the Stock Market when share prices are rising and when the economic outlook is optimistic.

*Capitalisation issues*   The capitalisation of reserves into new shares which are distributed pro rata and free of charge to the existing shareholders. Also known as scrip issues or bonus issues.

*Close company*   The name given to companies whose control is in the hands of five or fewer 'participators'. Close companies have special provisions relating to their taxation.

*Convertible loan stock*   Fixed-interest loan stock which is convertible into ordinary shares of the company at specified rates and specified times.

*Cost structure*   This is the description of the different types of expenses that a company has to bear. Typical breakdowns include fixed, semi-variable and variable expenses, and individual expense items which account for a significant part of total costs.

CPP   Current Purchasing Power.   This relates to the ASSC's recommended method of accounting for inflation. The accounts are adjusted for inflation by the index of retail prices (IRP) and is known as the Current Purchasing Power method. The ASSC's Provisional SSAP No. 7 'Accounting for Changes in the Purchasing Power of Money' contains the recommendation.

*Cum dividend*   Purchasing a share and receiving the forthcoming dividend.

*Cum rights*   Purchasing a share and receiving the rights entitlement.

*Current market value*   This refers to the current realisable price that could be obtained for a company's individual assets. For many assets there is no adequate market and so current market values may be difficult or impossible to establish.

*Cycle*   This is the term given to economic and business indices which fluctuate regularly between peaks and troughs.

*Deferred revenue*   This refers to income received by the company which is not included in that year's profit, but is delayed until a future period.

EFFAS   European Federation of Financial Analysts' Societies.

*Elasticity*   This measures the responsiveness of a variable to a change in an influencing factor. For example, the elasticity of demand measures the percentage change in the quantity of goods purchased by the percentage change in price.

EPS   Earnings per share.

*Ex ante*   Before the event. For example, the derivation of an investment strategy and testing it on future data.

*Ex dividend*   Purchasing a share without receiving the forthcoming dividend.

*Ex post*   Retrospective. For example, the derivation of an investment strategy and testing it on past data.

*Ex rights*   Purchasing a share without receiving the rights entitlement.

*Fund management*   Synonymous with portfolio management.

*Gearing*   The relationship between fixed, semi-variable and variable expenses. This analysis is most commonly carried out with respect to fixed-interest borrowings: gearing in this case also includes the relationship of the net assets of the company to the fixed-interest borrowings. The other main 'gearing' analysis undertaken is that relating to a firm's cost structure.

*Gilt edged*   These are securities which are issued and guaranteed by the UK Government. It is sometimes used as a general description of a very safe investment.

ICA   The Institute of Chartered Accountants in England and Wales.

*Imputation*   This is the description given to the current method of taxing company profits. A company pays corporation tax at a uniform rate but the shareholder is entitled to have part of the company's tax imputed to him. This is used to discharge the tax which the investor would otherwise have to pay in respect of dividend income.

*Insider dealing*   This is the name given to transactions made by investors who make use of information which is not publicly available at that time and which is supposed to be held in confidence.

*Intangible assets*   Those which have no material existence. The existence and valuation of these assets is often difficult to ascertain.

*Liquidity of assets*   The ease of conversion into cash at no loss.

*Glossary of terms*

*Market capitalisation* The number of shares of a specified class in issue multiplied by the current share price.

*Memorandum of Association* This is the document forming the constitution of the company and defining its objects and powers.

*Moving average* This is a statistic which is computed by adding a time series of recordings and dividing by the number of recordings. This evens out the possible erratic nature of absolute figures.

*Net assets* A term often applied to the total of the shareholders' funds. That is total assets minus total liabilities (including preference capital).

*New issue* This is the term given to the issuance of shares by the company for consideration (usually cash but occasionally the acquisition of assets or takeovers).

*Nominal value* The monetary description allotted to a share. Except in special circumstances a new issue of shares cannot be made at a price below the nominal value.

*Option* The right to acquire shares in a company at some later date. There is a small but active market in options for many of the larger quoted British companies.

*Overspill relief* This is special relief given to companies with heavily-taxed overseas income. This is available until April 1977.

*Portfolio* The description given to the total holding of a number of different shares or assets.

*Prospectus* An invitation offering to the public shares in the company upon payment of a specified amount.

*Replacement value* The valuation of assets at their replacement value, i.e. the cost of replacing an existing asset with a new asset producing identical output.

*Rights issue* The offering of new shares for consideration to existing shareholders pro rata to their existing holdings.

*Share* The name given to an individual unit of capital in a company. This share entitles its owner to certain rights.

*Share splits* The reduction of the nominal value of the shares in issue and increasing the number of shares in existence so as to maintain the Issued Share Capital.

*Stagging* The name given to the operation of buying shares offered in a new issue and selling them shortly afterwards. These investors have no intention of holding the shares as a medium- or long-term investment.

*Stock* The name that is given to capital consolidated into bulk, which can be made divisable into any monetary fractions. Stocks and shares are usually used synonymously and this is so in this book.

*Stochastic*   Random.

*Trading rule*   An investment strategy which is used mechanically. Typically the rule gives triggers for investment decisions and investment timing.

*United Stock Exchange*   The various Stock Exchanges in the UK have united to become the United Stock Exchange. The separate physical markets still retain their individual names.

*Warrant*   An option to buy a specified number of shares at a stated price.

# Index